NEPAL

MAHARAJA CHANDRA SHAM SHER
JANG BAHADUR RANA,
Prime Minister of Nepal.

NEPAL

PERCEVAL LANDON

IN TWO VOLUMES
VOL. II

WITH ILLUSTRATIONS AND MAPS

Published by

Gyan Publishing House
5, Ansari Road
Daryaganj, New Delhi-110002
Phone: 011-47034999, 9811692060
E-mail: books@gyanbooks.com

Distribution Network
gyanbooks.com
India, USA, Canada, UK, Australia, France

© **Publisher**

ISBN : 978-81-212-3815-1 (Set)
ISBN : 978-81-212-4698-9 (PB)
First Published, London, 1928

2nd Impression 2020

Printed at: Gyan Press, Delhi.

Nepal Vol. II
Author: Perceval Landon

CONTENTS, VOL. II

LIST OF ILLUSTRATIONS, VOL. II

PAGE

MAPS

NEPAL

CHAPTER XI

UNKNOWN NEPAL

§ 1

THE TOWNS

BEYOND the narrow limits of the Valley of Katmandu Nepal is and will probably long remain a land unvisited by those of Western birth. It is only, indeed, under the strictest regulations that the Nepalese permit even their own cousins of India and Tibet to thread their way along their mountain paths or use the long undulating tracks that painfully link together the towns of outer Nepal.[1] As I have said, before, the Tarai is not subject to this absolute prohibition. For purposes of sport and archaeology Europeans have been from time to time admitted into this surge of hot rank jungle which, like a green sea, washes against the foot of the Himalayan crags. Occasionally also for state purposes, such as forest development or engineering installations, the Maharaja not merely permits but welcomes therein the presence of English experts. But along a clear line defined by the outpost ridges of the Himalayas a barrier exists and has always existed against all foreigners.[2]

[1] There is no general prohibition directed against Asiatic travelling within Nepal. Large numbers of outsiders, chiefly Indians, are welcomed in the sacred centres and at the many *melas* or general fairs, which are usually held in the Tarai. Moreover, the Maharaja's policy of extending the industrial activities of his country has led to the introduction of representatives of Indian trade, who are permitted to travel extensively throughout the country for the purpose of organizing their business.

[2] In the first half of the nineteenth century Brian Hodgson made an excursion eastwards to the Sunkosi, and a few miles westward to the bank of the Trisul Gandak. The only other European who has in comparatively recent years travelled into "outer" Nepal beyond the foothills of the Himalayas is Dr. Hooker, the famous naturalist. In November 1848 the latter proceeded up the valley of the Tamor, afterwards climbing up the bed of its tributary the Yangma. Later he reached the pass of Walanchun. His description of the view from the Tangla above the Tamor valley is quoted by Sir Clements Markham. "Kangchanjanga," he writes, "was nearly due north—a dazzling mass of snowy peaks intersected by blue glaciers which gleamed in the slanting rays of the rising sun, like aquamarines set in frosted silver. To the east was a billowy mass of forest-clad mountains, on the north-east horizon rose Donkya and Chumolhari, to the

The present Prime Minister was once asked by an Englishman, who was a personal friend of his, whether he might be allowed to visit Gorkha, the cradle of the reigning dynasty of Nepal, about sixty miles west of the Valley. Chandra Shaṃ Sher's answer was as characteristic and courteous as it was final: " I could indeed give you permission to go, but it is my friendship that makes me refuse. I should have to send with you at least a company of my soldiers, and that," he added, with a smile which those who know him can readily picture, " would be unpleasant for you, and perhaps unpleasant for myself also." [1]

This sense of being a kingdom apart is, so far as the higher ranks of the Nepalese are concerned, a carefully thought-out policy. " Where the Englishman comes, he stays," is a maxim that would be recognized throughout Nepal, and of all the States of the world, there is probably a no more fiercely patriotic country than Nepal. This is natural enough. Excepting Afghanistan, there is no kingdom within the long scope of the interests of the Indian Government that has not, sooner or later, agreed to accept a semi-sovereignty in return for the great boons of an absolute protection from abroad and an absolute guarantee against any British or other interference in their internal affairs. The situation of Afghanistan is wholly different from that of Nepal. It has secured its independence chiefly because in no circumstances, short of absolute necessity, would the Indian Government have ever made itself responsible even for the line connecting Kabul and Kandahar. Partly also it is due to the fact of the slow encroachments of Russia from the north; and the dexterous policy adopted by Abdur-Rahman, which in its essence was identical with that pursued by

west Mount Everest." Mr. Douglas Freshfield, in the course of his climb round Kangchanjanga, also marched some way along Nepalese paths, but made no attempt to leave the high mountain tracks.

[1] I may perhaps add as a personal reminiscence the answer that the Maharaja once made to me when I asked him why he maintained so sternly the complete seclusion of Nepal. " My friend, the English have at times difficulty in the government of India," he said. " Those difficulties arise in no small measure from the fact that in these days of easy travel all English sahibs are not sahibs. Now I am convinced that the prosperity of Nepal is bound up with the maintenance of British predominance in India, and I am determined that the sahib who is no sahib shall never enter Nepal and weaken my people's belief that every Englishman is a gentleman." I do not suppose, nor did the Maharaja intend me to understand, that this was the one and only reason for the exclusion of foreigners from the country, but as an acute realization of one of the causes of our trouble in India to-day, the comment is characteristic of the shrewd observation of Chandra Sham Sher. The Indian Government has frankly accepted and respected the wish of Nepal to be left alone, and those who see in straws the direction of a wind may find in the visitors' book in the dak bungalow at Raxaul the betraying comments of those who have wished to force themselves upon Nepal and have been unwilling to believe that both the Gurkha and the Englishman were grimly in earnest when they refused them permission. It is also true that one or two of these remarks go far to justify the Maharaja's belief that many of those who travel in India are not sahibs.

Abdul Hamid in Constantinople. A third feature, which wholly distinguishes the relations of the two States, is the presence between them of a lawless No Man's Land peopled with well-armed tribes, the habit of whose life and the poverty of whose soil has always tended to make them gangs of robbers rather than workers.

It has been suggested to the writer on more than one occasion that it is the influence of the Brahmans which so completely bars the door against travel in Nepal. But it may be as well to explain that this forbidden tract does not extend to the full southern limit of Nepal. The Tarai has never been considered as part of the taboo. It is not, of course, true that Englishmen or other Europeans are welcomed indiscriminately, even in what the Nepalese call the Naya Muluk. But the presence of foreigners is welcome when specially invited to take part in one of the magnificent big-game shoots arranged by the Maharaja, and at least tolerated when it is necessary for experts to travel in the district, who have been called in by Nepal for such purposes as the organization of forestry, or the improvement of mechanical transport, or the identification of ancient sites of interest. None of these has ever been considered as in any way an infringement of the sacrosanctity of the country. The line of absolute prohibition may be said to extend through Butwal to Hetaura, and thence along the crest of the foothills parallel to the Bengal border. In old days there were indeed travellers across these forbidden lands. Sir Joseph Hooker, the famous botanist, was permitted, after great difficulty and a certain amount of regrettable action on the part of the Indian Government, to follow the eastward route from Katmandu through Ilam to Nagri and Darjiling in British India.

But those were different days from ours. The practical and political objection felt by the ruling classes of Nepal to the visit of any foreigner to any part of Upper Nepal is reinforced tenfold by the determination of the men in the outlying towns and villages that the sanctity of their country shall not be defiled by the presence of a stranger. There the matter rests—and by the cordial co-operation of the British. The prohibition is stricter to-day than it was a hundred years ago. Unless I am mistaken, it will be stricter still after the death of the present Prime Minister. But no one can read the future of Nepal, and our oscillations may involve her in certain expansions which may in turn alter the wholesome rules of seclusion which now exist, and by which in a large measure she has consolidated her present position, not merely as a sovereign and independent State but as an Ally, on whose unfailing loyalty the British Empire has had every reason to congratulate itself for many years.

The old kings and the modern statesmen of Nepal chose well when they selected the Valley of Katmandu for the centre of their government. The position is central, the climate is temperate, the soil fertile, the locality consecrated by a hundred traditions, religious and political. The result is shown in the fact that nowhere else in Nepal is there to be found a tithe of the noble buildings that adorn, or the practical comfort that enfolds, the Valley. In magnificence of scenery alone does outer Nepal hold its own against the Valley of her kings.

Of the provincial towns of Nepal there are but three which, by any stretch of the word, can be called important centres. These are Butwal, Palpa, and Pokhra. It will be noticed that they lie within a comparatively small area in the Gandak basin; and, as will be seen later, they owe their distinction to various causes—partly to the existence of flat cultivable land, partly to their importance as administrative centres, and partly to the fact that the old high road between India and Tibet supplied them not only with the daily custom that a garrison brings with it, but no small advantage from the foreign trade that made its way painfully north or south beneath their walls. Other towns there are such as Salyana, Jumla, Dhankuta, Dipal, otherwise known as Silgarhi, Ridi, Baitadi, and Ilam, which possess a certain notability as the chief towns of districts, as goals of pilgrimage, or as military headquarters; but of all the places outside the Valley, the three first-mentioned towns are of the greatest consequence. It will therefore be interesting to take the reader along the road from the southern edge of the Valley of Katmandu to Butwal and thence into the hills in a northerly direction through Palpa and Ridi to Baglung. Then, returning in a generally east-south-east direction, he may glance at Pokhra and the Marsiangti district before visiting historic Gorkha and Nayakot lying deep below the edge of the Valley. He will then have some acquaintance with the general features of the most important area of outer Nepal.

One leaves Katmandu by the iron bridge over the Bagmati, and, after threading one's way through Patan, follows the southward course of that river. At Khokna the metalled road ends—with the exception of a few miles to be noted presently. From this point, until the Valley is again reached, there are merely tracks impossible to wheeled vehicles, though except in a few places it is possible to use pack animals throughout the entire journey. From the edge of the Valley beside the gorge there is, at sundown, as beautiful a view as any that Asia can boast. At one's feet the Valley—seemingly as flat and green as the lake that it once was—lies dotted with pleasant villages and the white breasts of splendid temples. Beside the rivers and the roads are fields of verdure which here and there lose themselves in wide pools of close forest or in the upsweep of the vegetation clothing the slopes of the sheltering hills. The sharp violet outline of the northern and eastern hills with their countless ravines and screes catches the golden light, while above them the white summits of the Himalayas indent the purple sky. Close by is Pharping, where is the power-house which

connecting Jalhar with Pachari Mojua would help to increase the output of the mines at the latter place.

At Narayani, as well as at Ridi and Muktinath, the sacred shaligrams are found, which are described later in connection with the town of Ridi. Hunting for them in the river-bed forms, therefore, no insignificant part of the local industries. From this point the jungle becomes less over the stretch between Narayani and Butwal, and after descending the Sameshwar fold the track into the latter place is comparatively good going.

Before reaching the town itself, incoming goods are examined and have to pay duty at octroi posts in the jungle.[1] Butwal, on the edge of the Tarai and therefore interested in agriculture and forestry, is also an important centre of traffic and transport from its position at the entrance of the long · mountain trail that leads up to Muktinath and the Photu Pass. To the south, a few miles nearer India, is the unprogressive little village Bethri.[2] Here there is a brick court-house, a gaol, and a few other official buildings. It is the residence of a Bada Hakim with two subas under him. A few sentries are detailed from Butwal to guard the Nepalese Government treasury here. Bethri is a fair example of many smaller towns in this district. Situated along the northern side of the Tarai, and in the danger zone, they act as centres of commerce without, at the same time, attracting any considerable number of inhabitants. During the summer the place is almost empty. Markets are held twice a year to which villagers come in from over a wide area. They bring in large quantities of rice, pulses, vegetables, and fruit, and barter them for the produce of the hills and of Tibet. The place is almost encircled by extensive jungles, and a few mango topes close to the Kachari, or court-house, render the town picturesque. Still, as was once said of a famous bridge at Cambridge, Bethri is eminently a place of transit and not of lounge, and the small colony of permanent inhabitants in the reed houses pay a heavy toll in human life for the trading profits, considerable though these are. It is one of the places like Hetaura, of which the permanent existence, despite climatic defects, is secured by its position on the high road just where the under-features of the Himalayas burst up through the Tarai, and further progress must be made along one track alone.

[1] See p. 6. This illustration gives a fair idea of the lesser undergrowth and younger timber which are spreading along the foothills of the Himalayas, and are now being developed by English experts. There is probably no valuable Indian timber tree that does not grow better in Nepal than in India. In the Tarai wheat is sown largely, and other crops include peas, (muzzar?) barley, gram, and rice; wheat is grown on the rice stubble and thrives. There are two crops of rice, one of which is produced by artificial irrigation. This ripens in May; the other is more dependent on the rains. Miles of dhub grass are utilized for cattle grazing. [2] This is spelt Bhetehi on some maps.

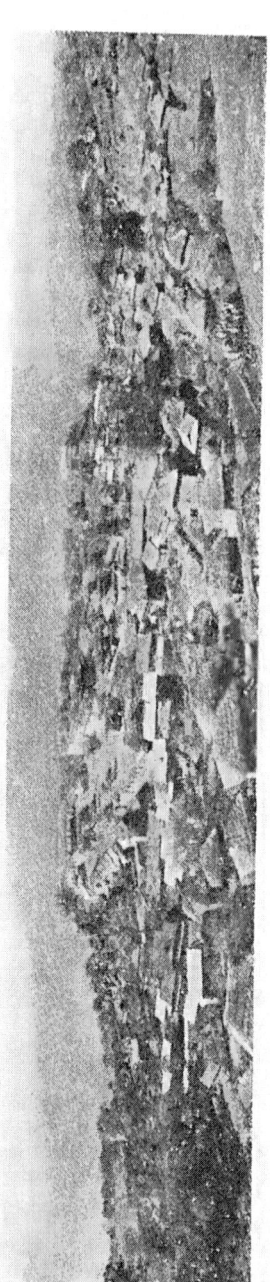

BUTWAL

8

§ 2

Butwal.—Butwal itself is a town of importance. Here there is a Residency, a couple of parade grounds, and several military offices. Three regular battalions of Nepalese troops spend the winter in Butwal and are moved up to Palpa in the hot weather. As is usual in Nepal, the parade grounds are as level as Lords' and kept in almost as perfect order. Large though the town is, its appearance is not imposing as the majority of houses are merely temporary structures of sun-baked brick with corrugated iron roofs. It is possible to live in Butwal all the year round, though the climate cannot be said to be healthy and epidemics of *awal* occasionally paralyse

A STREET IN BUTWAL

its industries. During the campaign of 1814-16 the strategic importance of Butwal and its retention by the British afterwards were matters to which Nepal attached no small value. Eventually, however, the place was given back to the Nepalese, and has remained in their hands as an administrative, military, and commercial centre. For justice and for trade alike the mountain folk come into Butwal from great distances. It is a natural halting-place for all travellers or caravans before the trans-Nepal route from India to Tibet is attempted, or after it has been traversed. But the great days of this road are gone, and the thin trickle of traffic which still uses the road through Katmandu to Kirong scarcely adds to her importance. But Palpa and Pokhra, towns of considerable consequence, as well as the lesser districts of Musikot and Baglung are centres for the collection of goods which are afterwards sent down into Butwal for transport to the Indian railhead at Bridgmanganj.

Besides the insufficiently explored ruins in the forest to the south of the town at Sena Mena—locally known as " Buddha's Darbar "—and Rummindei,[1] Butwal has a local fame for the growing of plants and shrubs of medicinal repute and for the production of many elixirs which both Nepal and Tibet consume in large quantities. Ghi, or clarified butter, is made here. The normal food crops, with the exception of rice, wheat, and Indian corn, grow scantily, but of these, together with certain pulses and vegetables, enough is grown for local needs. None of them is exported. The octroi yields an annual income to the State of one hundred and fifty thousand rupees. The place needs a better water supply, and I understand that the educational requirements of Butwal and a new system of sanitation are at this moment under the consideration of the Prime Minister. The plate will give a fair but not a flattering idea of the appearance of one of the main streets of Butwal.

§ 3

. *Palpa.*—Hereafter one turns one's back upon the rich vegetation of the Tarai and almost at once the characteristic scenery and vegetation of the Himalayan foothills is encountered. Immediately above the town is the fort of Nayakot. This is kept in better repair than the corresponding defences of Sisagarhi on the main road from Raxaul to Katmandu. A new track twelve inches wide permits the traveller to make his way up to Palpa; but strangers, even of Indian nationality, may only use it by express permission of the Maharaja. The jungle rapidly decreases as the ascent is made. No sal is found above Nayakot and the growth on the hills hereabouts is chiefly of use for fuel and as shelter for game. At Chitawan there is good shooting. The length of this path it is difficult to estimate. I have before me notes of a journey which make the distance from Butwal to Tansing only fourteen miles, which is certainly an underestimate: it is probably about twenty miles from Butwal to the adjacent town of Palpa. Though it cannot be regarded as better than a mule track, there does not seem to be any special difficulty.

Palpa is the name generally employed by writers on Nepal for the town which is often referred to in Nepal as Tansing. As in the case of many other districts in the country, " Palpa " is used both of the province of the city itself, and of the town which has gathered round the Governor's offices at a little distance—perhaps four and a half miles—which is locally known

[1] For a description of Rummindei, see chapter i. As permission to visit it is occasionally extended to European archaeologists, I have not inserted any account of it here. Notes of Sena Mena have appeared in the publications of the Archaeological Department of the Indian Government.

as Tansing, and generally as Palpa-Tansing. As the name Palpa is applied to the whole of this official area, it has been generally employed in these pages instead of Tansing.

It lies high on the crest of undulating hills of some steepness. There is a military cantonment here with a large parade ground lying at the back of the administrative offices of the Governor's palace.[1] In front of the palace is a long, well-kept lawn studded with trees, and containing a few shrines or memorials dating from different periods; none, however, is of great antiquity. The traveller will note as a proof of Palpa's prosperity

PALPA
Asantol quarter of Tansing

that here and in the older quarters of Tansing, nearly all the houses are built of kiln-burned brick.

All round this official centre the shingled or corrugated iron roofs of the town creep up or down from all sides. There is not an active market here, though, like Butwal, the place acts as a collecting centre. Palpa owes her high position among the outlying towns of Nepal to her administrative importance. The population of the town is said not to exceed six thousand, but it is difficult to believe that this can be the case, as besides the civilian officials permanently in residence, there are between 1,500 and 2,000

[1] The guns that Nana Sahib brought across the Nepalese frontier in 1857 were at once confiscated by the Nepalese and are said to be still at Palpa.

soldiers quartered here or at Butwal alternatively. It will be found by referring to the census returns [1] that the whole district of Palpa is actually more populous than even the Valley of Katmandu; the above figure should perhaps be taken with reserve. The town is well drained and rarely suffers from epidemics. She needs a better supply of good water and one would have thought that as an official centre she would have provided herself with a better system of primary education. The healthiness of her inhabitants is proverbial; a recent visitor was enthusiastic over their good looks: "all her men, women, and children have rosy cheeks and golden complexions and seem stout and strong there."

The Governor of Palpa has authority over the whole of the territory made sacred by the birth and childhood of Buddha, and it will be remembered that General Khadga Sham Sher—who afterwards fell by his own unwisdom—rendered great assistance to the archaeological department of India when Nigliva and Rummindei were discovered and partially explored. Of the local shrines, two of the most famous are the temples of Kal Bhairab and Palpa Bhairab,[2] which stand high up in the mountains about two miles from the city. The locality produces little in the way of cereals, though here and there in the shelter of watered valleys the ground is well and successfully tilled. There are many mango topes, and in the summer the flowers and fruits necessary for worship at the many shrines of Palpa are supplied by sweet-scented gardens and orchards.

About eight miles north-west of Palpa is Ridi, where the Kali Gandak is again met. The road to it is of the same uncomfortable nature as that which winds up from Butwal to Palpa. The vegetation dwindles all the way and the characteristic mountain scenery of Nepal closes in the horizon before one. From time to time the majestic icy peak of Dhaulagiri shuts in the view to the north, and from its southern shoulder a long bare rocky buttress leads to the outskirts of Ridi. Here its ravines afford a home for many companies of religious devotees. It lies at the confluence of a mountain stream and the Kali Gandak, which turns sharply to the east at this point.

§ 4

Ridi.—The most important characteristic and aspect of Ridi is its sanctity. It is regarded by the Nepalese as being almost equal in holiness to Benares, which is too far distant for any but the wealthier among the Nepalese to visit. But when their strength is failing them, many old men and even old women of Nepal will attempt the long journey into India in order that their bodies may be burnt at holy Kashi and their ashes assimil-

[1] Appendix VII, vol. i.
[2] This temple contains a figure of Bhairab which is identical with a figure in the palace square of Katmandu, before which officials were sworn in after the annual "paijni."

RIDI

ated with the waters of the thrice-sacred Ganges. At Ridi there is held out to them that after death the ashes of the faithful may become compacted and incarnate in the famous shaligram stones of the Gandak. The shaligram is a symbol of cardinal importance throughout Nepal and a large area of northern India. They are found at Ridi, upstream at Muktinath, and,

A STREET IN RIDI

as we have already seen, downstream at Narayani—all places on the Kali or Black Gandak. They are composed of a compact silica roughly spherical in shape and greyish black in colour. The surface is marked with white or yellow bands or spirals, and they roughly resemble a large unpolished onyx. But it is no shaligram unless it has a hole—or by a happier chance still, two holes—pierced completely through it. These are called by the Nepalese its eyes. For many centuries the curious little formations have been regarded as emblems of Narayan or Vishnu, and during worship before his shrines they are held up in the hand to sanctify the making of a vow. In the temples they are generally contained in a small copper cup, holding also Ganges water and a few leaves of the tulsi plant. At Ridi the last rites are performed, as at Pashpati. The dying man is placed upon a slanting ledge with his legs in the stream, and after death the body is burnt and the ashes strewn upon the running water.

Ridi is a well-built town with several good residential houses near it. The recesses of the hills are densely wooded, and in the small flat valley which surrounds it there is some scanty vegetation. The main building of the place is the Rikheswar temple, where there is a famous statue. This is

INTERIOR OF THE RIKHESWARA NARAYANA IN RIDI

an image of Rikheswar Rishikesh Bhagawan, one of the avatars of Vishnu. Local tradition has it that this statue was at the time of its discovery of the size and nature of an infant boy, but that it has in the course of years assumed the appearance of an adult god, and there are many old men and old women here who will testify to this miracle.

The town is huddled together between the high bluffs through which the mountain stream has cut its way, and the banks of the Kali Gandak, and only in one or two places is there a convenient descent to the level of the stream. On the crest and in the recesses of the hills above Ridi are the retreats and temples referred to. Religious men from Nepal or India are given shelter here and daily offerings are made to the god Bhagman by all. Besides acquiring general merit by their pilgrimage, the visitors expiate their sins by bathing in the sacred water that flows below the town. As is the case in most places of pilgrimage, the sale of articles of food and clothing to the devout comprises the larger part of the trade. Little rice or wheat is to be seen, and few vegetables appear to be cultivated in this rocky soil. To a great extent the food has therefore to be brought in from outside. In other circumstances Ridi might perhaps have been developed, for it enjoys a cold bracing climate and sanitation is an easy matter. Moreover, the general health is good, and from its position it might become the hill-station for the central Tarai.

Education in the English sense of the word is not provided here, nor is there either a post or telegraph office. Administratively Ridi is a dependence of Palpa, but, so far, it is her holiness only that has attracted any attention to the place. The architecture is more characteristically Nepalese than that of the other towns through which we have passed since leaving Katmandu. The illustrations on pages 13 and 14 will show how well the sacred town has maintained the Nepalese ideals of construction—ideals which for use and beauty are scarcely surpassed by those of the architecture of any other country in Asia. I am glad to be able to give a good photograph of the interior of the holiest of the shrines here—the temple to Rikheswara Narayana. In general it corresponds to the arrangement of the more famous temple near Bhatgaon, though it is probably much later in date. It is useful as a specimen of the architecture of the smaller temples of great local reputation that may be found in many places in the outlying districts of Nepal.

§ 5

. From Ridi a journey of about seventeen miles to the north-west takes one through Taksor, a dependence of Gulmi, to Tunghas. The track is bad from the beginning, though one which, in an emergency, can be used by tanjams. From Gulmi it is worse. Riding is impossible, and even while walking, both ponies and men are exposed to considerable danger. Tunghas is a small town on a plateau in the middle of a valley surrounded by well wooded hills where there may still be seen the traces of old bismuth workings. It is no great distance from this point to the " Kashmir of Nepal," at Musikot and Isma, though the journey may take five hours. These two towns are three miles apart on a well cultivated plain watered by the Badiya river surrounded by tree-covered hills eight thousand feet high. The district is rich in minerals. Bismuth, copper, antimony, and cobalt ores are all found here, and the presence of sapphires and rubies, though those found so far are of poor quality, suggest that a more systematic development of the place might repay the Government. Musikot offers another example of those collections of straggling townships that assume a common name to the bewilderment of travellers accustomed to greater precision of nomenclature. It spreads itself over an area about six miles long from east to west and about five miles wide from north to south. Within this space there are about ten large or small villages each known to itself as Musikot. Indeed, it is difficult to make any real distinction between Musikot and Isma, which is often included in the former designation, though it actually lies about a league west-by-south of central Musikot. Other villages claiming individuality are Nesti and Chali. A poor track about twenty miles long takes the traveller from Musikot to Baglung. It is known as a " mul sharak " or main road, but that is only joined five miles farther on when Kusma is reached. Seven miles beyond Baglung chairs cannot be

SYANGJA (NEAR POKHRA)

used; the path is fit only for those on foot. At Kusma the Modi stream from Dhaulagiri is crossed.

§ 6

Baglung is a busier centre of industry than any that we have seen hitherto. The women here weave a country cloth that is in great demand locally, and in 1924 there was a considerable cultivation of rice, wheat, mokaye (Indian corn), kodo, jowar (pulse), pumpkins, mustard, mangoes, plantains, and papayas. Fowls are kept by all except Brahmans and Chattris. In the dry season Baglung suffers from a grave disadvantage, for the wells dry up and the inhabitants have to descend a thousand feet to the river for their water.

From Baglung we begin the return journey to Katmandu. A little way south of Baglung, the Kali Gandak is crossed at Dhamarzung. This village on the left bank is about fourteen miles distant from Pokhra. The road is bad but picturesque, and the pine-clad hills that border it possess great stores of coloured mica.[1] Twelve miles on from Dhamarzung one passes the village of Henzabanzi, and from this point to Pokhra the road is so perfectly level that even in its existing state it might be used by motors.

§ 7

Pokhra.—Pokhra is the second city in Nepal—it would be more accurate to say it is the most important city outside the Katmandu group. It contains perhaps ten thousand inhabitants[2] and lies in a wide flat plain encircled by hills—the largest plain in Nepal except Katmandu and, possibly, Dumja—on the right bank of the Seti river. The plain is covered with lakes of considerable size—the only real lakes in all Nepal—which are bordered with trees. It contains important temples, notably those of Vindhya Basini—which is reported to be larger than the greatest temple in Patan, a comparison which probably refers to the temple of Machendranath—and of Durga. The town is characteristically Nepalese both in architecture and in the composition of its inhabitants. The illustration on page 19 gives as good a view of the bazar as could be obtained for me. It is a centre of administration, and possesses a Court of Justice and a military cantonment. Water is laid on in the main streets. It is not a place of wealth or of political importance, but its size, its fertile soil, and its position on the central east-and-west road of Nepal, combines with its official character to make it a town that is destined to play no small part in the future industrial development of Nepal. Hodgson makes the remark that the only other valley in Nepal at all comparable with that of Katmandu is the Jumla, which is smaller in area and at a considerably greater altitude. Here barley is grown whereas rice is the staple product of the metropolitan area. At a

[1] I give without comment the positive assertion of a traveller that the lumps, which are chiefly found at Namarzung, are red above the water level, while below it they are pink. Here, said the same authority, are also found rubies for the Lhasa market. It is not unlikely, considering the wealth of corundum strata in this district that these may be of genuine quality, but Mr. B. L. Shaw of Calcutta, the Indian traveller who has been kind enough to contribute much to this account of the towns in the Gandak district, and who is himself a known geologist, is of opinion that they may be spinels. The true ruby and the spinel ruby are alike crystals of corundum, but the latter is of octagonal crystallization while the true ruby is hexagonal. A trace of magnesium may also be found in the spinel, and its specific gravity is less. Otherwise it is indistinguishable from the no more beautiful stone which the world has decided to buy at a far greater price. The "Agincourt" ruby in the crown of England is really a spinel.

[2] A good illustration is thus offered of the manner in which almost the entire prosperity and commerce of Nepal is centred in the Valley of Katmandu. Each of the three greate towns of the Valley have a population slightly above or slightly below 100,000.

much lower elevation, not much higher than that of the Tarai, is the valley of Pokhra. This contains the lakes that are referred to elsewhere, from which, indeed, the name of the town is derived. The highest level is, however, so much lower than that of the valley that irrigation can only be effected by a large pumping plant. Jang Bahadur had a scheme for installing these pumps and hoped that he might secure an annual income of thirty or forty thousand pounds thereby. But the presence of an European engineer was regarded as essential, and the traditional hatred of the presence of foreigners, even Jang Bahadur did not care to challenge. It is already a producer of copper in considerable quantity, but the hills

THE POKHRA VILLAGE BAZAR

that surround it are full of other minerals. Its agricultural advantages will supply a vastly increased population, and if the industrial possibilities of Nepal are fully developed, the place will one day become an important mining and smelting centre.

§ 8

The road to the east turns south for a short distance and follows the edge of the Ulani lake. It afterwards accompanies the left bank of the Seti, which has the characteristic white opacity of snow water.[1] The view westwards from the point beside the lake where the roads divide is of

---

[1] It is said locally that even if bottled and put aside for a long time the water of this stream never recovers its limpidity.

extreme beauty. The flat plain of grass and water-grown willows with Pokhra lying low to the right, throws into relief the rugged heights that surround it, while the majestic mass of white-crowned Dhaulagiri dominates the higher peaks of the north-western horizon. At Durgahashi the track turns in a somewhat more easterly direction, and after passing Deorali Bhanjyang at fourteen miles, reaches Tarkughat at about twenty-eight. This village is of no importance beyond the fact that from this point two routes climb up one on each side of the river Marsiangti to the famous salt mines. These tracks are in places but six inches in width and wind their

JIMRO STREAM
Two miles from Pokhra

way among and across slippery sloping boulders. All vegetation stops two or three thousand feet above the level of Tarkughat, and at eleven thousand feet snow remains permanently in the ravines that score the mountain side.

Brine Springs.—The salt mines, or rather the brine springs from which the salt is evaporated, lie on the right bank of the Marsiangti. It is impossible to obtain any accurate estimate of their height, but they are probably from fourteen thousand to sixteen thousand feet above sea level. The largest are at Panu Khani and have been worked for about ninety years. In spite of the great difficulty of extracting the salt at a temperature that is rarely above freezing point, and where fuel [1] is scanty, a considerable amount is brought down to Pokhra, and a certain number of Tibetans make their way across an almost impracticable pass—nearly twenty-one thousand feet in height—to purchase it. The workers there say that it is a two days' journey from them to the Tibetan frontier—an estimate which would justify the higher of the two figures just given as the probable altitude of the brine springs.

The Marsiangti is crossed by two bridges; one of wood at Udaipur, and a suspension bridge—the gift of Suba Norjang—at Bhulbulia. There is another bridge across the stream at Udaipur, but this is regarded as

BANDIPUR
Headquarters of the district of Tanhung

unsafe. The river is generally about eighty-five feet wide. The eastern bank of it is in most cases almost a vertical cliff of rock, but the right bank is continually slipping into the stream, and there is a proposal to support it by a retaining wall. The track is of a dangerous nature and a new road

[1] The salt is obtained by boiling the brine in copper pans heated over fires fed by dora or brushwood. It is estimated that salt of about one-eighth the weight of the brine is extracted here. The process seems to be conducted under unnecessary difficulties. Were the brine pumped into an open channel and dealt with lower down, where evaporation is normal and the supply of wood sufficient, it would be possible to extract a far greater amount than is at present obtained. At Panu Khani there is no possibility of making full use of even what little evaporation takes place, because the ground does not permit of the construction of wide flat pans.

will have to be constructed if the salt industry is to be seriously developed.[1] Pack animals are at present impossible. The suspension bridge at Bhulbulia is approached over enormous water-worn blocks that constitute a danger in themselves. Two miles downstream from this point the Khudi stream falls into the Marsiangti and gives its name to a small village where there is a rest-house. The skill of its inhabitants in wood-carving is well known, and some of the finest temples in Pokhra have been decorated by the men of Khudi.

From this point the road to the capital passes villages of the normal type. The architecture—or the lack of it—does not differ from that already

VILLAGE OF KHOPLAN

illustrated in the plates. In the centre of each cluster of houses is a circular stone platform from which a pipal grows to give shade to travellers during the midday halt. Here there are always chattis of water, and generally there is a red-sprinkled image or symbol of Mahadeo, or a bell slung from a stone frame. The villages themselves are clean, and the villagers are simple and friendly to those who speak their language. One of these villages, Bandipur, is the military centre of the district of Tanhung. The traffic upon all Nepalese routes is small except upon those near the Valley of Katmandu or upon those which give access to railheads in India. In

[1] Generally speaking Nepal is badly supplied with salt, and it is from Tibet that the larger part is obtained.

remoter districts the wayfarer will often find himself in solitude for hours together.

§ 9

Gorkha.—There are two roads from the Marsiangti to Katmandu, of which the northern constantly crosses the affluents of the Seti. The highest watershed is crossed, and the Darwadi basin reached at last. At the bottom of the hill to the north is the picturesque little village of Khoplan Bhanjyang[1] where the road divides. The lower track pursues an east-south-easterly direction, and after about eight miles passes through Gorkha, the historic capital and cradle of the ruling dynasty of Nepal.

GORKHA

Gorkha [2] lies at the foot of a semicircle of hills which enclose a wide and well cultivated plain. Here there are barracks for two battalions of soldiers. Like other Nepalese towns it is of a straggling nature, and it is only near Pokhri Tol that the buildings combine to make any considerable effect. A house, once the home of Bhim Sen Thapa, is still pointed out. There are several interesting shrines here, though none of great size. By

[1] See p. 22.
[2] It is now generally accepted that the word "Gorkha" was in its origin identical with the title of "Gaekwar" which is assumed by the Maharaja of Baroda. It seems, therefore, to trace the warlike race back to a time when their occupation was less that of arms than of the peaceful tending of the holy cow—a very long period. Doctor Oldfield considered the term Gorkhali applied to all natives of the Gorkha district irrespective of their class. The term has since been roughly, but irregularly, extended to cover any military tribe from which the Gurkha battalions in the Indian army are recruited.

the side of a deep rectangular pool are two temples, one of early date with two roofs, and the other of the much later square dome-crowned style,[1] to which reference will be made shortly. The hills round Gorkha are fairly well wooded, the plain, which it commands, is carefully tilled, and the areca palm grows here without much difficulty. But it is not in the agricultural aspect of the place that the chief interest lies.

Long before the days of the invaders from India Gorkha had been a place of refuge, and there still exist traces of very early fortification on the conical hill whereon are placed the darbar buildings and the Bhawani temple—a situation which in old days it must have been difficult to take

GORKHA
The Pokhri Tol

by storm. Gorkha thus maintained its independence for many centuries in the uncertain manner in which so many other Nepalese fastnesses asserted their petty sovereignties, until the upward movement of the migration from Rajputana, driven north from the plains by Mohammedan invaders, flowed over the under-features of the Himalayas. The farthest point reached by the Mohammedan tide was not decided only by the difficulty of fighting with mountaineers within the shelter of their own hills. There was also a height at which the Himalayan winters proved too rigorous for the invading Moslems. Those whom they drove before them, those almost unwilling Rajput invaders of Nepal, had no choice but to adopt

[1] Perhaps the best and largest illustration of this style may be seen in the temple built by Jang Bahadur on the banks of the Bagmati in Katmandu.

the policy of permanent occupation. Return to the plains they could not; nor was it possible for them to live strung out along the series of Nepalese valleys where there was a chance of cultivation without putting their isolated cities of refuge into some state of defence. So one by one they occupied and strengthened the small kots or hill forts which proved, in

SANGU (NEAR NAYAKOT)

their hands, a still more sufficient defence against the unskilled and spasmodic assaults of neighbouring tribes. In 1559 Gorkha was captured and held by Drabya Sah. He could then, of course, have had no prevision of the great extension of the power and prosperity of his people among the Nepalese mountains, although by this annexation he laid the foundations for them. The present King of Nepal is the descendant of Drabya Sah, and, young as he is, it would be rash to prophesy that he would himself join his ancestors without having witnessed—if not achieved by his own hands—a further extension of the kingdom that had its rise in this half-deserted little town of Gorkha.

Of the Darbar building itself and the temple of Bhawani there is little to note except the final ascent to the latter through three archways, a feature which is found nowhere else in Nepal. Before the Bhawani temple is gained a remarkable flight of steps about one hundred and twenty feet in height and about seventy-five feet in width, has to be scaled.[1] The decoration of the shrine is ornate. In striking contrast to its elaboration is the holy of holies of the Gurkha race, a little crude sanctuary hidden in a cavern to which access is almost impossible except on hands and knees—the shrine of Gorakhnath. Here, beneath an overhanging stream, housed in the natural recesses of the rock, and with little adornment beyond the ceremonial tridents, flags, halberds, trumpets, and other insignia of all such places of worship, is the image of the god. The contrast between the high-built temple, with its majestic flight of stairs, and the humble simplicity of the divine habitation below it, recalls a curiously similar juxtaposition in Europe—Lourdes. There is little in the town to-day to attract attention. The glory, if not the sanctity, of Gorkha is departed, and, except for scanty business traffic, there is little travelling along the road that connects Gorkha with Katmandu.

§ 10

Nayakot.—The track to Nayakot now follows the northern road. A more direct track from Gorkha to Katmandu has been made which avoids Nayakot, and makes its way through Dhading to Kakani on the north-western edge of the Valley; but it is reported to be difficult and liable to damage during the rains. Along the northern track there is not much to detain the traveller, though as he approaches Katmandu he will welcome the picturesque beauty of the little town of Sangu, where the northern and western roads from Katmandu divide. The general aspect of the hills through which this route perpetually ascends and descends differs in no way from that of other mountain landscapes in Nepal. The road is bad throughout until the Trisul Gandak is reached. Making one's way across it by one of the suspension bridges which the present Maharaja has substituted for an old unsafe wooden bridge, one is confronted by Nayakot.

Nayakot lies on a spur descending in a south-westerly direction from Mount Dhaibung, about a mile distant from the Trisul Gandak in the west and the same distance from the river Tadi to the south and east. The town, which at one time was more prosperous and of greater importance than it is to-day as the winter residence of the Gurkha kings until 1813, consists for the most part of about sixty three-storeyed houses. These are apparently

---

[1] See vol. i, p. 65.

rather in the style of those in Kirtipur which Hodgson calls the Chinese style of Katmandu.

There is only a single street lying in an indentation of the cross of the ridge, and it is consequently invisible from below. The upper Darbar building and the temple to Bhairab are placed on somewhat higher ground and may be partially seen. It is a straggling area shut in on all sides by precipices except to the south-west, where a flat plain intervenes between the two rivers. The general difficulty of obtaining water has turned the Nayakot area into a realm of orchards and mango topes. The King of Nepal owns important plantations of the latter fruit. Lower down on the river level are fruit gardens where almost anything can be grown from pears, apples, and plums to cocoanut, betel, and the supari, which we know at home as the cape gooseberry. Its oranges and pineapples are famous and rice is grown, some varieties of which cannot be raised in the much higher fields of the Valley.

Nayakot is only about two thousand feet above the level of the sea. The lakes from which the two rivers, Trisul Gandak and Tadi, rise lie ten thousand feet higher, just below the line of perpetual snow. This descent has to be made within thirty miles. The frequency of vast spates as well as the normal rapidity of their current may be imagined.

The town of Nayakot is now more famous for its gardens and orchards than for its political significance. But the illustration on p. 63, vol. i, of the Darbar at Nayakot is of interest because it was from this town that Prithwi Narayan Sah directed his attack upon the Nepal Valley in 1768 and 1769, and it has its niche in history as one of those places in which, however humble their subsequent lot, destiny was fulfilled and the first words of a new chapter written. Until the occupation of the Valley by Prithwi Narayan, and indeed for a long time afterwards, low-lying Nayakot was the winter residence of the wealthier classes of the Valley, and generally of the Court also. But that is almost a thing of the past; whatever exodus there now is during the cold weather seeks a lower altitude still; the Tarai or India itself is preferred. The many-storeyed houses—outside the Valley and the Tarai, only here, at Pokhra, and at Palpa are there generally found buildings of more than one storey—bear witness to a vanished importance. The town is to-day merely a double line of houses along a depression in the hills. Only the Darbar structure and a temple to Bhairab break the view to the spectator from a distance. Compared with Katmandu, Nayakot lies low, but it is eight hundred feet above the rivers at whose juncture it is placed, and the difficulty of obtaining water has in the long run contributed to the development rather of the river-banks than the town itself. The watersmeet is presided over by a flattish decline of which the lowest part is occupied by the famous mango topes belonging to the king. Here, however, the dreaded *awal* reigns as virulently, though not for so long a period, as in the Tarai. Picturesquely enough, the Nepalese believe that at the close of the great festival of Bhairab the Destroyer in the middle of April, who is therein worshipped in the form of a tiger, the local goddess releases the man-destroying plague upon all who dare to trespass upon the tiger's favourite haunt of the Tarai. The difference of altitude between Nayakot itself and the warm damp valley below it is shown also in the different races that inhabit the two districts. Newars from the Valley are in a majority in Nayakot, while only the immune or semi-immune tribes of the Tarai and the Bhabar—or intermediate zone—can live in the malarious atmosphere of the Trisul Gandak and the Tadi.

As a garden community Nayakot has no parallel in Nepal. The markets of Katmandu are supplied with mangoes, tamarinds, bels, guavas, bananas, and custard apples, and sections of sugar-cane—all denizens of the hot Indian plains, but all improved by the touch of autumn chill which adds a flavour unknown in Bihar. Of the "temperate" fruits the pears, apples, apricots, and plums rival those of Kashmir.[1]

From Nayakot the journey into Katmandu is simple enough. The track descends a little towards the royal mango groves and then, crossing the Tadi, follows the left bank of the Trisul Gandak for a little way. It then ascends a little valley by a stony track until, not far from the British Envoy's summer bungalow, it joins the western road that accompanies the Trisul Gandak all the way to Tribeni and the Indian frontier. From this point there is a fairly steep descent to Jitpur and an easy path down to Dharmathali and Balaji on the western edge of the Valley. From Balaji a flat and good avenue leads to the north-west corner of Katmandu city and Thamale, not far from the Legation lines.

"Thamale" is the local pronunciation of Thambahil, a suburb of Katmandu, wherein the priests ceremonially plant every year the first rice of the season.[2]

[1] Dr. Oldfield records that in his time peaches were unknown there: they have since been grown with great success.

[2] Thamale extends from the north-western point of the city of Katmandu across the plain which divides the Vishnumati from the ground on which the British Legation is placed. Rather fancifully, a resemblance has been detected between the shape of this extension to the Scarf of Honour which is by custom attached to the hilt of the oriental sword.

CHAPTER XII

UNKNOWN NEPAL

THE TRACKS

WE have now roughly described the most important outlying towns of Nepal; we have followed two characteristic roads leading westwards out of the Valley; and we have seen the nature of the country from Bethri in the hot Tarai to the chilly salt mines fifteen thousand feet and more above the sea and within two stages of the Tibetan frontier. We have noted the characteristics of several different towns such as Ridi with its holy associations; Butwal the frontier station, unhealthy in climate but essential for purposes of trade and of guarding the Indian border; Palpa, a city of officials and a kind of commercial collecting station for many miles round. Farther up, in the healthier upper area, we have touched upon the plain of Musikot, which seems likely to become the centre of a valuable mining district; Baglung the industrious, perched sixteen hundred feet above the Kali Gandak; Pokhra, the best example outside the Valley of a Nepalese centre of administration, and probably destined in the future to become far more commercially important than she is to-day; finally, we have noticed Gorkha, the home of the ruling race, and the diminished glories of Nayakot itself.

It is now necessary to refer briefly to the two great trade routes that lead out, north and north-east respectively, from the capital into Tibet. These are respectively known from their last passes as the Kirong and Kuti roads, though neither village is actually within the present limits of Nepal, and they have had a historical and practical influence on Nepalese history which is shared by no other road leading into her seven-hundred-thousand-square-miled neighbour.

§ I

Kirong.—The Kirong road, which we will take first, is the more westerly of the two routes. From Katmandu one makes one's way through the avenue of willows to Balaji and then ascends the river bed of the Mahadeo khola through Dharmathali. From Dharmathali there is a path at an easy gradient to Jitpur. The scenery of this route increases in beauty as one rises slowly above the level of the plain. From Chandragiri it is possible to obtain a magnificent view of the Valley of Katmandu, but the picture thus gained is inevitably obstructed by the dense forest growth that fills the ravine down which the track descends. From Jitpur there is unrolled a wider and an even more beautiful view. To the right are the forests of Balaji and Mount Nagarjun; filling the centre of the landscape is the sweep of buildings and temples which make up Katmandu, Thamale, Deo Patan, and Pashpati; and the long panorama is happily finished at each end by the great white domes of Swayambhunath and Boddhnath. On a clear day the view from higher up is plotted out over a far greater area and with greater distinctness. But many prefer the graceful composition of a landscape to the merciless flat accuracy of an ordnance map, and it is from the reasonable height of Jitpur that the finest view can be had of the Valley of Katmandu.

Immediately above Jitpur the road becomes steep, loose, and difficult. The following extract from a letter will perhaps give a sufficient description of this track. " We walked to Jitpur for the most part along smooth paths fringing the river. There we got into chairs and were lifted up a steep road with an ever-widening map of the Valley before us [1] all the time. One could even detect an outburst of smoke in the heart of Katmandu which suggested a house on fire not far from the Darbar Square. The Tundi Khel was pasted down like a flat green leaf.

" As soon as we got out of the Valley and on to the south-western slopes of Kakani, we were among forty-foot rhododendron trees largely furred with orchids, though these were less profuse than those on the south-western slope of Chandragiri. We passed through scattered groups of houses, for the most part thatched and red-ochred cottages, with pipals of honour set in brick circles for the wayfarer's rest in the middle of the road; and goats, coolies, poultry, and family parties made up indiscriminately the inhabitants of the low stoeps. The houses were generally of two storeys, and the conversation on the threshold below was frequently corrected by the outspoken comments of the elderly ladies at the windows of the first floor. The loads that the coolies were carrying seemed even heavier than those which are taken up the treacherous southern slope of Sisagarhi. A baulk of wood, ten feet long and six inches square, seemed to be regarded as a fair burden for a single man. We turned aside to the Envoy's summer bungalow, on a spur of Kakani, just where the main track begins to trend downhill towards Nayakot."

The Envoy's summer residence at Kakani is placed upon a flattish crest, extending altogether about four hundred yards in length, and varying between fifty and one hundred and fifty yards in width. The bungalow itself is a white structure with an open pillared porch extending the width of the house and providing a cool sitting-room. The window frames are painted a bluish green, and the grey galvanized iron roof blinks at the sun. To the English visitor the most remarkable feature of Kakani is the

[1] We were of course carried up backwards.

SCENE NEAR CHANGU NARAYAN

fact that there is a daring miniature golf course laid out on the slightly levelled mountain crest. For all practical purposes the links are less than two hundred and fifty yards long by, at most, a hundred yards wide. On all sides the ground descended rapidly, but to the north-east the wooded precipice dropped so fast that a mere twelve-handicap man could without much difficulty have driven six hundred yards.

There are many other places in this most interesting of all Asiatic valleys, and perhaps not the least attractive are the hot-weather stations at Kakani and Nagarkot, on the north-western and eastern hills respectively. Here, while the temperature of the Valley surges about 90° Fahrenheit, there is always a cool wind, and the nights are free from mosquitoes. Moreover, from these crests the enormous range of the Himalayas, culminating in a far-off mound of snow and ice, which the world knows as Everest, fills the eye from sunrise to dusk. From no other habitable spot can such a panorama be seen as this long expanse of the ice-bound backbone of the world. One has only to walk a few paces in the other direction to look down on the other side upon the wide, peaceful Valley of Katmandu, with its clustering red-brown towns, its white domes, and the broad, even spaces of its lawn-like parade grounds. In all directions the surface of the plain is intersected by meandering river-beds, and the woods that cover the western and southern slopes rise like a tapestry of verdure masking the terrible paths by which alone this, perhaps the most beautiful of Himalayan valleys, communicates with, or is protected from, the outer world. You may see the chimney of a power station, or trace perhaps the obelisks of steelwork that support the ropeway that supplies Katmandu with her necessities from India and with her comforts from the entire world.

The main road to Kirong, which we have abandoned for the moment to pay a visit to the Envoy's bungalow, pursues a more or less steady descent for about three thousand five hundred feet, and from Kakani may faintly be traced at the bottom of the valley into which the Tadi Khola runs. Across this stream is visible the tip of the flat strip of land, to which I have before referred in speaking of the royal mango groves south of Nayakot. The track turns upstream beneath that town and rises and falls till at Sangu the routes diverge. That which we have just traced from Pokhra goes off to the left, the other, which we are about to follow, trends to the north-east along the eastern bank of the Trisul Gandak.

Pursuing the latter, one comes in about seven miles to Betravati.[1] This village lies at the confluence of the Trisul Gandak with the stream which played a famous part in the last stage of the war with China in 1792. I quote the story in the words in which it was told to me.

" The crossing of the Betravati, according to local tradition, brought disaster upon the Chinese army at the time of its invasion of Nepal. The

[1] The name is shown as Betravali on most maps. This is the local pronunciation.

Gurkhas, under Damodar Panre, secreted themselves on the opposite
shore, and thence attacked the Chinese troops, who were crossing a narrow
bridge over the stream. Pressed from behind by their own troops, and
opposed in front by the Gurkhas, the small bridge became over-congested,
and at this critical moment it either gave way or, as the tradition goes, the
Gurkhas cut the mooring chains, and thus a number of Chinese were thrown
into the surging water below. The Chinese advance stopped at this place,
and peace negotiations were begun." [1]

It will be remembered that Nayakot lies at a much lower elevation
than Katmandu, and the rise in the track is not considerable until Betravati
is passed. Here a steep ascent begins. The track keeps consistently to the
left bank of the river and makes its way over a large number of mountain
tributaries. The road presents little of interest except the rugged scenery
and the countless swirling rapids of the river which even in the winter
remains of a milky hue. At Ramcha there is a military post. This place
is only fifteen miles from Nayakot, but is three thousand four hundred feet
higher. The road then skirts a village at the river end of a small plain
known, as in Katmandu, by the name of Tundi. Eight miles on is Shabru,
one of the halting-places of the route. This is a small village which supplies
a neighbouring outpost with provisions. Here the road divides, and a track
running to the north-east communicates with Gosain kund, which will be
described later. The actual ascent to the lakes, which is very steep, begins
a mile or two farther on at Kundi, whence there is a steady and severe
climb for seven miles before the first of the pools is reached.

Eight miles farther along the main or north-western route to Kirong
there is for some distance a " trang," cut for the most part in the mountain
side and quite impassable by night. Beyond this lies the frontier post of
Rasua Chok, five thousand seven hundred feet above the sea. Here there
is a customs house and a garden. Many more feet, however, have to be
climbed before the pass is reached. It will be remembered that after the
Chinese war a considerable portion of land on the Nepalese side of the
watershed at both Kirong and Kuti was annexed by the Chinese. The matter
remains the cause of a not ill-founded complaint on the part of Nepal. At
both places the Tibetans—who have assumed the territorial rights obtained
by China in the Treaty of 1792—would be able to surmount the actual pass
at their leisure and descend some ten miles into what geographically speaking
should be Nepalese territory before reaching the actual frontier. In military
operations this might give Tibet such an overwhelming advantage that the
threat of any such concentration would justify Nepal in securing the outer
pass herself. Certainly in Katmandu it would be regarded as a natural
precaution.

After crossing into Tibet the road, still keeping to the left bank of the

[1] See vol. i, pp. 68-69.

Trisul Gandak, which here takes the name of the Jongkha Changpo, arrives at Kirong itself, a fortified place without attraction of any kind whatever. It has, however, played an important part in Nepalese wars and is occupied by a small detachment of Tibetans who are drawn from the larger military centre of Jongkha Jong, forty miles away by road to the north. Kirong was described by one of the pandits bent on Tibetan travel as a place with a fort, a good-sized temple, about twenty shops, and a population of between three and four thousand. It is interesting to note that wheat and barley were then grown round the town, and that the place acted as a trade exchange for Tibetan salt and Nepalese rice.

From this point the road runs in a north-easterly and easterly direction following the right bank of the mighty Tsangpo, which, after circumnavigating the eastern massif of the Himalayas and sweeping down some six thousand feet in a series of rapids from Tibet to the jungles of Sadiya, becomes the Brahmaputra and joins the Ganges, less mighty than itself, at the familiar watersmeet at Goalundo in Bengal.

§ 2

Kuti.—The other main road into Tibet is that through Kuti, or Nilam. To this place the route from Katmandu runs eastward through the Valley, leaving Bhatgaon on the right hand and making the first halting-place at Sankhu. This village is still within the Valley, which is not left behind until the Chautaria pass is reached, about fourteen miles from Katmandu. Once over the rim we follow the descent to the Mulanchi river which, after about ten miles, falls into the upper waters of the Sunkosi. If the Kirong track offers little attraction beyond scenery it must be admitted that its rival presents even less. The changing scene is not without grandeur, though continuous unclad slopes and peaks of rock, however enormous, become in time more monotonous than any other natural spectacle. The route threads its way through a large number of small clumps of houses, with here and there a place worthy of the name of village, all of which support themselves on the necessities of the travellers. None of them, however, offers any especial interest except to the ethnologist. It is among highly placed Himalayan villages such as these that the persistence can be observed of eight or nine different races of Tibetan origin, all Nepalese subjects and all insisting upon speaking their own tongue— generally a greatly modified but recognizable form of Tibetan. They carry their racial jealousy to such an extent that in some villages the inhabitants of neighbouring houses or huts are actually unable to understand each other. This, of course, is a needless addition to the work of administration, and the Nepalese Government, in providing an official and universal language for use throughout the country, is slowly breaking it down. But so difficult of access are these peoples, so remote from the world of business, and so proud of their individual descent that it may be long before success is achieved. Sometimes the probable origin of the inhabitants of a given village may be deduced from its name. Thus it is said that the little village of Newar, which lies beyond the Bisingkhar pass; represents an unmixed colony from the Valley of Katmandu. By all accounts the Kuti track, which has suffered even more than the Kirong route from the competition of the Çhumbi Valley, is so little used that it would scarcely be worth while to do more to it than has been done by the present Government, which is satisfied if the bridges along the track are kept in reasonable repair, and the " trangs " made safe.

Soon after leaving Newar the road runs along the right bank of the Sunkosi, which is here known as the Bhotiakosi, and climbs rapidly to a height of about ten thousand feet. Much of the road is hacked out of the cliff, and in places it consists of a mere foothold supported on iron and wooden beams driven into the hill-side. The name Chaksam, which is also found as the name of a village in the upper reaches of the Budhi Gandak to the west, indicates a place where men using the Tibetan tongue had at one time thrown iron chains across the gorge to support a temporary foot-bridge.[1] The Kuti Pass track was recorded by an Indian traveller to Tibet as one of the most dangerous in the whole Himalayan range.[2] He describes the route as passing through a fearful gorge where the road crosses the river no less than fifteen times; thrice by iron suspension bridges, and twelve times by wooden bridges, some of which were sixty paces long. At one point the rocky sides of the gigantic chasm were so close that a bridge of twenty-four paces spanned it. At another a path is supported along the perpendicular wall of rock on iron pegs let into the face of the rock. The path, of stone slabs covered with earth, is only eighteen inches wide, one-third of a mile long, and one thousand five hundred feet high above the roaring torrent.

The present Maharaja has done all that is possible to keep alive this historic route, but it is doubtful whether this track is available for animals, loaded or not. From the frontier station of Kodahari the path still climbs steadily upwards for twenty miles across the plateau to Kuti or Nilam at a height of thirteen thousand nine hundred feet, from which point the road descends slightly and again climbs to Tingri, which is about the same

---

[1] The best surviving example of these bridges is that which crosses the great Tsangpo river about forty-two miles south-west of Lhasa. This, too, gives the name Chaksam to the village on the southern bank, and it may be added as a curious testimony to the enterprise as well as the skill of the ironworkers of the fifteenth century, that the links are as good to-day as when they were forged.

[2] Father Grueber and Father Dorville, Jesuit missionaries, visited Nepal in 1662. Grueber records the tremendous precipices across the face of which he scaled the Kuti Pass and reached Katmandu.

height as Nilam. From this point there is an up and down track joining the Tsangpo road at Shigatse.

While upon the subject of the Kuti road it is worth while to record the inaccurate but picturesque description of Father Georgi who—quoting from Father Cassien's narrative—says that it is twelve miles from Katmandu to Sankhu, through which place all travellers to Tibet are obliged to pass. For which reason, says Father Cassien, Sankhu is the apple of discord among the kings of the Valley. Eight miles from Sankhu, Langur is reached after crossing the river Koska. From Langur to the next halting-place, Sipa, is eighteen miles, and the same distance separates Sipa from Ciopra. We are now fifty-six miles from Katmandu according to Father Georgi. Even admitting a certain looseness in the estimate of Father Cassien, it is difficult to identify some of these places, as his record of the length of the stages is repeatedly wrong. At the seventy-sixth milestone is the village of Nogliakot, with many chaityas, stones engraved with the formula *om mani padme hum* round the pagoda. Eight miles farther on is Paldu, and at the fourteenth mile Nesti, or Listi, is reached, a name that appears more than once in the record of the campaigns between Tibet and Nepal. At a point four miles on, he says that rice is cultivated—a most unlikely form of agriculture. His description of the difficulties of the road is picturesque. At the hundred and sixth mile—I quote from M. Lévi's translation —the very narrow track lies along the edge of precipices and is continually turning the corners of extremely lofty mountains. Often the yawning gulfs between the rocks are bridged by narrow and trembling constructions of sticks and undergrowth. The traveller shudders to see underneath him immense sheer precipices and to hear the noise of the water tumbling at the bottom among the stones. There is one specially difficult point which reduces timid or inexperienced men to terror, and the more they fear, the greater is the risk of a fall. Here a prominent rock about sixteen feet long slopes downwards over an abyss, and is the more slippery from the dripping waters which continually wash and polish it. It is true that holes have been hacked out upon its surface where the traveller is able to place, if not his entire foot at least the ball of it; but Father Georgi does not seem to think that this much reduces the terrors of the passage. The river Nohotha is spanned by iron chains. Here people cross in safety upon the footway of the bridge grasping, on the right hand and on the left, two cables which are riveted into the rock at each end, but the oscillations of this rough bridge are fearful—especially when there is added to them the vibration caused when several persons are passing at the same time out of step. Then, says Father Cassien, one can scarcely endure the terror. Sixteen miles farther on is Khangsa, or Khasa, which still gives its name to this portion of Nepal irredenta. Once more the fathers encountered a wretched and dangerous path, worse even than that of the day before. There were no less than twenty-nine gangways to cross, and the mountain side to which they clung in desperation was as dizzy as ever, and the hazards more numerous.[1] At last, after passing Dhairab kund, a spring of warm water, Kuti is seen, the last outpost of Nepal. Georgi's comparison of this pass with that of the Jelep in Sikkim is based on no knowledge of the latter, but it is interesting to recall his statement that the Sikkim road was in old days, as it is again to-day, the easiest route from India to Tibet. Father Cassien records the causes and the conditions of the temporary cession of Kuti to Tibet. They include the establishment of the Nepal currency in Tibet, the grant of extra-territoriality to Nepalese living in Kuti, Shigatse, Egantze, and Lhasa, a regular tribute of salt and Nepal's right to appoint the head men of the villages along the track between " Nepal " and Kuti.

§ 3

Gosain kund.—More important than any other religious centres outside the Valley are those of Gosain kund, or Gosain-than, and Muktinath. The former lies high up among the mountain ridges which ultimately join to form the buttresses of the holy Himalayan range. There is a mountain called Gosain-than ten or twelve miles beyond the frontier [2] in Tibet, but Nepal can boast of the sacred lakes—which are generally known to Europeans by the same name of Gosain-than—the cause of some confusion. They are magnets for a perpetual pilgrimage throughout the kindlier months of the year. Mention has already been made of the road from Nayakot to Dungsay where the tracks, to the pass and the lakes respectively, diverge. The latter road is naturally not only attended by sacred traditions but is adorned also by carvings of a religious nature. One of the most curious natural features of Nepal may be found between Rapcha (Ramcha) and Dungsay At a little Tibetan village called Taria an immense rock overhangs the road and forms the roof of a large natural cavern capable of sheltering between two and three thousand persons. It is largely used as a halting-place during the pilgrim season.

Of these lakes there are said to be twenty-two. The largest of them is known as Gosain kund, or Nilkhiat kund, and is of interest because it is the source of the river Trisul Gandak. The water falls into the lake from

[1] Father Marc does not attempt to give the length of the stage of this journey, but his description of its terrors is even more remarkable than that of Father Cassien. So terrible, he says, is the crossing of some of the chain bridges that many travellers are blindfolded and bound to a plank, which is slung to the cables and manœuvred across by a local expert.

[2] It is an imposing peak of twenty-six thousand three hundred feet, though its apparent height is dwarfed by the ice-crowned summits that attend it. It is known to the Tibetans as Shisha Pangma. It will be noted that the frontier line, as traced on the Nepalese maps includes access to the summit of this mountain.

a rock on the northern side by the three springs which have suggested the special name of the river. During the winter the lakes are thickly frozen over, but the stream of the Trisul continues to run. Gosain kund seems at first sight a curious place to have chosen for pious travel and adventure; except on the principle that the Himalayan gods—or, it would perhaps be better to say, the gods in their Himalayan aspect—prefer to live apart and unmolested by men. Seldom do these austere divinities sanction such

GOSAIN KUND

direct access as is permitted at Gosain kund or Muktinath. It is interesting to remember that within a radius of a hundred miles of Mount Everest most of the villagers, Nepalese and Tibetans alike, probably believe that the patience of the deity was at last exhausted when for the third time an attempt was made, in 1924, to violate her icy shrine, and that the deaths of Mallory and Irvine were directly and certainly due to the displeasure of that lonely deity.

But the lakes of Gosain kund, encircled by glaciers and fed from the scanty annual wasting of their eternal ice, offer a sanctioned avenue to these remote Powers of good and evil. Of these pools, the highest and most sacred lies on a great rocky bluff. In its centre is a tawny-coloured rock, which Oldfield describes as of an oval shape, the rounded top of which can be seen, sunk a foot or more beneath the surface of the tranquil and transparent water. " The pious worshippers of Shiva, as they stand on the edge of the sacred lake, look on this unhewn rock as a divinely carved representation of Mahadeo [1] and fancy they can trace out in it a figure of the deity reclining full length upon a bed of serpents. This rock must have been deposited in its present position when the lake was filled by an ancient glacier, and, sunk as it is in the centre of the ice-cold waters, it can never have been touched by mortal hands." [2]

The difficulties which attend the pilgrimage to Gosain kund have occupied the attention of the present Maharaja. The Government has appointed

THE TEMPLE OF MUKTINATH

officials to deal with the more arduous aspects of the journey, and the enterprise is not to-day the hardy and often mortal adventure that it used to be.

[1] For the curious identification with Shiva of this submerged symbol of Vishnu found in the similar pool shrines at Balaji and Nilkantha, see vol. i, pp. 226, 227.

[2] The following legend explains the existence of Gosain kund. Once upon a time the Kalakuta tide of poison was destroying the world. Three hundred and thirty million gods then prayed to Mahadeo, imploring him to protect the earth and, it seems, themselves also. Mahadeo good-humouredly assented and, to destroy its power, he sucked the tide into his own mouth. Instead of swallowing it, however, he kept it in his throat, which became blue from the effects of the poison—hence his name Nila-kantha. Feeling feverish, he went to the Himalayas, but even there the cold was not sufficient to bring him relief. So he struck his trident into the mountain side and at once three streams gushed out. He lay down and let the ice-cold water flow over his head—and there he lies to this day.

Muktinath.—The other great sanctuary in the Nepalese Himalayas, Muktinath, may be approached from Pokhra by a track running over the

MUKTINATH

The Jwala Mayi, or Chief Deity of this place of pilgrimage

Radnaga la. Afterwards a high altitude is maintained among the mountain peaks confronting Dhaulagiri until Deorali Bhanjyang is gained. Thence the path descends sharply to Sik on the banks of the Kali Gandak, about sixteen miles above Baglung, where the path from Ridi joins it. Perhaps, from the point of view of a European, the best thing that can be said about the route is that, for nearly twenty miles, the road and river make their way round the base of mighty Dhaulagiri, a gigantic and detached peak which ranks with Chumolhari and Siniolchu, Nanga parbat and Kang-chanjanga, as one of the five most beautiful mountains in the Himalayan range—and if in the Himalayas, then in all the world. From here the ascending road follows or crosses the bed of the river, and there is nothing to report of this merely arduous journey until Phala and the outskirts of

MUKTINATH
The 108 sacred springs

the much larger town of Kagbeni are reached. Muktinath lies six miles from the river south-east of Kagbeni, and in that distance the track ascends no less than two thousand two hundred and twenty-five feet.

In August, when the largest number of pilgrims undertake the enter-prise, there is not sufficient accommodation for them at Muktinath, and the surrounding villages, of which Santal is the chief, offer such scanty hospitality as this remote and unfertile region can afford. The shrine, of which the two views on pp. 38 and 39 give an adequate representation, ranks, in the view of the Nepalese, with Gosain kund, Pashpati, and Ridi as one of the four great places of Hindu sanctity and sin-remission in Nepal. It attracts also large numbers of pilgrims from India and from Tibet, offering to both creeds alike a large indulgence in return for the arduous and often fatal expedition by which alone it may be visited.[1] As will be seen the shrine stands beside a holy pool which is fed by a hundred and eight springs. This number corresponds with the number of times that the name of the exalted god should be preceded by "sris." Hard as the journey to it is, Muktinath is visited by thousands every year. Doubtless it owes no small part of its original sanctity to the fact that the thrice-sacred shaligram is found in remarkable abundance in the waters of the Kali Gandak at this point.

§ 4

Central route.—Of other main roads the greatest of all, that which leads from Darjiling in Bengal to Pithoragarh in Kumaon five hundred miles away and more, is, as may well be imagined, for the most part a merely local convenience. For any long distance it is easier and quicker and, it may be added, cheaper for a Nepalese to make his way either to one of the railway stations on the Indian border—of which Darjiling, Pratapganj, Raxaul, Nepalganj, Bridgmanganj, Chandanchauki, and Bileri are perhaps the most used—and there join the Indian railway system for an excursion east or west even when his destination is in his own country. But the long route needs some mention, though no European eye has seen more than a twentieth of it and it is difficult to obtain any description of it from the Nepalese themselves.

India and Nepal meet about half-way between Darjiling and Ilam, the frontier post being at Simana, a few miles north of the source of the Mechi or Telpani river, which, for a large part of its course, forms the boundary between Bengal and Nepal. It is a bad route from the start, obstructed by many steep ascents and descents, and during flood time practically impassable. These remarks apply to a large part of this long track. A small party might perhaps push its way through in spite of all difficulties, with the help of local assistance in the matter of rope bridges, ferries, and other means of crossing swollen rivers. But the entire length of the route runs through the under-features of the Himalayas—under-features which, in any other country, would be hailed as mountains of importance—and the pace is necessarily slow. Nor is it possible, without previous arrangement, to secure provisions locally. On the whole a fair number of Nepalese powahs or lodging places are to be found. It need hardly be said that any attempt to use this road without the permission of the Nepal Government would be entirely impossible, and that such permission would certainly not be given to a European under any conditions whatever. Moreover, as has

---

[1] It will be remembered from the chapter dealing with Nana Sahib in the preceding volume, that the mysterious visitor of princely importance from India, who was seen by the Panjabi fakir beside the Khundi khola, was then, nominally at least, on his way to Muktinath.

been said before, the Nepal Government and the Indian Government alike are totally opposed to the intrusion of foreigners or strangers of any kind within the territory of the king of Nepal—and the arm of the Sirkar is long.

THE KUNWAR KHOLA

About forty-five miles from Ilam the road, which has been clinging to the northern side of the Morung mountain frontier to the north, runs through Dhankuta after a steep descent of above two thousand three hundred feet into the upper waters of the Kankai river. From this valley there are alternative roads for threequarters of the way to Katmandu. That to the south has become neglected for any through traffic, so difficult is it. It may be said generally to ascend the right bank of the Sunkosi river. The northern road which we will follow makes a steep ascent and descent into the Arunkosi, which is not without interest because, within the basin drained by it are many of the descendants of the Kirantis who once reigned over a large portion of Nepal.

Another reason that lends interest to the Arunkosi is that during the recent attempts upon Mount Everest the upper or Tibetan valleys of the Arun offered to the surveyors, naturalists, and ethnologists of the party an interesting field of study. These districts down to the frontier near Lungdung in the Arun gorge and Popti la have been accurately surveyed by the Expedition. The track running over the Popti la, better perhaps known as the Hatia route, that being the name of the customs station, was never one of great importance. It appears in history as the scene of the disastrous withdrawal of the Nepalese army from Tibet in 1791. Fifteen miles farther east are the twin passes of the Tipta la, 19,000 feet, and the Kanglachen, 18,365 feet, within seven miles of each other. The former is known also as the Walanchun. Although the lower of the two, travellers are advised not to attempt this pass at the end of November, but to use the Kanglachen route. Again to the east another pass, the Jongsong la, of over twenty thousand feet, and about twelve miles north of Kangchanjanga, connects with the Sikkim roadways.[1]

§ 5

North-eastern Nepal.—Sarat Chandra Das adds incidentally to our knowledge of north-eastern Nepal in his description of his journey from Darjiling to Lhasa. He started early in November 1881, and at the Chambab, 18,280 feet, the frontier between India and Nepal. His account of this pass is probably characteristic of nearly all the higher passes in this region. It was heavily covered with snow at the time of his passage, and the method taken by his guide of throwing down a bale of clothing to see what would happen to it, and in the event of its bringing up safely at the bottom, of following it at full length, is not an unknown device in other mountainous regions. Patches of grass amid the snow were succeeded by occasional plants of the " blue lotus." Rhododendrons and junipers followed soon, and at last the traveller reached a brook about four feet wide, said to be the head waters of the Kabili river of Nepal. After some

---

[1] Besides these three passes there are Pangu la, the passes of Kuti, Kirong, Pangsing la, and Photu la sixty miles north-north-east of Dhaulagiri; the frontier posts of this track are at Changrang and Lo Mantang. The last and most westerly pass of all is sometimes known as the Taklakhar or Yari la. It takes advantage of the channel cut by the Karnali river not far from Simikot. It is an extremely difficult pass, and is scarcely used at all.

up and down work of no great difficulty Semarum was reached, and the traveller makes the note that both to the south and west the Semarum pass is overhung by a very rugged cliff resembling the outspread wings of an eagle both in colour and shape. From the top of the Semarum pass Chomo Kankar was visible, and the tracks of hares, snow leopards, and snow pheasants were here seen. The road at this point became difficult, but in a short time vegetation was again reached. At Namga Tsal, near Kangma, a halt was made for a night under the protection of a great cedar. A cave here enjoys no small vogue as a place of Buddhist pilgrimage. On the following day the Yalung was reached. This is spanned by a strong bridge of cedar logs and silver fir planks. Turning north-north-east the ascent of Chunjorma was begun, and Das noted specimens of the green pheasant recorded by Dr. Hooker.[1]

Three miles to the west of the road lies Yalung itself. This seems to be the residence of only twelve families, " who spend their summer in tending yaks at Yalung, and their winter at Yanku tang, in the valley of the Kabili." After attaining the summit of Chunjorma by the Nango la some more high crags are reached, of which one resembling a horse's head has naturally been called after Tam-drin. Junipers and rhododendrons were found on the other side, and Das stayed the night at Mudang Phug. Again descending, full forest vegetation was seen in the deep glens of the streams which here cut into the mountain side. In the Yamatari valley the rhododendron bushes were fluttering with the white and red strips which are so universally found in and near Tibet as the offerings of travellers. Das's servant, Phurchung, said that in a flat grassy valley near this place his parents had met Dr. Hooker, who not only treated his father for snow blindness, but gave his mother a coin to hang about Phurchung's neck, who was then a baby in arms. Beyond the Yamatari bridge is a small village, Kangpa-chan, where Phurchung was received by his relatives with a hearty welcome and much Tibetan beer.

Kangpa-chan (Hooker's Kambachen) is picturesquely situated on the lower slopes of snow mountains. Juniper and rhododendron bushes surround the village, broken by patches of barley, radishes, and potatoes. Mr. Das reached the place on the 24th November and was earnestly advised by one of the villagers not to attempt to get into Tibet by the Walang pass as it was too late in the season. The Jangma and the Kangmachen passes were still possible. In the village Phurchung's uncle, Pema Zang, owned a house of some pretensions containing a well painted shrine. " Pema Zang

---

[1] In November 1848 Dr. Hooker was permitted, at the urgent request of the Indian Government, to ascend the Kosi river in Eastern Nepal to its confluence with the Tamor, which he then followed in a general north-easterly direction. He made his way up the Yangma river and crossed the Walanchun and Yangma passes. (See *Himalayan Journals*, vol. i, p. 205. Murray, 1854.)

had long, thick, and tangled hair. He wore gold earrings in the shape of magnolia flowers, and his looks and talk were grave and serious. He often sits in deep meditation for the purpose of arresting hail and other storms by the potency of the charms he is able to pronounce."

Here snowshoes had to be bought and provisions put up for the hard journey that lay before the travellers. Kangpa-chan was once a far larger centre. But as punishment for the murder of an oppressive Magar chief, nearly the whole population was exterminated. His widow revenged herself by inviting the Sharpas, who had been guilty of the crime, to the funeral feast, and there poisoned nearly a thousand of them. The Tibetans, with whom the Sharpas are racially connected, sent an army to avenge this too rough justice, and the Magar chieftainess found herself besieged. The Tibetans seem to have been unable to take the place by storm, and therefore cut off the water supply. To deceive them the chieftainess employed a device as ancient as it is world-wide. She opened the reservoir in the castle and let the water flow out in full sight of the Tibetan troops. Thinking she must have abundance, they then raised the siege and retired; the lady, however, rashly made a sortie and fell herself in the melée. In the long run the Tibetans finally expelled the Magars from the Kangpa-chan and Tamor valleys, which were restored to their former owners. The place where this massacre was carried out is still known as Tongshong phug—" the Place of a Thousand Murders."

On leaving Kangpa-chan the road takes a north-westerly direction through Yangma to the Kanglachen pass. At Manding Gompa, short of Yangma, it became necessary to deal with the Nepalese authorities who closely scrutinized all travellers. There was apparently a discussion in the village as to the identity and standing of the pilgrim from India. The head Lama admitted that he had no orders from the Nepalese Government to prevent the pious from making their pilgrimage to Tibet. Phurchung seems to have proved himself a diplomatist of no mean order, and after a slight test of his master's knowledge of Tibet and the Buddhist religion, and the completion of a small financial transaction, they were allowed to go on their way. An hour or two afterwards Yangma itself was reached. Hooker dismisses it as a miserable collection of two hundred to three hundred stone huts.[1] Das seems to have been as little impressed. He says that the houses could be distinguished from the boulders everywhere strewing the ground only by the smoke issuing from the roofs. He was of opinion that, in 1881, there were not more than a hundred houses in the village.

The road now lies along the Yangma, which here flows either in deep gorges or else spreads itself in wide lakes. The real ascent now began, though Yangma itself lies 12,789 feet above sea level. Po-phug, a mere

[1] See *Himalayan Journals*, by Hooker, vol. i, p. 238.

collection of huts, lies at the foot of a steep ascent, where the head waters of the Yangma river were passed. Das notes that the limit of vegetation is reached at Tsa-Tsam. The track now lay across a large glacier a quarter of a mile wide and more than three miles long, and up a great curtain of bare black rock. The cold, the fog, and the darkness made it impossible for the party to reach the regular halting place, the White Cavern, so the night was spent in the open, and we may well believe Das when he says that it was the most trying night he ever passed in his life. Next morning they discovered that they had halted for the night only a furlong from the White Cavern, which, as a matter of fact, is nothing more than a crevasse between detached rocks.

It is interesting to set as a parallel with the accounts given of other high Himalayan passes by Father Grueber and Father Cassien the description by Mr. Das of the hardships he suffered at Kanglachen. " How exhausted we were with the fatigue of the day's journey, how overcome by the rarefi-cation of the air, the intensity of the cold, and how completely prostrated by hunger and thirst, is not easy to describe . . . and so with neither food nor drink, placed as if in the grim jaws of death, in the bleak and dreary regions of snow where death alone dwells, we spent this most dismal night."

The summit of Kanglachen is a small plateau from which a magnificent view of snow-clad peaks is to be seen. " On all sides there was nothing visible but an ocean of snow. Innumerable snowy peaks touched with their white heads the pale leaden sky where stars were shining. The rattling roar of distant avalanches was frequently heard; but after having succeeded in crossing the loftiest of snowy passes, I felt too transported with joy to be frightened by their thunder." The next day's road is easier. The rhododendrons and junipers reappear. The frontier town of Tibet is apparently Tashirabka, where the remains of a high stone wall, erected by the Tibetans during the Nepalese war, are still visible. It crosses the whole valley, its ends being seen high up on the sides of the mountain. From this point Mr. Das's route lay in Tibetan territory.

A reference should be made here to the Sharpas who live in this district, and from whom the various expeditions for the climbing of Mount Everest [1] were largely drawn. The praise which both Norton and Odell have bestowed upon these Sharpa porters will not soon be forgotten in England, while Odell's very gallant rescue of a small body of these men from a height of nearly 27,000 feet, where they had fallen exhausted and were waiting for death, will never be forgotten by their kinsmen. During the exhibition, in 1925, of the films taken during this last attempt to scale Mount Everest,

[1] The frontier line between Tibet and Nepal runs over the crest of Mount Everest. The name given to the mountain by the Nepalese differs, but in Katmandu it is known as Chomo-Kankar, whether the name would locally be accepted as applicable to the highest peak or not. The name means " Lady White Glacier."

nothing has been more popular than the interlude in which a personal introduction was made to the audience of one of these Sharpas, of whose courage, tenacity, and loyalty the lecturer could not say enough. It was by these Tibetan Nepalese—and they are proud and jealous of their Nepalese nationality—that work was done for the expedition, which, for endurance and loyalty, has never been equalled on any other mountaineering enterprise. It may also be added that the Sharpas would unhesitatingly refuse to render these terrible services to any but the British, whom they had come to know and most absolutely trust. Without their help—which can never be secured by any but men with whom they are familiar, whom they trust in any emergency, and who have proved their willingness to risk their own lives in keeping faith with their porters in a desperate hour—it would have been impossible for the results to be secured which have already justified this attack upon Mount Everest, high as the price was that had to be paid for them.

Of other records dealing with this extreme north-eastern corner of Nepal there is the narrative of Mr. Douglas Freshfield who, in his journey round Kangchanjanga, crossed from Jongri, in Sikkim, to Kangbachen, in Nepal, by the Kang la. At Kangbachen he touched Sarat Chandra Das's route, but continued his journey through Lhonak to the Jongsong la to the north-east and so regained Sikkim. Sarat Chandra Das continued his journey through Yangma to Kanglachen.

The Buddhist temples in this part of Nepal are also designed on the model of the Tibetan sanctuaries, having been founded by the great Lama, Lha-tsun, of the Red Hat school. Apparently Walang is the senior temple and Kangpa-chan second. The Manding Gompa—which is the monastery near Yangma—is of a special sanctity. Elsewhere he asserts that the Yangma and Walanchun districts belonged at one time to the Raja of Sikkim.

To return to the great east and west track of Nepal. The road between the Arunkosi and the Dudh-kosi crosses a range of mountains, and at Kumdia passes within three miles of a well-known temple—Halasi. I could obtain no description of this place, which is held in great repute in eastern Nepal as one of the abiding places of Padma Sambhava.[1] Beyond the

---

[1] In A.D. 747 this man was sent for from India by Thi Srong Detsan, King of Tibet. On his arrival he reorganized the Buddhist church, founded Lamaism, and established the Sakya monastery. In the course of much travel and many surprising miracles, the Most Precious Teacher visited Boddhnath and the cemetery called Shun-grub-brtsegs-pa in Nepal. Waddell notes that Halasi is on a continuation of the Siwalik range and contains the characteristic fossils of that formation.. Among these are the remains of the "sabre-toothed tiger" which is almost peculiar to this range. It would be an interesting study to compare the figures assumed by devils in animistic or semi-animistic regions with the fossils to be found in them. To Padma Sambhava is due the credit of having introduced in Tibet the Tantric form of Buddhism, which quickly spread into Nepal ; Lamaism, the

Dudh-kosi the track makes its way across numberless tributaries of the Sunkosi and the lesser mountain streams which only deserve the name in the rains, but are then impassable. The Tambakosi is crossed not far from Rajgaon; here the southern track, which has been ascending the right bank of the Sunkosi, is seen beyond the river, which is crossed at Bhataoli, and the two merge into a path along which a day's march will take the traveller to the wide and well cultivated plain of Dumja. This is a town of some local importance, but it is of course dwarfed by its

ARGHA

The residence of the Rajas in Lamjang

proximity to the Valley, the edge of which is only about nineteen miles distant. Barley and rice grow in the plain, but it cannot compete with Katmandu, though in extent it ranks second or third in Nepal. The road runs through Charangphedi and Banepa to Bhatgaon, and so on to the capital. The Valley is entered at Sanga, a little town on the north-eastern slopes of Ranichok.

The road through eastern Nepal has been of the same character throughout. Here and there passes have to be crossed, as at Chakawa (6,870 feet), Kumdia (6,300 feet), Wakhaldunga and Kanjia (4,620 feet), but a poor track

particular form of sacerdotalism that he created, has never taken root there, either in the form of the Red discipline or the Yellow.

for the most part winds up and down round mountain spurs well clad with small woods and cultivated in sheltered recesses.

From Katmandu, the west-bound traveller may pursue the path that I have already described through Gorkha to Ridi, though a rough track to Palpa, crossing the Kali Gandak at Kibrighat, is actually shorter. A third track and perhaps the best, though less interesting, runs down the left bank of the Trisul Gandak through Maisiduhan to Bichraltar, where a cut across fairly level country is made to Deoghat.[1] Here the river is crossed, and three stages more will bring Palpa into view. Ridi lies eight miles on.

Thence the track makes its way to Piuthana, which lies about one hun-

JHARKAN

dred and twenty-five miles west of Katmandu as the crow flies, a route of steep ascents and descents crossing the Chitrabasi near Wangle. Here there was at one time a considerable musket factory. Large quantities of gun-powder were made, the saltpetre required being taken from the village of Musinia Bhanjyang not far away. The manufacture of arms and ammuni-tion is now almost entirely concentrated in the Valley of Katmandu. From here in about five stages, Salyana is reached. The Madi river is crossed at Kimulchaur. Salyana, like Jajarkot, was at one time the capital of a small mountain clan, which, like all the others in this district, was finally absorbed by the Gurkha conquerors towards the end of the eighteenth century. Salyana is of interest because it is the capital of the province in which the more privileged of the refugees of the 1857 Mutiny were allowed to find

---

[1] On the way the fort of Upardangarhi is passed.

temporary shelter. Jajarkot contains a fine ruined castle which was once the stronghold of an aristocratic chief claiming Rajput descent, with the descendants of whom the Prime Minister's family has intermarried.[1]

With the exception of Jumla, Salyana is the most western of the important civil headquarters in the west of Nepal. Other centres, such as Dipal, Dailekha, and Baitadi, the extreme frontier post confronting Pithoragarh, are chiefly military stations. Owing to the difficulty of transit among these never-ending hills a certain amount of independent authority is conceded to the Subas and other officials in the small towns, constant reference to the capital being difficult. The road from Salyana threads its way along mountain sides and crosses the Sanubheri river before reaching Dailekha. This is the centre of the district of that name. Reference to the census figures[2] will show the relative importance of these sparsely populated areas. Not far from Dailekha is a pass—the Kachal la —which has been described to me by a Nepalese as one of the most impressive and beautiful of all the passes of his country. This praise was the more remarkable because natural beauty is not the matter which appeals first to a Nepalese, or indeed to any Oriental in describing his own country. One may ask a Nepalese about the length of a journey, the difficulty of the track, the number and nature of the different stages, what will be found at the villages along the route or should be provided when a river has to be crossed or an unusually steep ascent or descent has to be made—and in general you will receive plain and trustworthy replies. But the scenic beauty of Nepal is less regarded by them. Although these highlanders live in the midst of the most magnificent scenery in the world they would, I am convinced, prefer to cultivate the orderly but somewhat dull levels of northern India, could they but bring with them their independence, their climate, and, above all, their government.

From Dailekha the road runs through to Bilkhet on the eastern bank of the Karnali river. From this point one track runs up in a northerly direction—and chiefly on the right bank of the river—through Banda and Simikot to the Tak la, which has already been referred to in this chapter. The western road from Bilkhet crosses the Bheri at Sanpiaghat and, proceeding westwards, threads the military centre of Dipal or Silgarhi; thence again it pursues its way among passes and along occasional river flats to

---

[1] The following are the heads of a few of the chief families resident in outer Nepal.

Salyana.   Raja Sham Sher Bahadur Shah.

Jajarkot.   Raja Upendra Vikram Shah. (He is married to the niece of the Prime Minister.)

Bajhang.   Raja Devi Jang Singh. (Ex-Raja, was son-in-law of Prime Minister. He has left the country and is now living at Bangalore.)

Bajhang.   Raja Jai Prithwi Bahadur Singh.

Bajura.   The widow of Raja Dip Bahadur Shah.

[2] Appendix VII, vol. i.

Chuma[1] and Baitadi. From here it is but a short stage to the Kumaon frontier of India.

A rival track, leaving the frontier at Bargaon twenty-five miles north of Baitadi, and one that is said to be more often used though it is much longer and impassable in the wet weather, runs—roughly parallel to and north of the track that has just been noted—eastward through Banda—where it crosses the Tak la road—and Jumla, a considerable administrative centre. From Jumla it makes its way first over high passes and then along the tortuous Bheri river to Charka among the snows, and thence to Kagbeni

THE GAHRAUN KOT

These kots or forts are built on the tops of hills commanding towns in the west of Nepal

on the Kali Gandak, where the eastward path to Muktinath climbs up from the river. This road is in its lower parts fairly well wooded, but some of the passes exceed fourteen thousand feet.

From Kagbeni northwards there is a track which has in the past been used as a route into Tibet over the Photu la but is now almost impassable. As has been suggested elsewhere, the traffic over all the Nepalese northern passes has fallen off to a great degree since the engineers of the expedition to Lhasa of 1904 completed the regrading, and for the most part the reconstruction of the roads running over the sister passes, the Jelep la and the Nathu la, from Sikkim into the Chumbi Valley. Bad as the roads soon

[1] Dadheldhura, a military post, lies in the hills about five miles south of Chuma.

became, they were and still are so superior to the Nepalese passes that the merchants of Nepal have found it cheaper to send their goods down into India to be transferred by rail through Siliguri to the Tista, where the routes to these passes begin.[1] To this inevitable drift of traffic along the line of least resistance is due one of the existing difficulties in the relations between Nepal and Tibet. By treaty Lhasa may not charge customs upon Nepalese goods crossing the passes into Tibet. It is apparently not sufficiently stated in the agreement whether the passes of Nepal only were referred to. The Lhasa Government is now taking up the attitude that Nepalese goods, accompanied by Nepalese merchants—which are franked duty free through India and Sikkim by the Indian Government—are liable to the Tibetan customs at Yatung, because they have not entered Tibet directly over Nepalese passes. Against this action Katmandu protests most vigorously, but the matter is one which, were it the only difference of opinion, could be settled in a friendly way. But there is no doubt that at this moment the slightly unstable conditions that prevail between Lhasa and Katmandu are not rendered easier by this desertion of the Nepalese trade-routes. The Photu la was never of great trade importance, though it possesses, close to the Tibet frontier, a couple of mountain military posts.

These northern uplands of Nepal are inhabited by the quasi-Mongoloid tribes, to which reference is made in Appendix XVII. They are comparatively few, and the cultivation of crops is, as we have already seen, attended with much difficulty, even at a lower altitude. Until the level of perpetual snow is reached, the rocky buttresses and ridges, which hold up the enormous heights of the Nepalese Himalayas, spread themselves out like the sticks of gigantic fans dividing streams frozen for a certain part of the year and always of the clouded whitish green of snow water—which, by the way, gives its special name to the Dudh-kosi, the river of milk. These ridges are sparsely overgrown with small timber. That much could be done to improve the forestry of Upper Nepal is no doubt true, but a serious obstacle is that in the urgent need for fuel, undergrowth of any description is naturally, if not always lawfully, regarded as the perquisite of the nearest village. Life among these mountains is one of hard work and inevitable monotony, but the racial distinctions are kept up with a pride that would seem worthy of a better object. In conclusion, among these cold mountain ravines life is scarcely more than a long struggle for existence, and it is to the lasting credit of these mountaineers that by common consent they remain true

---

[1] Sir Charles Bell (*Tibet, Past and Present*, 1924) remarks : "Through the Chumbi valley, as through the neck of a bottle, is poured half of the entire trade between India and Tibet. The trade of all other routes, west and east from Kashmir to Assam, a distance of nearly two thousand miles, totals barely as much as that which passes along this one road."

to the Tibetan tradition of hospitality which they have kept alive in spite of their exile from their original homes.

In these two chapters nothing more has been possible than a description of the more important centres of outer Nepal and a general picture of scenery and road characteristics that do not vary very greatly. The photographs with which I am able to add to the interest of the narrative have been selected with the view of illustrating the chief localities of interest. Outside the limits of the more important towns and shrines the scenery of Nepal is of uniformly beautiful character, so much so that it almost becomes monotonous.

THE SETI RIVER DISAPPEARING UNDERGROUND

CHAPTER XIII

MAHARAJAS RANA UDIP, BIR, AND DEVA—GENERAL DHIR SHAM SHER

§ I

ALMOST the last action of Jang Bahadur had been to send a messenger to Rana Udip Singh warning his brother of his own approaching end and delivering into his hands the control of Nepalese affairs. It may be convenient here to explain the manner in which the office of Maharaja, Prime Minister, and Supreme Commander-in-Chief descends in the Rana family. Jang Bahadur during his lifetime made an arrangement somewhat similar to that of descent through the eldest agnate which prevails in Mohammedan countries.[1] By this scheme, which is in force to-day, a Maharaja is not succeeded by his eldest son—as is the case at the demise of the crown in Nepal. The Prime Ministership descends, in order of birth, from one brother to another, or one cousin to another, until all the survivors of a generation have succeeded in turn. On the death of the last brother, the succession passes to the earliest born son of the deceased males of the previous generation. Thus the descent from one generation to the next is not necessarily to the eldest son of the eldest brother.[2] The descent of the office in this second generation is throughout decided by priority of birth. The plan was devised by Jang Bahadur to insure that at no time should the government of Nepal be left in the hands of an immature member of the family. On the other hand, two defects are latent in the arrangement. One is that mere age is no guarantee that the eldest survivor of any generation is necessarily fit for the responsibilities of the post. The second is, that this rule of descent is likely to cause jealousy and foster a perpetual state of family intrigue. Moreover, it may well be that at some future date the dignity of Maharaja will pass in turn from one member to another of distant branches of a numerous family, not all the members of which can be expected to have had the special training needed for such high

---

[1] The orders of succession drawn up by Jang Bahadur and the present Maharaja may be seen in Appendix III, vol. i.

[2] At the present moment there is an illustration of the working of this rule. After the death of the present Maharaja's youngest brother, and certain of his elder nephews, the office of Prime Minister will descend not to his own eldest son, but to General Padma, the son of a younger brother, the present Commander-in-Chief, because General Padma was in point of time born before any of the sons of the Maharaja.

54

office. We shall see later that the former difficulties soon made themselves felt.

On the death of Jang Bahadur his eldest brother, Badri Narsingh, was as a matter of fact still alive, but it will be remembered that he and his son had been cut out of the succession; consequently Rana Udip succeeded. He was the fifth brother of Jang Bahadur and the sixth son of Bala Narsingh, and had been born on the 3rd of April 1825. In spite of his own *jeunesse orageuse*, Jang Bahadur had consistently done his best to educate and train his young brother during the turbulent years that led up to his grasp of the supreme power. Thereafter Jang naturally took the first opportunity of distributing well-paid offices of high responsibility among his brothers. During his visit to Europe Rana Udip was entrusted with the government of the Eastern and Western Provinces of Nepal, and on the discovery of Badri Narsingh's plot was charged with the duty of bringing the Mahila Sahib, Prince Upendra Vikram, to hear his sentence of imprisonment. In 1855 Rana Udip became Master of Ordnance during the Tibetan war, an office practically identical with that of our Quartermaster-General, and in 1857 he accompanied Jang Bahadur into India as second in command. In 1863, on the death of his brother, Krishna Bahadur, Rana Udip became Commander-in-Chief in Nepal[1]—a position which he held until his succession.

The new Maharaja, as his pictures and statue suggest, was a genial, easy-going man, but an excellent worker when under the strict supervision of his brother. On more than one occasion he had proved himself a loyal and capable lieutenant of Jang Bahadur, but there was entirely lacking in him his brother's magnetic personality. This was the more natural as it had been impossible for anyone in the kingdom to take any initiative in any direction during the late Maharaja's administration—especially, perhaps, for the brother who was destined to follow him in his office and dignity.

On hearing the news of his brother's death, Rana Udip acted with celerity. He secured from the King a formal ratification of his succession to the office of Prime Minister, summoned a strong military guard, and then broke the news to the sons of Jang Bahadur. He sent the sanction needed for the latter's cremation and the sati of his widows to Patharghatta by General Dhir. His promptitude was justified by the fact that Jang Bahadur at his death left ten sons who were, of course, in the order of succession and who, from the position of high dignity and authority they had enjoyed during their father's lifetime, had begun to assume among themselves that the descent of the Prime Ministership would in practice become a matter of primogeniture in the same manner as that of the royal dignity. There

[1] On 1st January 1876 he was invested as a K.C.S.I. by the Prince of Wales—afterwards the King-Emperor Edward VII. This was a belated recognition of the services rendered by Rana Udip during the Mutiny.

was another reason also for prompt action. During the long ministry of Jang Bahadur a younger generation of Thapas had come of age, and these cadets were sullenly awaiting an opportunity to revenge the death of Mathabar Singh at Jang's hands. With them were ranged the relatives of those who had lost their lives during the massacre of the Kot. More-

H.H. MAHARAJA RANA UDIP SINGH

over, the effect of women's intrigue was once again making itself felt in the affairs of state. The Jitha Maharani [1] and, strange to say, the second wife of Rana Udip himself, were both in league with the latter's enemies.

From the first the new Prime Minister, now an easy-going, middle-aged, childless man whose delight was in personal comfort and domestic life, depended largely upon his younger brothers. Jagat Sham Sher, the Commander-in-Chief, and the next in succession to the Prime Ministership,

---

[1] Jitha Maharani was the eldest wife of Prince Trailokya Vikram, step-mother of King Prithwi Bir Vikram and own sister of Jagat Jang.

died, however, in 1879. This raised Dhir Sham Sher to the position of Commander-in-Chief, and the indolence of the actual Prime Minister forced him to become in many ways the Chief Executive of Nepal. As will be seen later in this chapter, Dhir was a hard-working, capable, and far-visioned man. He had served so long and faithfully with Jang Bahadur that he understood better than any the special needs of a State like Nepal, which was still hovering between the old regime and the new. His personality was strong, and his influence in the administration of affairs of state soon became evident.

It was not long before the sons of Jang Bahadur began to intrigue against the authority of their uncles. Like many other great commanders and leaders of men, Jang Bahadur had not sufficiently taken into consideration that the world in which he lived and which he controlled so autocratically would not die with him. He seems to have allowed his sons to grow up without discipline beyond subservience to himself, and without any adequate preparation for the life that sooner or later they might be called upon to lead. It was perhaps to the knowledge that their father would be succeeded by their uncles and not by themselves that much of the inclination of Jang Bahadur's children to live a more or less free and easy life was due. There was discouragement in the knowledge that for many years after his death they would be allowed to have no share in the government of the State; they may even have felt that, as the children of a man who had so long kept out of office the new ruler, any endeavour by them to take a prominent part in public affairs would by no means be encouraged by the authorities. This lack of discipline was quickly apparent. The eldest son of Jang Bahadur, Jagat Jang, soon allowed himself to mutter complaints against the descent, not only of the office of Prime Minister, but of the title and estates that accompanied it; and almost at the same time the Jitha Maharani began to raise her head in revolt. Rana Udip was, however, loyally helped by his brother the Commander-in-Chief, and for a time the trouble was kept in hand, though the death of the heir apparent, Prince Trailokya Vikram Sah, in 1878, and the devolution of his royal rights upon his infant son opened another easy channel of intrigue.

In 1880 Rana Udip imitated his brother by making a visit to India. He had not Jang Bahadur's tact, however, and created some needless inconvenience by taking with him a retinue of almost four hundred persons. This number of guests did not matter much in the larger towns, but it was a cause of much trouble in smaller places such as Rameshwaram, and as soon as their accommodation became difficult it was clear that there was little or no organization to control these followers. In itself it was a small matter, but it indicated an inability on the part of Rana Udip to handle a minor situation that was soon to be reflected on the larger stage of his Nepal authority.

§ 2

Immediately after his return to Katmandu Rana Udip was confronted
by a situation caused by the death of King Surendra. Jang Bahadur would
have instantly put upon the throne the six-year-old grandson of the
late King, and placed the still surviving Rajendra under surveillance. But
Rana Udip was of a weaker mould. He was not strong enough to overbear
the querulous opposition of the ex-King Rajendra, and a quarrel ensued
which, however, was ended by the sudden death of this perpetual aspirant

KING SURENDRA

to long forfeited royal honours. On the 1st December 1881 the child, Prithwi
Bir Vikram Sah, was formally placed on the throne.

Soon after, Jagat Jang thought himself strong enough to protest against
the assumption of power, place, and property by Rana Udip Singh, though
there was not the slightest legal ground for his action. No doubt whatever
exists that Jang Bahadur, when accepting for himself the title of Maharaja
of Kaski and Lamjang, endowed the title with those two estates, and laid
it down once for all that in future they were to be the appanage of each
successive Prime Minister in turn, whoever he might be.

But Jagat put forward the right of primogeniture, and was supported
not only by his brothers, but by others whom the existing system had
disappointed. The exact character of the plot that was concocted was not

known at the time, but enough has since leaked out to make it clear that both the Maharaja and Dhir Sham Sher, the Commander-in-Chief, were to be put to death by the conspirators. Jagat Jang, it is said, had also bought the assistance of the Jitha Maharani by promising to place her daughter upon the throne in the place of the boy King. But he was not alone in the field. This antagonism within the Rana family had the inevitable effect of encouraging the hopes of the descendants of Mathabar Singh also, to whom the Bashniats and other people with grievances soon joined themselves. Their programme was drastic indeed. The intention of these new conspirators was to throw out the existing king and to put in his place his uncle, Prince Narendra, the brother of Trailokya, the late heir apparent. They proposed to destroy the Ranas of both factions. Neither Rana Udip, nor Jagat Jang's party, nor Dhir's family were to be left alive. But the close intermarriage of the few distinguished families that exist in a State like Nepal has always proved the bane of palace revolutions. Through a nephew by marriage Jagat Jang received complete information of the Thapas' plot, and the policy he adopted, however savage, was not without shrewdness. He intended to allow their scheme to mature, but to hold himself in readiness, when the latter should have put Rana Udip and Dhir's family to death, to set upon the Thapas in a fury of simulated justice and destroy them also root and branch. On the other hand, should the scheme of the Thapas fail and the party of the Maharaja gain the day, then Jagat Jang proposed to intervene with his full strength and make a clean sweep of his kinsmen.

The 6th January 1882 was fixed for the execution of this scheme. The murder of the Commander-in-Chief and several of the members of his Council was to be first carried out; assassins were afterwards to be sent to finish off the Maharaja—who was then in the Tarai—and the sons of the Commander-in-Chief. Jagat Jang was kept fully informed of every detail of this intrigue; but he remembered that his own life was threatened also, and with a timidity that one would hardly have expected from his father's son, he dared not await in Nepal the issue of the conspiracy, but made the best of his way with a few friends into India, leaving subsequent action in the charge of Bombir Vikram.

But the usual traitor was forthcoming. A grandson of Gagan Singh betrayed the plot to the Commander-in-Chief, who had no small share of his great brother's promptitude and thoroughness. He at once arrested all the conspirators that were to be found in Nepal. He caused a searching enquiry to be made into the charge of complicity brought against Jagat Jang, in the course of which the other conspiracy was brought to light. A document was found signed by many of the conspirators and setting out in full the object and course of the plot, whereupon some of the guilty ones made a full confession of the crime. Jagat Jang was then summoned from

India to clear himself, but this he prudently refused to do. As a result of this enquiry, twenty-one of the leading councillors of state were put to death. Prince Narendra and General Bombir Vikram were, as usual, handed over to the Indian Government to be interned at Chunargarh, and the names of Jagat Jang, Padma Jang, and Bombir Vikram were erased

STATUE OF MAHARAJA RANA UDIP SINGH

from the succession roll. The accident of the destruction of certain papers enabled other guilty brothers of Jagat to escape punishment. Padma Jang was interned, but through the influence of his sister, the mother of the King, he was ultimately replaced in the succession. Thus, thanks to the strong action of General Dhir, the forces of rebellion were scotched if not killed, and the Nepal Government had leisure to press forward certain much needed reforms.

Shortly afterwards Rana Udip started the militia system which still remains part of the military organization of the country and proved to be of the greatest use in the enlistment of tens and even hundreds of thousands of recruits into the regiments that were raised for the late war. It was not, however, originally established for such a purpose. The ill-inspired but not infrequent requests of the British Residents in Katmandu that the country should be opened to European development were the immediate cause of this military provision. Although the subject has already been explained in other chapters the present seems a fitting occasion for a further reference to the Nepalese policy of seclusion. It is not to be wondered at that Nepal has always been steadily opposed to the intrusion upon her territory of Western men and Western manners. It is only within the memory of living men that Japan and China themselves have been opened up for Occidental travel and residence. Tibet and Bhutan are still to a large extent closed countries. Different reasons have contributed in different countries to this prejudice. Probably at the root of it is a religious jealousy that is found in a greater or less measure in all creeds. Certainly the tradition that seals Nepal against visitors had its origin in a natural intolerance of the presence of infidel Europeans at or near her holiest shrines—and all Nepal is holy in the eyes of the Nepalese. But there has always been a practical inducement also to keep the gates of Nepal shut. The Nepalese have had long occasion to watch the gradual extension of English power in India. They saw how, from a small settlement at Cuddalore and a glacis only so wide as a musket ball might carry from the petty fortifications of the town, the English had lengthened the cords and strengthened the stakes of their authority over more and more and yet more of the land of India. In the course of a century from Plassey the proudest States had gone down before them. Nepal's neighbour Audh had fallen, and the widow of Ranjit Singh was a refugee at Thapathali to remind them that the best fighting races had been subdued, and that indeed, as Bhim Sen had once said, "England is a power that crushes thrones like potsherds." The recent Mutiny, which would have thrown out a lesser race, had resulted only in the final extirpation of the Imperial name at Delhi and the confirmation of English rule, absolute and unquestioned, throughout the entire peninsula. Is it a wonder, then, that Nepal—the only state of Indian sovereignty which had survived this slow but certain conquest—believed that by any concession in this matter of exclusion she was sealing her own ultimate doom?

The Nepalese frequently quote a well-known saying that the musket follows the missionary. There was no real fear of differences with the Indian Government on the score of religion, for Jang Bahadur himself, in one of his communications with an Indian prince, roundly asserted that the charges of insulting religion which had been brought by his correspondent against the English, were totally and notoriously untrue. But the question of trade was one that even the loyalty of Jang Bahadur looked upon with suspicion. He traced the spread of English influence—this time not in India alone but over the entire world—and saw how the English had first introduced their goods, their trading stations, and their trading rights, and had afterwards, when necessary, supported the latter by force of arms. Therefore, with a wisdom it is difficult to overpraise, he peremptorily forbade the entrance into Nepal of any visitor of any Western race unless he had both the invitation of the Nepal Government and the guarantee of the Indian Government. Nor was the visitor permitted to see any part of Nepal except the Valley of Katmandu and the road to it. The Resident himself and the Residency surgeon Jang Bahadur was indeed obliged, by the Treaty of 1816, to admit. The Resident had, and has, a small native escort, and it is necessary that a British officer should proceed to Katmandu yearly for some months to train these men. Moreover, from time to time technical experts connected with the Indian Public Works Department make brief appearances in Katmandu for the purpose of reporting upon the fabric and any necessary improvements at the Legation. Besides these formal visitors, the Nepal Government recognizes the necessity for the assistance of European engineers in the instalment of electricity, water power, telephones, ropeways, and other modern conveniences which tend to increase the comfort, capacity, and strength of the Nepalese people. It is not certain how soon this custom began, but it is clear that the Gurkha dynasty invited a Frenchman to install and direct an arsenal at Katmandu as early as the beginning of the nineteenth century.[1] Besides these classes, there are the rare guests of the Maharaja and the guests of the Envoy. In a very real sense the latter are also the guests of the Nepal Government, for the Maharaja has the right, which he would not hesitate to use, to refuse admission even to guests suggested by the Envoy.

In an appendix will be found a list of those to whom official permission to visit Nepal has been accorded in the last forty-six years.[2] It is therefore a list which includes practically all living Europeans who have made the journey, and it is not without interest to glance at its composition. It will be seen that no Viceroy's name appears in it. This omission is best explained by a story. Lord Curzon, during his period of viceroyalty, was naturally anxious to pay a visit to a country that had so loyally befriended

---

[1] Even earlier than this Prithwi Narayan enlisted the services of Francis Neville as head of the arsenal in Katmandu. He is generally called a Frenchman, but as a matter of fact was a half-caste. He was assisted by another white, or semi-white man, M. Dilbensee, and was making cannon on the river "Tookihur," a mile south-east of Katmandu. This is the stream Tukhucha which runs through and under the royal palace ground and finds its way into the Bagmati beside Thapathali. No magazine exists on its banks to-day. It is said that M. Dilbensee had with him a French colleague whose name was Vincent.

[2] Appendix XXIV.

India, had so often occupied his attention in the sphere of foreign affairs, and possessed such beautiful cities. His great interest in antiquarian research also prompted him to suggest to the present Maharaja that he would like to have the opportunity of making the acquaintance of the Valley of Nepal. Chandra's answer was courteous but unmistakable. He expressed his gratification at the suggestion, and assured Lord Curzon that the very day after he ceased to be Viceroy he would be welcomed in Katmandu—welcomed if he would allow it with all the ceremony and honour that could be accorded to him were he to pay the visit as Viceroy. But His Highness regretfully explained that so long as Lord Curzon remained Viceroy, it was impossible to extend to him an invitation. A precedent would have been set, of which subsequent Viceroys would most certainly have availed themselves. A visit to Katmandu is the most interesting of all expeditions in or near India, not only for the reasons that have been suggested in the introduction to this book, but because the welcome of the Maharaja and his warm hospitality in everything that can in any way minister to the comfort of his guest are things that seem to belong to another—a past and almost a lost—period of Asiatic life.[1]

Whether the Residents in Katmandu, who, in the nineteenth century, expressed their hope that Nepal would allow its great natural wealth to be developed by Occidental methods, were acting on the direct instructions of the Indian Government, it is hard to say. At the present moment, however, such a policy would be at once disowned by Simla. The Government of India recognizes, and recognizes with gratitude, the policy of isolation which has been more strictly enforced than ever during the last half century. The rare invitations of the Darbar are extended on the understanding that the visitor is on his honour not to attempt to traverse

---

[1] But the same reserve did not apply to the Commander-in-Chief in India, and it is curious to notice the visits of "His Excellency Sir F. Roberts" in 1892, and of Lord Kitchener in 1906. Lord Rawlinson, the late Commander-in-Chief, was more than once invited to shoot in the Tarai, and was on the point of paying a visit to Katmandu at the time of his sudden death in 1925. Of other visitors it is interesting to note the names of Sir Richard Temple, who is put down as having visited Katmandu as the guest of Mr. Girdlestone, Resident between 1872 and 1888—the exact year is not recorded; Sir Charles Elliott, also Lieutenant-Governor of Bengal, November 1894; "Colonel W. R. Birdwood, Military Secretary," November 1906; Mr. R. E. Holland, 1907 and 1919; "The Honourable C. Hobhouse of the Royal Commission on Decentralisation," January 1908; Mr. Percy Brown, the Principal of the Government School of Art, Calcutta, October 1910, the author of a very attractive and well illustrated book, *Picturesque Nepal*; Prince Antoine d'Orléans, April 1911; Lady McMahon in March of the same year; Mr. Kawaguchi, 1913; Baron and Baroness Maurice de Rothschild, 1913; Dr. Thomas, Librarian of the India Office in London, 1921; and, of more importance to Nepal perhaps than the other distinguished persons whom I have mentioned, M. Sylvain Lévi, 1898 and 1922. The full list is worth the study of anyone who is interested in the relations between Nepal and the outer world.

beyond the precise limits which the Maharaja opens for his friends and visitors.

Rana Udip sent a Mission to Lord Dufferin in 1885 to offer the military services of Nepal to the Indian Government should the rumour prove true that the Russians intended to continue their advance through Afghanistan. Lord Dufferin returned his warmest thanks for the offer which, in the form in which it reached him, he felt himself obliged for the moment to decline. But the incident raised a question which was not in the Maharaja's mind when he despatched his representatives. The Viceroy, in his reply, invited the Nepal Government to assist the Indian Government in obtaining recruits for the Gurkha regiments that were included in the Indian Army. This had always been rather a thorny question. The original Gurkha battalions had been formed at the time of the Nepal war with ourselves, 1814-1816, and in 1885 there were nine Gurkha regiments in the Indian Army, but the necessary recruiting for them in Nepal was a matter upon which the two Governments had never seen eye to eye. Rana Udip recognized the advantages to both countries of an understanding in this matter, and a general permission to enlist in the Gurkha regiments of the Indian Army was published from Katmandu. As a collateral understanding attached to the Treaty of 1923, this consent was ratified and confirmed in the fullest manner.

But the days of Rana Udip's quiet rule were now threatened.

§ 3

In 1884 General Dhir Sham Sher, Commander-in-Chief and the power behind the Prime Minister, fell sick, and after a brief illness passed away, and with him all hope of the continuance of peace. This good servant of Nepal deserves more recognition than is suggested by most writers, though the especial honour done to his memory by the erection of an equestrian statue on the maidan in Katmandu is proof that by his own people he alone is counted worthy to rank in honour among the Maharajas of his country. Politically, he was the arbiter of Nepal; personally he was one of the most attractive of his family, and had won from them the nickname of " San-nani." Laurence Oliphant records his own impressions in the following words: " Colonel Dhir was the most jovial, light-hearted, and unselfish being imaginable, brave as a lion—as recent events in Nepal have proved—always anxious to please and full of amusing conversation. . . . I know of no one I would rather have by my side in a row than the young Colonel, and his brother Jang evidently thought so too when he chose him to assist in the capture of the conspirators in the attempt on his life."

In an especial degree Dhir had always been the selected companion of Jang Bahadur in all his most important adventures and trials. In many

ways General Dhir was the finest soldier that Nepal had produced since
the days of Amar Singh, Ochterlony's opponent in 1814, and the part
played by him in the expedition against Tibet has already been referred to.
Kuti was captured by Dhir without the loss of a single life. In it was taken
a large amount of stores and the young General received from his brother
the warmest official congratulations. " Your occupation of Kuti," ran the
despatch, " has been a brilliant piece of work. For it detracts somewhat
from the credit of a commander when a battle gained is attended with
heavy casualties among the soldiers under his command; while you have

STATUE OF COMMANDER-IN-CHIEF
DHIR SHAM SHER JANG BAHADUR RANA

saved your troops and have won a great victory at the same time. I have
been immensely pleased with the valour and wisdom you have displayed in
taking possession of Kuti."

This success was followed by an advance upon Suna-Gompa (the
Golden Temple), a fortified post commanding the road between Shigatse
and Nepal. By a display of tactics to which the Tibetans were entirely
unused Dhir overcame an obstinate resistance and occupied the fort. His
victorious advance was only checked by orders from Jang Bahadur that
an armistice had been arranged at the request of the Chinese Amban. In a
letter ordering the return of Dhir's troops from the foot of Bhairab Langur
to better protected winter quarters, the Maharaja again expressed his great
satisfaction with the work of Dhir.

II   F

Negotiations between Jang Bahadur and the Tibetans were interrupted by a sudden attack delivered by a large Tibetan force upon Jhanga and Kuti during the absence of Dhir in Katmandu.[1] The result was disaster for the Nepalese troops. General Dhir immediately hastened from Katmandu with a small force to the relief of his men. He met the fugitives and out of them was able to reorganize five regiments, which, added to the five regiments he had brought with him from Katmandu, made up an expeditionary force of some size, the prestige of which was increased by the fact that it was led by the General whom the Tibetans had almost come to regard as invincible in the field.[2] The Tibetans fell back before him to the outskirts of Kuti. Outside the walls of that place Dhir delivered an allocation of singular force which deserves record in these pages. He praised the troops whom he had asked to undergo one of the most rapid and most difficult marches in the history of Nepal. He reminded them that as die they must one day, death on the field of battle, bringing to them not only earthly glory but heaven itself, was far more to be desired than a lingering death on a sick bed. He said that the Maharaja had ordered him to retake Kuti at any cost, and he pledged himself before them all that if he failed he would not leave the place alive, but would immolate himself in the ruins of Kuti as satis did on the funeral pyres of their husbands. Dhir placed in the van the very men who had fled from Kuti but a few weeks before, telling them that they had been given the place of honour in order that they might have an opportunity to rehabilitate themselves; and he added a grim incentive to valour by assuring them that if any one of them attempted to fly he would at once be shot down by the ranks in the rear. It was a great assault. The dispositions of Dhir were made with skill, and he ordered his men to hold their fire till the Tibetans had discharged their muskets, and then to clear them out of their entrenchments with the kukhri and the bayonet. These instructions were carried out, and the Nepalese only fired upon their enemies as the latter began to retreat. Not only was Kuti retaken, but General Dhir reported with satisfaction the recapture of everything in the place that had been lost, except part of the store of the wood and rice which had been consumed by the Tibetan garrison. Once again he received from his brother a letter of the warmest congratulation, in which the note occurs: " You have been true to the salt you have taken of your sovereign. You have studied to good purpose the manners and

[1] This tendency of Tibetan authorities to renew action while terms of peace were being discussed was later exemplified in 1904 when Col. Younghusband's Mission at Gyantse was besieged without warning by Tibetan troops while an armistice existed for the purpose of negotiations with the central Tibetan authorities, and peaceful—even friendly —relations prevailed between the expedition from India and the inhabitants of the Gyantse plain.

[2] From the rapidity of his movements he had earned among his opponents the title of "The Flying Kazi."

customs of the English in England itself. You have achieved great glory by adopting the military tactics by which the great commanders of Europe made their conquests and routed their enemies with very little loss to their own forces." [1]

References have already been made to the services of General Dhir during the Indian Mutiny. It was under his command that Ambarpur was taken and all the rebels who stayed to defend the fort cut down to a man. The subsequent work of General Dhir in India has been recorded by Malleson and other writers of this period. On the return of Jang Bahadur to Nepal General Dhir was left in command of the Nepalese army co-operating with the Indian troops. He was given by the Indian Government a personal salute of thirteen guns for his services at this time.

After the Mutiny he was employed in sweeping out the rebel fugitives from the Tarai, and the courtesy as well as the efficiency with which, for that purpose, he co-operated with Brigadier-General Holdich was mentioned in the latter's despatches. It is worth noting that Dhir Sham Sher protested strongly against the line that Jang Bahadur took up against the Resident, Lieut.-Col. Ramsay. The position that the Commander-in-Chief then held in the country cannot be better expressed than by a letter written by Ramsay to Dhir after the former's return to England. " At the time of my departure from Nepal, when I had gone to bid adieu to Maharaja Jang Bahadur he told me that it was only you who had advised him not to take any steps or make representations to the Government of India against me and for my withdrawal from the Residency, as that would bring nothing but humiliation to him. How very true your words subsequently proved to be. I admire your wisdom and forethought and hope you will continue to assist your able brother in his administration with your wise counsels and suggestions."

Internal affairs now claimed the attention of General Dhir, and an increasing share in the administrative work of the country fell to him. We find that the first serious attempt at public school education was inaugurated by him. He also caused the old road from Churia to Bhimphedi to be built ; and made special provision for the education of poor Brahman children.

In January 1877 General Dhir was sent to represent the King of Nepal at the Imperial Darbar at Delhi. On his return to Katmandu in the middle of February he found that Jang Bahadur was absent in the Tarai. The news was sent to him of his brother's illness; but he could not reach Patharghatta until after Jang Bahadur's death. To Dhir was

---

[1] An incident occurred at this time which is characteristic of both the brothers. One Major Pahlwan Singh had behaved with such conspicuous gallantry on this occasion that General Dhir, defying the military law upon the subject, created him a colonel on the spot. Jang Bahadur confirmed the appointment, but at the same time imposed a heavy fine on his brother. This was subsequently remitted.

entrusted the supervision of the cremation ceremonies of Jang and his three wives. He was strongly opposed to the practice of sati and had done his best to dissuade the Maharanis from immolating themselves, but he found it impossible to move the determination of the senior Maharani and two of the secondary wives. The senior Maharani, however, joined Dhir in forbidding the two younger Maharanis to sacrifice themselves.[1]

As has been said, Jang Bahadur's brother, Jagat Sham Sher became for a short time Commander-in-Chief after the succession of Rana Udip, but Jagat's death soon promoted Dhir to the official position of Commander-in-Chief, and practically also to that of Prime Minister. The duties of the Commander-in-Chief in Nepal are not confined only to military affairs. He has many civil functions to perform, and the lack of administrative and organizing faculties which the new Prime Minister soon betrayed left many grave decisions in the hands of Dhir. Burdensome as this double office was, the Commander-in-Chief found occasion to give his children a first-rate education, and he imposed on them a kindly but iron discipline; in short, to the utmost of his power he gave them the training which Jang had so signally omitted to give to his own sons. There can be little doubt that from the moment of the death of Jang Bahadur, General Dhir could have imposed his authority upon the country as Prime Minister had he wished to do so. Rana Udip and Jagat were weak and comparatively unpopular characters; and the sons of Jang Bahadur were wholesomely afraid of this idol of the army. Never for a moment did Dhir entertain the thought. It was not perhaps to his country's good that he should have so loyally accepted the arrangements made by Jang Bahadur, and in particular the Order of Succession that his brother had settled, but Dhir never swerved from what he conceived to be the path of his duty. With all his severity he had a share of that greatness of vision which led both his brother Jang Bahadur and his son Chandra to overlook and pardon even gross acts of disloyalty. He did not live to assume the highest honours— earned by the work he had performed so long and so honestly. He died on the 14th October 1884, and with his death the inevitable crisis was precipitated that had overhung Nepal so long and had been averted only by Dhir's strength and foresight.

§ 4

The removal of the Commander-in-Chief's strong hand led at once to the resuscitation of Jagat Jang's intrigues. Rana Udip had been unwise enough to consent to his nephew's return from exile and his reinstatement in the roll of succession, and at once the old political groups began to dominate and overcloud the situation. There was no great change in the

---

[1] The ceremony of sati has never since been performed in the Rana family, and it is now forbidden by law.

parties or their leaders, except that Bir Sham Sher took the place of his father, the late Commander-in-Chief, as head of the Sham Sher party, and the Narsingh adherents, realizing that unaided they could never hope to achieve their end, were soon persuaded to unite their forces with those of Jagat Jang, son of Jang Bahadur. The issue was thus narrowed down to the struggle between the latter and the sons of Dhir Sham Sher.

Jagat Jang's course was, however, not so easy. His recall and his intemperate intrigues had caused dissensions in his own party. His younger brother, Jit Jang—who had automatically become Commander-in-Chief after the death of Dhir—resented the possible reinstatement of Jagat Jang and did not come back to Nepal from India, where he had gone for medical help, prior to the latter's return. From Allahabad he wrote a remarkable letter to Rana Udip in which, after protesting against the apparent lack of confidence in himself shown by the recall of Jagat, he adds that, if his supersession were insisted upon, he would prefer in future to reside in peace in a sacred place and sing the praises of God.[1] In his letter Jit quotes the following curious words used by the late Jang Bahadur: "I have salvaged the Nepalese ship of state, which had been sunk by the Panres, the Thapas, and the Sahis by putting their trust in outsiders to the exclusion of their own near relatives. I have established a constitution unknown in the annals of Gods or Emperors by setting up a covenant, and you should not think of acting in contravention of the Order of Succession. Even if your superior and master takes to tying up goats to elephants' posts or *vice versa,* or to paying no heed to merit, do not oppose him, but rather forsake the country and retire to a sacred place. Let your mind dwell upon no other course of action and do not act thoughtlessly."

In order to prove that he had not acted in an underhand way, Jit Jang reminds Rana Udip that when he and Her Highness, his august aunt, were in the garden osier house, he had represented the impossibility of carrying on the duties of Commander-in-Chief in a restricted manner. "It is not wise to repeat the same thing over and over again to the mighty, but . . . I laid this supplication before you not once but time and again, whenever I had the opportunity both out of doors and indoors." He therefore had falsely represented his visit to India as a mere temporary urgency. He concluded his despatch by an earnest prayer that if only to avoid bloodshed the Maharaja would still carry out the instructions of Jang Bahadur—and restore the Order of Succession established by him. It was clear that the nephews were prevailing over the weak uncle, and the ultimate result was the revolution of November 1885.

[1] During the illness of Dhir the Bada Maharani of Rana Udip, who had always been in sympathy with the aspirations of Jagat Jang, had made use of her position to bring about Jagat Jang's return to Nepal, and this, coupled with the probability of his reinstatement if he once came back, had caused great uneasiness in the mind of Jit Jang.

Before dealing with this violent rearrangement of authority in Nepal, it is worth while to note the personalities of the party that thus found itself in opposition, both to Jagat Jang and to Rana Udip. They were the sons of the late Commander-in-Chief, Dhir Sham Sher. The eldest son was Bir Sham Sher, who was born on the 10th December 1852. His father was not a man of great wealth, and Bir Sham Sher had been practically adopted by his grandmother for many years. He spent some time at Doveton College in Calcutta, but does not appear to have attained to a knowledge of English, or indeed the power of writing and reading his own language fluently. But literary attainments have never been a guide to the innate character of either boy or man. Bir lived in an atmosphere of intrigue, and had inherited from his father not only a considerable military capacity but a power of striking at the right moment, which, in those unrestful days, was perhaps more valuable than any other talent. He married in early life the daughter of the traitor Mahila Sahib Upendra, the next brother of King Surendra.

In Nepal, although the practice is now being relinquished, there was no surprise when a man of high position married more than one wife. Nor was it in any way implied thereby that the junior wives belonged to a lower class or caste. This custom did not escape criticism in India, but it has remained as a characteristic—and it may be added a complication—of the succession of the Maharajaship to this day. Elsewhere[1] will be found a chart pedigree to which a note is attached indicating three recognized classes of wives. The first are those of equal caste with their husbands. These have not been distinguished in the chart by any accompanying symbol. Below them are wives taken from a caste which had every right of association with the caste of the husband other than that of eating rice together. The third class consists of wives drawn from castes with which no eating in common is possible. In the interests of all concerned, and certainly that of the country, the present Maharaja has only permitted those to be added to the roll of succession who are children by wives of the first class. But he has been unable to make this decree retrospective: he has not amended the list of succession which he received from his pre-decessor. It will therefore be seen that in the line of near succession to the Prime Ministership are three candidates for the highest office in the State who do not fulfil the qualification laid down by Chandra for future observ-ance. These are the sons of Maharaja Bir Sham Sher by wives who were not of the same caste as his own. In view of the new and stricter conception of the descent of the title and powers of the Maharaja, it is obvious that difficulties are not unlikely to arise when these candidates have a claim to assume one of the senior offices in the State.

At the age of eighteen Bir Sham Sher was chosen by his uncle, Jang Bahadur, to act as the representative of the Government of Nepal in

[1] End of vol. i.

Calcutta—and Jang Bahadur did nothing idly or without purpose. So far as that lonely man could be said to be so with anyone, he was, as we have seen, on terms of friendship with, and indeed of all his relatives relied most upon, Dhir Sham Sher; and it is not unlikely that the great Maharaja deliberately trained the latter's son with an eye to the certainty that some day he would hold high, and perhaps the highest, rank in the State. His own children had disappointed him. They had been unable to bear the heavy trial of being the sons of a great man. It was therefore to the sons of Dhir—it will be remembered that Rana Udip had no children—that Jang Bahadur naturally looked for the ultimate maintenance of authority in the State; and there could be no better training for Bir Sham Sher than to be in charge of the relations between Nepal and India for a twelvemonth. Two years later he was sent to succeed the notorious Badri Narsingh as Governor of Palpa. We need not credit Jang Bahadur with powers of divination in thus watching carefully the development and supervising the training of a boy who early showed a definite personality and was, in fact, destined to influence in no slight degree the history of Nepal. We may, perhaps, also see in this attention a silent criticism of his own sons.

Bir remained at Palpa for five years. After Jang Bahadur's death he returned to Katmandu, and acted as Chief Secretary to his father, the Commander-in-Chief. On the death of his father the whole position was reversed, largely owing to feminine influence at headquarters. As if conscious that Dhir had been the real Prime Minister and autocrat of Nepal, Rana Udip, freed from his restraining influence, took the opportunity offered by his brother's death to make a change in the national policy that, had he been alive, would have been opposed vigorously—and successfully— by Dhir Sham Sher.

On the return of Jagat, Jit Jang abandoned his position as Commander- in-Chief, as we have seen, and the feud between the two parties was openly recognized by everyone in Nepal. We have noted the course that Nepalese politics had generally taken in the past, and the Sham Sher brothers—Bir, Khadga, Rana, Deva, Chandra, Bhim, Fateh, Lalit, Jit, and Judha—soon found themselves confronted with a flat choice. Either they must at any cost make themselves masters of the government of Nepal, or their lives would lie at the scant mercy of those whose hatred had been accentuated not merely by a sense of exclusion from authority in their early lives, but by the smarting recollection of a long exile in India.

These brothers were men of no ordinary mould. They deliberated upon the situation long and coldly. They watched the gradual increase of power of their bitter enemy, Jagat Jang, and his growing domination over their weak and therefore dangerous uncle the Maharaja. They decided to strike, and they allowed little time to be lost between the decision and the stroke. On the night of the 22nd November 1885 the Sham Sher brothers went to the palace of Maharaja Rana Udip and put him to death. Jagat Jang and his son Judha Pratap Jang suffered the same fate. Immediately afterwards Bir Sham Sher and his brothers, taking with them the infant King and the Queen-Mother, hurried to the Tundi Khel. There, in the face of the army which had been hastily mustered, Bir Sham Sher proclaimed himself Prime Minister of Nepal.

It is interesting to know the evidence upon which Bir and his brothers acted. Of the general situation and of the reality of the danger that threatened the sons of Dhir there was no doubt. But precise details were only obtained after the *coup d'état*.

I quote from Nepalese official sources the following letter written by General Kedar Narsingh, son of Badri Narsingh, and nephew of both Jang Bahadur and Rana Udip. " I, Kedar Narsingh, do hereby declare that, with a view to setting up Jagat Jang who had once been cast off on a charge of conspiracy against the person and throne of His Majesty the King, the honour of Her Majesty the Queen Mother, and the lives of the Prime Minister and other bharadars, I, in collusion with Jagat Jang's brothers, Ambar Jang and Dhoje Narsingh, approached Her Highness the Bada Maharani [Maharaja Rana Udip's second wife] and won her over to the plot. Her Highness then secured the consent and approval of Maharaja Rana Udip also." Kedar Narsingh, truthfully or not, protested that he refused to join the conspiracy, and was given the option of going away with his family and property to India.

He became aware that Jagat Jang had been sent for with a view to reinstating him in the roll of succession to the office of Prime Minister, " some seven or eight days before the death of Maharaja Rana Udip." The second wife of the latter assured Kedar Narsingh of her determination to place Jagat Jang in power. To this Kedar opposed a natural protest in view of the fact that Jagat Jang had jotted down in his notebook a vow that he would " kill Kedar Narsingh and flay alive cousin Khadga Sham Sher." He was, however, reassured by Jagat himself and allowed it to be thought that he was on the side of the conspirators.

Two days later Rana Udip openly stated to Kedar his conviction that if free Jagat Jang would certainly kill General Dhir Sham Sher's sons, and harm the Queen Mother and her sister Kanchha Maiya, both of whom were in favour of General Bir.[1] In reply to Kedar's questions Rana Udip replied that he had made all arrangements to guard against any such revenge on the part of Jagat Jang and that he would look to it. This is just the inconsistent answer to be expected from a man of Rana Udip's weakness. After a few days Kedar, becoming more and more uneasy, joined with

---

[1] There can be no doubt that the Maharaja was on the point of reinstating in blood, privilege, and office both Jagat Jang and Jit Jang. But he had apparently convinced neither of his *bona fides*, and Jit Jang declined to return to Nepal.

Padma Jang and Ranbir Jang, and, at the Maharani's request, went again to Rana Udip to persuade him to reinstate General Jagat. The Maharaja was unwilling to say anything definite, and asked his visitors to submit a statement in writing of the advantages and disadvantages of the course they recommended, adding that he would consult the sons of Dhir. The statement was prepared and sent in, and on the following night a message from Rana Udip summoned Kedar to Narayanhiti. On arrival there, Dhoje Narsingh—who had thus used the Maharaja's name—informed him that the Maharaja was dead. Both men then took refuge at the Residency, where Ranbir Jang and Padma Jang joined them.

From the Residency a telegram was sent to Jit Jang in India, and another to the Resident at Sagauli to the effect that Rana Udip had been murdered: would he kindly inform the Viceroy? The senior Dowager Maharani then appeared at the Residency. She at once sent a telegram, apparently to the same address, saying that the Maharaja was murdered in her presence, and that she had taken refuge at the Residency. A little later Kedar Narsingh surprised the Maharani in the act of writing a letter to the Viceroy of a most indiscreet nature. Kedar prevailed with her not to send it. So far as can be made out from Kedar's rather involved narrative, the Maharaja, pretending that he had the willing consent of all of the Jagat Jang faction, said he would consult with Bir Sham Sher and Khadga Sham Sher as to the day for the departure of the Maharaja on tour. Two days before this departure Jagat Jang was to be sent as Governor to Palpa; no definite announcement would be made as to his reinstatement in the succession, but it was apparent that Rana Udip intended to reinsert his name. Dhir Sham Sher's sons consequently decided to act two days before the departure of Jagat Jang.

The actual death of the Maharaja Rana Udip was described by the senior Dowager Maharani in more or less the following words. The Maharaja at the time was lying on his bed with his breast on the pillow, and facing east had begun the familiar " Rama, Rama " that prefaces a letter. On the left the Maharani and three other ladies were seated. On this side also was Mahila Babu, and two maidservants were anointing the Maharaja's feet. Choutaria Babu then knocked at the door and said that Khadga Sham Sher wished to have an interview with the Maharaja on a matter of business. Rana Udip then told an officer to open the door. No sooner was the door opened than Dambar Sham Sher, Khadga, Chandra, Rana, and Bhim entered the room and, resting on his right knee, Dambar produced a rifle. He made the apparently nervous comment that it was a rifle of a new pattern, and at once fired at the Maharaja. Whether the wound was fatal or not could not be discovered, for Khadga Sham Sher fired also, and his action was followed by others of the Sham Sher brothers.

This is the Maharani's story. On another occasion she accused the present Maharaja of having incited his brothers to kill her as she was attempting to fly. It is impossible that Chandra should have suggested this outrage against the divine law of Nepal which in the most categorical manner classes the killing of a woman with the unspeakable sacrilege of killing a Brahman. It is to be noted that Kedar is careful to make a distinction between his own knowledge and the statement made by the Maharani. It has been denied that Chandra Sham Sher was present in the room at all. I think it only right to say that he has, in the fullest manner, placed at my disposal the various official records referring to this palace revolution. The matter is not one of the first importance. Chandra Sham Sher, whether he actually fired or not, would be the last person to deny that, after the fullest consideration of a situation which must end in the death of one party or another, he was entirely at one with his brothers in the action they found themselves compelled to take.

Mr. Digby records that soldiers were then sent to Manaura where Jagat Jang was living, and to Thapathali, the residence of Judha Pratap Jang. Both of these men were put to death. There is some doubt here of the action of the Resident, Colonel Berkeley, at this crisis. Mr. Digby asserts that the refugees from Katmandu were treated with great harshness, and that the King's uncle, Narendra Vikram, was refused shelter. Mr. Digby was avowedly a partisan of the family of Jang Bahadur, and his book was written as a criticism of the Indian Government's action in not intervening on behalf of Jang Bahadur's descendants. If allowance be made for this undoubted bias one may perhaps understand that Colonel Berkeley, like his predecessors, maintained the strictest neutrality possible in the circumstances.

The new Maharaja Bir Sham Sher set to work at once. Naturally a large number of changes were made in the personnel of the higher offices; he also cancelled the roll of succession drawn up by Rana Udip, and exiled a large number of partisans of Jagat Jang. With a constitution such as that which prevails in Nepal, there is no other course open to the autocrat who establishes himself by violence but to secure his position by the absence of those whom he has indeed expelled from power, but whose resentment and intrigues would entail a wearisome and probably ineffectual surveillance were they permitted to remain in the country.

Like his uncle Jang Bahadur, within sixteen months of his assumption of power Maharaja Bir discovered another conspiracy directed against himself and the young king. This time it was headed by his own brother, Khadga Sham Sher, the Commander-in-Chief and heir to the Prime Ministership. Khadga was inclined to overrate both the services he had rendered to the new regime and his own capacity. He was a vain man and had already begun to assume greater authority than his position justified. In March 1887 Khadga and his maternal uncle, Kesar Singh, joined with

H.H. MAHARAJA BIR SHAM SHER

Kanchha Maiya, the sister of the Queen-Mother, in a plot which resulted in the internment of Kesar at Salyana and the exile of the lady to a hill district in eastern Nepal. He was a man of curious contrasts—a bully and a keen student of antiquarian research; useless as a leader he was a capable enough man in carrying out readily and efficiently a scheme thought out by another and entrusted to him for execution, as had been seen in his share in the plot against Rana Udip. But his impatient vanity was such that there are on record against him no less than four separate attempts to overthrow a Prime Minister of Nepal. Khadga was interned in a hill district near Palpa, of the name of Thada. It was not a severe punishment for his disloyalty, and two years later, by that curious mingling of mercy and mercilessness which so often characterized the Nepalese, he was appointed Governor of Palpa. In that position, it may be remembered, he offered willing and effective service to the explorations conducted by Dr. Fuhrer and others in the district of Rummindei and Tilaura Kot. But intrigue was in his bones, and we shall see later that he caused trouble both to Maharaja Deva and Maharaja Chandra.

Bir Sham Sher continued his policy of expelling from Nepal or interning therein all those who were likely to cause him trouble; in some cases this was accompanied by confiscation of property.[1] These were difficult days for the new Maharaja. It may be conceived that, if his own brother was willing to lead a plot against him others would be found to do the like. Early in 1888 Ranbir Jang, son of Jang Bahadur, led a foolish and easily crushed expedition into the Tarai from India. He was defeated at Butwal. At the same time he induced his nephew, the son of Jit Jang, to start a mutiny among the garrison at Palpa. The latter movement resulted in the immediate arrest of its ringleader. He was sent to Katmandu. Of those involved with him, numbering in all fifty-four, five were sentenced to death; a certain number of Brahmans, who may not be put to death for any cause whatever, were either imprisoned or—a far more terrible thing—had to submit to the hideous rites which accompanied their defilement and degradation from caste.[2]

[1] In November 1887, according to Mr. Digby, Dhoje Narsingh, who was the adopted son of Maharaja Rana Udip, sent in a claim to the Nepal Government. He asserted that his losses included a head-dress or pagri of brilliants and rubies valued at 250,000 rupees, and a necklace of fourteen large emeralds valued at 72,000 rupees. He also complained that silver plate sufficient for 170 guests had been taken from him, and adds the curious charge of 51,000 rupees for "emeralds supplied by my late mother [wife of Badri Narsingh] for the King's head-dress—not paid for." He also demanded one year's undrawn allowance belonging to the late Maharaja at the time of his murder. It is not clear whether this sum represents the revenues of Kaski. Altogether he claimed no less than 13,535,040 rupees.

[2] Captain Vansittart states that another plot was discovered early in 1888, and that after its failure the conspirators were put to death. But this is denied by the present Maharaja, and may perhaps be a misreading of notes connected with Ranbir's rising.

After the deposition of Khadga, Rana Sham Sher, as next in succession, held the office of Commander-in-Chief until his death in 1887. He was then succeeded by Deva Sham Sher. Considering the unhappy use that he afterwards made of the position of Prime Minister, it is only fair to note that General Deva seems to have carried out his work as Commander-in-Chief with willing co-operation in the matter of the recruitment of Gurkhas for the Indian Army. A proclamation issued jointly by him and the Maharaja states quite frankly that men who have acquired military training in British regiments will be in a position to help their country on their return.

In February 1888 Maharaja Bir Sham Sher was received in Calcutta by Lord Dufferin with full honours. On his return he sanctioned the arrangements for the marriage of the King of Nepal to two more wives. The King had been married for the first time in 1887 to two queens from Rajputana. Bir now wished the King to marry his two daughters by his Kanchha Maharani. The senior Dowager Maharani, however, wrote to the Viceroy to protest on behalf of the Nepalese refugees in India. In her letter she asserts that the mother of the intended brides is a woman of very low caste whose children under the Hindu law of marriage are absolutely ineligible for marriage into the superior castes, much less into a Kshatriya or royal family. As the senior member of the reigning family of Nepal, she asked Lord Dufferin to intervene. At the same time she charged the Prime Minister with having concluded a secret treaty with China which was opposed to the interests of the British.[1] But Lord Dufferin replied with the utmost correctness and reserve. The old Maharani seems to have been implicated at this time in a good many other intrigues in India, all directed against the existing regime in Nepal.

In 1889 the Maharaja received the decoration from the Chinese Emperor of T'ung ling ping ma kuo kan wang. In the following year Prince Albert Victor, Queen Victoria's eldest grandson, visited the extreme western end of the Tarai jungles for a shooting expedition. In the same year a German named Otto E. Ehlers came to Nepal with the request that he might be allowed to climb Mount Everest from the south. In the friendliest but most unmistakable manner, the Maharaja declined to give him this permission.

Much progress was made with the supply of water to the Valley during Maharaja Bir's period of office. The new works were put in hand in 1888, and the opening ceremony took place at Katmandu in the autumn of 1891. Bhatgaon was supplied four years later. In the winter of 1892-3 Bir Sham Sher paid a visit to Lord Lansdowne at Calcutta. He made an extended tour as the guest of the Government of India, and in the

---

[1] It may be remarked that in this letter the Maharani asserted that the Nepalese allegiance to China was nominal.

following. autumn was invested by the Resident with the insignia of a K.C.S.I.

After spending some years in useful administration of the country and improving the educational, sanitary, hospital, and traffic requirements of Nepal—among his constructions being the suspension bridge at Khuli-khani and the clock-tower on the Tundi Khel—he turned his attention to a general supervision of the efficiency with which the existing law was carried out. In June 1897 he was given the Grand Commandership of the Star of India, and in 1899 he paid another visit to Calcutta to meet Lord Curzon.

A little difficulty was raised by the attitude of the Indian Government towards their guest. Nepal had always insisted that the head of a Nepalese Mission on such occasions should be recognized as an Ambassador from the King of Nepal; the Indian Government regarded the visit as a " complimentary mission to Lord Curzon." Nepalese opinion perhaps regarded the matter in too serious a light. There could have been no reason for any change of attitude towards the State of Nepal. But the essentially watchful attitude that has always characterized, and still characterizes, the relations of Nepal with all neighbouring countries, saw in a description of this journey as a complimentary mission to Lord Curzon, a derogation of the position and dignity that had always surrounded the rare visits of the Prime Ministers of Nepal to Calcutta. These subjects of misunderstanding have now been finally rectified, and the relations of Nepal to India run no risk of alteration so long as Great Britain retains her responsibility for the government of the peninsula.

For the remainder of Maharaja Bir Sham Sher's rule he devoted himself to internal affairs, and he continued to discharge this primary duty until the end of his life, which was not long delayed. At the beginning of the new century his health suddenly failed, and on the 5th March 1901 he died from an aneurism.

He was a capable and earnest ruler. In moments of emergency he acted with rapidity and firmness. There was no particular occasion during his rule to emphasize either the military strength of Nepal or the constant friendliness which existed between Nepal and India. There was indeed only one threat of war during his time of office. Once again the Tibetans proved hostile. The occasion was insignificant—a mere dispute about a supply of salt. The only important aspect of the matter is the fact that as a result of this trifling difference the Tibetans continued to maintain an attitude of suspicion towards Nepal.

Bir Sham Sher died in peace, a matter which was regarded by his own countrymen as a proof that he had earned the approbation and the confidence of his own people. Were one entirely certain of the cause of Jang Bahadur's death in 1877, Bir Sham Sher might be set down as the second Prime Minister of Nepal who had died a natural death. As it is, there are some who think that the privilege may be claimed for him of being, the first. He was a great builder and no mean musician. His house at Narayan-hiti is a fine building based upon Government House in Calcutta. Of his nominal other tastes Lord Roberts writes: " The Maharaja is extremely musical, and has several well-trained bands taught by an English band-master."[1] He was equally devoted to the encouragement of Indian music.

The following description of General Bir Sham Sher by one who knew him and his work well, is not an unfair estimate of the personality of one who helped to fill in the interval between the two great administrators of modern Nepal. " In personal appearance General Bir Sham Sher just fell short of what might be called a heavy man. He was endowed with a sound common sense, which he brought to bear upon every question before him and thus helped him to a solution which, though it might not have been brilliant, was in most instances on the right side. Reserve was one of his special characteristics, even to the point of making him appear grave and rather gloomy."

§ 5

Maharaja Deva Sham Sher.—In strict accordance with the roll of succession, Bir Sham Sher was succeeded by his brother Deva Sham Sher. His period of office was so short that it is not necessary to record of him more than one or two of the outstanding facts of his life and work.

He was born on the 17th July 1862. He was a well educated man, and spoke English fluently. His character seems to have been unmarked by any of the vices that proved so great a temptation to some of his relations. Unfortunately it was also unmarked either by strength, judgment, or foresight. He was a frivolous man. As a second-in-command he had done his work sufficiently if not remarkably well. He had been brought up as the adopted son of the wife of General Krishna Bahadur, Jang Bahadur's brother, who had lost all her own children. His adoption was, however, merely nominal, for he continued to live in his father's house. The opinion entertained of him by his more active brothers may be gleaned from the fact that in 1885 he was allowed to have neither part nor lot in nor even knowledge of the conspiracy which placed Bir Sham Sher on the Prime Minister's throne. In 1887 Khadga's misbehaviour and dismissal thrust greatness upon Deva Sham Sher. He became Jang-i-lat or Senior Com-manding General.[2] But, as we have seen, General Rana Sham Sher,

---

[1] *Forty-One Years in India*, p. 536. For an account of a great Jalasa held by him at Bagari in the Valley, the reader is referred to a report in the *Amrita Bazar Patrika*, 7th February 1900.

[2] In India the title "Jang-i-lat" belongs exclusively to the Commander-in-Chief. In Nepal it is not the Commander-in-Chief but his immediate junior in the succession who takes this title. This is largely due to the fact that the Commander-in-Chief has other duties, which make it impossible for him to devote his time exclusively to military work.

Commander-in-Chief, died only three months later, and Deva succeeded to that post and thus became immediate successor to his brother.

H.H. MAHARAJA DEVA SHAM SHER

Under the direct supervision of Maharaja Bir, Deva seems to have exercised his functions satisfactorily. During the fourteen years of his control of this office, he introduced considerable improvements in the Nepal Arsenal at Nakhu. He also laid on water for the use of travellers to

Katmandu along the main route from India. Between Simra and Bichako he constructed five tanks fitted with hydrants. He did the same at Bhimphedi. He built at his own cost two good rest-houses, one at Bichako and the other at Bhimphedi.

But despite his adequate administration of the office of Commander-in-Chief, Deva himself remained a luxury-loving and lazy man. Immediately after his succession he wasted both time and money in a series of darbars, triumphal processions, and other celebrations. The magnitude of the task entrusted to him was never realized. He spent his time in sport and amusements, and left the government of Nepal without any directing head.

Deva Sham Sher was a man of kindly and useful tendencies. He was, however, wholly inadequate to the position which he was now called upon to occupy. An ill-balanced man, he sank the administrator in the prince, and sought to magnify his office, less by vigorous and unceasing work than by devising new splendours for his frequent days of ceremony. Then, tired of these inaugural pomps, he abandoned his capital and chiefly devoted himself to a life of easy sport at Nagarkot.

When he did introduce a measure it was unfortunate and often premature. By a stroke of the pen his thistledown wit inaugurated thirty primary schools in the country. A third of these died out within a few months. It is to the credit of his heart if not of his head that he anticipated the present Maharaja in an immature scheme to free the slaves of Nepal. But like his other work it was based upon nothing more substantial than mere sentiment. Hastily and without foresight he attempted to emancipate female slaves, not only in the states of Kaski and Lamjang, over which he had immediate and personal control, but in Katmandu itself. The time was not yet ripe for such a measure, and an uproar arose which compelled the withdrawal of the scheme.

Among other defects Deva Sham Sher had no sense of the reticence which must be observed by the governing authority under such a regime as that of Nepal. No man could suggest a reform for his consideration without the fear of its being published to the world on the following day; and, though perhaps he has been hardly judged as one who took pleasure in the humiliation of others, he alienated the confidence as well as the affection of all classes alike—and his brothers, who from the first must have regarded his succession as a hazardous experiment, rapidly decided that he must be replaced by a man of greater dignity, breadth of view, industry, and, above all, of greater strength of mind.

The end soon came. On the 26th June 1901 Deva was invited by his brothers to go to the palace of Bir Sham Sher to settle a domestic dispute concerning the partition of the building among the sons of the late Prime Minister. Once inside the house, his brothers presented him with an ultimatum. Deva promised to reform and made a desperate but ineffectual

II   G

attempt to retain his place; one account says that he was actually in tears when he at last consented to sign his abdication in the presence of the King. He was of course succeeded by the eldest and ablest of his brothers, Chandra Sham Sher, the present Maharaja.

Deva was interned for a short time at Dhankuta, but shortly afterwards was allowed to escape to India. He lived for the most part of his remaining years at Mussoorie.[1] He accepted his new life with philosophy after having—like other exiled Nepalese officials—made an almost traditional attempt to murder his brother, the new Prime Minister. He took advantage of Chandra's attendance at the Darbar in Delhi in 1903 to launch this plot. He met with no support, and the perfectly informed Indian Government—the good-natured gaoler of all such Nepalese offenders —interned him at Benares so long as Chandra remained on Indian territory.

Four years later the two brothers met in Calcutta, and Deva, with his weak and loquacious good nature, assured Chandra that he was glad of his deposition, because, he was good enough to say, Nepal under him would never have become what she was under Chandra. This did not, however, bring about any permission to return to Nepal, and on the 20th February 1914 the ex-Maharaja died in India. His sons were admitted by the present Maharaja to fitting posts in the army, and their family property was restored to them. A well-written and judicious estimate of his personality that I have received from a Nepalese source, ends with these words: " Such is Maharaja Deva, whose tenure of office as Prime Minister was of short duration; the only prominent relic of his ministry which survives in the country to this day, is the midday gunfire that was first ordered by him."

[1] Chandra sent his weak brother down to Mussoorie with 4,000 rupees a month pocket money. It was the latter's wife who conceived the idea of supplying water to travellers on the Bichako-Simra-basa road, and as she died before the idea could fructify, Deva started and completed the works in memory of her pious desire. The artist had the happy inspiration of modelling the lever which releases the water in the shape of her wrist and hand.

MAHARAJA CHANDRA
In Chinese Robes.

CHAPTER XIV

MAHARAJA CHANDRA SHAM SHER

EARLY LIFE—PERSONALITY—INDEPENDENCE OF NEPAL—LHASA MISSION
OF 1904

§ 1

CHANDRA SHAM SHER, who thus succeeded to power, consolidated his position by rapid and judicious action. He at once held a reception of the military and civil officers of the Government, and their instant welcome convinced him that the country entirely endorsed the *coup d'état* which had just been carried out. As may be imagined, his advent to the supreme office was received with enthusiasm not only by the hierarchy of Church and State, but by the rank and file of the army also, with whom and for whom he had worked for years.

The King at once confirmed the new situation by a formal act and, as a final endorsement of the ministerial regime under which Nepal has prospered so well, it is interesting to note here the large extent of the authority thereby conferred upon the new Prime Minister and Marshal. The proclamation runs thus:

" He is given full authority in respect of passing sentence of death, deprivation of caste, imprisonment for life, confiscation of property, banishment or deportation, conferring or deprivation of honours, control of the Treasury, together with plenary powers in all affairs of the State." No ceremony of state was omitted. He was installed in the high office of Prime Minister; the status of a Maharaja was confirmed to him together with the title of Marshal. The King formally agreed that he would in advance accept all public acts done by him as having the full royal approval. By another edict of the King, the whole Nepalese people were conjured to be active in their loyalty to the new minister. Those who showed themselves remiss were to be regarded as disloyal, and Chandra Sham Sher was enjoined to punish such persons by decapitation or death, by deprivation of caste, by disgrace, by imprisonment for life, by confiscation of property, and by deportation or banishment. Intimation of the change thus affected was at once sent to the Government of India through the recognized channel of communication, the British Resident in Katmandu.

Furnished thus with absolute power Maharaja Chandra assumed supreme control of all things Nepalese, and began the work in which he is to-day as vigorous and as unlimited in his authority as at the time of his

H.H. MAHARAJA CHANDRA SHAM SHER IN CORONATION ROBES AS
MAHARAJA OF KASKI AND LAMJANG

accession. Henceforth the history of Nepal is the history of his administration, his reforms, and his policy in all things, foreign and domestic alike.

The following estimate. of *The Englishman* in 1905 deals fairly with Chandra's appointment to the highest office in Nepal: " The manner of his accession to power was a pleasant contrast to that of many of his predecessors. He acquired his position, not by the sacrifice of other lives in order to satisfy personal ambition, but because his ability, high character, and good qualities marked him out as the best man for such a position of responsibility."

Before dealing with the record of Chandra Sham Sher's long administration as Prime Minister of Nepal, his earlier years require some notice. He was born on the 8th July 1863. He was the fifth of the legitimate sons of Jang Bahadur's youngest brother, General Dhir Sham Sher, who, as we have seen, held for a long time the actual office of Commander-in-Chief and practically that of Prime Minister also. At the age of nine he began the study of English under Nepalese tutors, and no doubt he owes the unusual clarity and flexibility of his spoken or written words to this early introduction to the language. English is now spoken by the chief personages of Nepal with fluency, but when Chandra was a child it was rare to meet with any of his countrymen who possessed more than a halting acquaintance with the English tongue.

Like his uncle Jang Bahadur, Chandra, as a boy, was carefully and rigorously trained in the manly and military sports that then took the place of the athletic training which Nepal has now adopted for her own soldiers from the system of the army in India. His general progress was as satisfactory as even his father expected. In the year 1878 he was married to a bride from a Thakuri family, and not long afterwards, before completing his nineteenth year, he had an opportunity of showing the stuff of which he was made. Jagat Jang's plot of the 6th June 1882 was prevented by the strong hand of Dhir Sham Sher, and his father's successful action was admittedly due to some extent to the decision, courage, and discretion of young Chandra. Immediately afterwards he went down to Calcutta to go through a course in English and other subjects, and in 1883 the annual speech of the Vice-Chancellor of Calcutta University contains a reference to " a young student who holds a high military command in the army of Nepal, and has shown on this occasion that he can handle the pen not less efficiently than the sword." He was the first of his family to matriculate in this manner, and his success stirred him to further academic ambitions. But the sudden illness of his father compelled him to abandon his schemes. He returned to Nepal and remained by the bedside of Dhir Sham Sher until the end came in 1884.

The death of his father proved the turning-point of Chandra's life. The administration of his uncle Maharaja Rana Udip had been almost wholly directed by Dhir and proved uniformly successful so long as the stronger nature of the latter was there to assist the judgment and galvanize into action the easier nature of the elder brother. As has been related, Dhir's death immediately released the intrigues and backstairs work which had been crushed during the administration of Jang Bahadur and the earlier years of his successor.

Not long after the *coup d'état* of 1885 which ended the dangerous situation caused by Jagat Jang's ambition and Rana Udip's weakness, the important position of Senior Commanding General was inherited by Chandra on the death of an elder brother. The duties of the Senior Commanding General, as has been explained already, are similar to those of the Commander-in-Chief in other States. In his charge are the supreme services of recruiting and training the Nepalese army. Chandra was thus placed, by incident and accident alike, into a position of responsibility that was of especial importance in a country where the ultimate sanction of the Government lies greatly in the efficiency and loyalty of its troops. In Chandra's case the work to be done was scarcely less than the entire reorganization of the military forces of Nepal, but it was work after his own heart, and in 1892 Lord Roberts noted the excellent drill and discipline of the Nepalese regiments that were reviewed by him at Katmandu. He says that he had been informed that Chandra Sham Sher had almost lived on the parade ground for weeks before his arrival, and just as Sir Henry Lawrence, fifty years earlier, had noticed the promise of Jang Bahadur, Lord Roberts seems to have been impressed with the vigour and capacity of the twenty-nine-year-old director of the training of the Nepalese army. To the end of his life the aged Field-Marshal remembered Chandra's *cri de cœur* on that occasion. " We have forty thousand soldiers ready in Nepal, and there is nothing to fight." But Lord Roberts did not die before he had seen the opportunity of great work given in full both to the army of Nepal and to the man who uttered this proud complaint. It was not only in this field of service, however, that Chandra was attracting attention. Owing to Deva Sham Sher's lack of initiative, although the Prime Minister, Bir Sham Sher, on the occasion of his visit in February 1888 to Lord Dufferin in Calcutta, left the acting prime ministership of Nepal to the former, he showed a greater trust, not in his next brother and heir apparent, but in Chandra, whom he appointed to look after his personal interests and household, and whom he requested to live in the Prime Minister's Palace for the whole period of his absence from Katmandu.[1]

So it came about that shortly afterwards Chandra, at his own request, attacked the thorny problem of public education in Nepal, and to this task

[1] This was the beginning of his prominent association with the Prime Minister in nearly all administrative work from this time onward, and was the first public indication of the opinion of the Rana family as to the relative capacity of Deva and Chandra.

the Prime Minister soon added the administration of much of the work of the Nepalese Foreign Office. Of the matters that occupy the attention of this department, the relations between Nepal and India are of course by far the most important. At the moment of his taking over control of the office, Chandra found that a certain formality characterized the relations between the two countries. No complaint could be made that India was interfering in any way in the internal affairs of Nepal, and Chandra not only saw the advantage of establishing a more cordial feeling, but a way to do it. Naturally enough he had recourse to the field in which he had won his first laurels, and which to this day is probably nearer his heart than any other department of his supreme administration. At that time the number of Gurkha regiments in the Indian army was nine. Chandra at once provided for the enlistment of four more, and in 1891 the total was increased to fifteen.[1]

During the tours of inspection annually carried out by the Prime Minister of Nepal, it was Chandra who was summoned to accompany the Maharaja. We can therefore understand that little by little Chandra became not merely his brother's right hand, but almost an equal associate with him in the government of Nepal. This practical equality of responsibility if not of status was, of course, known only to a comparatively small circle. Chandra's loyalty to his elder brother was unfailing, and in public, whatever his real credit, he willingly surrendered it to the Maharaja and took a secondary place. Thus the great project for the supply of water to Katmandu that has been already mentioned as the work of Bir Sham Sher, was in fact largely carried through by Chandra's activity. The same remark applies to a large portion of the public administration and to some of the foundations that marked the government of Bir. The hand was the hand of Bir, but the voice was the voice of Chandra.

His next experience was concerned with the foreign relations of his country. For some time there had been trouble in Sikkim. The Maharaja of that State, prompted by his friends and co-religionists in Lhasa, had assumed an attitude of scarcely veiled hostility towards the Indian Government, and had even attempted to prevent the establishment of a British political officer at Gangtok. This phase was brief. The Indian Government gave Sikkim to understand that no nonsense would be tolerated, and in 1889 the Maharaja of Sikkim fled from Gangtok. He attempted to make use of Nepalese territory, though it is not clear whether he did so to obtain shelter or merely as a convenient means of communicating with his friends in Lhasa. The Prime Minister of Nepal at once turned him out. His action was courteous enough, but the princely escort which Bir provided

---

[1] At the present moment there are twenty battalions of Gurkhas in the Indian army, this number having been reached by the addition of battalions between 1902 and 1908, for which also, of course, Chandra was responsible.

for the return journey of the Maharaja did not conceal from Sidkeong Namgyal that no support of his action against India was to be expected from Katmandu. The behaviour of the Nepalese Government at this time, strictly correct though it was, is thought by some to have left its traces in the uneasy relations that still exist between Nepal and Lhasa. But those relations are due to deeper causes, though the unmistakable determination of the Gurkhas not to be drawn into any quarrel with India should have been remembered by the young Dalai Lama who very soon afterwards took into his own hands the government of Tibet.[1] Chandra, as director of the Nepalese Foreign Office at this time, had therefore considerable knowledge of the internal affairs of Tibet when, in his turn as Maharaja, he offered the assistance of Nepal in connection with the Younghusband Expedition of 1904-5.

In 1892 Bir and Chandra visited India. The illness of the Prime Minister compelled his younger brother to take his place on many occasions, and Lord Lansdowne admitted to the latter his knowledge that it was he rather than his elder brother who was responsible for the large reforms that had been carried out in Nepal, and that Chandra was perhaps the better qualified of the two to explain the existing position in that country to the Indian Government. Characteristically enough, the first result of this visit to Calcutta was the receipt in Nepal of about eight thousand Martini-Henry rifles and a few mountain guns, which the Nepal Government were allowed to purchase in response to Chandra's plausible argument that the Gurkhas could not come effectively to the assistance of India in any emergency unless they had been trained in the use of modern weapons. The Sikkim trouble broke out again shortly afterwards. This in itself was dealt with quickly and finally by Katmandu, but the aftermath was a renewal of the old dispute with Lhasa which gave Chandra the opportunity of once more overhauling the military efficiency of Nepal, though there was no actual breaking off of relations.

In return for the constant service received from Chandra, the office of " Senior Commanding General " was raised in dignity and a special flag and special salute were granted to it, and when on 5th March 1901 the sudden death of Maharaja Bir put an end to a loyal and useful alliance in the service of Nepal, it was obvious that only Chandra was qualified to take over the heavy responsibilities of the office of Prime Minister, though in

---

[1] There is a curious note to be made here. For several generations the Dalai Lama had not lived long enough to come of age and take into his hands the autocratic administration of Tibet. In plain words, during the nineteenth century the Regent and Council of Four at Lhasa had retained their authority by putting the Dalai Lama to death. When Tubdan Gyatso, the present Dalai Lama, attained his majority about 1893 Tibet was claiming independence of China, but not by an open denunciation of the suzerainty of the Emperor. Had a new reincarnation taken place at this time it would have necessitated the submission of the infant's claim for ratification by Kuang Hsü or a refusal to submit it, which meant open rebellion. So Tubdan Gyatso was allowed to live.

point of precedence Deva was technically senior to him and was permitted, as we have seen, one or two months in which to prove his incapacity.

§ 2

Personality of Chandra.—Before attempting to describe the far-reaching changes that have been effected by the present Prime Minister of Nepal and the incidents of his administration, it is almost essential to have some idea of the presence and personality of this strong man in Asia. Of Chandra's administrative power, his foresight, and his devotion to the purposes of his life—the vindication of his country's complete independence and sovereignty and the steady improvement of the conditions of life and work among his people—sufficient evidence will be found in the pages of this volume. Nor will it be less clearly shown there that in him, in a degree equal to that possessed by his famous uncle, are to be found the personal ascendancy, foresight, and tenacity of purpose which alone can maintain and develop the interests both internal and external of a kingdom like Nepal. He has been accustomed throughout his entire period of government not merely to deal in detail with the affairs of his State and of the more important classes therein, but to make himself thoroughly acquainted by personal and unofficial contact with the lives of the poorest of his compatriots.[1] In him alone in the world to-day an absolute autocracy is vested: almost alone also is his insistent and minute observance of everything that goes on in the houses of the poor and in the fields of the peasant. Nothing is too small for his notice, yet his grasp of the greater questions that affect Nepal is broader and farther sighted than that of any man who has directed her affairs. He is at once the most accessible official in his own country and the most removed from all possibility of coercion or rivalry. He is his own parliament, and the powers that were given to Jang Bahadur in 1858— powers so great as to constitute him the master, guardian, and tutor of every soul without exception from the Kali river to the frontiers of Sikkim —have been maintained intact in his hands. Nay, use and tradition have helped to make his position stronger than was ever that of his famous uncle. I am inclined to repeat here what I wrote seventeen years ago, that of the force of his personality there can be as little doubt as of that of Cecil Rhodes.

In person he is somewhat above the stature of the aristocracy of Nepal. His figure is still strong and wiry, and though he has been obliged to abandon some of the more vigorous exercises of earlier days, he is capable of as hard a day's work on the hills or in the jungle as any of his own sons. A glance at the illustrations in this volume[2] will show his personal character-

[1] His friend Scindia, Maharaja of Gwalior, who died in 1924, had much of this resemblance to Harun-er-Rashid in his character.

[2] The coloured pictures of the Maharaja in full dress and in his Chinese uniform give a fair, but not, perhaps, a flattering portrait of him.

FAMILY GROUP

istics—the broad forehead, the steady glance of the penetrating eyes, and the determination that is marked in every feature. Few who have met Maharaja Chandra will ever forget the geniality of his smile and conversation; yet the former probably deceives no one into thinking it a sign of easy acquiescence, and the courtesy of the latter is the courtesy of a strong and certain mind. His manners, his discourse, and, in a singular degree, his letters are alike graceful. He gives the impression of a man who has never thought it worth while to lose his temper about anything; and though at times he has found it necessary to take off the velvet glove, it is probably true that his judgment has never been affected by anger or the disappointment of the moment. In general he dresses quietly in a kind of undress frock-coated uniform, and does not, except on the greatest occasions, use the magnificent diamond head-dress or the other insignia of his high office.[1] His clothes have the plainness of distinction, and it is no doubt in recognition of this dignity of simplicity that the King himself rarely appears except in similarly restrained garb. His Majesty's portrait appears as the frontispiece of this book attired in the State robes proper to his rank, but on the rare occasions when he appears in public he is generally dressed in a plain double-breasted European suit of dark blue, wearing the triple emerald necklace, a crescent of huge stones on his breast, and a jewelled badge upon his cap. He wears ear-rings composed of a single large diamond and ruby.

In conversation the Maharaja has the power of setting any man at his ease, and his manner is as good as his manners. He is far from that type, common to the West as well as the East, which after providing the fullest hospitality for his guests, is content therewith. He anticipates their wishes and provides to the utmost of his power for the satisfaction of their curiosity, or the carrying out of their researches. Beyond the domain of his own work and interest he is ready to discuss with adequate information and with shrewd sense most of the social and nearly all of the political problems of the West.[2] Yet no man presumes upon this good humour and grace. Liberties are not taken with the Maharaja of Nepal.

The scope of his interests is wide. It is to be regretted, however, that though he recognizes that in the Western world the study of the past has become an absorbing passion, his practical mind does not allow him to attribute more importance to it than the material and religious needs of his

[1] Instead, he often wears a scarlet peaked cap with gold embroidery, carrying, not infrequently, a diamond bow, once a favourite jewel of his late Maharani.

[2] Lord Morley, when Secretary of State for India, received the Maharaja. He writes : " I had an ordinary round of talk with him. He is certainly much more than an ordinary man. His little speech to the King [Edward VII] was admirable and the King was much taken by it." This testimony from a man as unwilling to recognize distinction in other living men as Lord Morley, and from such a supreme judge of human nature as the late King, will be sufficient for any man who had the fortune to know either.

country suggest. But he puts no obstacle in the way of such investigations as may be carried on by foreign archaeologists within the Valley and in the Tarai. It will, of course, be understood that the value of the remains, architectural, cultural, and epigraphic, in those two districts is probably many times greater than that of all the rest of Nepal put together. Certain places exist, however, of which we have no adequate knowledge, and it would be of great interest to the world if, failing European expert assistance, qualified Indian natives were permitted to make a thorough examination of such centres as Muktinath, Butwal, Gorkha, and Dhankuta.[1] In giving any such permission, the difficulty with which Chandra Sham Sher is confronted is no doubt that with which he has always had to deal in effecting any reform. No man has been more scrupulously careful not to offend the religious susceptibilities of any of those for whom he is responsible. As we shall see later the conventional Nepalese eye has at first looked askance at some of his reforms. That convention, which is characteristic of all Nepalese life and thought, may be said to be a deeply rooted—and from the point of view of those who find their plans miscarry, an over great —fear of permitting strangers or the customs of strangers to enter Nepal. That this is largely based upon religious prejudice is clear, and the due respect which the Maharaja has always paid to this obsession has delayed many of his reforms though it has not prevented their achievement. The story of the abolition of slavery which is told in another chapter is a good illustration of the manner in which these special problems are dealt with by the Maharaja. He is tireless in presenting and pressing the case for a reform, but in that presentation he has not failed to be just to those whose assent he could not at once obtain.

By a mere stroke of the pen Chandra might have introduced many of his reforms. The army is with him to a man, and there is no one living who can gainsay his authority. But he has not read history in vain, and the peculiar descent of authority in Nepal renders any change that is not freely accepted by the people and by those who are destined to succeed him only too likely to fade out after the reformer's death. With all things pertaining to the sovereignty, security, communications, trade, and general well-being of Nepal he can deal without hesitation and he does so. The preservation of law and order, the prerogative of mercy, the maintenance of an efficient and loyal army, and the collection of the national revenues and their expenditure are matters within the scope of his personal authority. He listens readily to suggestions, but to no man does he delegate his final authority. Where it is necessary to enlist the co-operation of his people,

Other places than Katmandu have been at one time or other centres of government, religion, and art, and their exploration might throw light not merely upon the tangled and contradictory chronicles of Nepal, but upon the origin of the many races that compose its population.

he takes them with him in a manner that admits of no misunderstanding. A story was told to me by one who had long been associated with the Residency, that several years ago it was found that the " white ant " was increasing its ravages in the Valley. Chandra was advised that the plague could be arrested if measures were taken instantly. He therefore caused numerous exhibits to be made showing the nature of the " queen " of the white ants. These little carcases were officially sent round the Valley to every house and the inhabitants warned that the severest punishment would await any man who did not personally take steps to discover and destroy every queen that was to be found in or near his buildings. This method of making every householder sweep the street in front of his own door was effective. Thousands of the prolific little beasts were killed, and as the remedy is one of permanent application, the Valley now may be said to be almost free from one of the curses of the East—a curse of double potency in a land of wooden houses. Chandra is a well read man and believes in the saving grace of education. His own library probably affords him the greatest pleasure of his few spare hours and the personal notes with which he corrects, amplifies, or illuminates his volumes are often terse and poignant.[1]

His daily life is simple. He rises between six and seven and after a religious service begins with his secretaries to prepare the work of the day. In the early morning he gives audience to any officials who may present themselves, or be summoned, for special instructions. Then come the petitioners whose cases have been already inquired into and passed as worthy of his attention. These cases have been summarized carefully and impartially by the Niksari Commission, and the Maharaja's decision is given rapidly and finally. After this audience he deals with letters and despatches till about ten o'clock, when he performs the daily religious rites of his caste. He goes to his first bath of obligation where soap is used that is of ceremonial purity. After being anointed by purified pastes, he enters a new bath into which a few spoonfuls of the sacred Ganges water have been poured. He then goes to the room set aside for his spiritual observances and there makes his daily symbolic offering to Brahmans of five rupees and eight annas—which represents the nominal price of a cow—and a cup of bell

---

[1] I may perhaps be allowed to give an illustration. Dr. Oldfield was the guest of Jang Bahadur on a shooting expedition, and had remarked to his host that he had had no breakfast that morning. At once Jang sent off a messenger to Thapathali, and a hot breakfast of stewed and curried fowls, pork cutlets, pilaw of pheasant, eggs, cracknells, chapattis, and fruit was prepared and despatched to meet the returning party. Unfortunately Dr. Oldfield, in recording the incident, notes that after breakfast he distributed cheroots, " of which the Nipalese are very fond, especially when they do not have to pay for them." Many different comments might have been jotted on the margin of this page, but it would be difficult to surpass Chandra's quiet pencil note, " Did Oldfield pay for the breakfast?"

metal containing about four ounces of ghi, or clarified butter. He then repeats his prayers and goes to his breakfast.

After a short rest he sees the Kazi [1] and the heads of the more important departments such as the Commander-in-Chief or his secretary, the Senior Commanding General, the General in charge of the Council office, the Foreign Secretary, and others who come in fixed rotation. This work continues till three or four in the afternoon. At four o'clock in fine weather he sits on the lawn and takes up appellate cases. In the presence of both the appellant and the respondent the clerk presents the facts of the dispute, appending to it the decisions of the courts that have already dealt with the matter. Native judgment and long experience enable him to deal rapidly and justly with the issue of the moment. A certain number of high officials are generally in attendance and he does not hesitate to consult them whenever matters affected by local custom are involved. Few complaints of the justice of his final decision have ever been made, but one result of this national confidence in their ruler is a large increase in the number of appeals. Some vicarious administration of this final court must soon be devised. Attractive as paternal administration of justice in the open air is, the sphere of civilization which Nepal has now entered will soon make it impossible for the Prime Minister to continue to bear this growing burden. Saturdays are for him a holiday; and it is this weekly day of rest and such recreation as big game shooting during his annual tour can afford that form the only relaxation in a life of hard and unending work.

The Maharaja's private tastes induce him to live in a simply furnished suite of rooms in the palace that he has erected. As can be imagined, he is a strict disciplinarian and exacts scrupulous obedience from those who are *de facto*, if not *de jure*, his subjects. Admired and loved as he is by the people, few of the Nepalese ever enter his presence without a sense of respect in which awe plays no small part. He examines work done for him impartially and thoroughly and is not easily pleased or displeased, for he has sound intuition about men and rarely makes a bad choice. He is rigorous with himself as with others. He was an inveterate smoker until the age of forty-five, when within twenty-four hours he abandoned the practice for ever. It would be impossible to close this estimate of the Maharaja without referring to the story which is told elsewhere of his having at last given in to the continued requests of his dying wife and taken a secondary wife for a short period. It is to be regretted that the example of monogamy which Maharaja Chandra has for a long time shown to the

[1] There were originally four Kazis or state councillors, but of these only one now remains, Marichi Man Singh. Bharadars are councillors and are generally drawn from the highest civil and military officers. Sardars are officials both military and civil and have a diamond in a gold badge. A Mir-Suba or major has seven jewels in a gold badge, and a Suba or captain has two jewels in a gold badge.

H.H. MAHARAJA CHANDRA SHAM SHER AND HIS SONS

Nepalese should not as yet have borne its full fruit. Still the custom is spreading and it is to be hoped it may become the universal practice of the country. In order to lead the way in a campaign against drink—once the curse of the Valley—he has become the strictest of teetotallers.

That Maharaja Chandra is popular with the officials at Court, with the soldiers in the field, and with the merchants in the cities is true—so true that one would almost be glad to have a note of criticism from one or other of these sections of his people, but of such criticism there is none.

At his own repeated request I have, in using the full material that he has placed at my disposal, written what I believe to be the truth, and I have not hesitated to record his direct complicity in the plot against his uncle Maharaja Rana Udip. But the English as a nation as well as individuals are an undemonstrative race, and when all is said, Maharaja Chandra remains the man whom the British Empire has delighted to honour above all living foreigners.

§ 3

The Rana Family.—A note of the personality of the Prime Minister's family may not be out of place. An important personality requires first notice. The Maharaja's next brother, Bhim Sham Sher, the Commander-in-Chief, is his natural successor as Prime Minister. It is difficult to form a personal opinion of this man. He is naturally less accessible than the Maharaja, and his work, all important as it is, is concerned with less conspicuous matters than those which his brother has to decide. But he is the Maharaja's trusted adviser and should he survive Chandra, by common consent he will prove a worthy successor. Full of dignity and a man of resource, he has contributed to his brother's work the most loyal and efficient help that any Prime Minister of Nepal could desire. In some respects he is probably less inclined than Chandra to press forward the introduction of the conveniences and comforts of Western civilization, and those who look for any relaxation under his regime of the present strict exclusion of foreigners from Nepalese territory are likely to be disappointed. His heart is in his brother's work and in his hands the great structure built up by Chandra will be worthily and efficiently maintained. A word must also be said of General Padma, his son. He occupies a position of importance not only because in the roll of succession by the accident of an earlier birth General Padma precedes his cousins, the sons of the Maharaja, but because of the excellent work that was done by him in India as Commander of the Nepalese troops in that country during the Great War, and the indefatigable way in which he has thrown himself into matters of such primary importance as the carrying out of Maharaja Chandra's schemes for the development of mechanical transport in Nepal. Those who know

THE THREE BROTHERS

(Maharaja Chandra Sham Sher, Commander-in-Chief General Bhim Sham Sher, and Senior Commanding General Judha Sham Sher)

him best expect most from him, and in the not distant future he may play a very great part in the fortunes of his country and in her relations with India.

The third and last brother of the Maharaja, Judha Sham Sher, who is now Senior Commanding General and enjoys the title of Jang-i-Lat—a dignity which, though equivalent to that of Commander-in-Chief, is not used by General Bhim, the heir apparent—is naturally less in the glare of publicity than are his two elder brothers, and it is enough here to note the confidence with which the Maharaja has entrusted to him the supervision of the Nepalese army.

Chandra's eldest son, General Mohan Sham Sher, is responsible for the organization and smooth running of all matters within the Singha Darbar, and if success on a smaller stage is a test of what a man can do on a larger one, there is much to be looked for from General Mohan should he succeed in due course to the high office that his father holds. General Mohan possesses the order of K.C.I.E. The second son, General Baber Sham Sher, who is perhaps the best known to Europeans of all the second generation, bears upon his breast sufficient testimony to the high regard in which both India and England hold him. He has been invested with the G.B.E. (Military Division), the K.C.I.E., and the K.C.V.O., besides minor decorations. Elsewhere his work in India is referred to, and the position he holds in the Valley has been bestowed upon him by his father after long trial of his capacities. His hospitality is proverbial, and the intimate relations which he maintains with his friends at home and in India is a good index of a cosmopolitanism which is perhaps more characteristic of him than of his brothers or cousins. The third son is General Kaiser, who combines an astonishing width of reading, knowledge of the world, and general culture with a reputation as a first-class shot and an expert knowledge of the fauna of Nepal. He has been commissioned to make the arrangements for the great big game shoots which take place from time to time in honour of distinguished visitors, and if the organization of the camps and general sporting strategy of that which was attended by the Prince of Wales in 1922 is an indication of General Kaiser's capacity, his future career will be watched with no little interest not only by India, but by Western Asia. The Maharaja's fourth and fifth sons, General Singha Sham Sher and General Krishna Sham Sher, are not as yet entrusted with any civil administrative work, though they are carefully trained for their high positions in the army. The three younger children, sons of the second Maharani, Vishnu Sham Sher, Shanker Sham Sher, and Madan Sham Sher, are too young to have given proof of any special aptitudes.

§ 4

Chandra in office.—It was usual and not unnatural that each previous *coup d'état* in the chronicles of Nepal had been followed by a wholesale change in the officers and officials by whom the Government had been carried on. But Chandra made no such sweeping revolution. During the three months of his Commandership-in-Chief he had had time to check and amplify an estimate of the work of these officials based upon a far longer experience in the highest administrative service of Nepal, civil and military; and in a certain measure the composition of the non-commissioned ranks in that service already reflected his own judgment and experience. To assist him in his work of regeneration he appointed commissions to inquire into the more pressing reforms that were needed; of which the first began its sittings in May 1902, eleven months after his accession to power.

It was a great work that confronted him. Apart from the general question of the standard of purity in public affairs and the extirpation of corruption in every branch of the administration, Chandra found it necessary to reorganize many of the existing departments of State, redistributing the work and, in many cases, establishing new offices for the handling of certain public services that were either created for the first time by the new ruler or were judged by him to be inconsistent with the scope of the department to which they had hitherto been entrusted.

During the early months of unremitting and often ungrateful work the new Prime Minister found his time and talents fully occupied by this internal reorganization, of which the fruits will be found recorded in their proper place on many pages of this work. Of domestic incidents there were few. The people of Nepal accepted with unconcealed relief the advent of a strong and far-sighted ruler, and there was a comparative absence of those counterplots and family intrigues which in the past had always clouded the early months of a new administration in Nepal. But reference should be made to the unwise activity of his brother Khadga Sham Sher, who had for some years been Governor of Palpa, and whose absence from the centre of Nepalese life had perhaps led him to misinterpret the solidity of the new regime. Whatever the real intentions of Khadga may have been, his military energy at this moment laid him open to suspicions that would have been more than enough in other days to bring about immediate punishment. But it is only the uncertain who are compelled to have recourse to drastic action, and Chandra was so sure of his ground that he dealt with the situation with a courteous diplomacy that deceived no one less than his unwise brother. A request was sent that Khadga's crack regiment, the Sabuj corps, should be sent to Simra-basa to take part in certain manœuvres that the Prime Minister had ordered. An intimation was also given that, owing to Chandra's impending visit to India, it was advisable that the strength of the military organization in Katmandu should be increased by the subsequent presence of the Sabuj regiment. At the moment Chandra had not before him full evidence of his brother's intentions, and it was the immediate flight of Khadga to India that set the seal of confession upon a foolish and hopeless intrigue. The plot itself collapsed and Chandra, after reviewing the facts, found justification for the dismissal of a small number of junior officers. He treated his brother with generosity, and made arrangements by which Khadga could live in retirement and comfort at Saugor in the Central Provinces.[1] A formal reconciliation took place between the two on the return of Chandra from England in 1908; and though Khadga was not permitted to return to his life and duties in Nepal, places were found for his sons in the administration, and he himself was allowed to pay brief visits to the country in order to meet the Prime Minister. Khadga, who seems to have turned his thoughts to other things in his advancing years, died on 22nd December 1921 at Benares, and but a few months before his death referred, not ungracefully, to his relations with Chandra by comparing himself to Balaram passing his time in spiritual meditation while his younger brother Krishna was ruling the kingdom.

The accession of King Edward VII was celebrated with full honours in Katmandu on the date that had been arranged for his coronation in Westminster Abbey—26th June 1902. It is a curious comment on Nepal's remoteness even in these days of rapid communication between all parts of the world that the news of King Edward's sudden illness, two days before the " solemnity " should have taken place, did not reach Katmandu until after the 26th, and that therefore in this capital alone of all civilized centres, the prearranged ceremonies were carried through in their entirety. Shortly afterwards, an invitation was received by the King from the Government of India, informing him of the coming Imperial Darbar at Delhi on 1st January 1903, and requesting the presence of a Nepalese representative at this high ceremony. In reply His Majesty intimated that his " other self," the Prime Minister, would attend the Darbar on his behalf. The story of the Darbar of 1903 is one that belongs to Indian history, but the presence of Chandra Sham Sher among the representatives of other independent states such as France, Portugal, Holland, Siam, and Afghanistan [2] lends to it a special interest for the student of Nepal's steady consolidation of her position among independent states.

§ 5

Foreign Relations.—Before proceeding with the record of the representation of Nepal at the King-Emperor's Darbar it will be as well to discuss the

---

[1] Maharaja Chandra presented his brother Khadga with certain terms, and offered in the event of their acceptance that his children should be restored to the succession. This offer Khadga refused, and therefore his children are excluded from the succession.

[2] The full independence of Afghanistan and the relinquishment by India of all responsibility for her foreign relations followed the Third Afghan War in 1920.

question of the relations between Nepal and India, but it may be pointed out here that there never has been any real misunderstanding on this point on the part of either the British or the Indian Government. It is true that a singularly unfortunate mistake was made by the compiler of the 1907 edition of the Official Gazetteer of India,[1] but that blunder has been atoned for, and the complete and sovereign independence of Nepal is now a recognized international fact. It is, however, one thing to have this matter settled once for all as an international fact: it is another to make the individual understand it. It is scarcely an overstatement to say that not more than one-half of the officials in the Foreign Offices and Chanceries of the diplomatic world could offhand state with precision the exact relations between India and Nepal; and it is certainly within the mark to say that the same proportion of non-English writers on international affairs, either out of carelessness or ignorance, generally discuss a situation in south central Asia as though the English possessed the right to control or at least to advise upon the foreign action of Nepal. The English have not this right and have never had this right. At the treaty of Sagauli in 1816 there was no pretence whatever that the agreement then made was other than a contract between two independent parties—and the spirit that governed that agreement has governed that of 1923. It is to be regretted that certain other countries which, had they controlled India themselves would probably have taken advantage of the geographical position of Nepal to let their influence weigh at her council-board, seem unable or unwilling to believe that Great Britain has no more power to guide the policy that Katmandu may think fit to adopt towards Tibet, let us say, than she has to advise the Dutch about their affairs in Sumatra.

While dealing with this question of the complete independence of Nepal, it is as well to note her relations with China. These have been regarded by some interested persons as affecting her status as an entirely sovereign kingdom, but, as will be seen from the following record, there is no justification for this view.

In 1792, after her unsuccessful war with China, Nepal agreed to send once every five years a Mission to Peking, bearing to the Emperor the good wishes and gifts of the King of Nepal. I have before had occasion to note that the progress of this Mission through Tibet was at times accompanied by hardship and even by the intentional ill-treatment of the Tibetans; but the Mission continued to exist, though at times it was nearly two years before the survivors of the party regained Katmandu. The Mission was not without its commercial side, for the members of it enjoyed the special privilege of exemption from *likin* and customs duties of all kinds during their passage to and from Peking. Moreover, the Emperor of China distributed among its members gifts far more valuable than those which they

---

[1] Vol. iv, chap. iii, p. 501.

had brought from Nepal. So far then as profit was concerned the Nepalese had the best of these exchanges, but China is China and for some time there remained a sense that the outer world regarded Nepal as being in tributary relations with China—of which the bitterness was largely mollified by the consideration that this nebulous tie with Peking, which exacted nothing but a profitable giving and receiving of presents, could be always invoked were it necessary to impress the Indian Government with the absolute disconnection of Nepal from India.

It is perfectly true that the gifts from Nepal were officially described as tribute. No doubt in their origin this adequately enough represented the views of the Celestial Court, but the extreme vanity of the Chinese Emperors induced them to apply the same phrase to presents brought or sent by the Envoys of other States, such as Great Britain, or the princes of Magadha. The Maharaja's opinion on this matter is worth quoting.

" This claim—that the deputation proved the vassal character of Nepal —is not only an unwarranted fiction but is also a damaging reflection on our national honour and independence. The missions that proceeded from this country to China were of the nature of embassies from one court to another and have invariably been treated with the honour and consideration due to foreign guests, and their expenses were entirely borne by the Chinese Government. The presents they carried for the Emperor can never be regarded as tribute, as they are mere sougats bringing forth counter-presents from the Court of China. They are merely channels by which we tried to keep up our friendly intercourse with distant China, to express our regard and respect for the Celestial Emperor and to cultivate the good-will and friendly feeling of the Chinese Government, especially on account of our heavy stakes in Tibet." [1]

The last Mission to Peking was received by the Emperor in 1908. It was really regarded there more as a picturesque anachronism than as representing any real bond between the Chinese and the mountaineers, and the Waiwupu was not anxious to lay stress upon any supposed vassalage. Since the establishment of the Republic, no Mission has been sent by Nepal. When I was in Peking in 1924 I asked the then Foreign Minister, Dr. Wellington Koo, what the present attitude of China was towards this visionary Nepalese tie. He said that he would have to look up the matter,

---

[1] The Mission sent by Nepal to Peking was in no sense one implying vassalage. Presents were indeed exchanged and a nominal offering of money presented to the Imperial Court. But this is no more than prevails in the relations of other Oriental countries.

Indeed, it seems that the only danger Nepal has to fear from China is that the reassumption of Chinese power in Tibet would give the Celestial Republic the power to cancel the ex-territorial and other privileges enjoyed by Nepal within Tibet.

and a few days later I received from his secretary at the Waichiao Pu the following letter, dated 7th March 1924:

" Waichiao Pu,
" Peking.

" DEAR SIR,
" Referring to your letter of February 22nd and my reply of February 25th, I beg to say that the last tribute from Nepal was in the 34th or last year of Kwang Hsu in the 3rd month [April 1908]. No tribute has come under the Republic. In the early days of the Manchu dynasty tributes came once in five years, but on account of the distance between Nepal and Peking it was agreed that they should come once in twelve years instead.

" Yours sincerely,
" W. P. WEI.
" Perceval Landon, Esq."

It will be seen that the Chinese, true to their policy of surrendering no territory over which they have ever had even a transitory influence, have invented a mutual agreement to enlarge the interval between the Missions to twelve years. Of this agreement the Nepalese Government knows nothing, as of course no such agreement exists; but it is only right to say that when I discussed this matter with the Prime Minister of Nepal in June of the same year, he admitted that, were the old conditions in China to be restored, Nepal might think once more of sending the traditional mission of courtesy.

That this Mission involves no condition of subordination to China is evident. The nominal suzerainty, which China thought she had forced upon Nepal in 1792, has long vanished. Moreover, the revolt of Tibet against China has created an entirely new situation by severing all geographical connection between Nepal and the Chinese Republic.[1]

There is no question of anything but a complimentary exchange of gifts between China and Nepal, and any tie that may have existed in the past must now be regarded from the Nepalese side in much the same light as the " tributes " which Burma was allowed by Calcutta to send to Peking long after the British annexation;[2] and from the Chinese side in the same light as the nominal claim, put forward by Britain until 1801, that the

[1] This loss of a very large portion of their territory has not of course been officially accepted by the Chinese. But, as I was assured at Loyang in 1924, those who are chiefly responsible for the military policy prevailing in the Chinese Republic have practically ceased to take Tibet into their consideration either as a Chinese province or even as a tributary State.

[2] Both Burma and Hunza-nagar in the north of Kashmir sent political missions to China after they had admittedly come under British rule.

King of England was also King of France. To this day similar shadowy claims are to be found. Thus the King of Spain, whose territories are very precisely and notoriously defined, still claims to be King of the two Sicilies, of Jerusalem, of the Eastern and Western Indies, of India, and " du Continent Oceanien." But these matters are taken more seriously in the East, ánd though there was but one more mission sent to Peking after the Darbar of 1903, and though Chandra expressly denied to the Indian Government that any state of vassalage was thereby either symbolized or implied, it was a good thing that the representative of Nepal should make his formal appearance at the Imperial Darbar among the accredited envoys of independent powers.

Chandra took a deep interest in this mighty Soenair, and himself contributed much to the universal picturesqueness of the occasion.[2] But it need not be said that he regarded this definite assertion of the independence of his State as the most important matter in the glittering ceremonial, and he was right in so doing. The Viceroy was not slow to recognize the importance of this friendly but wary mission, and later in the same year, 1903, the Maharaja received an invitation from Lord Curzon to pay him a visit in Calcutta.

He arrived on the 25th January 1904, and was received with full honours in the Indian capital. Hastings House had been specially arranged for his reception, and on the following day formal visits were exchanged between the Viceroy and the Maharaja. The visit was not entirely one of courtesy or informal diplomacy. To Chandra, not the least interesting of the incidents of his visit was a thorough examination of the Calcutta Mint, for the coinage of the Nepalese currency was and is still a matter in which he takes a more than usual interest. During his stay in Calcutta he and Lord Kitchener met more than once, and the mutual respect of the two strong men found expression in a practical form when, ten years later, the employment of Gurkhas far and wide in the theatre of war was arranged between them.

At this time the Tibetan mission under Colonel Francis Younghusband was still awaiting the opportunity of moving forward from the cold plateau of Tuna. Several questions involved by this determined attempt to come to an understanding with Lhasa were discussed between Lord Curzon and the Maharaja.

§ 6

Lhasa Mission of 1904.—It is necessary here to refer to the relations between India and Tibet and recall the incidents that led up to the despatch

---

[1] Almanac de Gotha. This is a noble counter to the admission that another of his seigneuries—Gibraltar—is "temporarily in the possession of the King of England."

[2] The Maharani accompanied her husband to the Darbar.

of Younghusband's Mission. It will be remembered that in 1792, and again in 1856, definite treaties between the Nepalese, the Chinese, and the Tibetans respectively had reduced to some sort of order the relations between the three countries. In 1890 the Chinese acknowledged the British claim to Sikkim and settled the boundary of that State so far as Tibet was concerned. Three years later a trade agreement was signed between the two Empires regulating the exchange of goods through the Chumbi Valley and opening official markets at Yatung and other places.[1] In 1895 the Tibetans, already filled with a spirit of self-determination, refused to abide by these agreements on the ground that they had been no party to them. An attempt was made by India in that year to delimit the 1890 frontier by the erection of pillars. But these were at once thrown down by the Tibetans and an acute cause of trouble arose in June 1902 when the raids of the Tibetans upon Sikkimese grazing grounds and the loss of Sikkimese life caused thereby created a problem that could no longer be left unsolved. The Viceroy's letter to the Dalai Lama was returned to him unopened. Representations to the Chinese Government met with the usual explanation that the Tibetans were really very tiresome partners, and that the blame was entirely due to them and not to any slackness on the part of Peking. However, the Chinese Government consented to appoint a special Imperial Resident to discuss the matter with the British at Khamba Jong in Tibet in July 1903. But no Commissioner arrived, and nothing could be done with the Tibetans in their existing mood. They were determined to challenge Chinese suzerainty and did not consider the task of defeating the British Empire also beyond their power.[2] In this they were encouraged

[1] The Yatung Maritime Customs Station was opened in May 1894, and closed, as a Chinese post, in 1912 by order of the Lhasan Government. As a Tibetan post it continues to control the traffic of the Nathu la.

[2] There is a touch of humour in the fact that when the Dalai Lama was awakened from his attitude of apathy or contempt, he asked what and who these English really were. He had just sent back Lord Curzon's letter unopened, and may have had some qualms. The reply that he received reassured him though it would probably have been accepted by no other ruler. It is known that the Indian Government has long made to the State of Bhutan the allowance of a certain number of thousands of rupees a year in return for her keeping order along the frontier between herself and Bengal and Assam. The Dalai Lama was now informed that the British Empire was a vassal of Bhutan, and was obliged by that miniature State to pay tribute regularly every year. But in June 1910 the Chinese Government waxed more arrogant still. It claimed Nepal and Bhutan as feudatory states. But by this time the treaty between the Indian Government and Bhutan had been completed, and with the aid of Nepal the Himalayas were definitely established as the limit of Chinese influence. The suzerainty of China over Tibet was neither admitted nor denied by Simla. In December of the same year Sir John Jordan informed the Chinese Government in Peking that Nepal and Bhutan were both independent of China, and that since the conclusion of the Treaty of Bhutan, the latter's external relations were under the British Government, which would tolerate no attempt by China to exercise influence over either of these states.

by the support that was promised to them by Dorjieff, a Buriat Lama who produced an extraordinary effect at both ends of a long line of travel. In St. Petersburg he made the Emperor believe that His Majesty was regarded by the Lamaic Church as Maitreya—the expected reincarnation of the Buddha: in Lhasa the Dalai Lama was assured that the Tsar was a convert to the Buddhist faith—and in both he averred that no real difference in aim and morals existed between the Christian and the Buddhist churches. On one occasion he displayed before the doubtless astonished eyes of Tubdan Gyatso the full pontificals of an Orthodox Bishop, which had been sent to His Holiness by the Tsar's personal order. Convinced of the effective help of so mighty an ally, the Tibetans hardened their hearts and refused to allow anyone, Tibetan or Chinese, to deal with the English. Therefore Younghusband went back from Khamba Jong into Sikkim and waited.

Now these things were of primary importance to. Nepal. A clear head and a strong hand were needed to keep the situation free from complications and indeed from danger. By the Treaty of 1856 it will be remembered that Nepal had undertaken to come to the help of the Tibetans were they unjustly invaded. On the other hand Chandra saw, better probably than anyone, that the military strength of China would certainly not be exerted in favour of the Tibetans in their existing mood, and he had also conceived a very clear idea of the slow but practically invincible-strength of the Indian Government in such a matter as this, and he had no wish whatever to disturb the friendly relations with Calcutta which it had been his chief aim at his Foreign Office to strengthen and consolidate. In short, he was in no mind to be drawn away from the great policy of friendliness to India which has throughout his administration been the backbone of the Maharaja's handling of foreign affairs.

Soon afterwards Great Britain received an astonishing communication from the Russian Government to the effect that any alteration in the *status quo* in Tibet that might be caused by the Younghusband Mission would be of such gravity as to oblige St. Petersburg to take measures to protect Russian interests in those regions. This was going altogether too far. The despatch did more than justify the expedition; it made it necessary. The British Foreign Office naturally asked for an explanation, and in reply the Russian Government, without any longer pretending to possess interests in Tibet, declared that they wished the *status quo* to be maintained there, because it was an integral portion of the Chinese Empire. What the Dalai Lama thought of this manner of championship has never been known, but it was too late now for him to reconsider his brave words against India. The Mission was reorganized and again set forward through the Chumbi Valley to Gyantse and eventually to Lhasa. After a vain attempt by Chandra to avert the trouble by a letter of advice to Lhasa and an explanation of his position to Calcutta, it became evident that Nepal could not entirely disinterest herself in the crisis. The clause in the Treaty with Tibet (1856) in virtue of which the Tibetans demanded the help of Nepal against India, runs as follows: " Tibet has become solely a dwelling place of Lama-monasteries and celibate religious hermits, therefore from now onwards when a war maker from another Court arises in Tibetan territory the Gurkha Court shall protect Tibet as far as possible." [1]

There was a small section in Nepal that felt that on whichever side the right happened to be, help should be extended to the Tibetans. To this the Maharaja was opposed, and after careful examination he set the matter before his Councillors in the form of four questions: (a) Was there justice on the side of the Indian Government? (b) Did the Mission intend to annex any portion of Tibetan territory? (c) Would the utmost effort of Nepal prevent the English from achieving their object? (d) Would such intervention by Nepal place that country for the future in a disadvantageous position as regards its relations with India? These questions he could answer in only one fashion. He believed that the Tibetan Government had insulted and was intriguing dangerously against British interests; after communication with England and India he was convinced that those Governments had no intention of annexing one acre of Tibet; he did not believe that armed assistance sent from Nepal could in the long run prevent England from coming to terms with the Grand Lama in some place and at some time, however long the delay might be—nor did he wish to prevent such an understanding; and finally, he viewed with grave misgivings the exchange of a policy of friendliness and confidence with India which had secured so much already for Nepal, for one that must involve strained relations for many years between Calcutta and Katmandu.[2]

It was clear therefore that this determination of the English to have an agreement with the Dalai Lama could scarcely be called an invasion, and in the circumstances did not call for the intervention of Nepal. At the

---

[1] The full text of this treaty with the variations between it and the Nepalese text and comparisons between the translations and comments of Sir Charles Bell, Mr. C. U. Aitchison, and the Nepalese Government will be found in Appendix XXII.

[2] The following quotation from Sir G. S. Baker's edition of H. W. Halleck's *International Law* is of some importance. " In a defensive alliance made before the war, *casus foederis* does not take place immediately on one of the parties being attacked by an enemy. The other contracting party has the right, as indeed it is his duty, to ascertain if his ally has not given the enemy just cause of war; for no one is bound to undertake the defence of an ally in order to enable him to insult others or to refuse them justice. If he is manifestly in the wrong, his co-ally may require him to offer reasonable satisfaction; and if the enemy refuses to accept it, and insists upon a continuance of the war, the co-ally is then bound to assist in his defence." Perhaps the simplest illustration of this rule is the fact that Italy, in spite of the Triple Alliance, declined to co-operate with the Central Empires during the late war.

same time the Maharaja was indefatigable, both in his advice and warnings to Lhasa and in his intercessions with the British. He decided to adopt what was indeed the only possible attitude for him to adopt—one of benevolent neutrality. Any acquiescence by India in Russian influence in Tibet would merely have transferred to Nepal's north-eastern frontier the anxieties with which Afghanistan had been watching the slow advance of Russian territory towards her own frontiers, and Chandra's attitude was well understood by the Government in Calcutta. The words of an official despatch written on the 8th January 1903 are worth recording.

" We believe that the policy of frank discussion and co-operation with the Nepalese darbar would find them prepared to assist our plans most cordially. Not the slightest anxiety has been evinced at our forward operations on the Sikkim frontiers,[1] and we think that, with judicious management, useful assistance may confidently be expected from the side of Nepal. Our anticipations on this point have been confirmed by a recent interview between His Excellency the Viceroy and the Prime Minister of Nepal, Maharaja Chandra Sham Sher, at Delhi. The Nepalese Government regards the rumours of intrigue in Tibet with the most lively apprehensions, and considers the future of the Nepal State to be primarily involved; and further, the Maharaja is prepared to co-operate with the Government of India in whatever way he thought most desirable, either within or beyond the frontier, for the frustration of designs which he holds to be utterly inconsistent with the interests of his country."

Shortly afterwards Chandra wrote to the Viceroy a letter in which he sums up once for all the policy of Nepal towards the Government of India. It may be taken to represent his constant and determined attitude, and it may also be said that it is as true to-day as when it was written. " I shall take this opportunity of assuring Your Excellency's Government that I shall always deem it a sacred duty and a valued privilege, not only to cultivate and continue unimpaired the friendly relations subsisting between the Government of India and Nepal, but to strengthen and improve them, so that we may realize all those expectations which the association with a Power like that of England naturally raise in our minds. I am fully conscious that our interests can best be served by the continuance of friendly relations between India and Nepal." These cordial assurances were greatly appreciated at home, and through the Viceroy a letter of thanks was sent to the Government of Nepal. At the same time it was

[1] This is perhaps an over-statement. I have received information in Katmandu which shows that some of those who were in the confidence of the Maharaja viewed with mistrust the movement of an armed Mission through Sikkim. The Nepalese, as we have already seen, are prone to suspect the complete altruism of the Indian Government, and there were misgivings in certain quarters; some being even inclined to suspect in it the intention of the Indian Government to render Nepal helpless against a subsequent attempt to deprive her of her sovereign status.

clearly understood that Nepal did not intend to support the advance of the Expedition by any military operation whatever. Still the Maharaja not only permitted the Indian Government to purchase yaks in Nepal, but he made a present of 2,500 animals to that Government for the purposes of Younghusband's Mission. Both sides were permitted to purchase material from Nepal. The first and second yak corps, numbering 2,300 beasts, the gift of the Nepalese Government, set out to join the Mission in the autumn of 1903. A third yak corps of about 1,700 followed them. Ultimately of these 4,000 animals only 150 survived. Anthrax, rinderpest, foot-and-mouth disease not only laid them low in hundreds, but the fear of contagion compelled Capt. Wigram, who was in charge of them, to use unfrequented and dangerous paths. Many hundreds died from heat in the comparatively low Sikkim valley. Forage was inadequate and little could be bought along these solitary tracks. A somewhat unfair jibe of the time suggested that the Indian Government believed that yaks were capable of sustaining life on pure snow. In 1904 the Nepalese Government furnished many thousands of highly efficient porters for carrying our supplies upon the long line of communications.

In February 1904 Lord Curzon telegraphed to the Secretary of State the opinion of the Maharaja about the Mission. His prophecy turned out to be more correct than that of other observers. " He informed me that the Tibetans would oppose the Mission, and he expressed the opinion that we might be compelled to proceed to Lhasa to conclude a treaty, unless the Tibetans made an attack upon us and received severe punishment, in which case they might be willing to negotiate at Gyantse."

But Chandra had not confined his advice and help to the side of the Indian Government. From the beginning he sent instructions to the Nepalese Envoy in Lhasa, Captain Jit Bahadur, to convey to the Dalai Lama and the Council of State the necessity of meeting the British delegation early on their journey in order to prevent the serious consequences that might otherwise ensue. But the replies of Jit Bahadur were by no means encouraging. He said that he was given no opportunity of conveying the Maharaja's message to the Dalai Lama himself, and that the Council of State was too weak to deal with the question, urgent as it was. He had indeed obtained an assurance that the rumour of an agreement between Russia and Tibet was untrue, and was of the opinion that it had been set on foot to create friction between Nepal and Tibet.

The Envoy in Lhasa having failed to secure the attention of the Dalai Lama, the Maharaja wrote directly to the four Kazis of Tibet in the autumn of 1903 before the advance of Colonel Younghusband's Mission to Gyantse. After reproaching the Tibetan Government with its failure to send plenipotentiaries to Khamba Jong and Tuna and with the silence with which his own representations had been received, he went on to offer the Tibetan

Government serious and well-informed advice. He accepted the assurance made to the Nepalese Envoy by the Kazis that there was no truth in the reported agreement between Tibet and Russia, but his letter did not leave them in any doubt of his view that the treaty between his country and that of the Dalai Lama justified him in gravely warning the Tibetans of the folly of their action. It was improper, contended the Nepalese Prime Minister, to declare that the treaty of 1890 was not binding upon the Tibetans because it had been made by the Chinese and not by themselves. It had, he said, been settled at a time when the foreign relations of Tibet were entirely in the hands of the Chinese. Unless the Tibetans were willing to face the results of a rebellion against China and a total repudiation of all treaties entered into on their behalf by Peking, Tibet was bound to carry out the agreement of 1890. The Prime Minister of Nepal also pointed out that the experience of his own country had convinced the Nepalese of the fair dealing of Britain. The observance of the terms of the treaty of 1816 by both sides had been advantageous to the Government of Nepal; and, he added, their religious interests had not suffered in any way. Since that treaty was made the British Government had on different occasions restored to Nepal territories lost in the war of 1814-16 which were now producing a revenue of many lakhs of rupees. The British had consistently helped the Nepalese to maintain the independence of their country, though if they had wished to act in an unjust manner they might without doubt have deprived them of it. A notable feature in the relations of the Nepalese with the British was that the latter had held sacred all Nepalese religious and social prejudices. Hence, if the Tibetans would even now take time by the forelock, settle the questions in dispute, and behave to the British in a friendly manner, he was sure that Tibet would, like Nepal, derive much benefit from the alliance. That the British Government had any designs upon the independence of Tibet was supported by no evidence, and was contrary to common sense. " It is well known that the sun never sets upon the British dominions, and that the sovereign of such a vast empire should entertain designs of unjustly and improperly taking the mountainous country of the Tibetans should never cross your minds." The Maharaja followed up this sage advice by an unveiled warning that should it be neglected by the Lhasa Government, he would decline to assist them in the trouble which would inevitably ensue. The Indian Government, he said, was acting within its rights and it was as unwise as it was unjust to treat Colonel Younghusband as an enemy. He concluded with the remark that the Tibetan Kazis were assuming a heavy responsibility in rejecting the counsels of the Chinese Amban, or Resident, in Lhasa.

The Tibetans refused to send an envoy of any description to treat with Colonel Younghusband, and despatched troops to oppose by armed force the forward movement of the Mission at the Hot Springs near Tuna, in

Red Idol Gorge, in the Gyantse valley, and on the Kara la. The most serious danger consisted in the persistent bombardment from Gyantse Jong of the Mission in Chang lo post during the absence in India of a large part of the escort and at a time when an armistice had been agreed to by both sides. This was continued for two months, and rendered it impossible for the British Government to accept any other issue of the Mission than a thorough understanding with the authorities in Lhasa.

The Maharaja saw the gravity of the situation thus produced and informed the Resident that he had received a letter and some presents from the Dalai Lama, who, however, made no reference to the Mission. This omission led Chandra to think that the Dalai Lama was kept in ignorance of what was going on,[1] and he wrote an outspoken answer. He did not hesitate to warn the Tibetans of the folly of challenging a great Power like India, and suggested, though with diplomatic correctness, that the incarnate Buddha had not been made fully acquainted with the facts of the situation. Once again he asked that a fully authorized representative should meet Younghusband and bring about a peaceful settlement. From the point of view of Nepal it was, as Chandra saw, essential that Tibet should not be so weakened by a struggle with Great Britain that China should find her an easy prey.

But the Tibetans hardened their hearts. They insisted on the return of the Mission to Indian territory before negotiations should begin. The British naturally replied that they had waited many years in their own territory for the promised negotiations, and saw no reason to suppose that the Tibetans had any greater intention then they had had before of dealing seriously with the diplomatic questions that had arisen. Chandra made yet another attempt to bring the Tibetans to reason. In June 1904 he wrote a personal letter to the Dalai Lama. In it he referred to the advice which he had tendered in the previous year and which the Lhasan Government had rejected; and he again represented the folly of attempting wantonly to oppose the manifest weakness of Tibet to the strength of the British Empire. He went on to say that he could not believe that His Holiness had been given proper information on either of the points in dispute between India and Lhasa, or of the hopelessness of opposing the Mission by force. But the Dalai Lama proved as obdurate as his councillors, and the result of his obstinacy is a matter of history. Once the British expedition had arrived in Lhasa the Nepalese representative rendered invaluable service in the cause of peace and a better understanding between Tibet and Simla. On his return to India Colonel Younghusband wrote officially to testify to the goodwill shown by the Nepalese Envoy during the con-

---

[1] We have since discovered the political and diplomatic capacity of Tubdan Gyatso, and it is not now believed that ignorance of any kind explained His Holiness's action at this or any later period.

versations which led to the signature of the treaty, and this appreciation was followed by expressions of gratitude from the Government of India and from Lord Curzon.[1]

A little known but amusing incident of this campaign was the attempt of the Tibetans to make the British expedition believe that Nepal had sent its Gurkhas to the assistance of the Tibetans. The latter dressed up about five hundred of their own troops in an imitation of the Nepal uniform, and though the imitation was of no great accuracy, the British Mission was actually in some doubt about the matter. Representations were accordingly made in Katmandu, and the Resident was of course told that, on the face of it, the supposition that any Gurkhas had been sent to the aid of the Tibetans was absurd.

The formal thanks of the Government of India and the Viceroy's congratulations on the large part he had taken to bring the Tibetans to their senses were duly sent to the Maharaja. It is curious to note that, shortly before his flight, the Dalai Lama sent a despairing message to Chandra asking for the despatch of an experienced Nepalese official to assist in concluding the treaty. It was, however, too late to do this, and Jit Bahadur therefore acted upon the general instructions of the Nepal Government.

This was the first occasion on which the diplomatic insight and political prevision of Maharaja Chandra Sham Sher were highly tried. His position had at times been one of extreme difficulty, and from first to last he made no false step. Throughout the long expedition the part played by him was of good augury for the future. He maintained an impartial attitude. In trying to obtain for the British a peaceful hearing and a settlement of the points at issue with the Tibetans, he in no way forfeited the friendship and esteem of the latter. Indeed, towards the end of the negotiations in Lhasa the counsels of Chandra were admitted by the Tibetans themselves to have had great weight in the settlement which was then made.

It is the more to the Maharaja's credit that he undertook this office of peacemaker, because there is no doubt that one of the results of this settlement, the opening of the direct Chumbi Valley route between Tibet and India, has to a great extent diminished the volume of trade that had

---

[1] I may perhaps be allowed to quote here a reference to this Envoy which appears in my book *Lhasa* (1905):

"The Nepalese Resident met us when we reached Lhasa. . . . His overcoat was one of the most gorgeous pieces of Oriental embroidery that I had ever seen. Quietly dressed in all other respects, and personally an unassuming man, his outer garment made him recognized at the distance of a mile. It was of delicate pink satin sewn all over with silver and gold lace and imitation pearls, latticing down some really very fine embroidery in myrtle green and rose. He is a shrewd man and we owe him a debt of gratitude for the commonsense advice he always gave the Tibetans."—P.L.

HOUSE FRONT, KATMANDU

hitherto ebbed and flowed along the Kirong or Kuti roads through Nepal.[1] Nor was the Marshal blind to the probability that as a result of the expedition and the consequent weakening of Tibet's power of resistance the Government of China might be aroused, and might even re-establish its waning authority in that country in a manner that would not fail to affect the interests of Nepal. But confident, not merely in the military strength of his country but in the excellent relations which had been established between Nepal, India, and Tibet, Chandra did not hesitate to adopt the policy of intermediation which has been described. He was justified in his decision by the event, for though an immediate, and temporarily successful, effort was at once made by China to re-enforce its suzerainty over Tibet, the internal upheaval (1911-12) which resulted in the establishment of a Republic in China made it impossible for any efficient control to be permanently exercised over this remote province. It is indeed merely the pride of the Chinese which refuses to admit the diminution of their territory by an acre which still maintains their claim to the sovereignty over this organized state, of whose determination to vindicate her independence against all comers there is no question. At another time the collapse of the Celestial Empire would almost certainly have entailed the vigorous intervention of Russia. But the outbreak of the Great War and the subsequent Soviet revolution paralysed for the moment all effective interference on the part of Moscow. Even now there seems to be a new orientation of Russian interests in China. After long continued effort and the most careful and expensive propaganda the Soviet goal, as the result of its recent successes, seems to be nothing less than China proper. It need not be said that the absorption by the way of outer and inner Mongolia and of Sinkiang and Kansu will be none the less complete when Russia has time to consolidate her new territory. But at the moment she is entirely taken up with her penetration into the valley of the Yangtse and the Yellow River, and has neither time nor ability to deal with the Tibetan problem which she regards in exactly the same light as that in which she looks upon Afghanistan—as one of the two postern gates of India. Indeed, it was always rather the personal credulity of the late Tsar than any considered imperial policy that smoothed the way for Dorjieff's strange intrigue. With China Nepal remained, and remains, on friendly terms. Shortly after the assumption of power by Maharaja Chandra the Emperor of China conferred upon

[1] In discussing the effect upon Nepal of the establishment of direct relations between India and Tibet, Sir Charles Bell remarks how that Nepal's friendliness has at times led to her own injury. " Her trade routes have suffered ; her position as an intermediary is gone. Still she treats these matters as side-issues and remains our true friend and ally. She allows us to recruit twenty thousand soldiers for the Indian Army, and that army knows no better soldiers than the twenty battalions of Gurkhas. During the world war some twenty per cent. of the adult males between the ages of eighteen and fifty were taken out of Nepal to aid the British and Indian forces."

II   I

him the honorary title of T'ung ling pingma kuo kan wang,[1] the highest rank in the Manchu army, and in 1903, on the occasion of the return of the quinquennial mission, special emissaries were despatched from Peking to Katmandu with robes of honour and other presents.

It may cause surprise to students of Asiatic history that at this moment there should be any need for anxiety in Nepal about the strenuous efforts that Tibet is making to free herself from the last trace of Chinese suzerainty or influence. If the matter is looked on from a military point of view, Tibet would have little chance should it come to actual war between herself and Nepal. It is true that a few Tibetans have been trained in elementary drill in Gyantse, and it is also true that the Indian Government has permitted the Tibetan Government to add to a small present of rifles the right to purchase a larger quantity. The policy of Simla in this matter is perfectly simple.[2] But the Tibetans have no arsenals worthy of the name, the flouting of their traditional link with China prevents them from obtaining the least military equipment from that country, and the experiences of the Mission of 1904 has proved the helplessness of Tibet against any invading force that can solve the problem of its own supply and transport. Therefore, with the deliberate intention of putting Tibet into a somewhat better position to defend its frontiers, and with an equally strong determination to interfere in no way with the internal affairs of that country, the Indian Government—now not merely a friend but the Power to which Tibet looks for its development and for its very existence—has conceded certain small privileges to Lhasa.[3]

The policy in foreign affairs which has been adopted by Maharaja

---

[1] See Appendix II, vol. i.

[2] The Indian Government could not disinterest itself in the avowed intention of Peking to turn Tibet into a Chinese province. Any such advance of Chinese military strength would have given India a North-Eastern as well as a North-Western question. Moreover, India was concerned in the maintenance of Tibet as a buffer State against Russian ambitions in India.

[3] A danger—"proximus Ucalegon"—that Chandra had foreseen as a result of the 1904 mission—the renewed predominance of China in Tibet—did indeed take place with startling rapidity. During the next few years Tibet, deprived of the presence of its Grand Lama, received such a double set-back to its self-confidence that the victorious Chinese re-asserted themselves in Lhasa. It was admitted by the Chinese Government that their intention was to reduce Tibet to the position of a mere province of China—and Nepal stood next in the line. It is difficult to foresee what the position might now have been had not the Chinese Revolution of 1912 upset all the calculations of Central Asia. As a result of that *coup d'état* the Chinese were obliged to withdraw their helpless troops from Tibet, and from that moment such apprehensions as still exist are concerned chiefly with an occasional threat of reprisals for Tibetan monastic arrogance on the frontier. It should, however, be borne in mind that the immunity from Chinese pressure that Tibet now enjoys is largely due to the internecine strife that is now (1927) distracting all China, and especially the province of Szechuan.

·Chandra Sham Sher has just been dealt with at length. Briefly stated it is a continuation of the attitude of friendship and co-operation with India that his famous uncle originated. The vindication and maintenance in its last detail of the independence of Nepal has been the mainspring of her foreign policy for the past one hundred and ten years. For the last eighty years it has been seen that that end was best secured by a generous policy of friendship with the Indian Government and a readiness to lend the latter all possible support when, as has not infrequently happened, the mightier of the pair had sore need of the assistance of the lesser. This policy has now been crystallized in a Treaty which is given in Appendix XXIII.

With Tibet the relations of Katmandu have remained friendly. If it were not that the whole question of Tibet seems likely to be again discussed between the Indian and Chinese Governments, it might be sufficient to leave the story of Nepalese relations without further comment. But until the destiny of Tibet as an autonomous State free from interference by China is definitely and finally settled, Nepal will be compelled to keep a watchful and sometimes an anxious eye upon the fluid policy and chequered fortunes of Lhasa. That this is recognized by Great Britain is clear enough. It is perhaps necessary only to recall here the protest which was made on 26th February 1910 by.the British Government.

" Great Britain, while disclaiming any desire to interfere in the internal administration of Tibet, cannot be indifferent to disturbances of the peace in a country which is her neighbour and on intimate terms with neighbouring States on her frontier and especially with Nepal, whom His Majesty's Government could not prevent from taking such steps to protect her interests as she may think necessary in the circumstances."

Here we have the root of the matter. There is not the slightest fear, so long as Chandra Sham Sher is arbiter of the destinies of Nepal, that any ill-considered movement against the interests of Tibet will be undertaken. But it is necessary to remember that should any policy, wise or unwise, be decided upon by Nepal, either during the Maharaja's lifetime or afterwards, the Indian Government would be unable to oppose it. At this moment[1] the exact position of Tibet still remains undecided and there seems little prospect that it will crystallize into any form of autonomy known to diplomacy for some years to come.

The Maharaja's first and last care has been the furtherance of the interests of Nepal. It is for that reason—the absence of all pretence on the part of the Maharaja that this has not been the touchstone and guiding principle of his life—that the Englishman trusts the Maharaja of Nepal as perhaps he trusts no other foreigner alive. Chandra has believed that in and through the English he could attain the security and prosperity for his people which are his only incentive and his only goal. When

[1] 1927.

necessary he has maintained against the English a curious firmness, which has been as little misunderstood by Simla as he has misunderstood the occasions on which the British Government has been unable to respond fully to his wishes. The two Governments have faced each other as man to man and have spoken the same language. Brothers are they, and the bond between them now is so great that it cannot be broken.

In conclusion the situation may be summed up thus. Although India is anxious to make of Tibet an inviolable buffer against any hostile movement directed against India, she is as loyal as ever to the long tradition of alliance and friendship that has existed between herself and Nepal. As is said elsewhere, the only policy which she maintains towards Nepal is a policy of friendship, and we have already seen in what a generous spirit Nepal responds to this kindly feeling. We shall see in the next chapter that in a day of high trial Nepal, more perhaps than any other State in the long Allied line, gave, without hesitation and with full knowledge of the heavy blood tax that would be exacted from her; all that she had in men, in money, in food, and in Asiatic diplomacy, to help the English in the war for civilization.

CHAPTER XV

MAHARAJA CHANDRA SHAM SHER

DEATH OF THE MAHARANI—VISIT TO ENGLAND—KING-EMPEROR IN
NEPAL—THE GREAT WAR—TREATY OF 1923

> "Your magnificent response to the call to arms in this hour of trial will
> never be forgotten by me or my people."— KING GEORGE V (1914).

§ I

ON the 11th February 1905 the Maharaja, to his intense and lasting grief, lost the companion of his life. The part played by women in the Orient is generally one of two things. Rarely it is one of dominating autocracy—almost universally it is one of complete insignificance. In the case of the Maharani it was neither. It is pleasant to remember that, secluded as she was, she had vindicated her personality far beyond the limits of her own home and had won for herself the cordial affection and reverence, not merely of the official circle that surrounded her husband, but of the inhabitants of the villages and fields of Nepal. She was an unselfish, loving, and resolute woman, and she never showed her devotion to her husband more practically than in her determination, during the last few months of a life which she always knew to be doomed, to provide the Maharaja with a helpmeet for the time as well as with someone who should take her place as a worthy companion and colleague after she herself was gone. Marriage of the kind known in European royal circles as "morganatic" is an accepted practice in Nepal, but Chandra had never married more than one wife, and his disinclination for the left-handed alliances which were as common among the Nepalese as among neighbouring races, had no doubt helped to render the Maharani's married life happier than the bride of an Oriental potentate can always be certain of enjoying. A curious contest of wills therefore took place between the Prime Minister and his dying wife, each generously contending against the other's insistence until the illness of the Maharani won the day. Moreover she was able, twenty-four hours before she died, to obtain from the Maharaja a definite promise that her own place should be taken by a bride whom she had gone to great pains to bring to Nepal from Benares. The first Maharani's statue stands in Patan, which owes its pure water to her generosity, and her name is daily blessed by the people of this town for whose comfort she inaugurated the scheme at her own expense, though one cannot help regretting that she died just before the fulfilment of her merciful idea.

THE BADA MAHARANI

In the same year Nepal suffered a keen disappointment. King George V, then Prince of Wales, repeated the visit to India which his father had made many years before. His Majesty is notoriously one of the best shots in Great Britain, and he had looked forward with keenest anticipation to taking part in one of the great " shoots " of big game which Nepal, alone now of all the countries in the world, is able to organize in honour of a distinguished visitor. But this pleasure was to be postponed. During the months of preparation required for one of these great enterprises cholera broke out among the tens of thousands of beaters that had been collected. On hearing of this disaster the Prince at once recognized the necessity for abandoning the proposed sport, and in the letter in which he expressed his regret that the kindly intentions of the Maharaja had been defeated by circumstances beyond his control, he was careful to convey his sincere sympathy with those upon whom the pestilence had fallen.

Lord Kitchener, then Commander-in-Chief in India, paid a visit to Katmandu in the autumn of 1906. Reference has been made to the mutual friendship and esteem of the Prime Minister and Lord Kitchener, and it was a happy idea of the authorities of both Great Britain and Nepal that this visit should be made the occasion of exchanging between the visitor and his host the rank of General in the armies of which each was already so distinguished a commander. At this time Chandra was also made Honorary Colonel of the 4th Gurkha Rifles. General Woodyatt has written an account of Lord Kitchener's surprise at finding before him as he descended Chandra-giri an intensively cultivated valley, dotted with flourishing little villages and houses that reminded him of Swiss chalets. Lord Kitchener, he says, in *Under Ten Viceroys*, had been carried down Chandragiri in a dooly— really a chair—while the present Commander-in-Chief, Sir William Bird-wood, walked down—but couldn't raise his legs without pain for three days afterwards. Lord Kitchener's comment upon Katmandu is not without interest : " There I found marble palaces, lighted by electricity and full of Nepalese officers who are . . . always in uniform like a continental nation. The Maharaja was kindness itself, and meted out to us the most splendid hospitality, while his big review was excellently carried out by very soldierly-looking troops." A full parade of the Gurkha army was held in honour of the Indian Commander-in-Chief, who requited the courtesy with words that must have seemed to the Nepalese as great a compliment as the chary and discriminating Field-Marshal ever paid to any foreign corps.

" Should it fall to my lot to be appointed the leader of troops in case of serious war I should feel proud to have under my command the army of Nepal and to associate it with the Gurkhas of our army, who have long been recognized as some of our bravest and most efficient soldiers." The time was to come when his wish was fulfilled to the letter, and when the " Hampshire " went down with Lord Kitchener off the far northern islands, the minute guns in the Valley that paid him the last and greatest of military honours were ordered by one of his greatest admirers, and were sincere tokens of the regret that for a moment stunned Nepal as well as others of the allied States.

Early in 1907 the Prime Minister went down to Calcutta to pay a visit to the Earl of Minto. Full honours were again paid to him by the Indian Government, and he was once more lodged in Hastings House. The 4th Gurkha Rifles, his own regiment, took this opportunity to present him with an address, and begged his acceptance of a sword of honour.

§ 2

Visit to England.—But wider travel than this was in store for the Marshal. Recognizing that personal observation was the only means of acquiring a thorough knowledge of the civilization of the West, or of so much of it as could profitably be absorbed by his people, Chandra, like his uncle, suggested to the Indian Government that he should pay a visit to Great Britain. Besides the purpose just referred to, there were many points concerned with his external relations that he wished to see finally cleared up—points which could best be discussed in London directly between the British Government and himself. Above all, he wished to make clear once and for all the status of Nepal as an absolutely independent and sovereign state.[1] But more practical considerations were not missing. The Maharaja was also anxious to secure—and the Indian Government were not unwilling in this matter to have their policy reconsidered by the direct attention of the British Government—a continuous and unconditioned supply of ammunition and other munitions of war, for which the special assent of the Government in Calcutta had hitherto been necessary. Finally, in his anxiety to raise the standard of life and prosperity in his country, the Maharaja was also desirous of clearing the way for the free importation of industrial, agricultural, and scientific machinery into Nepal.

A cordial invitation from the British Government was at once received, and the news of the impending visit was published in London. The incident caused considerable interest in England. Other princes of Indian blood and religion had, it is true, visited England since Jang Bahadur. In most cases they had found it necessary to propitiate the prejudice of Hinduism which forbids the faithful servant of Vishnu or Shiva to cross the " black water." A justification, however, was readily forthcoming. The special

---

[1] In the fourth and the nineteenth volumes of the 1907 edition of the Imperial Gazetteer of India statements will be found which show that even then the compilers had failed to understand that the presence of a Resident in Katmandu was nothing more than the establishment of a diplomatic representative in the capital of an independent state. The mistake thus made did not, indeed, lead to any practical difficulty with the Indian authorities, who were well aware of the actual relations between themselves and the Himalayan kingdom. But it led to misunderstandings abroad in other countries, and was resented by the natural pride of the Nepalese. A technical difficulty due to a similar misunderstanding of the Maharaja's actual position as the ambassador of a sovereign state had arisen in connection with Chandra's visit to Calcutta in 1903.

relations between these princes and the British Government had been deemed to be a sufficient excuse for their travels, though in all cases the most stringent precautions were taken that the regulations of caste should be scrupulously respected. It was regarded in England as a more remarkable thing and a special courtesy to the King Emperor that an independent prince, who by birth, training, and personal preference was directly bound by the law and custom of his Hindu faith but was under no tie of allegiance or obligation, should attempt this enterprise. It is doubtful, however, whether anything of this growing interest reached the ears of Chandra, who had already established himself as one who, as a rule, did not encourage either compliment or criticism even from his immediate friends. To those who looked a little below the surface, the most remarkable part of this journey to Europe was, perhaps, the fact that the situation in Nepal was already so secure that the prolonged absence of the Chief Executive could safely be contemplated.

The Maharaja bade farewell to the King and to the Valley of Katmandu on the 6th April 1908 amid a scene of great enthusiasm. The occasion was graced by certain omens of a most auspicious nature. A local chronicler makes the note that whether these manifestations were indeed omens or not, " by the grace of a benign Providence, not one of the big party, which consisted of twenty-two members, had the least complaint—not even a slight headache—throughout the whole period of full five months' absence from home." The journey through India, which was characterized by a perfection of organization which a commander accustomed to good staff work must have appreciated, was so arranged as to afford an occasion of visiting certain religious and other centres which the Maharaja had not had the opportunity of inspecting hitherto. He broke his journey at several points and everywhere was received with full military honours. In Bombay he was joined by Major Manners-Smith, V.C., who had been detailed to act as his political attaché during the visit to Europe. He spent four days resting in a house close to the Governor's " village " at the extreme end of Malabar Point. On the afternoon of the 17th April a salute of nineteen guns announced his departure from India.

He had chartered the steamship " City of Vienna " for the voyage to England and had had extensive interior alterations made in her to meet the religious and social needs of himself and his staff. He took with him a suite of twenty-two persons, and the English section of the party, under Major Manners-Smith, numbered fourteen. It may be imagined that the passage of the Red Sea late in April proved somewhat trying to those of the travellers whose experience of hot weather had hitherto been tempered by the cool nights and mountain breezes of the Valley of Nepal. The " City of Vienna " arrived at Suez early on the 28th April, and Port Said was reached without any more serious accident than a temporary stranding in the Canal. Here the Maharaja went on shore, more for exercise than for sight-seeing—most of all, perhaps, to avoid the unpleasantness of coaling. The original intention had been to approach England through Constantinople and the line of the Orient Express, but this had been abandoned for the usual sea journey to Marseilles—a change which enabled the Maharaja to visit Malta, where the Duke of Connaught extended the heartiest of welcomes to him. He landed at Marseilles on the 6th May. The day was spent there and in the evening the Maharaja entered his special train for Calais. London was reached late in the afternoon of the 8th. A royal carriage awaited the Maharaja at Victoria Station, where a large crowd had collected to catch the first glimpse of a man whose position, personality, and Oriental setting had awakened great interest in England. Mortimer House in Halkin Street, Belgravia, had been placed at the disposal of the Maharaja by the British Government and thither he and his staff were at once driven.

It would be far too long a task to retell in full the story of the interest which the Maharaja excited wherever he went and of the popularity he achieved. A large amount of the time was of course taken up with ceremonial visits and sightseeing. But Chandra did not forget the chief purposes of his journey, and achieved the main objects of his long travel. He received with good nature the information that some of his minor ambitions could not be realized at once. During his visit to London he had been persuaded to cancel a large order for maxims. He took a graceful revenge by the instant offer of a certain number of machine guns to the British army as soon as the outbreak of the Great War in 1914 had demonstrated the urgent need that existed for these weapons.

His Highness naturally saw much of the King and Queen. King Edward was immediately attracted by this man of men, who for a moment threw the almost forgotten light of autocracy across the humdrum and beaten tracks of constitutional Europe. It chanced that his visit coincided with that of President Fallières; and it is not unfair to that excellent statesman to say that the dominating personality of the Maharaja—together, perhaps, with the magnificent jewels that formed part of his official uniform—lent him in the eyes of London crowds a distinction that it was difficult for the civilized representative of a great Republic—permitted to make an official appearance whether by day or night only in the severest of evening clothes —to rival. It was not only the Occidental that suffered in this comparison. One or two Indian princes were in London at the same time as Chandra, but the leading London newspapers had no eyes for them. Public interest concentrated upon the jewelled head-dress which the Maharaja wore on occasions of high ceremony. " The gorgeous jewels in the turbans of the Indian princes," said one, " were as nothing to the diamonds worn by the Maharaja. A kind of helmet, with an enormous sweep of osprey feathers, was one glittering mass of precious stones. The members of the Maharaja's suite wore almost as many jewels, so that even the most scintillating of the boxes at the gala performance of the Opera paled by contrast." [1]

On the 28th May Chandra visited Dover, where a fleet of about fifty warships was collected in honour of the visit of the French President. Soon afterwards the Maharaja inspected some of the great industrial centres. His visit to England was prompted by many motives, and though the organization of Nepal as an industrial state will bc left for his successors to carry out, he thus obtained a clear view of the standards that would guide him in laying the foundation for such a development.

Among the pleasantest reminiscences of his stay in England were two visits that he paid to Wilton House and to Longford Castle, both near Salisbury. A casual reader might imagine that the life within these characteristic English country seats would be an entire novelty to the ruler of a remote Himalayan kingdom. But as a matter of fact, not merely in his own palace at Katmandu but, in a lesser degree, among the residences of his own relations and the princes of the blood royal, the comforts and standards of life have, wherever the regulations of caste permit it, been closely approximated to those of Europe.

Among other distractions the Maharaja's interest in horses and in the motors which have nearly superseded them, took him both to the race-track at Brooklands and to the May Day cart-horse parade in Regent's Park. Soon afterwards he went down to Aldershot, where field manœuvres were carried out in and around the Long Valley, and there was subsequently a review on Laffan's Plain of all the troops engaged. To Chandra not the least interesting sight of the day was that of a contingent of Sikhs and of certain non-commissioned officers from other native Indian regiments who happened to be going through their training in Aldershot at that time and were greeted by him with a few straight words of encouragement and remembrance. A visit to Windsor Castle, where he was once more received with especial honour by the King and Queen; a dinner at which all his old friends then in London, chiefly officers of the Gurkha regiments, were present; an examination of the Port of London and of Woolwich Arsenal —which probably interested him far more; an afternoon at the great annual gathering of racing society at Ascot; an exhibition of naval tactics, viewed from the flagship of the home fleet, H.M.S. "Dreadnought"— these by no means exhausted the full tale of his visits, nor, it may be added, interfered with the real purposes of the Maharaja's presence in England.

The King made Chandra a guest of honour at a garden party given at Windsor Castle, and by his side witnessed the international horse show at Olympia. The Maharaja visited Oxford during Commemoration Week,

---

[1] The feathers are not those of the osprey but of the bird of paradise, and the reporter omitted altogether the most remarkable and historical features of this coronel.

in order to receive the honorary degree of Doctor of Civil Law from 'the hands of the Chancellor of the University, his old friend, Lord Curzon.[1] In connection with this visit the words of the Oxford *Chronicle* may be quoted: "The Prime Minister of Nepal was introduced by the Public Orator as a statesman who had guided the foreign policy of his country and added to the strength of its military position; he had also been in his time a student and had successfully passed the examinations in the University of Calcutta, of which Lord Curzon was chancellor during the six years of his viceroyalty. The King and Queen had already received their distinguished guest with a welcome due to a friend and ally, and the University now willingly added its meed of recognition." The next day the Maharaja paid a visit to Hackwood, one of the late Lord Curzon's country houses. In the uniform of a Major-General of the British army the Maharaja attended the picturesque ceremony of trooping the colours on the Horse Guards Parade.

The Maharaja, about whom were quickly woven sumptuous legends of an Oriental wealth and power that Harun-er-Rashid scarcely equalled, was soon a familiar figure to the public, not of London only, but of the whole country. His visits to Edinburgh, Sheffield, and Glasgow afforded those in Scotland and the provinces an opportunity of displaying a welcome not a whit less enthusiastic than that which Chandra had received in London. At Glasgow the Maharaja made a happy reference to the notorious sympathy that exists wherever the Gurkha and the Highlander meet in camp or field. After acknowledging the reference made by the Lord Provost to the association in arms of the two races, he went on to say, "But my experience here to-day and during the last few days in Edinburgh shows me that the friendship of the Scot for the Gurkha has a broader basis than mere comradeship in the field." On the return journey to London he made a halt at Sheffield and inspected with especial interest and attention the works of Messrs. Vickers and Maxim.

The last week of the Maharaja's residence in London was as busy as the rest of his visit. Scarcely anything of the first importance in the capital was left unvisited by him, and as a fitting climax to a most successful stay among the British people the King conferred upon the Maharaja the Grand Cross of the Order of the Bath. For this purpose the Maharaja, attended by his suite, went to Buckingham Palace on the 21st July, and the formality of investiture was gone through with full ceremony. The incident received the last touch of grace by the fact that, in recognition of the loyalty and friendly spirit that had always been shown by the Maharaja towards the British Government, the King, as a most exceptional honour, had had the star of the Order which he then pinned upon the Maharaja's breast set in diamonds.

---

[1] Subsequently the Maharaja presented a valuable collection of Sanskrit MSS. to the Bodleian.

On the following day the Maharaja left London on his return journey. He did not go without distributing large sums of money as subscriptions to the chief charities of London. Besides large gifts to King Edward's Hospital Fund and Queen Alexandra's Home for Officers' Widows, it is pleasant to remember that he forgot neither the poor who lived near Mortimer House in the parishes of St. Peter's, Eaton Square and St. Paul's, Knightsbridge, nor the Children's Holiday Fund. At his departure Chandra published in the *Times* of the 21st July a cordial letter of thanks to the King and. Queen, to the princes and officials with whom he had been brought in contact, and to the people of Great Britain.

" Wherever we have gone we have found everyone anxious to make us feel that we were friends. I have been able to-day personally to thank their majesties the King and Queen; and I want to, and do, thank the British people for all their kindness and friendship. Yours is a great country. I have seen with admiration your splendid fleet and am proud that it is the fleet of our ally. But to me the greatness of your country is best seen in the good it has done for our great neighbour, India; in the peace, security of life and property, justice, and numerous other benefits it has given to that country.

" So I take my leave, with the wish that God may prosper the people of this country and their work, and by again saying how much I and my people have enjoyed the kind hospitality which has been so fully extended to us and for which we are all so thankful."

Almost every newspaper in the country wished the Nepalese visitor God-speed as he set out upon his return to Nepal. This journey was broken at Paris, where the Marshal placed a wreath upon the tomb of Napoleon. Afterwards a pleasant travel across Europe introduced to the party the half-familiar mountain scenery of the Alps. They could hardly have guessed that ten years later by the shore of the Lake of Geneva there would be buried, beside his British comrades, like himself fallen in the war, a Gurkha soldier of their own kith and kin whose dying words in hospital expressed the pleasure that he had had in being cared for to the last moment among the ice-clad mountain ranges that brought back to him the memory of his own gigantic Himalayan peaks.

A halt was made at Milan and the Maharaja visited the famous cathedral. Later on, Rome detained him for a few hours, where St. Peter's and the Colosseum excited much interest. At last Naples was reached, where the " City of Vienna " was awaiting her passengers. An expedition was made to the site of Pompeii, and on the next day the Maharaja's party left for India.

Instead of Bombay, the goal on this occasion was Tuticorin, the extreme southern point of the peninsula. From this place an interesting journey was made by rail and boat to the island temple of Rameshwaram, where the Maharaja with his whole suite went through the necessary ceremonies of purification. The utmost care had been taken throughout the journey that in no circumstances whatever should the rules of caste be broken. But according to the strictly orthodox view, which the Maharaja holds as relentlessly as any man, it was inevitable that such long travel as he had undertaken might involve some unnoticed lapse from the high standard which it is customary and indeed easy for Kshatriyas to maintain at home. After the ceremony the Maharaja rejoined his steamer and proceeded to Calcutta. No halt was made here, and on the 25th of August, exactly a week after the visit to Rameshwaram, the frontier town of Birganj, just across the Raxaul stream, was reached. By the afternoon of the 27th, a day earlier than had been arranged, the Maharaja was again among his own people in Katmandu.

Great festivities welcomed the returned Maharaja-Marshal. Troops lined the roads and guards of honour awaited his arrival at every point. An official welcome was accorded to Chandra by the King in the Darbar chamber of the palace of Hanuman-Dhoka, whereat the fullest ceremony was observed. It began about three o'clock in the afternoon with the presentation in new form of an autograph letter from the King-Emperor to the King of Nepal, while the guns outside fired a royal salute of thirty-one guns.[1] The letter was dated from Buckingham Palace, 20th July,.and was as follows:

" My Friend,—It has given me great pleasure to receive the kharita which has been delivered to me by Your Highness's Prime Minister. I appreciate very fully Your Highness's expressions of regard and loyal devotion, and I am gratified by the friendly terms in which you recall the memory of my visit to Nepal in 1876. I have also to thank you for the beautiful and interesting tokens of friendship which you have sent for my acceptance.

" It is my earnest wish that Nepal may ever increase in prosperity, and that the friendly relations which have so long existed between my. country and Your Highness's State may be confirmed and strengthened.

" To this end it has afforded me great pleasure to receive the visit from

---

[1] This unusual number of guns is peculiar to India. The highest Indian chiefs receive the usual royal salute of twenty-one guns. The additional number is said to have been due to the forgetfulness of those who drew up the scale of salutes. Having given the four great Indian chiefs, the Nizam of Hyderabad, the Gaekwar of Baroda, the Maharaja of Mysore, and the Maharaja of Kashmir twenty-one guns each, it became necessary to give a larger number to the Viceroy, who was accordingly given thirty-one guns, the same salute as that fired in honour of the King at royal ceremonies in India.

When the King-Emperor is personally present in India his salute is one hundred and one guns on all official occasions. At ceremonies of the highest importance, such as the Imperial Darbar of 1911, this salute is fired not by single guns but by batteries, each gun being then represented by a salvo of six discharges.

Major-General His Excellency Sir Chandra Sham Sher, Your Highness's Prime Minister, who will, on his return to Nepal, be able to assure Your Highness of my good will towards yourself and good wishes for the prosperity of your State.

"I am, Your Highness's sincere friend

"EDWARD, R. et I."

The welcome of the Commander-in-Chief and the Bharadars, Gurus, Prohits, and the people of Nepal in general, was then read. After briefly reviewing the facts and distinctions of Chandra's life this address recalled with appreciation the industry, foresight, and efficiency with which the Maharaja had raised the standards of Nepal in all departments. The speech was, in fact, a record of the Maharaja's State services with which this and the following chapters deal at greater length. The Maharaja replied in fitting terms thanking the people of Nepal for their enthusiastic reception and laying especial stress upon the ability with which his brother, the Commander-in-Chief, had administered the State during his absence and had maintained cordial relations with the Government of India. After a brief speech, in harmony with the surroundings, by Colonel Macdonald, the Maharajadhiraja completed the ceremony by a brief but warm address of personal congratulation delivered from the throne.

§ 3

In the early months of 1908 the relations between Nepal and Tibet had become more strained than usual, and the possibility of hostilities was present to the minds of both parties. Now, Nepal lies under a certain strategic disadvantage which must be borne in mind if her attitude towards Tibet is wholly to be understood. Her contention is that the existing frontier is unduly favourable to Tibetan operations of war because at the northern ends of the two great passes of Kirong and Kuti there is a considerable indentation of Tibetan territory which had been wrested from Nepal in 1792.[1] Nor is this the only, or indeed the chief, strategic difficulty

---

[1] There is a difference as to the delimitation of the common frontier between Tibet and Nepal at several places. This dispute has not the importance that it would have on any other border line in the world. The fact that the frontier has been properly surveyed for but one-third of its extent, that it runs along watersheds that have not been properly traced, and the loose way in which well-known names such as Gosain-than, Kirong, and Kuti have been used, add to the difficulty. But the fact that diminishes the importance of the actual line is that for more than three-quarters of the whole frontier it runs through rock and snow, glaciers and ice-fields, which are entirely uninhabitable for any period in the year. Some time ago there was a suggestion that the scaling of Mount Everest and the proper surveying of its vicinity might have political as well as geological and meteorological interests. This is untrue so far as political interest is concerned. A

by which Nepal is faced. The existing frontier is so drawn that the Tibetans could, at their leisure, overcome many miles of difficult mountain and upland track and muster their forces at the head, say, of the Kirong pass, from which point there· is a short and not extremely difficult descent to Nayakot. The Nepalese would have no right to protest against any concentration of the Tibetans on Tibetan soil and, failing any legal right to protest against it, might be compelled to precipitate the issue. It might well be that Nepal could not help doing so should she be called upon to defend what could only be defended by an immediate offensive.[1]

But this was not the only source of trouble. Mr. Chang in the winter of 1907-8 was already stretching out his hand towards Nepal, whose representative he informed that Tibet and Nepal, " being united like brothers, under the auspices of China, should work in harmony for the mutual good "—a tentative assumption of Chinese suzerainty over Nepal to be pressed or disavowed later by Mr. Chang's Government according as circumstances might suggest. But at this time the last Mission sent by Nepal was nearing Peking, and it is noteworthy that Mr. Chang should have thought it necessary to make these overtures. In themselves they amount to a confession that no suzerainty over Nepal was implied by the sending of a Mission to Peking. Mr. Chang had urged upon the Maharaja the blending of the Five Colours—China, Tibet, Nepal, Sikkim, and Bhutan. He compared Nepal, Bhutan, and Sikkim to the molar teeth lying side by side in a man's mouth. Shortly afterwards China demanded the right to enlist in her Tibetan contingent the Nepalese-Tibetan half-breeds of which there are a large number in and near Lhasa. It will be seen that this claim also raised in an indirect manner the suzerainty of China over Nepal as well as Tibet. Chandra rejected the demand, not least because it had become of urgent importance in the Sino-Tibetan dispute. Moreover, he brought things to a definite issue by repudiating in other matters the Chinese claim to suzerainty over Nepal. In the course of communications with the Indian Government, the latter assured him that so long as the

survey from a much lower altitude has already defined the frontier, and it is partly for that reason that the map of Eastern Nepal in this book is of especial importance.

There is a frontier dispute at a place called Nya-nam. The Tibetan representatives eventually made an agreement with the Nepalese Government ceding the territory in question to Nepal. The Tibetan Government refused to ratify this agreement and suggested that a British officer should arbitrate. No doubt this was mere bluff, as the Dalai Lama was well aware that no British officer would be allowed on Nepalese territory. This offer was rejected by Nepal and the matter still remains unsettled.

[1] I do not wish to disguise from the reader my own conviction that in no conceivable circumstances could the Tibetans carry out an attempted aggression against Nepal. But it is necessary to record the fact that the traditional antipathy that exists between Tibet and Nepal has partly blinded the eyes of the Nepalese people to this obvious fact.

existing friendly relations between India and Nepal continued, the latter might count upon the assistance of her great neighbour should she be threatened—the phrase is to be observed—from Tibetan territory.[1] On 31st March 1911 China, then on the eve of the revolution that effectually checked imperial extension, again demanded the right of enlistment of the half-breed. On 24th May of the same year the British Government declined to recognize China's claim and said that it would resist any attempt on the part of Peking to enforce it. Lord Morley could not be induced to do more than express pious hopes that the Chinese should not station troops on the Indian frontier. He advised the Foreign Office, however, that China should be told that the British Government would protect the integrity and rights of Nepal, Bhutan, and Sikkim. This was done. About the same time China reminded Katmandu that another quinquennial mission was due to start in 1912. After consultation with the Indian Government the Maharaja replied that it would be better to defer the despatch of the mission to a more propitious date; at the same time he asserted in the clearest manner that its despatch had never implied and would not then imply any condition of vassalage.[2] China was informed that Britain would assist the Nepalese and would undertake the defence of Sikkim and Bhutan—with which little territory we had signed a timely treaty—and Chandra was advised accordingly. But China continued her encroachment[3] and a special supply of munitions of war was sent by Calcutta to Katmandu in December 1911. In April 1912 the Maharaja informed the Resident that Nepal wished to see Tibet restored to its proper status of practical independence and that Nepal would help Tibet to attain this by all means that were sanctioned by the Government of India. At the same time he observed that if England left China a free hand in Tibet and thus brought China down to the frontier of Nepal, the northern boundary of the latter country should be rectified so that it might coincide with the natural southern watershed of the Tsangpo. On this occasion also the reinclusion of both Kuti and Kirong within Nepalese territory and the matter of Nepal's strategic disadvantage was brought once more upon the *tapis*. In 1912 the overthrow of the Chinese

---

[1] Sir Charles Bell remarks that as the British, by their own action, had lost the means of making Tibet a bulwark for the Indian frontier, they had to fall back upon the barrier of the Himalayan States. It does not seem that this is a final statement of the policy of the Indian Government.

[2] It may be remarked that the Chinese Government temporarily abolished the extra-territorial rights of the Nepalese in Tibet during their short occupation of the country before the revolution of 1912.

[3] On the 22nd of December a letter from the State Council of Lhasa appeared in Katmandu. The four Kazis asked for help against the threatening attitude of the Chinese. The demand was repeated at the beginning of 1912, but the Prime Minister did not think it necessary to send troops to assist Tibet against a power which, as he had himself reminded the Council, still possessed certain rights over Tibet.

imperial regime encouraged the Tibetans to throw the Chinese out of the country and take over for themselves the Chinese Maritime Customs post at Yatung.[1] The undefeated optimism characteristic of the Chinese race was shown on this occasion.

During his somewhat ignominious retreat through India—as it was impossible for the Chinese force to return by any Chinese route the Indian Government allowed them the use of the road through the Chumbi Valley down to Calcutta; Gurkhas escorted them on their passage—the Chinese High Commissioner made an offer to Nepal.[2] But the Himalayas had not yet become the lower jaw of China. Maharaja Chandra returned him a most courteous and at the same time delicately sarcastic reply.[3]

But the friction between Lhasa and Katmandu did not end with the peace agreement of August 1912. Nepal demanded and ultimately secured compensation for the material losses suffered by her nationals during the Chinese intrusion.[4] But some heat had been engendered by the dispute,

[1] News of the revolution in China reached the Chinese troops in Lhasa, and in a spirit of Bolshevism which has not yet received sufficient attention from Chinese students, they immediately cashiered their officers and set up a pinchbeck Republic based upon what was scarcely less than a reign of terror. The action of the Tibetans was instant, united, and successful. They drove out the Chinese intruders with an ease which might have led to excesses. At once the Nepal Government intervened to prevent the only too patent danger of vindictive reprisals against their tyrants. The Chinese themselves had long recognized the influence that Nepal exerted in Tibetan affairs, and characteristically enough attempted to win over the Maharaja's sympathies by offering to bestow upon him the highest order in the Chinese Empire. This, however, was parried by the Maharaja with such dexterity that the point was never reached at which the offer had to be declined.

[2] General Chang sent the following note to Peking and communicated it directly to Chandra. " The present Maharaja is an exceedingly well-informed man and is doing all that is possible to secure for his country power and prosperity. His subjects are a million times happier than the Tibetans. But the country under His Highness is small and there is no navy, and if a union could be made with the five races of China, the prospect for the future will be very brilliant."

[3] With Oriental pleonasm he thanked the General for his good intentions but assured him that the ancient Hindu kingdom of Nepal could not for a moment entertain the idea of a union with the affiliated races which constituted the glorious Republic of China. Nepal wished always to remain on friendly terms with her neighbour so long as her independence was strictly respected. And it was natural for her to rejoice at the assurance of the continued amity of China, which, " no doubt," was the real basis of the well-meant suggestion that General Chang had made. The Dalai Lama when taking refuge in Darjiling denied that the relations between China and Tibet were of the nature of those between an overlord and a vassal. " The relations between the two," he said, " are those between a layman and his priest. The priest receives help from the layman but does not become his subordinate." His Holiness asserted also that China would not rest content with her control over Tibet, but would try also to draw Nepal, Sikkim, and Bhutan into her net.

[4] It is to the credit of the Maharaja that the amount claimed, 134,894 rupees of Tibetan mohar, was not in excess of the material damage that had been proved after the strictest inquiry.

and the Dalai Lama, now again on his throne in the Potala, countered by a revival of the Chinese claim—this time on his own behalf—to enlist the half-breeds. From China this pretension could be listened to if not accepted, but coming from Tibet, which had exercised no authority over Nepal since A.D. 880, and was still paying Katmandu ten thousand rupees a year as an indemnity for the war of 1856, it seemed to imply a deliberately hostile attitude.

The difficulty blew over for the time. But from the English point of view it is worth while to consider what would have happened had Chandra forestalled the Tibetans by announcing the occupation of the ends of the passes. Such a rectification would have affected only a few hundred square miles of cliff and glacier, and the Tibetans after a formal protest would probably have accepted the occupation while they denied the annexation. But a storm of outside criticism would have fallen upon England. She would have been represented by a world that is apt to be censorious where her Empire is concerned, as the real author and instigator of this enterprise, and our imperial history would have been ransacked for precedents of such high-handed procedure. As has been said the world does not fully understand that Great Britain has for many years recognized the complete sovereignty of the kingdom of Nepal.[1]

§ 4

The news of the death of King Edward VII on the 6th May 1910 was received in Katmandu with deep regret. The personal relations between the late King-Emperor and the Maharaja had been of an especially friendly description, and the memory of royal hospitality in England was fresh in Chandra's mind. One hundred and one guns were fired on the Tundi Khel as a last farewell to one of the best friends of Nepal. The Prime Minister sent a letter expressing his sorrow to the new King George. The latter, in his answer, referred to the friendly relations which had been so warmly established between the Governments of Great Britain and Nepal.

Not long afterwards the intelligence came that the new Emperor intended to visit India with the Empress in order to hold a Darbar and announce in person his accession to the throne. That meeting, which was held with the fullest state and the revival of a hundred Oriental ceremonies and symbols which could with propriety be used in the presence of the Emperor alone, took place at Delhi in December 1911. The Maharaja was glad to take this opportunity to renew the invitation to a great shooting expedition in Nepal, greater even than that which had been prevented by the outbreak of cholera in 1906. This invitation was conveyed to London

[1] M. Sylvain Lévi himself has recently fallen into the error of supposing that it is only since the Great War that the sovereign status of Nepal has been recognized by Great Britain (*Journal des Débats*, 3rd March 1924).

early in 1911, and in reply His Majesty expressed his sincere pleasure, and the work of preparation was at once put in hand.

It is difficult to suggest to a European the enormous size of these battues and the infinite care, industry, and expense which is involved in organizing them. An army of beaters is employed for weeks and even months before the opening of the sport in driving before them the beasts that infest the warm, damp, rich jungles of lower Nepal. Steadily and with minute care all the greater game over an area that in some cases may exceed a thousand square miles is beaten down towards the selected district in the Tarai. Under the close and searching activity of these long lines the jungle is combed out with a care that is possible only in such a country as Nepal and under the conditions that prevail there. Into the selected area are driven rhinoceroses, elephants, tigers, leopards, bears, wild boar, and indeed the entire fauna of this happy hunting ground of big game. Ultimately, within the chosen area, which may measure some thirty or forty miles in length and perhaps ten in depth, a multitude of animals is concentrated and allowed to grow accustomed to its new surroundings. The Nepal Tarai, where it has not been reclaimed, presents a scene of the thickest and most tangled vegetation to be found anywhere in the world. The very reeds and bamboo grass through which the elephants make their painful way are in many places eighteen feet high. Underfoot the going is treacherous. Swamps are frequent, and the natural prudence of the elephant, which mistrusts the effect of its own bulk upon any unsteady soil, adds to the difficulty of forcing a way through.

After the arrival of the Maharaja's guests, two score and more of points, according to the information received at headquarters, are arranged, where the kills are tied up, and news is immediately sent in of the presence of tigers and the other beasts the Maharaja has had beaten in for his visitors' sport. Part of the game thus collected is stalked or ridden down in the open. But the most characteristic feature, and that by which the Nepalese Tarai shoots are known to the outer world, is the enormous ring of elephants by which the tigers reported overnight from the various "kills" are encircled and held prisoner till the dawn and the arrival of the guns. At times as many as two hundred and fifty elephants are employed for one circle. As the tiger is approached, the ring is contracted until a living wall of elephants, side by side, prevents the escape of the brute from the enclosed jungle. Immediately upon the arrival of the visitors ten or a dozen specially trained elephants are introduced into the circle thus made, which may be anything up to two hundred yards in diameter. These proceed at once to form in line and march into the patch of jungle in which the tiger is hidden, snapping the smaller trees like matches and treading out the undergrowth. It is astonishing to see the skill with which the hemmed-in beast will often attempt to hide from this close search. But eventually, of course, he is discovered—much perhaps to the dismay of the particular elephant that happens to rouse him from his lair—and in making a dash for liberty the brute has to run the gauntlet of the waiting rifles. In any case he has but a scanty chance, and a moment's halt or hesitation is fatal. Sometimes, indeed, a tiger will charge the ring of elephants, and may succeed in creating a momentary panic, in the course of which he slips through to freedom. Sometimes he will spring upon the head of one of them and force him back out of the ring; but an elephant, though he may be desperately mauled, is quite capable of dealing with a tiger, and in few cases does the latter manage to make his escape. Leopards more often succeed, as the fear displayed by the elephants seems to increase in inverse ratio to the size of the animal making for them. It is amusing to watch the squealing panic that will at times be produced along a hundred feet of the elephant ring by the unexpected appearance of some jungle-cat no larger than a Scotch wildcat.

Once again a disappointment loomed on the horizon. While the guns were still sounding their salute at Delhi His Majesty the King of Nepal, whose health had been failing for a long time, passed away. No one had taken more interest in the preparations that were being made for his imperial visitor than the King, Prithwi Bir Vikram Sah. He had watched with satisfaction and pride the skilful and vigorous planning of the camps, the construction of the new corduroy road, the installation of telephones, and above all the slow concentration within the desired territory of the great game of his Tarai. Though he knew that his days were numbered, his greatest hope was that he might be allowed to welcome as his guest the Emperor of India. But after a long illness the feeble life flickered out in the early days of December. Before he died, however, he sent to King George, through the Maharaja, an earnest and heartfelt appeal that his death should not be allowed to interfere with the great preparations which it had been the pride of Nepal to make in honour of the Emperor's visit. The question was indeed a difficult one for King George to decide. A profound unwillingness to realize one of the dreams of his life at a moment when the host who had extended the invitation so warmly was no longer there to greet him fought with a sense that the last wish of the dying man was sacred. Consideration for the disappointment that would be caused to Nepal eventually won the day against his natural wish that the usual honours to a departed sovereign should be exactly and meticulously rendered, and at the earnest entreaty of the Maharaja, His Majesty consented to fulfil his engagement, and in spite of the cloud that naturally hung over the occasion, there was for the Nepalese the proud satisfaction that never in their history had the work of this unrivalled shoot been carried out so fully or with greater success, and their enthusiasm grew as the moment approached when, for the first time since the days of Asoka, an Emperor of India was to visit Nepal.

The camps were arranged at Sukibhar, about thirty miles west-north-west from the British frontier station of Bikhna Thori; one at Sukibhar itself between the Rapti river and the Riu river within four miles of the point where the two streams fall together into the Kali Gandak; the other was at Kasra, seven miles to the east of Sukibhar on the southern bank of the Rapti. The former is about one mile from the Indian frontier, and the

KING PRITHWI BIR VIKRAM SAH

latter is about four times that distance. This district was chosen as it was the best rhinoceros haunt in Nepal. Tiger, as is well known, may be met with in many places in India, but the rhinoceros, though found in Assam and in some parts of northern Bengal, is practically extinct elsewhere, and the only place within an easy distance where rhinoceros shooting may be had is in these royal preserves under the Sidhara range, just outside the Indian border.[1] As may be imagined, King George's special shooting camp

[1] Rhinoceros is regarded in Nepal as royal game *par excellence*, and may not be shot except with the direct permission of the State.

MAHARAJA CHANDRA SHAM SHER WITH H.M. THE KING-EMPEROR IN THE SHOOTING-CAMP AT KASRA, 1911

[To face page 134, vol. ii

was furnished with all the comforts of civilization, including electric light and hot and cold water. A far more necessary precaution was to be seen in the barbed wire entanglements which entirely surrounded the compound As may be imagined, if every beast of prey within a distance of sixty miles has been concentrated in a small area, it is necessary to guard against a counter attack. The Maharaja's own camp was situated a little lower down the Rapti. It held accommodation for twelve thousand followers, besides the elephants, and two thousand attendants upon them. The elephants used on this occasion—including a certain number borrowed from India—numbered more than six hundred. Five days of the ten spent in Nepal were passed at Sukibhar and were fully occupied by sport from early dawn till sunset. King George's own bag on this occasion was twenty-one tigers, ten rhinoceroses, and two bears; the total, including those secured by his party, being thirty-seven tigers, eighteen rhinoceroses, and four bears.[1]

At the same time a valuable Christmas gift was made by the Maharaja to King George. This consisted not merely of a large collection of Nepalese curios and manufactures of all kinds, including ivory carving and old silver, brass and woodcraft, but a considerable number of animals characteristic of all parts of Nepal. These included a rhinoceros calf, a baby elephant, and a tiger cub, besides adult specimens of tiger, leopard, bear, and snow leopard. Most remarkable of all was a specimen of the almost unknown Tibetan stag, of the Wapiti class, of which the heads had once or twice been secured by travellers, but of which no living specimen had ever even been seen, much less shot, by any white man until the Younghusband expedition to Lhasa broke into the hitherto virgin recesses of the Chumbi Valley. Besides these there were other kinds of deer and many cattle such as sambhur, thar, gharal, nilghai, and yak. A pair of single horned sheep made an interesting addition. General Kaiser had been chiefly concerned with making this collection, and King George expressed to him his great pleasure and satisfaction in becoming thus the owner of so many of the animals that were destined to fill needed gaps in the collection in the Zoological Gardens in London.

On Christmas Eve King George invested the Maharaja with the insignia of a Grand Commandership of the Royal Victorian Order, and at the same time gave him a gold Coronation Darbar medal. A more practical gift was that of two thousand Lee-Metford rifles and five million rounds of ammunition. Upon the Commander-in-Chief was conferred the K.C.V.O. Maharaja Chandra had received the additional honour of a salute of nineteen guns on Indian soil—a salute which will be rendered to all future Prime Ministers of Nepal on their visits to India. On the 27th December

---

[1] When King Edward visited Nepal as Prince of Wales the entire bag, including those secured by his companions on this occasion, was twenty-three tigers, of which fifteen fell to the Prince's rifle.

some fighting elephants were exhibited and two Mutiny veterans of the Nepalese army were presented. On the following day King George returned to India after having inspected four Nepalese regiments. He was escorted to the frontier station of Bikhna Thori by the Maharaja. The telegram that His Majesty sent is worth quoting in full. " Before the day closes I must again thank you from the bottom of my heart for all that you have done to make my visit to your country so happy. You have omitted nothing that could give to me and my staff the greatest possible enjoyment. You have shown me the finest sport in the world, which I assure you I have greatly appreciated : and its experiences will always be most delightful remembrances. In both the charming camps I was as comfortable as if in my own home. Dear Maharaja, I know I can always count upon you and your people as my truest friends." That this was a personal composition of King George and expressed his genuine feelings of gratitude and pleasure there can be no doubt.

§ 5

Death of the King.—The death of King Prithwi Bir Vikram Sah, which has been referred to, had been foreseen for a long time. The relations between him and Maharaja Chandra had been of the friendliest description, and it is not without interest to note the conclusion of a letter sent in acknowledgment of Chandra's congratulations on the occasion of the King's birthday in 1909: " With the never failing love and regard of him who prays for your ever increasing happiness and prosperity, and desires the continuance of your unbroken, kind affection." Exchanges of compliments between the higher officials of this world are often common form, but it would not be thought that the phrases just quoted were drawn from any conventional source. That at least the Maharaja believed in their sincerity is shown by the fact that he has enshrined the letter in a silver frame and placed it in his own writing room. But a more impressive proof of the deep gratitude entertained by the King for his great and principal servant is to be found in the speech which, on his death-bed, King Prithwi read out to the principal officers and officials of his kingdom. It is too long to quote in full, but in unmistakable phrases the dying King records his admiration for the masterly efficiency with which Maharaja Chandra had steered the " ship of State." After referring to the professional and spiritual assistance that had been evoked by the Maharaja to prolong the ebbing life, the King went on: " If you do not succeed do not be sorry. His will be done. You have done your best for me, for my beloved mother and family, and I am sure you will continue to do so in the future. Myself, my mother, and those of my race to come will never be able to repay you for what you have done. Should it please God I may welcome you back

H.M. MAHARAJADHIRAJA TRIBHUBANA BIR VIKRAM SAH AND HIS QUEENS

after the shoot. It is an onerous work that you have undertaken, and I hope I shall be spared to hear of the success of this work to which you have devoted so much time and labour. More I would like to say. The mind urges but the body fails. So long as God grants me consciousness—and may it please Him to allow me to take with me memories of you into the spirit life—I shall not cease to pray for the prosperity of one who ministered to my comforts more than my own father could. Maharaja, you have won my eternal benediction. Commander-in-Chief, Generals, and Bharadars, serve Maharaja Chandra Sham Sher faithfully. Remember that is your one duty."

The present King, Tribhubana Bir Vikram Sah Deva, was crowned on the 20th February 1913, and four days later the British Resident, Colonel Showers, presented to the boy-King the congratulations of the Government of India. The occasion was celebrated by the giving of dinners to about fifty thousand poor, military displays, public decorations, and a general amnesty to prisoners convicted of lesser offences. His accession made no change of any kind in the full authority with which Chandra Sham Sher continued to direct the whole policy of Nepal, foreign and domestic alike. It was a good thing, not merely for India, but for the Allies, that the affairs of Nepal were at this moment in strong hands, for though few were then able to read it, the warning of the Great War was already written on the wall, and the following pages will be devoted to the consideration of a national act on the part of Nepal far greater both in its extent and in its results than any that stood before in the records of this Himalayan State.

§ 6

The Great War.—Earlier than many even of those who were at' headquarters in London the Maharaja-Marshal seems to have recognized the inevitable character of the coming conflagration in Europe. That the assassination of the heir to the Austrian throne was likely to lead to the long dreaded explosion of European rivalries was an opinion expressed by him more than once in the course of the month of July 1914. On the 3rd August he sent a letter to the Resident expressing his fears. In it, more correctly than even some of the members of the British Cabinet, he summed up the inevitable action of the people of Great Britain should war actually break out; and then followed the offer which will remain for all time as one of the finest expressions of friendship between two peoples, differing in religion and custom but essentially one in their standards of justice and right, of which the East holds record. " I have come to request you to inform His Excellency the Viceroy, and through him the King Emperor, that the whole military resources of Nepal are at His Majesty's disposal. We shall be proud if we can be of any service, however little that may be. Though far from the scene of actual conflict we yield to none in our devotion and friendship to His Majesty's person and Empire. We have spoken of our friendship on many occasions; should time allow, we speak in deeds. May I say I am speaking to you in double capacity: firstly as Marshal of the Gurkhas, and secondly as Major-General in His Majesty's army."

It was not until the 6th August that the news came to Katmandu of the declaration of war between England and Germany. The following words by a chronicler of Nepal express well the attitude of the Gurkha people. " The deliberate disregard of the recognized principles of justice and freedom by Germany, supported by elaborate preparations extending over a quarter of a century and guarded by well thought-out schemes, clearly indicated a speedy termination of the war to be out of the question, and naturally put a terrible strain for the time being upon the neighbouring state of England. German intrigue carried the flame of the European conflict to Asiatic soil. The Great War gradually extended its field of operations until it comprised a dozen theatres of conflict, from Flanders to China. In such a dark hour for England the cloud that hung over its political firmament was marked by a silver lining—the true consistency and splendid loyalty of all her subjects at home and abroad and the devotion to her cause of her friends and allies everywhere. Nepal, as a small friendly state outside the borders of India, rose to the height of the occasion under Chandra Sham Sher, and rendered every assistance and help that was possible, considering the limited resources she possessed. Her help adds more to her glory when we consider the spirit that moved her to action. That spirit has nowhere been more appropriately and admirably described than in the words of Mr. Asquith at the Guildhall meeting held on the 19th May 1915: 'It was not founded on obligation but upon goodwill and sympathy.'"

This time there was no false pride and no delay. The British Government at once accepted with gratitude Nepal's offer. The first step was a request for a loan of six thousand troops from Nepal for general service within the borders of India. The Maharaja at once organized the drafts required, and, characteristically enough, was better than his word. Seventy-five hundred men left for India on the 3rd and 4th of March, in two detachments under the direction of General Baber Sham Sher, the Maharaja's second son, who was appointed Inspector-General of the Nepalese contingent and was attached to Army Headquarters in India. These four regiments, under the command of Commanding General Padma Sham Sher, the Maharaja's nephew, proceeded at once to the north-west frontier, while two other regiments—the crack battalions which constituted the personal bodyguard of the Maharaja—were attached to another force stationed in the United Provinces under General Tej Sham Sher. This great loan of the finest troops in Nepal was increased by the gratuitous offer to the Government of India of the whole stock of Lee Enfield rifles which the State possessed at that time. These men replaced a larger number of British and other troops who were at once transported to the various theatres of war. The Maharaja fully understood that the need for his men would be continual, and he had no sooner despatched the first contingent than he set about training another. At the end of December three fresh regiments of a thousand men each left Nepal under the command of the Maharaja's third son, General Kaiser Sham Sher. Of these, two, under the command of Major-General Shere Sham Sher, the Maharaja's half-brother, joined the troops under General Padma in the north-west. A fourth battalion that followed six weeks later remained in the United Provinces. Here again the generosity of Nepal was marked. She had been asked for four thousand; she sent four thousand seven hundred and fifty-seven.

But it is not sufficient in war merely to send battalions; they must be kept up to their full strength; and from time to time new drafts were dispatched from Katmandu. Six hundred and fifty-eight men were sent in December 1916; ten hundred and fifty about a year later. A third draft of seven hundred and seventy-nine left in February 1918, and a fourth contingent of eighteen hundred men was on the point of marching south when the end of the War disappointed it of the hopes of service. Their chance was, however, still to come.

Thus we have in all a total of sixteen thousand five hundred and forty-four soldiers of first-rate quality freely loaned by Nepal at this crucial moment in the history of India. The Maharaja-Marshal addressed each one of these contingents on the eve of its departure. He impressed upon them that during their absence they would be not only fulfilling their duty to their sovereign and their Prime Minister, but would be serving their own country in the measure in which they served the cause of Great Britain also. In India their conduct was admirable. They were denied the thrill of the active service which their kith and kin were enjoying—there seems no other word to express the keen delight of the Gurkhas when the last diplomacy is finished and the guns begin to speak—in other fields. But it must not be supposed that their duties were merely the duties of peace. The north-west frontier offered only too many opportunities for the display of the characteristic Gurkha military efficiency. And more than once the Maharaja received from the Commander-in-Chief in India warmest congratulations upon the gallantry of his men. But the greatest service that Nepal rendered by its gift of men lay in the perfect freedom thus afforded the Indian Government to strip the country of troops that would otherwise have had to be retained. The presence of these men was more than a mere material help in the preservation of peace. It was a moral lesson. It was an encouragement to the orderly and the loyal and it was a significant warning to the discontented. Nor was the generosity of Nepal shown only in this practical addition to the forces of a friendly neighbour. The Maharaja assumed a risk in thus depriving her territory of practically the whole of the finest fighting regiments in her army. A writer whom this double generosity did not escape sums up the characteristic qualities of the Gurkhas in words the truth of which will be recognized by all who have had to do with these mountaineers in arms. " They are very good shots, expert with the bayonet, most excellent hill fighters, and, in fact, regular first-line troops. They are extraordinarily well behaved and disciplined—crime being conspicuous by its absence—very pleasant to deal with, and, like all Gurkhas, the greater the hardships to be suffered the more cheerful they become."

In more stately terms the Viceroy of India expressed his appreciation of the qualities of the Gurkha contingents in a speech at the beginning of February 1919. After reciting the services to which allusion has just been made, His Excellency went on to praise the work done by the commanding officers in general and of General Baber Sham Sher in particular. He had been attached to the staff of the Commander-in-Chief as Inspector-General of the Nepalese contingent, and proved of the utmost assistance during the four years in which the good order of India was largely maintained by the generous support of his fellow countrymen.

But it was not only in India that the Gurkhas had done work for which the Viceroy expressed his deepest gratitude and admiration. " In France, in Mesopotamia, in Egypt, in Palestine, and Salonika your fellow country-men have covered themselves with glory and worthily maintained the high fighting traditions of their race."

After the conclusion of the Viceroy's speech General Baber Sham Sher expressed the appreciation of the Nepalese contingent for the courtesy and consideration which had been extended to them during their stay in India.

It must be remembered that the supply of these contingents for service in India was only a small part of the help rendered to the fighting lines of the Allies. There were, in 1914, about twenty-six thousand Gurkhas forming part of the regular Indian army. These regiments, who naturally suffered a vastly greater wastage than those who remained in India, had to be kept up to their strength, so that, including non-combatant contin-gents, the number of men who actually left the country for all military purposes amounted to more than two hundred thousand. Mr. E. Candler quotes the words of a Gurkha during the War. " Asbahadur told me that he had met very few men of his own age near his home. In his village the women were doing the work, as they were in France; garrisoning of India by Nepalese troops had depleted the country of youth. He only met old men and cripples and boys." To obtain such numbers the whole country was quartered by Chandra and a new and intensive system of recruiting was put into force.

Another service rendered by the Maharaja was the issue of an official notification of mobilization to men of Gurkha regiments in the Indian army who were at home in Nepal. A special Nepalese mail service carried the warnings throughout the country, and the strict injunction of the Nepalese Government was added to this notice of recall. They were warned that the British recall would be enforced as rigidly and the penalty for refusal would be as severe as would have been the case in the Maharaja's own army.[1] To render this summons less troublesome special measures were enacted by which a moratorium was granted, through which the judicial rights of the absentees, the security of their holdings, and a compassionate treatment of overdue rents was secured. Local officers were appointed to deal with cases of hardship among the families of the men on service, and arrangements were made for the free carriage and distribution of the mails.

But a thing which to a Gurkha was more important than anything else remained still to be dealt with. We have seen that the Maharaja himself was obliged to undergo a special form of purification before he returned to Nepal from his journey overseas. This purification or dispensation is called Pani Patia, and the widespread importance of this rite when tens of thousands of Gurkhas were being employed abroad, led to a special arrangement between the Prime Minister and the supreme religious authority in Nepal, the Raj Guru. It was formally arranged that this dispensation should be granted automatically to all Gurkha soldiers who had proceeded abroad under the orders or with the consent of the Nepalese Government. To this there were two reasonable conditions attached. No man was wantonly to prolong his absence abroad beyond the absolutely necessary period: and each man was required to produce a certificate signed by a British officer that he had observed the regulations of his caste during his time of service abroad. It may be difficult for the Western reader to understand the nature of the boon that was thus secured by Chandra for the Gurkhas fighting by our side in extra-Indian fields, but of its magnitude there can be no question.

These precautions did not, however, prevent occasional ill-informed and even malicious comment upon the religious observances of the Gurkhas, and indeed of all Indian soldiers on foreign service. General Sir O'Moore Creagh, an ex-Commander-in-Chief in India, wrote to protest against these foolish reports.

" In every oversea expedition that leaves India complete arrangements are made to meet the caste and religious requirements of the men, both on

[1] Between August 1914 and November 1918 Nepal supplied no less than fifty-five thousand recruits for the Gurkha battalions of the Indian army, in addition to those furnished to other units such as the Assam and Burma military police, the Dacca police battalion, the Army Bearer Corps, the Labour Corps, and other similar formations.

board ship and at the place of its destination. This is the case in the present expeditions to France, Persia, and Africa. For example, beef is supplied to no Indian troops. When meat is used by either Hindus, Sikhs, or Moslems, it is the flesh of goats killed either by the men themselves or by camp followers of their caste. In the case of other food and water everything is done to meet the requirements of those concerned." He went on to point out that there was no truth whatever in the statement that the Gurkhas were given dispensation to eat beef and drink porter when they were camping, just as if they were British soldiers. "The Gurkhas in Nepal are Rajputs. They observe strictly all the Hindu customs of their most noble clan. To say they eat beef is an insult to them and is absolutely untrue; to say they could get a dispensation to do so when campaigning is equally untrue and mischievous; to lead it to be supposed that their British officers would—even in the impossible event of the men desiring to do so—countenance such a gross breach of caste and religious observance is equally wicked and injurious to these brave men and the government they serve."

Of the individual achievements by Gurkha regiments during the war it is invidious to speak, but the following words from Mr. Candler's book, *The Sepoy*, are a just and eloquent recognition of the sturdy gallantry of these hill fighters.

"The hill men of Nepal have stood the test as well as the best. Ask the Devons what they think of the 1/9th Gurkhas who fought on their flank on the Hai. Ask Kitchener's men and the Anzacs how the 5th and 6th bore themselves at Gallipoli, and read Ian Hamilton's report. Ask Townsend's Immortals how the 7th fought at Ctesiphon; and the British regiments who were at Mahomed Abdul Hassan and Istabulat what the 1st and 8th did in these hard-fought fights. Ask the gallant Hants Rowers against what odds the two Gurkha battalions forced the passage of the Tigris at Shumran on February 23rd. And ask the Commander of the Indian Corps what sort of fight the six Gurkha battalions put up in France."

On the last point we will follow the advice given and record the evidence of General Sir James Willcocks, the Commander referred to.

"Of the Indians who served with me in France, the Gurkhas were the first in the permanent trenches to bear the shock of a German attack. They laboured under great disadvantages in taking over trenches too deep for their stature, and that at a time when rain and slush made it impossible to remedy the defect. They took time to accustom themselves to the uncanny conditions, but the soldier from Nepal has a big heart in a small body; he has the dogged characteristic of the Britisher; he will return if he can to a trench from which he has been driven, and it will not be easy to turn him out a second time. After the first shocks they pulled themselves together. Taciturn by nature, brave and loyal to a degree, the Gurkhas ended, as I knew they would, second to none."

Some notice of the work involved to support these contingents both in India and overseas may be given in order to keep in perspective the effort of Nepal compared with that of the Princes of India. In September 1914 the Nepal Government made a contribution of three hundred thousand rupees, which sum was increased by a donation from the Maharaja's private purse of two hundred and fifty-five thousand rupees. On the 1st January 1916 and 1917 a further sum of three hundred thousand rupees was offered through the Viceroy for any purpose in connection with the War. In the following year yet another two hundred thousand rupees was presented in honour of the silver wedding of the King and Queen.

But this offer of money was only a small part of the contribution of Nepal. Over five thousand maunds (four hundred thousand pounds) of cardamons, eighty-four thousand seven hundred pounds of tea, and a large quantity of army blankets and two hundred thousand broad-gauge sleepers contributed to the Indian railway free of royalty were included in this generosity. Reference has already been made to a great gift from the Maharaja in June 1915 of thirty-one machine guns. The number was gracefully decided by that of the imperial salute in India, but there must have been many who remembered that it did not differ from the number of machine-guns which Chandra had attempted without success to buy during his visit in 1908, and the free use of which without doubt would have been added to the other services which Nepal was rendering to the Allies at this moment. Another act of courtesy was the loan by Nepal of one hundred and twenty-five lakhs of British and Nepalese silver coins at a moment when the war scare had once more driven half India to the old and deplorable habit of burying specie beneath their hearthstones.

We may rest assured that the ultimate victory of the Allies was the greatest recognition and reward that the Maharaja could have wished to receive, and Nepal has indeed reason to be proud of her generosity and the unfailing support which she gave to the Indian Government. On the other hand it may fairly be said that British rule in India has never received before so deep a compliment as that which is implied by the willing and unprejudiced help given to it from outside its own dominions by a friendly people, who not only had every right to retain their soldiers and their funds for their own possible need, but deliberately and without hesitation threw themselves on the side of the English at a time when half Asia was secretly convinced that victory was a foregone conclusion for Germany.

A writer has summed up in words that it would be difficult to improve the nature of this alliance between Nepal and Britain. " I often wonder how many Englishmen have realized the extent of the sacrifices that this mountain principality, tempted by the specious promises of our enemies and bound to us by no compact, made for Great Britain in the cause of freedom. I doubt if any of the belligerent powers directly interested lost so big a proportion of their fighting men. To little peaceful hamlets hung on the mountain side or nestling in Nepal's remote and lovely valleys, very far from the enthusiasms and excitement of mobilization and the contagious turmoil of military preparations, and threatened by no danger, the call came; and the hill men poured down, they knew not why save that they were summoned by their Government and their brethren. One saw them in the mud of Flanders, in the deserts of Mesopotamia, on the rocky slopes of Gallipoli, in the forests of Persian Gilan."

§ 7

The War was over, the Gurkha regiments had returned during the latter half of February 1919, and the Maharaja in an admirable allocution expressed the deep thanks of Nepal to God, who had restored to Nepal its legions, and the satisfaction and pleasure with which the Nepal Government looked back upon the gallantry and good discipline of the troops for whom it had been proud to be responsible. This appreciation of the honourable way in which the Nepalese had justified themselves in the battlefields of the Great War took the practical form of the distribution of two and a half lakhs of rupees among the men on service in India as well as overseas. An increase of pay was also hinted at, leave was granted to every man at the rate of one month clear at home for each year's service in the line, and altogether it seemed that the Gurkha battalions were about to enjoy the long and undisturbed rest to which their hard work had entitled them.

Bare as this description is of the help that Nepal rendered to the Empire in the days of her greatest trial, a reader, however casual, cannot fail to understand the importance of this free-will offering of lives, service, goods, and money in a cause with which Nepal was only connected because of her unwritten but long alliance with the Indian Government, Put into a few words it means that to the last man and the last mohar this mountain kingdom, without necessity or obligation of any kind, and knowing full well the results to herself should the Central Empires win the day, stood by our side from the first day until the last.

Nay, it is not enough to say the last. After the War was over when half the world was content to retire exhausted to its homes and, as a Nepalese said to me, lick its wounds, the foolish invasion of India by the Afghans two months later again raised an ominous cloud of trouble on the north-west frontier. This trouble the Maharaja, whose private information of frontier conditions is no whit behind that of the Intelligence Department in Simla, foresaw and suggested that the disbanding of the extra troops, raised in his country during the late War, should be postponed as well as the leave granted to the troops who had just returned. Still following the ancient routine in this matter, the offer was received with gratitude but considered unnecessary for the moment. But the Maharaja's intelligence was right. Six months later—in May 1919—the Indian Government found itself face to face with a new Afghan war, and, unwilling as it was to call again upon the strained generosity of Nepal, had no other course open to it except to make another request for help, when the folly of Amanullah Khan darkened the Afghan border. The circumstances were peculiarly difficult. The regular Indian army was still largely depleted by the contingents that had remained overseas, and the suddenness of the attack from Kabul was rendered doubly inconvenient by the almost simultaneous outbreak of sedition in the Panjab. These two assaults upon the Indian Government had been intended to synchronize but, as is almost invariably the case with these hot-headed and ill-considered movements, each of them went off-at half-cock. Though no co-ordination between them was actually achieved, and the internal revolt was crushed without difficulty, matters wore for three months an ugly complexion along the north-west frontier, for the Amir left no stone unturned to increase the religious prejudice of that turbulent district. The Maharaja under the circumstances might have found some difficulty in providing at once an adequate force to send to the assistance of India. But when fighting is in question there is never any trouble in obtaining the ready and cheerful—almost the gleeful—co-operation of the Gurkhas. Two thousand men moved at once from Katmandu on 2nd June 1919. Three days later the Maharaja, in a letter to the Viceroy, reviewed the situation in India. He expressed his admiration at the vigorous measures taken to restore law and order within the Empire and his amazement at the foolhardy action of the young Amir. Speaking of the leaders of sedition in India and the apostles of Bolshevism outside it he uses phrases that are not without importance in view of future possibilities as well as of the freedom from Swaraj intrigue that Nepal has enjoyed. " If any of the persons responsible for this attempt entertained the absurd idea of outside help and encouragement in their unholy work, they must know how utterly absurd such an idea is to every sane man of every government. In case it should recur, or the peace of India be threatened from outside, and any assistance from us be needed and asked, then Your Excellency and your Government may rely upon the Nepal Government and myself for rendering such help as is possible for us to give."

The two thousand Nepalese troops moved up to the Afghan front under the command of Commanding General Padma Sham Sher; and General Baber Sham Sher resumed, at his father's instructions, his position at the Army Headquarters in India. The mobilization of a large contingent was at once set on foot, but the Afghan War ended as rapidly and as foolishly as it had begun, and the Nepalese contingent was able to return home after an absence of only three months. Nepal had, however, shown her readiness to face out the new trouble to the end, however long it might take, and the shortness of the service does not diminish the credit that is due to her for once again proving, even in a moment of exhaustion, her affection for the English and her deep-seated confidence in their rule. In all history it is hard to find an exact parallel for the self-devotion of the Nepalese. Germany had, of course, done its worst in Nepal as in every other State that bordered on India. The beginnings of the War seemed to promise success for the German arms, and no one was in any doubt as to the treatment that would be accorded by a victorious Germany to those who had thrown in their lot with the Allies. There was no promise or understanding that compelled the Government of Nepal to come to the help of the British in any way whatever. Assuredly there was none that made the gigantic sacrifice of our mountain neighbour anything but the gratuitous proof of a practical alliance that will not lessen so long as the British Government shall have effective control of India. And, we might add, the reality of a friendship that would survive even the disaster of our retirement from full responsibility there.

Recognition of the great work done by Nepal has been as complete and as sincere as it lay within our power to make. The Maharaja, who in 1915 had been promoted to the rank of honorary Lieutenant-General in the British Army, was raised to the rank of full General soon after the termination of the War, and the Grand Cross of the Order of St. Michael and St. George—our Imperial Order *par excellence*—was bestowed upon him. On the occasion of the conferment upon the Prime Minister of this dignity, the relations between England and Nepal were thus summed up by the British Resident, Colonel Kennion: " I venture to think there is a vast difference between the relations existing between the two Governments when His Highness first assumed the reins of office nearly two decades ago, and the relations that existed at that momentous time, the autumn of 1914. During this period, thanks to goodwill on both sides, but mainly, I think, thanks to His Highness's political vision, sagacity, and, I may add, patriotism, the relations between the two Governments steadily improved. Frankness, confidence, and mutual understanding took the place of the somewhat suspicious friendship that previously existed. I cannot attempt to enumerate all that His Highness did during those four years of war and after. Let it suffice to say that in this great war, if the expression may be allowed, Nepal pulled her weight, and more than pulled her weight.[1]

---

[1] It would be interesting to know what meaning this expression, so full of significance to any Englishman, actually conveyed to the minds of the Resident's hearers; for there is scarcely a country in the world in which there are so few pieces of water, and boat racing is entirely unknown.

I should wish specially to mention here the distinguished services of General Sir Baber Sham Sher Jang and General Sir Padma Sham Sher Jang, and the magnificent contingents that His Highness sent to India. As for the Gurkha troops in the Indian Army, whether enlisted before the war or specially sent by His Highness for the war, they fought all over the world, and, as ever, maintained the grand tradition of their race for valour and self-sacrifice.... His Highness in 1901 found existing a limited, conditional and somewhat lukewarm friendship; he transformed it into a brotherhood, sealed by the comradeship of war in a righteous cause which, please God, will last as long as the British Empire and the Kingdom of Nepal endure.... General Sir Baber Sham Sher accompanied the Nepalese contingents to India as Inspector-General, in which capacity his work at headquarters was of an administrative kind. On prospects of active service occurring, true to Nepalese instincts, he at once went to the front. In both capacities his conspicuous talents won him the highest praise as an administrator among administrators and as a soldier amongst soldiers."

But it was difficult to devise any full recognition of such services as Nepal had rendered during the Great War. Of personal honours Great Britain was lavish to all who had taken a leading part in this struggle. But for a time the two Governments found it difficult to discover any form of national recognition that would in the slightest degree reflect the gratitude of England and her sense of the concord which, forged in these days of trial, links together the interests and the future of the Empire and the Kingdom. After many diplomatic enquiries and many courteous replies the Government of India came to the conclusion that an annual and unconditional gift of one million rupees in perpetuity would, in the long run, prove of greater benefit to Nepal than any other token that it was in the power of India to give. In Katmandu an addition of territory would probably have been more welcome than any monetary recognition. But this it was not in the power of the Government of India to grant. The settlement of Indian territory had progressed fast since 1858 when the last cession of Indian soil was made to Nepal, and this annual gift—for the Nepalese Government regards the word "subsidy" as inapplicable to this present and is anxious that it should not be used—was accepted in graceful terms by the Nepalese Government as the most useful alternative.[1]

[1] The exact phrase used by Lord Chelmsford, Viceroy of India, in communicating this offer to the King of Nepal in his letter of the 27th of December 1919 is of importance. "I am now addressing Your Majesty in order to convey to you the cordial thanks of my Government and to inform you that, as a recognition of the services (which have been rendered by the Nepalese troops during a period of nearly four years) and in testimony of the friendship which unites us, I am offering to Nepal on behalf of the Government of India, an annual present of ten lakhs of rupees to be paid in perpetuity unless and until the friendly relations which so happily subsist between the two countries are broken off. No other conditions whatever are attached to the offer." This phrase has since been defined

A question of some importance arises in connection with this annual gift. At present the payment of this sum lies in the hands of the Viceroy himself as chief of the Indian Foreign Office. It is exempt from all opposition, criticism, or restriction in the Indian Parliament as a " reserved subject," but should Great Britain determine to grant a measure of Home Rule to India under which all subjects at present reserved would be annually brought under the consideration of the Parliament, it is not impossible, though not probable, that when the budget is discussed some question may be made in the Assembly about this grant to Nepal.[1] Than such a discussion nothing could be more distasteful either to the British Government or to the Government of Nepal.

In October 1920 the Viceroy of India addressed the Maharaja by the courtesy title of " His Highness." This change in style symbolized the recognition of the unique position of the Prime Minister and Marshal of Nepal, and raised him to a plenipotentiary rank implying direct and permanent representation of his sovereign that no other public office in the world bestows except as a temporary dignity. A great Darbar in Katmandu was held by the King on the 21st November 1920 in celebration of the event just recorded and to provide an occasion for presentation to the Maharaja and other officers and officials of certain British dignities and decorations.

to mean "such a serious difference of opinion between the two Governments on matters of vital importance as would entail the withdrawal of the British Representative."

In the Prime Minister's reply accepting this offer, a reference is made to the Viceroy's explanation that money is offered only because it is impossible to repeat the retrocession of territory which expressed the gratitude of the Indian Government for the services of Nepal during the Mutiny of 1857 to 1858. Lord Chelmsford had said that it was impossible that the reward should take that form, and Chandra accepts the annual present "as forming the best available substitute for any restoration of territory." The Government of India subsequently announced that this annual grant was absolute and depended in no way upon the policy that the Government of Nepal might think fit to adopt. The assurances of the Government of India make it clear that nothing short of the withdrawal of the Envoy—which would be tantamount to the existence of a state of war—would terminate this grant. In no way whatever is it to be regarded as offering the least excuse for interference with the sovereignty of Nepal.

[1] Such canvassing of a recognition of India's gratitude to Nepal is improbable, however short the memory of new India may be, because if and when Home Rule is granted to India the payment of an annual present securing the goodwill of a neighbouring State of such military efficiency is one of the last items on her budget that India will be inclined to criticize. Moreover, if by any access of folly this annual grant be refused by the Indian Parliament, the situation thus created would be of grave importance—indeed, of such gravity that the mere seventy or eighty thousand pounds a year involved would be scarcely worth consideration. Still, it would be perhaps to the advantage of all that this payment should be secured by the creation of some form of Consolidated Fund, the establishment of which is advisable for other Indian purposes also—which shall be guaranteed by the British Government and exempt from Indian Parliamentary criticism.

§ 8

At the end of 1920 the Duke of Connaught visited India and the Maharaja was, of course, glad to take this opportunity of seeing again an old and honoured friend. He went to Calcutta, where Belvedere House, lately the residence of the Lieutenant-Governor of Bengal, was opened for his convenience. The Duke did not fail to endorse in private conversation the cordial and sincere appreciation in England of the great services rendered to the Allies during the War by the Maharaja and his Government.

The Duke's presence in India was in substitution for the visit of the Prince of Wales. The latter, who had been unable to pay his long desired visit to India in 1920, was received by the Government and people of the Peninsula at the end of 1921. The Maharaja had inquired whether the Prince would like to have organized for him another of the great shoots in the Nepal Tarai with which the Darbar had welcomed his father and grandfather. A cordial acceptance of the offer was received and the Maharaja at once set to work to make the necessary preparations. His Royal Highness's visit took place between the 14th and 21st December 1921. The district of Chitawan was selected, and an elaborately furnished and palisaded camp was pitched for the Prince's reception at Bikhna Thori, close to the Indian frontier. Thirty-six miles of road were made suitable for motor-cars, extending twenty-nine miles to Kasra on the west of the camp, and seven miles to Shikaribas on the east of it. Thirty-two miles of telephone lines were also laid along the road. His Royal Highness's party consisted of the Earl of Cromer, Vice-Admiral Sir Lionel Halsey, Mr. G. de Montmorency, Colonel R. B. Worgan, Sir Godfrey Thomas, Lieut.-Col. F. O. Kinealy, Captain Dudley North, R.N., Captain the Hon. Piers Legh, Lieutenant the Hon. B. A. A. Ogilvy, Lieut.-Col. C. O. Harvey, Surgeon-Commander A. C. W. Newport, Mr. H. A. F. Metcalfe, Mr. D. Petrie, Captain E. D. Metcalfe, Captain S. F. Poynder, Lieutenant Lord Louis Mountbatten, Sir Percival Phillips, Professor Rushbrooke Williams, Mr. Perceval Landon, and Mr. E. Villiers, together with official photographers and cinema operators. Altogether there were forty-nine Europeans and two hundred and fifty-three Indians in the royal camp. Four hundred and twenty-eight elephants were collected for the shoot. The total bag consisted of eighteen tigers, eight rhinoceroses, two bears, and two leopards. Two rhinoceroses were subsequently picked up, one of which had been tracked and shot by the Prince of Wales.

The killing of a rhinoceros is an event of no small importance in Nepal. The shikaris of the jungle naturally perhaps maintain longer than their more civilized fellows the nature-superstitions of their forefathers. As soon as the great brute has fallen, the beaters and others rush in to celebrate the death and secure from the fallen beast the precious ointments and charms which are inherent in this emperor of all game. Everything that a man can detach or tear from his clothing is at once soaked in the thick blood oozing from the nostrils. It seems that this coagulated gore is used for a different purpose than that which ordains the smearing of the whiskers of a fallen tiger with his own gore. A few drops of rhinoceros blood smeared on the head of a dying man acts as a kind of viaticum and ensures for the sufferer a happy reincarnation. The head is then hacked off; which is a gruesome spectacle but one that is performed with extraordinary skill. The horn is credited with many magic properties, and scrapings from it are notoriously useful as an aphrodisiac. Otherwise the horn may be used for magic purposes and is therefore the first object coveted and taken away should an unguarded carcase be found in the jungle. Drinking cups are made of the horn, which are supposed to betray the presence of poison, but the associations are chiefly of a maleficent nature and are connected with putting spells upon or otherwise annoying one's enemies. Nor is this the full tale of the half-magic uses of a dead rhinoceros. There is a curious practice which seems to be connected with the conception of rebirth by which a symbolic entrance of the carapace of a dead rhinoceros by a man's descendants is held to assist his reincarnation. This is a belief that is widely held by the higher and lower classes of Nepal alike.

The days of the Prince of Wales's visit were spent in the pleasantest surroundings and in a luxury that was known to no Mogul on the march. The evenings were spent in concerts, exhibitions of Gurkha skill with kukhri and music, and General Baber and General Kaiser—who was responsible for all the arrangements of the shoot—often came into the Prince of Wales's camp and joined in the amusements of the night.

A valuable collection of beasts and birds had been got together for presentation to the Prince, and this was afterwards taken home and placed in the Zoological Gardens in London. In a letter to the Maharaja, written by His Royal Highness after his visit, he expressed his thanks for the infinite forethought and care that had provided for him so magnificent an opportunity for shooting big game. But he concluded by saying that more than anything else he valued the opportunity thus given of paying a personal visit to the kingdom of Nepal, which had rendered such assistance to Great Britain in the War, and of establishing personal relations with the Maharaja, in whose devotion and fidelity the King Emperor has reposed and continues to repose his grateful confidence.

§ 9

The Treaty of 1923.—During the next four years the steady progress of Nepal continued, and the policy, both domestic and foreign, that had been adopted by the Government was consistently pursued. The signature of a new treaty between Nepal and Great Britain, on the 21st December 1923, brought to a happy conclusion the friendly negotiations that had been on foot for some time. In full state the ceremony of signature was performed in the Grand Council Hall of the palace. The British Resident was received with full military honours, and after the signature the conventional attar and pan were presented by His Highness to the British Minister, and the ceremony terminated by the escort of Colonel O'Connor to the British Residency by a troop of cavalry.

Two days' universal holiday and a general remission of three months of their sentences to prisoners other than life convicts were announced during the ceremony; Katmandu was illuminated that night and a few days later, and the poor were befriended by gifts of food and clothing on the Katmandu parade ground. The Treaty, which is given in full in Appendix XXIII, recites in its preamble that true friendship had been mutually and consistently shown by the Nepal Government and the British Government for over a hundred years, and that with the intention of still further strengthening the good relations between the two Governments this new agreement had been drawn up.

The first article provides for perpetual peace and friendship and for the mutual recognition of the independence of the two Governments. The second confirms all the previous treaties and agreements since the Treaty of Sagauli of 1815, except in so far as they are varied by the present Treaty. The third article is cast in a more material shape. Both parties to this Treaty agree to communicate at once any misunderstanding or friction with neighbouring States likely to interfere with the friendly relations between Great Britain and Nepal, and to do whatever is possible to remove the cause of trouble. It will be seen that an actual defensive alliance is not contemplated, but the union between the two kingdoms is further secured by an undertaking that neither should permit its territory to be used to the detriment of the other. The fifth article provides that the Government of Nepal shall be free to import from or through British India whatever arms and warlike stores may be needed for the strength and welfare of the former country. This arrangement shall hold good in perpetuity unless and until the British Government shall have reason to fear that there is danger to the peace and order of India due to such importation. The Nepal Government on its side undertakes that there shall be no export of arms and warlike material across the frontier of Nepal either by the Nepal Government or by private individuals. This article is qualified by a proviso that should the British Government become a party to any future international regulation of the Arms Traffic, the right of importation of arms and ammunition by the Nepal Government shall await the adhesion of that Government to the Convention, and that thereafter such importation shall be made in accordance with the provisions of the Covenant.

By the sixth article it is provided that no customs duties shall be levied at British Indian ports on goods in transit to the Nepal Government, provided that a sufficient certificate to that effect is presented to the customs officer at the port. The certificate shall set forth that the goods are the property of Nepal, are required in the public service of that State, are not imported for the purpose of trade, and are being sent to Nepal by order of the Nepal Government. This concession on the part of the British Government was increased by a remission also of duties upon trade goods imported at British India ports for immediate transmission in bulk to Katmandu.

The Treaty was signed on the part of the British Government by Lieutenant-Colonel W. F. T. O'Connor, C.V.O., C.I.E., British Envoy, and on the part of the Nepal Government by the Maharaja. The speech delivered by the British Envoy after the signature of the Treaty recalled the uninterrupted peace and loyal friendship that had reigned between the two countries since the Treaty of Sagauli. Colonel O'Connor recapitulated the magnificent effort that Nepal had voluntarily made on behalf of the allied nations during the Great War. And he added the curious and significant comment that, in proportion to the resources and population of the country, it compared favourably with the effort of any of the Allies. It had been estimated, he said, that no less than two hundred thousand, or nearly one quarter of the total of those who, by any stretch of the term, could be called the fighting classes of Nepal, served in some capacity during the War. After noting the assistance given by the Nepal Darbar, he referred to the good fortune that Nepal and the British Government had alike enjoyed in possessing as their Minister and ally so enlightened a statesman and so loyal a friend. " Not only has Nepal stood the strain but it has emerged stronger than before. In helping the cause of civilization Nepal has at the same time confirmed her own sturdy independence and has enhanced a reputation already high and honourable among the nations of the world." In reply the Maharaja addressed first his people, praying that the friendship between the two Governments would continue unabated and grow in solidarity for centuries to come. To Colonel O'Connor he made a graceful acknowledgement of the pleasure that Nepal felt in listening to the assurance that an abiding place in the memory of the British nation had been carved by its gratitude for and appreciation of the effort of Nepal. He then paid a well deserved compliment to the share which Colonel O'Connor had taken in bringing about the conclusion of the new Treaty, and then laid stress upon the acknowledgement by the British Government, absolute and unequivocal, of the independence of Nepal. He went on to say that he valued greatly the military and industrial facilities granted by the British Government, and his speech ended with a repetition of the debt which Nepal owed to the courtesy, patience, and fairness of the British Envoy.

The news of the signature was telegraphed to Delhi, and the Viceroy, Lord Reading, wrote before nightfall to convey his warm congratulations to the King of Nepal upon the successful conclusion of the Treaty. Next day complimentary telegrams were exchanged between the two high officials.

With this graceful incident the more important aspects of Nepalese relations with the outer world may now be said to have been described. But that outer world—and the feeling was not confined to Englishmen—had to give still further expression to the high honour and respect in which it holds Nepal. On 30th March 1925 a pleasant ceremony was held in Katmandu. The French nation, through its representatives, M. Daniel Lévi and M. Garreau-Dombasle, presented the Maharaja with the insignia of the high dignity of a Grand Officer of the Legion of Honour, which had been conferred upon His Highness by the President of the Republic on 17th October of the previous year. M. Lévi, in the address he delivered on this occasion, referred in stirring terms to France's remembrance of the valour of the Gurkhas during the war for civilization and paid a warm tribute to the work done by the Maharaja in the fields of peaceful progress also. He made special reference to the imminent abolition of slavery in Nepal through the strong action of the Prime Minister, and to the constant assistance he has rendered to French scientific missions in the country. This allusion to the great research of M. Sylvain Lévi, the father of the chief of the mission, was received with cordial pleasure and referred to later by His Highness.

The Maharaja, in his reply, spoke in moving terms of the brotherhood that sufferings in common had cemented, when the sons of the two countries, along with those of their great friend and ally, Britain, fought shoulder to shoulder in many a hard-fought battle and in death lay side by side on the field of glory. The possession of this high grade in the illustrious Order, hallowed as it was with the immortal name—a name which yet sends an electric thrill through every true soldier—of Napoleon was, he said, very dear to him, and he asked M. Lévi to convey to the President of the Council, and through him to the President of the Republic, his grateful thanks. In conclusion he alluded to the splendid work done by M. Sylvain Lévi " in lifting out of obscurity the ancient and glorious history—as he calls it—of this little kingdom."

A week later the British Envoy, Colonel W. F. T. O'Connor, had a similar graceful duty to perform in presenting a number of decorations to distinguished Nepalese officers. In a speech in which he allowed a touch of personal regret for his approaching retirement to colour the purely official nature of the occasion, the Envoy referred to the ripening of the old historic friendship between Britain and Nepal in fields of peace as well as those of war, to the welcome given to the Prince of Wales, and, above all, to the conclusion of the new treaty between the two countries. The Maharaja, in his reply, alluded to the deep significance which the honours possessed —a significance which vastly increased their importance and the pleasure with which they had been received. He paid a well earned tribute to the work and personality of Colonel O'Connor, and referred to the very close ties of friendship and affection which bound him to the departing Envoy.

Perhaps, however, the words which will longest be remembered by that audience were those in which Colonel O'Connor summed up the attitude of Great Britain to the Maharaja himself, and it would be difficult to find a better phrase with which to close these chapters in which His Highness's activity and capacity in foreign matters have been studied and explained. " We all recognize that the guiding hand and the guiding spirit in shaping Nepal's destiny and policy are those of my friend His Highness the Maharaja Sir Chandra Sham Sher Jang.[1] My Government has frequently expressed its high appreciation of His Highness's services and character, and no public testimony to our mutual good relations would be complete without a tribute to his statesmanship and courage and to his loyalty to his friends and allies. I need say nothing more at this moment to assure His Highness that his services and support both in times of peace and in times of war will never be forgotten."

[1] Throughout this book the full sovereignty of Nepal has been in every case recognized. By a misunderstanding which has recurred in several cases, the distinctions awarded to Nepalese subjects have been supposed to confer the title of "Sir" upon their recipients. It cannot be too precisely or strongly laid down that no grant of an honorary title—and all grants of British titles to foreigners are honorary—confers the title of "Sir."

CHAPTER XVI

MAHARAJA CHANDRA SHAM SHER

SLAVERY—JUDICIAL AND SOCIAL REFORMS

"The Gurkhas are the best masters I have seen in India. Neither in the Tarai nor in the Hills, have I witnessed or heard of a single act of oppression since I arrived a year and a half ago, and a happier peasantry I have nowhere seen."—Sir HENRY LAWRENCE.

§ 1

SO far we have chiefly had under consideration the steps by which Nepal has vindicated its claim to independence in the family of nations and in particular the relations which it has maintained with its neighbours and with the British Government. It is now time to turn to the internal condition of the country, and it is perhaps in this section of the work that Asiatic students will find the chief interest which these volumes may possess. Reference has already been made to the fact that Nepal to this day presents the picture of an older India in many respects unaffected by the codes and administrative systems of the West, and it is therefore with special interest that the customs, standards, and progress of this Himalayan kingdom come to be studied. It should be said from the first that while the two great Maharajas of Nepal, Jang Bahadur and Chandra Sham Sher, have been strict in their maintenance of the natural development of their fellow countrymen along lines that are familiar to them, Oriental in their essence and uninfluenced by the theories and experiments of social life of other continents, there has been a steady and on the whole successful attempt to introduce into Nepal the material facilities and methods which a Western civilization has tested and found satisfactory. It is obvious that some of the inventions of modern science are inapplicable to a country which has no desire to adopt a democratic form of government, or to serve as a goal of travel, and little to act as a channel of communication between its neighbours. For example, it is not expedient to introduce there the doubtful blessing of the freedom of the press or mechanical transport for passengers. For the moment it will be of importance to note the manner in which, without infringing upon or even colouring with Western prejudices the national habits of thought in the people round him, Maharaja Chandra has endeavoured to guide along lines natural to the Nepalese not merely the progress that has been made in the material welfare, but such public opinion as can be said to exist in this contented backwater from the turbulent stream of modern history. " Of course," he said to me on one occasion, " it will take time, I am afraid, for the people of this country to look kindly upon innovations, but perseverance and tact are sure to carry the day in the long run." The use of the powers of even such an autocrat as is the Prime Minister-Marshal of Nepal may bring about discontent and friction if they are employed in a way which is foreign to the temper of those who are thus ruled. But neither the Maharaja nor his great predecessor made any such mistake. If the broad liberalism that has characterized the policy of the Government were the rule rather than the exception among the inhabitants of Nepal, the development of that kingdom would have taken a speedier course. But there is no need for haste. Asia is littered with foolish experiments in government, the failure of each of which is to be traced to the folly of implanting Western ideas upon people not merely unready to benefit by them, but of a traditionally different habit of thought in regard to government. The solid nature of Nepal's independence and progress has been due to a constant recognition on the part of her rulers of the need of making a people understand as well as obey. If, therefore, in the following pages there seems to remain in Nepal much that to a Western mind is difficult to understand, and even inconsistent with the international position and brilliant services of the Gurkhas, it should be remembered that education—in the only sense of the word in which education is of value—is a plant of slow growth, and that the well intentioned reforms which are or are not conferring benefits upon India are regarded in Nepal with a mixture of astonishment and incredulity —not unmingled with thankfulness that neither Viceroy nor Secretary of State has any power whatever of influencing her own development.

At one time the Nepal Government adopted a policy which, in the circumstances, was natural. A small number of the sons of the aristocracy were sent to Japan to be trained in technical knowledge, especially in modern methods of engineering. It was thought that thus the advantages of modern science could be enjoyed by Nepal without the corresponding danger of the introduction of men imbued with Western principles of democracy. Even this comparatively slight departure from the traditions of the land met with some little criticism, but the Maharaja had his way, though whether at this moment he is satisfied that the Japanese offer the best channel for instruction in matters which, after all, are largely foreign to Japan herself, is perhaps to be doubted. But this and other experiments, such as the establishment of a " shresta pathshala," were necessary in order to test by practical application the methods that were best suited for the development of a body of expert officials. In general the aim of the Government has been to draw into the public service those classes of high social position which in the past had been content rather to strive than serve. It is impossible to create overnight such a class of men as, let us say, the Indian Civil Service, but beneath the policy thus adopted by Nepal may be read a wish to draw into public life not merely the best brains in the country, but also and chiefly those to whose keeping the moral standards of Nepal could most safely be entrusted.

The administration of Nepal has followed lines which reflect its history. It will not be necessary to take the story earlier than 1768. Prithwi Narayan found it advisable to act much as William the Conqueror did in 1066. He created a feudal system of a military nature, assessed the revenues to be drawn from each part of the country in a rough but not unjust manner, and left it almost entirely to the feudal overlord to maintain order, collect and remit his dues to Katmandu, and execute justice. Brian Hodgson summed up the natural result of this policy as allowing the mesne lord and his soldiers to wring as much as they could out of the people. This, however, was not the hardship in an Asiatic country that those nursed in the liberalism of the West might imagine. A wise farmer has as little wish in the East as among ourselves to kill the goose that lays golden eggs, and there was, in case of absolute necessity, always an appeal to the despot in Katmandu who, for his own sake, was anxious that the revenues of the country should be encouraged rather than checked by unjust oppression. Moreover, here as everywhere else rough justice was secured by the rivalries and jealousies that existed between these feudal chieftains. The parallel with William might be continued in the habit of rewarding the officers of a victorious commander with land rather than money, but all tenants of freehold held directly from the King. The earlier administrators of modern Nepal have had scanty time in which to develop any consistent reformation of this rule of thumb government, and it has been only in recent years that the internal order of the country has enabled the Government to attempt a steady amelioration of the law. ·

The first thing that was needed was a reformation of the public departments of the State. Into these ancient channels a new spirit was breathed, and honesty and competence in administration gradually filtered down from Katmandu to the remotest village lost among the · Himalayan snows. The spasmodic and uncertain right of appeal to the Government was confirmed and extended. Although the Maharaja has maintained in his conduct of State affairs something of the inaccessibility that has throughout all time been a feature of the administration of Oriental potentates, it is, as a matter of fact, easier for an aggrieved labourer on the land to obtain a direct hearing from Chandra than it would be for a ryot in a similar position to attract the personal attention of even a Commissioner in India. This is a system which works excellently well where a man of insight and experience forms this court of appeal, but the danger of any autocratic method of government often lies more in the uncertainty of the nature of his successor than in any real mistrust of the personal altruism or fairness of the man who has won his way to power. The Indian administration thus provides the one necessary check upon a beneficent autocracy. It sees to it that a man's successor shall, if possible, be as good as himself. Reference will be made to the methods by which the land revenues are collected and the judicial and administrative needs of the country provided for. They work well beneath the eye of a man of capacity and determination. But it would be unwise not to realize that in spite of all the improvements that have been made, the administration of these departments would be looked upon by a globe-trotting Member of Parliament merely as an example of the manner in which the East understands Government—and is alas! contented with it. He would regret to find therein no illustration of the Occidental methods that many in the House of Commons are still attempting to foist upon an unwilling Orient. But, at any rate for many years to come, in this matter he would be wrong and Maharaja Chandra would be right. Against corruption in the public service the Nepal Government has taken a vigorous and steady stand, and so far as possible the Maharaja has seen to it that the wheels of good government shall continue to revolve long after his own steadying hand has been removed.

It will be remembered that Nepal has long been accustomed to the annual renewing of all appointments. It was at one of these paijnis that Bhim Sen first realized the weight of the opposition he had to encounter in spite of a brilliant and unhampered administration of the affairs of the country for some thirty years. This ceremony continues to-day in a much improved shape. It is the Prime Minister, the actual governor of the country, who thus reviews year after year the work of those who serve with him. Naturally the changes that are annually necessary become fewer and fewer as it is realized by public servants that industry and capacity alone will secure the retention of their posts. In old days when a new man was appointed as the head of a public office he used his position for the wholesale rewarding of his supporters and the discomfiture of his opponents. His action was rarely questioned, and the amount of injustice thus done was exceeded only by the instability and want of continuity thus imported into the public service. But in these days the Government would take prompt action were there even a suspicion that anything had been done by the head of a department from a motive other than that of the public service. The present Maharaja has again and again impressed upon the members of the various departments of state that their service may be regarded as permanent until by their own misconduct or incapacity or idleness they compel the Government to make use of its right of abrupt dismissal. It is to be regretted that civil Government posts in Nepal carry no pension. Apart from the obvious justice of providing for the declining days of those who have given their lives in the service of the Government, the prospect of losing a comfortable allowance in old age would stimulate all concerned to a greater determination to give satisfaction to the powers that be.

A point of great importance was the resumption by the Government of a large amount of land which had at one time or another been granted in return for military service. Of course, compensation has been given in every case, and the conversion of these interests has always been a matter for the consideration and approval of the man owning the *jagir*. The only matter that deserves record is the abolition of the bad old system by which, in a greater or less degree, any Government official was permitted to requisition both goods and service on nominally State business. The *corvée* has been suppressed. Even for the tours of inspection by the

A MODERN FARMHOUSE

Prime Minister himself unpaid labour and unfairly cheapened goods are things of the past. The peasant of Nepal is no longer compelled to furnish the beasts required for the annual sacrifices of the Durga Juja festival at low or even nominal rates. Nothing perhaps has brought so directly to the knowledge of the people the new spirit which actuates the Nepal Government than this relief.

The Tarai, wherein, of course, most of the agriculture of Nepal is centred, has vast forest domains. These forests are carefully supervised by a regular State department. The indiscriminate felling of trees has vanished *pari passu* with a far better protection of the woods from the danger of fire. The experience of the Indian Forest Institute at Dehra Dun has been drawn upon for this purpose, and increasing use is being made of the skill and organization that have made the Forest Department of the Indian Government famous throughout the world. Mr. J. V. Collier has been entrusted with the direction of this service, and it has largely been due to his energies that the roadway which is now being constructed from Raxaul towards the capital has been enabled to achieve its existing success. Mr. Collier is also to be credited with the reclamation of large tracts of the Tarai, especially in the districts of Morung, Mohotari, Sarlahi, Chitawan Surkhet, and Kailali-Kauchaupur.

The recent treaty has settled the question of customs duties so far as the main avenue into Nepal is concerned. It will be sufficient to note here that the chief imports from India are naturally manufactured articles, of which cotton yarn and piece goods are the most important, other items being salt, petroleum, shawls, woollen cloth, rugs, Oriental silk, brocade, embroideries, sugar, spice, indigo, tobacco, areca nut, vermilion, lac, oils, a little fine rice, buffaloes, sheep, goats, sheet copper and sheet iron, copper and brass ornaments, beads, mirrors, precious stones, guns and ammunition, and tea from Darjiling and Kumaon. The exports of Nepal chiefly consist of rice, oil seeds, ghi, honey, cattle, falcons, talking birds, timber, musk, cheretta, borax, madder, turpentine, catechu, jute, hides and skins, furs, ginger, cardamons, chillies, turmeric, and yak-tails.

The duties upon these imports and exports provide a steady and important revenue to the State, and much has been done to unify the tolls, the anomalous nature of which caused a good deal of difficulty and discontent in old days. Local duties levied on goods in transport among the hill districts, resembling the inter-provincial imposition known as *likin* in China, were abolished in 1923, a boon which was greatly appreciated by the workers of the remoter districts. A similar exaction in the Tarai upon goods exposed for sale at the fairs in different localities had been discontinued since 1914. Dues somewhat of the nature of " octroi," that had long been imposed upon the transport of goods within the Valley of Katmandu have also disappeared, and other forms of taxation that were once customary along the Chitlong-Raxaul road have been done away with.

It has been less easy to deal with the trade with Tibet. Here the tendency to stand upon the ancient ways is more difficult to change, because of the absence of a strong central personality in the country of the Lamas. In 1923, however, a great advance was made by the nominal abolition of the posts at which dues were exacted at several points along the principal trade routes between Nepal and Shigatse, Gyantse, Lhasa, and other Tibetan centres. It may generally be said that relief has been granted in all directions in which the internal taxation was hampering the chief industries of Nepal.

§ 2

We come now to the most interesting section in this narrative, the life and work of the Nepalese people. The social laws and customs of a

II   M

people and their enforcement are perhaps the best test that can be taken by the historian of the success of an administration and the position which a country holds among civilized races. But the Eastern view is essentially different from that which obtains in Western lands. In Europe and America the almost complete separation between religious and civil rights has, so far as form is concerned, taken the shape of the full protection of any form of belief which is not opposed to the existing regime in the country or to public morals. Among Indian peoples religion has from the earliest days been regarded as a matter that has a right to the direct support and defence of the Government, and wherever, as usually has happened, a non-Hindu ruler governed India, by Mohammedan and Christian alike protection has been given—less in the case of an Aurangzeb, more in the case of a Victoria, but always sufficient to prevent religious war on any considerable scale. In the peninsula, however, there has been tolerance if not encouragement of other creeds. In Nepal, where, as we have seen, the tradition of life and thought is less changed from that of early India than elsewhere, the religious law still remains to permeate and, indeed, to form the foundation of the existing system of administration. However gross or infamous his offence, no Brahman may in Nepal suffer capital punishment; the traditions which still colour Indian life so profoundly in the matter of the sanctity of the cow are represented in this country by ranking the killing of that animal as a crime equal to that of the murder of a man; still, as much as ever, religion and religious prejudice and preference attend a man throughout his life from his birth to his funeral. But there is a strange thing also in Nepal. The Brahman has for so long been the senior caste that it has almost been forgotten except by students that there was a moment when the Kshatriya took precedence of him. Incidentally one may note the attempts that are now being made by the Brahmans to claim Prince Gautama as a Brahman. The attempt does little but emphasize the wish of the Brahmans that he had been of their caste. This seniority of the Brahmans may perhaps be the cause of the occasional recurrence in early Indian history, when the Rajput takes unquestioned precedence, of the right of a sovereign to interpret the absolute rules of the creed so as to reconcile them with the increasing development of the national intelligence and the rung of civilization upon which the people stand. Nowhere has this been as manifest as in Nepal, and it is interesting as being a surviving proof of a very early form of Hinduism. It implies the right of a sovereign to change the rules after consultation with the highest spiritual authorities, openly and without concealment. In Nepal the abolition of sati is of course the obvious illustration of this inherent right. In India the British simply laid down the law that sati was to cease, and in general it may be said that from that moment it ceased. The British authorities listened to not a word of the defenders of the Hindu practice. The abolition of sati in Nepal may be taken, with the modification of the law of purification after possibility of defilement during the War, as an illustration of the reasonable compromise that attends amicable discussions on points that may be affected by religious scruples whenever these seem to stand in the way of the advancement of civilization in the State. It is the more remarkable because in Nepal there had hitherto been no compromise of any kind for an offence which trespassed the laws of caste. To this day in India a man who loses his caste by infringing its cardinal regulations is sometimes permitted to remain unmolested within its fold by the connivance of the .priests. In Nepal, however, there is no escape, and the absolute need of purification in such circumstances is recognized and is a familiar part of the occasional ritual of the Hindu faith. This privilege is one which is based upon the highest and most ancient authority, and is jealously vindicated by prince and people alike. That a general indulgence was granted to all soldiers detailed for oversea military operations, provided they neither consciously broke the caste-law nor stayed longer than their actual work required, is an illustration of the extent to which the progress of its development has been harmonized with the strictest religious observances. But there is another and even greater proof of this spirit of adjustment which has just been realized, and that is the abolition of slavery.

§ 3

Abolition of Slavery.—At last the efforts of the Maharaja to raise not merely the military strength and the political sovereignty of Nepal but its moral and humanitarian standards also, have been crowned with success. The question of slavery is one that goes deep into the heart of all human society, and so long as any State tolerates it within its boundaries, it has to render a reason to the civilized world why this blot upon its fair name should be permitted to continue. Sometimes it is no easy thing to crush out. Slavery in such districts, for example, as Central Africa, or the border states of Burma, is a matter which it is practically impossible to extirpate except after many years of vigilant repression and often disheartening attempts at education. For slavery is apt to find itself sanctioned, justified, and even intertwined with religion. It is true that religion has probably been the means by which civilization has learned to treat and terminate the evil, but it is equally true that a religious protest against slavery has been in the nature of an afterthought after political liberty had rendered the conception of slavery impossible. The religions of the world did not view the practice with displeasure nor was the sense of justice of their greatest teachers affronted by it. We cannot therefore be surprised, considering that every one of the great creeds of the earth had its origin in the Orient, that the Oriental does not regard the system in the same light as his Western brother. Moreover, it is not to be forgotten that the East, with a deeper estimate of humanity than is always granted to the Occidental, declines to admit that so great a distinction as is often believed exists between the wage slaves of the West and the family slaves of the East.

The attitude of master and slave in Nepal strongly resembled—for the past tense is already justified—that which existed in the better-class country residences of the Southern States of America before the war of liberation. The slave was in many respects treated as a member of the family, and much liberty was granted to him should he prove able to advantage both himself and his master by skill in any particular trade or craft. However successful the slave might become, he rarely took advantage of any opportunity of separating his connection with the family of his master. It will perhaps surprise some who hold conventional opinions on this matter that not infrequently the slave who had made better use of his talents than his master, acted of his own free will as the bread-winner after any legal connection had been terminated. He was sometimes even appointed as guardian when the owner was a minor. The Nepalese did not, except in such rare cases as may be found in any civilization, ill-treat their slaves. It may be said that this is due merely to a wish not to injure their own property; but at least it introduced a pleasant incentive to kindly relations between the two, which in general tended to make the life of the slave a more tolerable existence than that of many a hard-driven and desperate worker in a nominally free country.

Jang Bahadur was the first who attempted to reform the old system. He made a law forbidding any free person to sell himself into slavery and making it illegal for a parent to dispose of his children. He also—moved no doubt rather by a laudable wish o get his new and rich Tarai soil cultivated than by any consideration of the feelings of the slave—ordered that no slave who had run away from his master and had settled in the districts of Naya Muluk and Morung should be returned to his owner. Neither of these enactments was of much use. It was found impossible to prevent men from selling themselves and their children when in desperation, and it is perhaps a pleasant commentary upon the system of slavery in Nepal that scarcely any runaways were willing to exchange the comfortable slavery of the uplands for the unhealthy liberty of the Tarai. Maharaja Deva Sham Sher made the first attempt to abolish slavery on any large scale. He issued a proclamation that the female slaves of Kaski and Lamjang, the two large estates attached to the office of Prime Minister, were free women. But he had reckoned without taking into consideration the inherent difficulties of interfering with any ancient vested interest. The scheme pleased no one. The old regime offered an absolute and flat refusal from the very beginning. Those who, owing perhaps to their official position, were compelled to make some show of deference to the order, retained their slaves under another name. Even among these owners there were but one hundred nominal liberations in the whole of Katmandu, where he subsequently issued a similar proclamation.

Chandra Sham Sher, however, has taken a characteristic line on the matter. His first action was to see that the nominal reforms of Jang Bahadur, prohibiting the inclusion in the ranks of slavery of any man or woman who was not born into it, were rigidly enforced. His next step was to make it impossible for any sale of slaves to take place without a due publication to their relatives of their right of pre-emption. Nor was the sum to be paid fixed by the arbitrary decision of the slave owners. For a payment varying from 25 to 120 rupees any slave might claim the right to his freedom should there be any attempt on the part of his master to dispose of him to another. The Maharaja also issued an order for the immediate freeing of all slaves that came into the possession of the Government by course of law. Thus, where a man was punished by confiscation of his property, his slaves, coming into the possession of the Government, were at once liberated. Nor was this all. Two enactments were published inviting any slave to become a free settler in a third and healthier district in the Tarai, that of Chitawan. No man had the right to prevent any slave of his who accepted the offer of the Government from taking up this work and his liberty at the same moment. An even more important order referred to slaves who had run away into India. In old days they had no chance of returning without being made to forfeit not merely an exorbitant ransom from their old masters, but probably also the entire amount of their earnings in India during the period of their absence. The new law compelled a master to accept from any slave who had been a runaway for the space of three years in any foreign country, the same small redemption fee as that which, as we have seen, could secure the freedom of any slave whom his master attempted to get rid of. If a slave remained a fugitive for a period of ten years he would return to Nepal as a free man without payment of any ransom whatever. These orders did more than merely offer freedom on liberal terms to a large number of individuals. By accustoming the Nepalese to take up a new and more civilized point of view they struck at the heart of the practice.

Within our own Empire the work has to go on slowly, though the field is now narrowed to but one or two districts, and the effective liberation of all slaves in the remotest quarters of our territory is already in sight.[1] With

[1] Arrangements have now been made for the release of nearly all of the slaves in the Hukwang Valley, in accordance with the arrangements made by the official expedition sent there in 1925. The owners are well satisfied with the prices offered for the redemption of the captives, many of whom are remaining with their masters, to whom they have become attached. It is hoped that the expedition will convince the Naga Chiefs of the Government's determination to stamp out slavery and human sacrifices.

a stroke of the pen we abolished slavery from all land under our administration in India, but we have never taken upon ourselves to criticize the retention of a certain form of humane slavery in such a country as Nepal where religion, tradition, and even national prosperity were largely responsible for its toleration. But the Maharaja has long been aware that the continued existence of thraldom in any form was inconsistent with the standards that he had set up for himself and for Nepal. Under date 28th December 1924 he wrote to me as follows: " You will be interested to hear of the bold attempt I have lately made to see slavery totally abolished in my country. For years past I have been directing my efforts to this end, commencing with the passing of laws at various times calculated to improve the lot of slaves and reduce the distinction between them and free men. I thought that the time was now ripe. Accordingly in an open-air meeting which was convened at Tundi Khel a few days before my departure from Katmandu, I made an earnest appeal to my countrymen to come to my support. . . . With the influence I have been and am trying to bring to bear on the question, the majority of views so far received has been in my favour, and I look forward to the day, which I earnestly hope will not now be many months off, when, by God's grace, I shall have the supreme satisfaction of witnessing the fulfilment of my long cherished desire to see, not only the inhuman practice inherent in the institution stopped, but also the legal status of slavery totally abolished throughout the kingdom."

What had happened was that on Friday 28th November 1924 the Prime Minister issued a reasoned appeal to the people of Nepal, in which he dealt with every aspect of slavery as it affected either the reputation for humanity, the sense of justice, or the economic position of his country. It will be useful to give in brief form the substance of this interesting contribution to the study of slavery, written by one of the most detached and disinterested as well as far-sighted observers. The Maharaja recognized that in this matter the civilized world was still reserving judgment upon a race that had come much more to the front than it had ever come before; and he recognized that that fact alone should be an incentive to his countrymen to maintain and increase their reputation as a brave, just, and humane people. He admitted the force of custom, but when customs become effete, he said, they must either be discarded or must yield place to others more vigorous, and he asserted in unhesitating words that the learned and religious authorities of Nepal sanctioned the abolition of slavery. " If such a custom is definitely prejudicial to the best interests of the people, the community, and the country, it is incumbent on us to change or abolish it forthwith for the common good."

A vivid picture is then drawn of the dreary and disheartening life of a slave deprived in childhood of the caresses and sympathies of his parents, and in later years a bitter observer of the distinction that marks him out from his fellow-workers, the hired men of the neighbourhood who have the right to " wear the dignity of labour as a diadem." The Maharaja readily admitted that there were households in which elderly slaves presided over family deliberations, and in practice directed family affairs during the minority of the heir; that in many households in the hills the business was managed by slaves during the absence of the owner; and that many kindly masters had, except for certain legal restrictions, practically abolished the distinction between themselves and their slaves. But on the other hand he pointed out that the law which he had himself promulgated in 1921, giving the right of ownership of property and devolution by succession to slaves, had been so far a dead letter. " How could it have been otherwise, seeing the time of the slave is wholly his master's? How can the slave find time to earn a stake in the country? You allow him to marry, but at any moment parents and children may be separated at the convenience of their master."

Dealing with the economic aspect of slavery, the Maharaja uses a vivid illustration to show the difference in the quantity of work done by slaves and that of free men. " The incentive to forced labour was the lash. Slaves, while they work, look behind to protect their back, while a free man labours looking forward to his hire, which he knows will be proportional to his work, and upon which rests his hope of provision for his family and himself." Another contrast between the work of the two classes appears in this well thought-out argument: A slave cannot be dismissed, his sustenance is assured to him whether he is slow or quick over his job, whether he is skilful or slovenly; he can never have the incentive of the free man. Experience gained in other countries proves that where servile labour is exacted with all the brutal means at a master's command, a free labourer is three times more efficient than a slave. Freely admitting that the Nepalese do not ill-treat slaves, the Maharaja estimates that among them one hired man is still about equal to two slaves. Turning to another aspect of the question, he reminded his hearers that at some time or other, generally always, all slave owners have to maintain unproductive hands—the old, the ill, the infirm, the mother, and the young; and there is always the risk of loss by death or desertion. Moreover, from a financial point of view, an employer has not to pay a lump sum down for hired labour as he has to do when purchasing slaves; his capital is free.

The expense of *bani*, or contracted labour, is contrasted in this treatise with that of slave labour, and the same result is arrived at—the hired labourer produces about twice the work of slave labour at the same cost. And the Maharaja adds the comment that the liberation of slaves in Nepal will in itself supply the *bani* servants that will be needed when this reform is carried through. His Highness did not depend upon mere oratory to press home his great intention. He deals directly with what he regards as the intolerable outrage of the sale of the children of slaves. As he says, " This inhuman practice is beyond all condemnation, and is rightly looked upon as the worst feature of the institution "—though he doubts whether there are not actually lower depths of infamy. The law in Nepal provides that the father of any child by a slave girl shall have the right to emancipate the child by payment of the legal amount of 35 rupees to the master of the girl. The framer of the enactment had trusted that the feelings of a father would be strong enough to compel him to act in such a case, but the hope had been vain. Nay, the Maharaja went on to say, it had been found, difficult though it was to believe, that certain masters, knowing that if the children of his women slaves were his own they would be automatically set free under the law, devised the inhuman practice of compelling the wretched women to submit to the embraces of any casual man who was known to be too poor to redeem the child—" and all this in a country where matrimonial relations are held so sacred under the laws that a wronged husband is allowed to impose a most severe and humiliating punishment upon the adulterer." It had become clear to him that a system which permitted of this abominable tyranny must be put an end to, and that soon. Then he turned to a curious side of the question—but a side which will be understood in all countries where there is an old tradition of aristocracy. Slaves were often white elephants to their owners, but family honour compelled each successive generation, whether it could afford it or not, to maintain the number of slaves that had been handed down to it by its forefathers; as a result the family estate had often to be mortgaged, or even handed over to the profit of the slaves themselves. But he admits that such families generally treat their slaves with unusual humanity.

One case, adduced by the Prime Minister, in which the system of slavery had resulted in intolerable cruelty, may be quoted:

" The mother, a slave, had given birth to seven children, and her master, despite her protests and tearful prayers, had already disposed of one daughter and four sons by sale. The woman in her petition through the Niksari Office wrote that the bitter lament of the children at thus being forced to separate from their mother sent a pang through her heart more acute than any she had ever suffered; that she summoned resignation to bear the misfortune and drew consolation from what was left her; that she submitted to it as the work of that fatality, the result of the accumulated *karma* of her previous births, which had followed her like a shadow to her present existence; but that when to her dismay the hard-hearted master arranged to take away the baby slave that was still suckling at her breast, her endurance broke down completely. She supplicated and prayed—as parents do pray, as you and I pray to the Gods on high when the dearest of our children lies in the clutches of grim death—to her master, the arbiter of her destiny, and to her as omnipotent in this crisis as fell Death himself. But all to no purpose. The adamant heart did not melt; the master completed the transaction. Then, maddened at a treatment which, is resented even by irrational beasts, she came all the way to see if the Maharaja, ' the common father of all people,' could do aught to allay the consuming sorrow at her breast. As this was so different from the ordinary run of complaints, the people concerned were sent for, and the matter on investigation turned out to be true to the letter of the petition; the child had been sold by a regular deed, the Parambhatta. The master was asked if he did not feel pity for the poor woman, though a slave; what would have been the feelings of himself or the mother of his children if such an infant of theirs were either forcibly taken away or sold elsewhere? What reply could he make to his Creator when summoned to His presence to answer this charge of inhumanity? He replied, and the purchasers replied, that that was the custom in the hills, and the law did not forbid it. Now what does it mean to us all? That so long as we permit this sort of thing every one of us must bear a part in the sin, must share the curse of the weeping mothers, inasmuch as we tolerate the custom and uphold such laws. The poor woman was given the wherewithal to free her sold children according to the law which provides that on the sale of slaves their kith and kin or those interested can liberate them on payment of the legal amounts to their masters."

The Maharaja then dealt with the general question of the possibility of an exodus of Nepalese freed men into India. He regarded it as improbable, and pointed out that it was the escaped slave who fell most easily. into the hands of unscrupulous labour-agents across the border, giving as an example the intervention of the Indian Government in a recently exposed case of press-gang labour in a colliery in Assam.[1] Naturally, a careful distinction was drawn by him between such servitude and the lot of Nepalese who take the opportunity to enlist in the Gurkha battalions of the Indian army and thus enjoy the steady guarantees of fair recompense and happiness offered by the Indian Government.

It is to be noted that the institution of slavery prevails in the hills only. This is probably due to the fact that,. in the Tarai and in the larger towns on the southern foot-hills of the Himalayas, means can usually be devised for a slave to break away into British territory. A curious estimate is here given of the very small number of owners and slaves in Nepal compared with the population of the country. There are 15,719 owners of slaves, and the number held in slavery is 51,419. The total population of the

[1] He notes the ignorance of the 1921 law that still denied to slaves the rights they then acquired. Any slave who had been resident abroad for three 'years was thereby given the right to emancipation on payment of the fixed dues to his late master; one who had been abroad for ten years was emancipated on demand without the payment of any dues.

country is estimated at about 5,573,788, and therefore 5,506,650—or nearly 99 per cent. of the population—are neither slaves nor slave-owners. " Now if 99 per cent. can carry on their everyday work as employees or employers without slaves, it is curious that the masters, who are a little over a quarter of the one per cent. remaining, should feel abolition as a hardship and be under the apprehension that their everyday work will come to a standstill."

With a wide knowledge of the experience of other countries at the time of a general liberation of slaves, the Maharaja pointed out that even in the comparatively inconspicuous matter of the necessity for the existence of slaves to do certain ritual in marriage and other ceremonies, other slave countries have suffered no trouble whatever from this cause. Indeed, it was too often forgotten that the liberated slaves must at once turn round and look for remunerative work by which to keep themselves and their families; they cannot afford to refuse any work that is fairly paid.

He noted also that, from the religious point of view, India herself has seen many changes in the traditional allotment of occupations. " Consider all honest work as dignified, and you will not lose in self-esteem."[1] What had really brought the question to the front more than anything else had been the spread of education. Slavery is doomed by the spread of knowledge; its abolition is merely a question of time. " Then why not anticipate what you cannot prevent, when by doing so you can cut your losses and become the pioneers of a patriotic and humanitarian movement in the country."

The appeal continued by a reference to the abolition of the custom of sati, a practice which was more intimately connected with religion than is slavery. In 1920 sati, in spite of the protests of an apprehensive minority, was definitely and resolutely forbidden by the Nepalese Government, and the Prime Minister challenged his critics to tell him what unwelcome results have followed this abolition. He clinched a forcible appeal by reference to the fact that large and increasing numbers of Nepalese living in Sikkim, Darjiling, and the adjacent hill tracts under almost identical conditions with those that prevail in Nepal, can manage without slaves.

" We alone labour under the incubus, when even countries known in the past as uncivilized have become free from it. . . . It is fervently hoped that the unanimous opinion of this assembly, representative of the best in the land, will be that this inhuman, barbarous, immoral, and worthless custom shall be put to an end."

The Maharaja then proceeded to state the practical steps that he considers necessary. The clauses of the new law are but three in number:

1. On and from a certain date, to be fixed as early as possible, in

---

[1] As early as 1839 the Nepalese Government had forbidden the enslavement of any free man, woman, or child belonging to the four castes and the thirty-six sub-castes.

consonance with general opinion, the legal status of slavery shall cease and terminate throughout the kingdom of Nepal.

2. Owners shall be given the statutory price for every slave held by them, according to the register, that is over whom their claim has been fully established.

3. Slaves freed from the fixed date shall be apprenticed to their former owners for a period of seven years: that is, the slaves shall be bound to labour for their masters, the latter in return providing them with food and clothing as at present.

During those seven years the money paid by the Government for each slave, if invested at 10 per cent. compound interest—which is a moderate rate of interest in Nepal—would be practically doubled, while at the "usually prevailing rate of interest at 16 per cent." it would be nearly trebled.

The *Pioneer* of 29th August 1926 states that the Nepal slave liberation scheme has been completed at a cost of 3,670,000 rupees (£275,250), an average of 70 rupees (five guineas) per slave, the total liberated with compensation by the Government being 51,782. Four thousand six hundred and fifty-one slaves were liberated by their masters without compensation; 1,984 died; 1,342 fled; 114 paid for their own release, thus accounting for the total slave population of 59,873.

The rates paid in compensation ranged from 20 rupees for a female and 15 rupees for a male under 3 years of age, to 100 rupees for a female and 75 rupees for a male between the age of 13 and 40. Prices after the age of 40 dropped to 50 rupees for a female and 30 rupees for a male under the age of 60, 41 rupees for a female and 31 rupees for a male over 60 years old. The Anti-Slavery Office actually started work early in 1925. The Prime Minister of Nepal, Sir Chandra Sham Sher Jang, who recently celebrated his sixty-fourth birthday, has thus been able to redeem the pledge he made to the world and realize one of the dreams of his life.

Tracts of cultivable land have been thrown open to the emancipated slaves in the hills, and reclamation and clearance works have been started in the Tarai, suitable advances of cash being made to the freed men by reclamation and agricultural offices. A remarkable feature in the successful execution of a scheme which took its origin in the Anti-Slavery laws passed in 1920 and, particularly, in the historic speech of the Prime Minister in November 1924, when he appealed to his countrymen to abolish a practice, on which rested the curse of God, is the extent to which the owners have co-operated. Out of 15,719 owners, only 467 desired the retention of slavery; 179 desired the emancipation of slaves under nine years of age; 1,281 volunteered to release their slaves without compensation; while only 498 demanded a higher rate of compensation than that given.

It is not for Europeans, to whom slavery has long been unknown, to criticize the precise form in which this great enfranchisement is to take place. The readiness is all; details concern Nepal and not the outer world, which is content to know that even as these lines are being written Nepal has wiped away the last miserable symbol of an old regime, and in this, the first of all human duties, can stand forward as in all respects the equal of her sister sovereign States.[1]

§ 4

Sati.—Chandra's reference to the abolition of sati needs a few words of comment. It will not be a matter of surprise that in Nepal, which represents better than any other existing district the law and custom of mediaeval India, great difficulty was found in an attempt to obliterate this ancient and evil custom. Before Jang· Bahadur's day the burning alive of a widow upon her husband's funeral pile was commonly practised in Nepal. It had been abolished in India by Lord William Bentinck in Council on the 4th December 1829, but naturally it was long before the practice itself was entirely stamped out, so deeply had it been identified with religious duty or, in some cases, family jealousy, in the minds of the people.[2] Jang Bahadur thought it must stop, and he issued instructions that in no case in which the widow was performing or was likely to perform valuable services to her children, her husband's family, or the State, was she to be allowed to commit this honourable form of suicide. Bir Sham Sher carried the movement a step farther. He insisted that the consent of the Prime Minister himself or, in his absence, of the highest legal authority, should be obtained before any widow was permitted to immolate herself. This did not, however, have the effect that was intended. The whole weight of public opinion was so often brought to bear upon the woman that in many cases she was driven to make the great sacrifice before the cumbersome machinery of the law could be set in motion to protect her. Not the least of the claims to the respect of the world that Chandra Sham Sher possesses is that on the 28th June 1920 he absolutely and completely abolished the whole practice of sati from one end of Nepal to the other. It is a tribute to his personal ascendancy that he should have been successful in thus " changing the squares of obsolete tradition into the circles of civilized enlightenment." With orthodoxy he has every sympathy; with bigotry he has none.

[1] It was natural that the congratulations of India, should have been universal and chalorous. It was not only in the peninsula that this recognition was forthcoming. When in 1926 the Maharaja succeeded in his object and was enabled to declare definitely and finally the freedom of every Nepalese subject, the abolition of slavery was noted with respect by all the more prominent newspapers in the world.

[2] The success which attended this order in India stands on record as one of the rare instances of a salutary meddling on the part of the Christian stranger with one of the most sacred rites inculcated by the religion of a country.

So far from attempting to interfere with the religious establishments of Nepal, the Maharaja has added largely to the stability of the Brahmans, and their chiefs the Gurujis have wealth, dignity, and an inviolate position, and it is interesting to notice the extent of the Maharaja's endowments in support of religious philanthropy and learning. Chandra has established an ecclesiastical commission, of which the prime duty is to see not only that all moneys and lands left to insure the performance of religious rites or instruction shall be held in trust for the Church, but that they shall be enjoyed only by a strict performance of the attached conditions. His

PEDESTAL AWAITING CHANDRA'S STATUE

personal generosity is famous. He has extended and organized the charitable institutions dependent upon various shrines of Nepal: he has arranged for the free supply of food at several of the more important places of pilgrimage: he has given houses and lands of great value to the Brahman community, and on special occasions he has distributed as many as one hundred cows among the poorer of this caste.[1]

[1] He has often presented both horses and—perhaps a more doubtful advantage— elephants to deserving persons, and twenty-seven poor people are fed daily at his palace gates. Nor has he despised the maintenance of one of the oldest traditions of India. On one occasion of Suvarna Tuladan he was weighed against gold. It took sixty-seven and a half seers (about one hundred and forty-five pounds) of gold to weigh down His Highness, and the whole of this was then distributed among the poor and destitute. Eight times also has the Maharaja performed the costly ceremony of Koti Homa. This

He has endowed the pilgrim roads from the plains of India, and the cardinal Hindu shrines—the Golden Temple at Benares, and those of Jagannath at Puri, of Ramanath at Rameshwaram, of Krishna at Dwarka, and the Kedernath temple in Garhwal—have all known his generosity. Except in the case of the shrine of Krishna at Dwarka each of these endowments has followed and put on record a personal pilgrimage to the place.

§ 5

Judicial System.—The Gurkha conquest of 1768 brought about the assimilation of local customs into the general law, but no attempt whatever was made to codify the judicial custom of the country until the days of Jang Bahadur, when an endeavour was made that did not greatly clarify the administration of this tangled system. Another effort was made by Bir Sham Sher, but it was left for the present Maharaja to revise the whole code on two occasions. The first aimed at the identification of the law in all parts of Nepal, while the second, besides carrying on this work, mitigated the severity of the punishments to be inflicted. Jang Bahadur had abolished the punishment of mutilation, but other undesirable features remained. For example, in the case of those of high social position the punishment incurred by the noble delinquent was frequently inflicted vicariously upon his agent or representative; there was no statute of limitations; to a large extent no distinction was made between criminal and civil offences. Moreover a prosecutor was able to have his case called by any court, provincial or superior, that seemed advantageous to himself.

The improvements recently enforced by the Nepal Government have humanized the administration of justice without weakening its authority. The code has been thoroughly revised. The hardships that have been referred to have been remitted and the law's delays have been largely curtailed. Chandra is, however, not satisfied with the improvements he has already effected and a third revision is now in progress. He is himself the official court of appeal and exercises the prerogative of mercy in every case in which it seems to him that equity demands its employment.[1]

is one of the holiest of Hindu ceremonies, and the religious merit thereby acquired is exceeded by no other exercise of that faith. One crore, or ten million prayers, and the same number of offerings of grain have to be made in the course of this rite, which lasts for about a month and a half.

[1] A curious point may be noted, that the Nepalese have a superstitious repugnance to being put in irons, not so much because it cramps their liberty, but because of the tradition that to be bound by anything made of iron brings about inevitable disaster to the sufferer. A change has therefore been made in the law, by which prisoners for civil offences are not put in chains during their imprisonment. To this privilege, however, an exception is made in the case of Government servants sentenced for embezzlement or bribery, and escaped prisoners.

Not less important is the accessibility of the new code. Printed copies are to be consulted at all magistrates' offices and can be bought for a low price, thus bringing it within the reach of rich and poor alike. Formerly only the courts and Government officials could consult it, and in consequence the mass of the people remained in ignorance of the law, unable to know in many cases when they stood in danger of breaking it, or what their rights were against a trespasser; they were largely at the mercy of unscrupulous men and unevenly administered justice. In the new code a careful distinction is attempted to be drawn between offences against the State or the person or property, and those which are transgressions of the religious ordinances of the people. But, as may be imagined, religious sentiment plays no small part in the first section also. For example, an injury done to a parent or a guru (spiritual adviser) is punished fifty per cent. more severely than a similar hurt done to a stranger. I have noted before that no missionary is permitted to enter the country. It is actually a penal offence to assist in the conversion of any man to a foreign religion.

As may be imagined in a land where polygamy is practised the matrimonial law is of an extremely complicated and special nature. Here, too, religion plays a large part. The law leans heavily against any marriage of a woman of a higher caste to a man of lower rank. In certain cases such an alliance is a serious misdemeanour and the punishment inflicted is greater in proportion to the difference in caste. A curious custom—and one for which the Nepal system is perhaps best known—is that by which an outraged husband held the right of killing the adulterer at any moment whenever and wherever he found him, subject to the curious right of the latter to be given a few minutes' start in a life and death race, the husband being permitted to carry a sword and cut down his injurer—who, of course, was unarmed—should he overtake him.[1] The curious point about this custom was that either man could be freely impeded or tripped up by the friends of the other. So iniquitous a tradition is now practically obsolete. but the husband has nominally the right of insisting upon this curious test, though he is allowed to put it in practice only after the matter has been submitted to the Prime Minister and all attempts at compromise have failed. Where the offender is a Brahman no such right exists, of course, but he is, after conviction, permanently expelled from his caste.

In certain sections of the community the marriage of widows is permitted and the marriage also of such as have been divorced. The essential difference of standpoint in matrimonial affairs that exists between the Western nations and these austere devotees of Hinduism could not be

---

[1] The adulterer might escape, however, if he publicly crawled beneath the raised leg of the offended husband. But, as may be imagined in a proud race like the Gurkhas, few availed themselves of this dishonourable expedient, which involved a social ostracism equal to actual outcasting—from which, too, there were no means of obtaining purification.

better illustrated than in the wholly different standards which regulate public opinion in this matter. From a European point of view it would perhaps be just to regard some of the older tendencies of much of the habit and custom of Nepal as due to religious prejudice and tradition rather than to any natural callousness. Child marriage was, and still is, common among Brahmans and the higher classes; though of course a child married at a tender age remains with his or her mother until of sufficient years to live with the child partner. Torture has long been abolished. The observance of the prohibitions of the Hindu religious law is supported by the State. The dining together of high and low castes, the eating of forbidden food, and other similar things are offences calling for special reference in the Nepal code. But it is only fair to say that in such cases extenuating circumstances are usually pleaded and readily listened to. The religious law dictates also the provisions dealing with inheritance and succession. In the latter case the complicated regulations of the code are still further tangled by the admission of local custom.[1] Male relations within three degrees of consanguinity inherit in preference to daughters; children in lawful wedlock take a larger share of the property than others; children of different wives take *per capita* and not as representatives of their mother; unmarried daughters have a lien on the joint property to the extent of their dower. As may be imagined, the partition of an ancestral estate in Nepal frequently gives rise to much discontent and litigation.

§ 6

The Justiciary.—It is not necessary to refer at length to the obsolete system by which four central courts or adalats—named respectively Itachapli, Koteling, Taksar, and Dhansar—were established to which were allotted particular jurisdictions without much regard to the similarities of their natures. Over them was the Adalat Goswara, a supreme court of appeal. In all of these tribunals the civil and criminal jurisdictions overlapped, and so much of the legal rights of Nepal depended upon local custom that assessors were frequently called in to assist the judges. In cases in which great difficulty was found in deciding a case, the court would sometimes order a trial by ordeal, an account of which has been given.[2]

The first action of Maharaja Chandra was to abolish the Taksar and Dhansar courts and to make a distinction between civil and criminal

---

[1] Of all the local customs of Nepal the strangest was that of the people of Doti, who for centuries enjoyed the occupation of State lands on condition that all the women of their families became prostitutes and were at the service of the troops quartered there. No Prime Minister had dared interfere with this ancient and dishonourable custom before the present Maharaja, who put an end to it in 1905.

[2] See vol. i, chapter v.

jurisdiction. The Adalat Diwani Koteling dealt with civil cases and the Fuzdari Adalat Itachapli with the latter. The principle was also established of separating the judicial work from the duty of carrying into effect the decisions of the court.

In 1906 a Bharadari court of from five to ten Bharadars—the officials of the State—or men of high position was created; and in 1908 the appellate jurisdiction was reformed. The new tribunal became the court of appeal from the decisions of the two Sadar courts just referred to. These latter, besides being courts of first instance, had previously acted as courts of appeal from the decisions of the provincial magistrates of the Gunda courts in the hills and the Goswara courts in the Tarai. This appellate jurisdiction was now taken from them and given to the Appeal Court.

This clearance of the wells of justice brought about an increase of litigation. It was found that the judicial work multiplied to such an extent that the Diwani Adalat was ultimately divided into four courts, while the criminal court was divided into two. In 1921 a new change was made. The possibility of appeal invited the litigious nature of the Nepalese. The appellate court gave place to a new form of an ancient Bharadari court of appeal. The English custom does not permit fresh evidence to be brought up on appeal. Where, in its opinion, the case has been wrongly conducted an order for a new trial is made. In Nepal, when fresh evidence is procurable, the court of appeal admits it, and may even consider issues not laid before the lower court. The overcrowding of the appeal courts of all kinds is due to the determination of litigants to have serious cases brought ultimately before the immediate consideration of the Prime Minister himself, in whom, as in all other matters, the final judicial authority is vested.

The following, therefore, is the present system of judicial administration in Nepal. One of the four Diwani courts above mentioned has been transformed into a Court of Registration, and does not deal with litigation. The remaining tribunals are known as the First, Second, and Third Diwani Courts. There is no limit to their civil jurisdiction, but an appeal lies against their decisions to the Bharadari court. The First and Second Fuzdari Courts decide criminal cases of all natures except those which the Sadar Jangi Kotwali, or court-martial, and the Thana[1] is empowered to deal with. It is to be noted that the latter has special powers to decide charges of sedition or of creating disaffection against the King or Prime

---

[1] The Thana is the police court executing the direct orders of the Maharaja. It deals also with cases of defamation, gambling, counterfeiting, adulteration of food, violation of the law of preserved forests, kidnapping, etc. Its authority to deal with cases of attempted conversion of the King's subjects to Christianity, Islam, or any other foreign religion, is practically of less importance than its direct subordination to the Prime Minister in matters affecting the stability of the existing Government.

Minister. Besides these there is the Amini Goswara Court [1] to deal with the reports of the courts of the Tarai, over which the Foreign Office has control. The Bharadari or main appellate court has lately been reconstituted. It is presided over by a general officer who must be a near relation of the Maharaja. There are four departments under four Hakims, who have certain powers of their own, but whose main duty it is to prepare and present the case before one of two benches, each of eight or more judges. The result is that minor appeals, dealing with sums below five hundred rupees, are considered respectively by the Hakims, one of the benches, the General—and finally by the Commander-in-Chief. The Prime Minister may only be approached in criminal cases in which the fine amounts to more than two hundred rupees or imprisonment of over six months and, civilly, in real estate cases concerned with land of more than five bighas or ropnis in extent. The appellate jurisdiction of the Prime Minister is administered in the following way. Petitions from suitors are first scrutinized in the Niksari court where the appeal from the Bharadari court is received. The Niksari judges are drawn from very high families, Generals or Commanding Colonels, the Chiefs of the subordinate principalities of Nepal, the family of the Raj Guru, and a group of men of long experience in law and practice. The Niksari office has the power to decide cases concerned with sums up to two thousand rupees or sentences up to nine years imprisonment, or fines up to four hundred rupees, or disputes about land up to twenty bighas in area. Above these limits an appeal must lie with the Prime Minister himself.

Besides dealing with these appeals, the Niksari office has a department which deals with petitions to the Prime Minister and is the means by which his Highness's equitable decisions in matters not provided for in common law are published. Last but not least, it acts as the Prime Minister's almonry through which in any case of great hardship he is able to come to the help of those suffering from the oppression of the official or the wealthy.[2]

The provincial courts deal with criminal as well as civil cases. Appeal lies from all their decisions, and the graver matters such as murder or sedition cannot be dealt with by them until reference to the Maharaja has been made and his confirmation obtained. Of these provincial courts there are twenty-eight Adalat courts in the hills and twenty-two Amini courts in the plains or the Tarai. Besides these there are in the hills ten Gundas and eight Goswaras composed of responsible military officers. Their chief duty is to see that justice is neither denied nor delayed in the provincial courts. Four of them are courts of First Appeal. Nine similar

---

[1] The Amini Courts are held in the Tarai, and they deal generally with cases in which one or both of the parties is a foreigner.

[2] Reference to this patriarchal dispensation of final equity by the Maharaja is made in chapter xiv, p. 94.

courts exist in the Tarai where the chief officers are styled Bada Hakims. There is also a Goswara court in the Tarai, serving as a court of First Appeal similar to that existing in the hills. The duties of the officers of this court are of similar nature to those of a Commissioner of a district in British India.

The Maharaja is well aware of the inconvenience of a system which, though it brings a fair trial within the reach of all, seems to indulge the natural litigiousness of his people. It is believed that he is now considering a revival of the village Panchayat in order to prevent frivolous and vexatious litigation. But it is regarded as doubtful whether the Panchayat—which would perform a function similar to that of a Grand Jury in England— would not at times allow local popularity or local prejudice to defeat the ends of justice.

§ 7

Education.—The progress of Nepal in social and educational work has been, of course, affected by the same religious rules and traditions that have coloured its judicial system. When Dr. Wright compiled his book on Nepal in 1877 he summed up the question of popular education with the remark that the subject might be dismissed as briefly as that of snakes in Ireland. For a long time during the present Maharaja's administration he did not see his way to make any great improvement in the few existing opportunities of education which had been painfully inaugurated by his predecessor Rana Udip Singh, and by General Bir Sham Sher, who was perhaps more closely associated than any of his forerunners with the attempt to supply this cardinal need of civilization. Deva Sham Sher in his irresponsible way proclaimed a system of universal instruction— for which however he made no provision of money and no organization, so it fell still-born. One or two schools were indeed founded in Katmandu but they did not at first meet with much appreciation from the Nepalese. In fact, the first beginnings of education were looked upon with something of the mistrust with which the mediaeval church of Rome heard of the activity of scientists within her fold. We have seen that the present Maharaja began a new regime by sending some of the sons of the aristocracy to Japan in 1902. In the sense that he and he alone is responsible for every action of the Nepalese Government, the Prime Minister is absolute. But it has already been suggested that no one realizes the folly of too rapid an advance more than he. In permitting the spread of knowledge he found opposed to him the traditional obscurantism or at least the jealous exclusiveness of a religion which had its roots deep not only in the minds but in the hearts of his countrymen. It required patience and tact to overcome this opposition, and the expense of sending these young students to Japan was enormously increased by the precautions that had to be taken for the due observance in the least detail of caste regulations during the journey and their residence in Japan. Although this experiment could not be called a success, a certain amount of credit is due to the boys themselves for the gallant effort that was made by them to overcome the difficulty in which they were placed by their almost complete ignorance of the Japanese language. At the meeting of Bharadars in 1905, the Maharaja tentatively put before the responsible officials of Nepal a proposal that students should be sent to study in Europe or America. The council advised against this scheme and suggested that it would be better to invite the help of Indian experts. In general this policy has been adopted, and the youth of Nepal have been sent in large numbers into India to take advantage of the excellent facilities for higher education which are offered there. In 1919 the Government established an English college in Katmandu, which is attended by several hundred students, who make a fair showing in the matriculation examination of the Sanskrit college at Benares. In the report of the work done at the Government schools in Katmandu it is significant that in 1901 the number of new students admitted into the English department numbered seventeen, whereas eighteen years later they had increased to one hundred and forty-two. Many of the men matriculated here have passed on to study in secondary schools and universities in India.

There are now many primary schools throughout the country, but the results of this somewhat sporadic and ill-organized instruction are not satisfactory, and the Nepal Government is again taking the matter into its consideration. There is no more ardent advocate of education in Asia than the Prime Minister of Nepal. He sees that it is not merely an important, but that it is a vital, aid to any permanent progress, individual as well as national, and he has especially interested himself in the technical side of such instruction. He is under no delusion as to the wide field that still remains to be covered, but he has already laid a foundation and is determined that his successors, if not himself, shall be enabled to build upon a well thought-out structure of national education. The Nepal schools are affiliated to the University of Patna, and the gratitude of Nepal to the Governments of India and of Bihar and Orissa for the privilege thus extended has been freely expressed. The Prime Minister's words to the students on one occasion may be recorded as a fitting illustration of the attitude that the Nepal Government has taken up in the task of fitting their youth for their work and life as men.

" Remember my advice. Be loyal to the institution. Make it your pride to support its name and fame throughout the country. Do not, in the vanity of your acquirements, forget or belittle the superior claims that your country has upon you, and the reverence that is due to your religion and institutions. Mere proficiency in a foreign tongue gives you no advantage unless you apply it in acquiring useful knowledge. Neither such proficiency alone nor the foolish aping of foreign manners will do you good. You can make for yourselves an abiding place in the history of your country and in the grateful memory of your countrymen only by devoting yourselves to their service. Recollect that education does not come to an end with your days in school and college or with the passing of examinations, and bear in mind that it is not designed as a means only to Government employment. A man lives to learn; he is a student all his life through. He must have the same passionate love for work afterwards as he had for his studies here. To whatever work he is allotted, high or low, he must bring to bear upon it the same concentration and the same well disciplined mind, the same honesty, the same integrity that should characterize him as a student. Do not feel downhearted if you are dull; patience and perseverance overcome all difficulties. If you are clever, do not shirk application, without which no one can ever acquire solid and sound education. Above all, learn to look upon knowledge as a prize in itself to illumine your path all through life."

§ 8

Social Reform.—In the wide field of social reform the same reactionary tendencies of such an inflexible faith as Hinduism are visible. A household in Europe would be appalled at the unremunerative expense which a Hindu will voluntarily incur on such an occasion as the marriage of a daughter; indeed, it is scarcely too much to say that the majority of the debt-bound workers in India have owed their first servitude to money borrowed for this purpose at ruinous rates of interest. Quietly and without drawing attention to his example the Prime Minister has set the fashion for a general reduction in the useless expenses of daily life, and through the Maharani he has been successful in replacing the costly and cumbersome gowns worn lately by ladies of the better classes by dresses of simpler materials and more sensible fashion.

From the first days of his rule there was a grave national fault for him to tackle. He found his efforts for the public weal impeded and hampered by the tendency of the Nepalese people as a nation to drink. Very sensibly he took no crude step towards prohibition. First of all he saw to it that, if his fellow countrymen must drink ardent spirits, those spirits should be the best and most wholesome that could be manufactured. Then the number of liquor shops was greatly reduced. The temptations offered along the main thoroughfares of the Valley and indeed throughout Nepal have been dealt with with fairness and firmness, and the exclusion of foreign-made liquor has marked another step on the road that has guided his people to sobriety. Such handling of a dangerous tendency was more effective than any Draconian legislation. Lastly, no liquor may be sold at any of the fairs and festivals held at the different holy places in the kingdom. Drunkenness is not unknown in the Valley, but I do not myself remember ever having seen any one who could be said to be disorderly or indeed noticeably under the influence of alcohol.

Opium is forbidden except under licence, and the poppy has practically been banished from the Tarai. A more difficult vice to deal with is gambling, for the Nepalese seem both by nature and tradition to be specially addicted to this insidious pastime. In general, gambling in public is forbidden, but an explicit permission to be found in the Shastras has prevented the laws of Nepal from prohibiting public gambling on certain festivals.[1] Much remains to be done in this matter, but the Maharaja has made a start by prohibiting any credit to be extended to the loser. Cash must be paid on the spot. It may be interesting to note that the gambling generally takes the form of playing with cowry shells. Sixteen of them, of equal size, are chosen, and the respective number that fall face up or face down determine the winner among the four parties concerned, each of whom is allotted one set of combinations out of the following four. Thus A takes the pool if one, five, nine, or thirteen shells fall face upwards; B wins should the number be either two, six, ten, or fourteen; C is given three, seven, eleven, and fifteen, and D stakes his chances upon four, eight, twelve, and sixteen. The game seems simple, apparently free from any possibility either of cheating or of the display of skill.

Personally the Maharaja is a Hindu of the strictest sect, not only by blood, but by instinct, training, and experience. Never in the course of his government has he failed to respect a genuine tenet of the Hindu religion, but for the abuses which are the inevitable parasites of every faith he has no sympathy. He has intervened sternly to put an end to the malversion of religious endowments. The Nepalese may now be assured that money left or given for any religious purpose will be employed for that purpose and for nothing else. A curious instance of his activity may be found in his rigorous overhauling of abuse in Janakpur—a place renowned as the birthplace of Sita, the luckless and maligned bride of Rama. A strict examination of the way in which the large funds of the shrines there were employed resulted in the discovery of a surplus, hitherto enjoyed by the Mohants, which has proved sufficient to feed and clothe one hundred and ninety-two poor men and, in addition, to maintain and educate one hundred and sixty-two students.

After consultation with the spiritual head of Nepal an end has practically been put to the bad old custom that compelled any man who crossed the frontier into India for military service, or any other purpose, to go through the " Patia ceremony " on his return. It was obvious that a journey to a

[1] During the Dewali and the Dasahra ancient custom permits universal gambling which is for the rest of the year sternly discountenanced.

neighbouring country more endowed with holy shrines than even Nepal itself, could not reasonably be regarded as a defilement. The matter is now placed on another basis. A small rite and the payment of a nominal fee are all that is now required. It may be that even these are imposed rather to mark the unwillingness of Chandra that Nepalese should lightly leave their own country than as any recognition of the need of spiritual purification.[1]

Nor has the Maharaja been less energetic in his spread of medical assistance throughout the country. His brother, Maharaja Bir Sham Sher, had established a central hospital in Katmandu, but the remainder of the State was without any organized centre to deal with general illness and the occasional trouble caused by epidemics. One of the greatest difficulties that the reforms of the science of medicine encounter in India is the obstinate and natural preference of the natives for their own Ayurvedic system of medicine, that properly controlled contributes its fair share of success to the healing craft, but has no knowledge or sympathy with advanced methods of treatment discovered by modern science. Chandra, whose travels and perhaps whose personal indebtedness to modern medicine and surgery have convinced him of the necessity of incorporating the results of present-day knowledge in the pharmacopoeia of Nepal, has treated both schools with generosity. He has established twenty centres in the

---

[1] The gifts of Chandra have been very great indeed. Besides the feeding of Brahmans in multitudes, the gifts to them on certain occasions of one thousand cows, the dedication to their use of elephants and horses so tricked out as to symbolize the holy mountain of the gods, and the distribution of food to twenty-seven poor persons daily at his palace, there are other and special examples of his liberality. The Koti Homa is one of the holy ceremonies of Hinduism. It is performed by Brahmans and lasts for about six weeks. The essential part of this rite is the offering by the sacred caste of handfuls of different grains—rice, sesamum, and barley, kneaded together with melted butter—to the fire of sacrifice which is never allowed to die out throughout the entire period. Each Brahman has to recite the Gayatri once before he makes his offering. This continues until one crore or 10,000,000 of prayers and offerings have been made. Gifts are afterwards made to the officiating Brahmans. Chandra has provided eight such ceremonies up to the present year.

He has invested one lakh (100,000), the interest on which is used to provide food and conveyance to needy pilgrims on their way to the shrine of Pashpati during the Shivaratri festival. Naturally this assistance is given over the most difficult part of the road up from India, that between Bhimphedi and Katmandu. It goes perhaps without saying that Benares, the holiest of all the cities in India, should have received his assistance on several occasions. Among his titles is that of Bharat Dharma Dhurim, or Supporter of the Faith, bestowed by the Sacred Bharat Dharma Mahamandal, or Great Council of Benares.

Other funds intended to help impecunious members of his princely house and others of high birth reduced by no fault of their own to penury, have been founded by him. He has taken under his especial care the infants and foundlings among his people and has instituted a foundling hospital, with an important out-patient department for maternity cases.

country districts which will be in charge of young men now completing their course of education in India. The Ayurvedic school in Katmandu will be reinforced by a new academy under the charge of four trained doctors. In opening the hospital at Bhatgaon in 1904 the Maharaja noted the impossibility of far distant Nepal taking full advantage of recent developments in the healing art, but added that it would be much to be regretted if the fullest use was not made of such new light as modern science had thrown and their limited resources were able to employ. In the Tarai there exist several hospitals maintained by charity under the charge of physicians from Indian Universities, and the mountainous regions of Nepal have not been neglected.

A bacteriological department has been established in Katmandu and electrical treatment is provided in an annexe to the General Hospital. Vaccination is not compulsory, but it is free to those who choose to avail themselves of this protection against a disease that, though never attaining the gravity of an epidemic, is rarely entirely absent from Nepal.

The last public ceremonial which I am enabled to record in the pages of these volumes is that of the opening of the War Memorial Military Hospital on Thursday, 9th September 1926. Not only was the occasion remarkable as a memorial to the thousands of Nepalese who died in the Great War—all voluntary sacrifices upon the altar of civilization—but it has completed, in a manner that will be envied by the majority of military stations in India, one of the best equipped hospitals in Asia. In plan the hospital is of the most modern and improved design. It is shaped in the familiar fashion of two " E's " back to back, and each wing is capable of being isolated. It consists of three wards on the three floors, each complete in itself. There are six wards of eight beds each for soldiers ; twelve cabins with one bed each for officers; and one ward of four beds for isolation cases; there being sixty-four beds in all. The last improvements in the matter of ventilation, open-air treatment, ambulances, etc., are provided according to the latest pattern. Over £24,000 has been spent upon this notable memorial to those who lost their lives in the war. It is also endowed with an annual revenue of £15,000 which, according to present estimates, will meet the recurring annual expenses.

In the speech in which the engineer communicated to the meeting the above and many other statistics, he sums up in an interesting manner the material benefits that have been showered upon Nepal during the reign of the present Maharaja. He refers to canals, roads, rail and ropeways, hospitals and other civil buildings, bridges, waterworks, electrical installations, tube wells, and municipal undertakings going on here, there, and everywhere. He incidentally stated that the Ayurvedic School of Medical Thought was not to be neglected. Candidates were to receive at the best centres in India the ayurvedic training that is especially the development of Indian physicians. These men when fully trained would be sent to stations in the hills and the Tarai.

But the speech that more fittingly than any other concludes this survey of the recent developments of Nepal is that which the Maharaja himself delivered. In form it was addressed to the King, but Western civilization will recognize behind this scanty veil the feelings of the Prime Minister himself. On 26th June 1926 His Highness completed the twenty-fifth year of his administration of Nepal, and in a touching discourse he explained that the aim of his life would be achieved " if posterity credits me with having done my level best for the uplift of the country and the removal of the sufferings and miseries of the people." He concluded his brief speech with a new announcement with which the second half of what we may hope will prove his years of jubilee will be well begun. Seven lakhs of rupees have been set apart to combat tuberculosis. A sanatorium will shortly be erected. As an eternal memorial to Chandra's work in connection with this great hospital, it will for all time bear his name, and as the Tribhubana-Chandra Memorial Hospital it has started on its long career of usefulness.

CHAPTER XVII

MAHARAJA CHANDRA SHAM SHER

THE NEPALESE ARMY—PUBLIC WORKS, ROADS, AND BRIDGES—TENURE
OF LAND—CONCLUSION

"There is nothing that cannot be obtained by man. Everything can be
got, provided the necessary exertion is made."—MAHADEO.

§ 1. *The Army*

THERE is perhaps no military establishment in the world which
has been so rapidly and so efficiently reformed as the army in Nepal.
In 1885 the present Maharaja succeeded to the office of Senior
Commanding General, which in effect gave him the responsibility for the
upkeep, drill, and discipline of the army. In 1892, when acting on behalf
of his brother who was ill in Calcutta, it will be remembered that he obtained
from Lord Lansdowne a gift of modern rifles which may be said to have
poured a new life into the military vigour of the home forces of the Gurkhas.
But long before that, as Lord Roberts testified in the same year, the
drill of the troops under Chandra had been improved in a marked degree.
The somewhat casual methods of his predecessors were scrapped and a
new regime instituted. It was hard work, for in military matters as in
others there was at that time no great willingness to adopt methods which
were obviously modelled upon those of the Europeans to the south. But
Chandra realized that the days of the old hit-or-miss tactics and mass
attacks were over with the invention of the repeating rifle and smokeless
powder, and set himself to ensure the utmost military efficiency that
could be got from one of the natural warrior-nations of the East. But as
has been said the task was not an easy one. He found at the outset an
almost complete want of co-ordination in the training of the army. There
were no regular text books. Manuscript notes ill arranged and insufficiently
understood formed the basis of the instruction given. His first work was
to compile a set of drill books in the Parbatiya language. These he based
upon the similar text books used in the British army, adjusting them to the
special circumstances of his country and his men. At the same time the
tactical efficiency of the officers was carefully considered. Examinations
were held and according to their result officers were chosen and commissioned. The highest ranks of all are to some extent still nominal, as the

sons of the Prime Minister while infants receive the title of General. But this almost honorary dignity does not in practice interfere with the working out of the army reforms. Promotion in Nepal depends upon efficiency. The organization and administration of the departments dealing with stores, equipment, ammunition, transport, and other necessities were also reformed, and the military law of the country has been supplemented by the compilation of an active service code which proved of great use when the Nepal contingents were sent to India during the Great War.

Before the present Maharaja's time, military service in Nepal had as a rule been recompensed by an assignment for life of land in different parts of the country. This system produced so many evils that Chandra gradually transformed this method of payment into a cash settlement—a custom which was already in vogue at out-stations. Where necessary an increase has been granted in recent days as the cost of living became higher. The service of porters, carriers, drovers, and other non-combatant corps has been entirely reorganized and a fair wage given in all cases. The Government of Nepal, like all Governments, reserves in times of emergency the right of conscripting labour as it reserves that of conscripting military service.

The Regular Army of Nepal numbers about 28,000 men. The Militia, which was first organized by Maharaja Rana Udip in 1879, varies somewhat from year to year, but may be taken at 13,000 men. The Reserve, consisting of all men who have had military training, is liable for service at the call of the Prime Minister, and though it is impossible to distinguish between those who undertook active military work during 1914-18 and those who served in a non-combatant condition, it is clear that the entire military strength of Nepal is very much greater than had been previously supposed. The following figures indicate the growth of the personnel of the army and the militia since the war with Great Britain in 1814.[1]

	1812	1841	1859	1922
Regulars:				
In the Capital ..	5658	10140	20048	22520
In other places ..	9029	9153	6014	6077
Militia	—	—	—	12860
	14687	19293	26062	41457

The following is a general indication of the distribution of the army:

Regulars.—Three battalions at Palpa or Butwal; one battalion at Baitadi or Dipal; twenty-six battalions in the Valley.

[1] It is perhaps necessary to remind some readers that these figures do not include the number of men serving in the twenty Gurkha battalions of the Indian Army.

MOUNTAIN GUN, 1924

LIGHT HOWITZER (1920) MANUFACTURED IN KATMANDU

Militia.—Two battalions are stationed at Dipal and two at Pokhra. The other chief military stations of Nepal garrisoned by militia or by regulars and militia are Ilam, Dhankuta, Sindhulia, Udaipur, Karphuk garhi, Bojpur, Pati, Wakhaldunga, Ramcha, Dhulikhel, Piuthana, Kuljung, Dailekha, Salyana, Dullu, Dhunaldhora, and posts in the Valley of Katmandu.

There are, or have been, arsenals at the following places: Nakhu, Sundarajal, Nayakot, Balaji, Themi, Piuthana, Dhankuta. Round Katmandu there are magazines at the foot of Swayambhunath and at the Laghan Khel near the southern stupa of Patan, as well as on the great parade ground of Katmandu, Tundi Khel.

There is compulsory service for three years with a right to remain in the army after that period on the recommendation of the commanding officer.

In the Nepalese capital the men of the army are not quartered in barracks—though their construction is now contemplated—and are permitted to live in lodgings in and about the town. The old practice of holding the first parade immediately after daybreak in summer has been changed, as causing some hardship to men lodging at a distance. This parade is now held at seven a.m. in summer and nine a.m. in winter. At Bhatgaon and Patan barracks have been built providing accommodation at each place for about 200 men. They have also been built at Birganj and Nepalganj, though on a smaller scale, for no part of the regular army is permanently stationed within the limits of the Tarai. The posts at the latter places were established in order to reinforce the local police when necessary and to check dacoity. It is probable that this principle, which has proved successful, will extend to other places in and near the Tarai. The essential principle of army organization is that it should be capable of indefinite extension in any time of emergency, and it will be seen that the system adopted by Maharaja Chandra proved equal to the enormous strain imposed upon it by the late war.

There had been a crude kind of arsenal at work in the Valley as early as 1770, but for many decades the Nepalese army depended for efficient firearms upon the gift or purchase of rifles and ammunition from the Indian Government. This was an unsatisfactory state of things. On the one hand Nepal naturally fretted against this dependency upon the generosity of her neighbour; and on the other the Indian Government on more than one occasion feared that by these gifts it might be implicated in the foreign ambitions and activities of Nepal. An arsenal was therefore fully equipped in Katmandu which is capable of turning out excellently constructed field guns, howitzers, mountain batteries, trench mortars, and all other necessary artillery. Even this, however, was not enough, and the friends of Nepal will congratulate the Maharaja on having obtained by the recently concluded treaty the unrestricted right of importation through India of arms and ammunition and of all necessary machinery.

At the conclusion of the war of 1914-18 the Maharaja announced a further increase in pay of the rank and file and of the lower grades of the officers to meet the increased cost of living that had been brought about by the hostilities.[1] Improvements in the medical arm and the immediate construction of a military hospital were then begun. The peroration of His Highness's speech on this occasion is worth recording as an illustration of the patriotism which burns not only in the heart of the speaker, but is expected by him to be the guide and lode-star of every man in the country, high or low.

" The hard life in the hills where we have to dig and delve to provide the necessaries of life may lead some of these loving men to leave their place of birth in search of ease and pleasure elsewhere. Their mistake is great and great is the wrong they do to their country. Our country's motto that one's mother and motherland rank even above heaven itself, appeals to everyone in every country—be your home in snow-covered regions, in sandy plains, among rugged rocks, in forest depths, or any conceivable spot in all the world. • The land of birth has the first claim upon us and a compelling charm to which we have given the name of patriotism. Even dry bread therein is sweeter and better relished than rich plenty elsewhere. What could be more sweet and sustaining to one than one's mother's breast? Be loyal and devoted to your country, and be straight and true to the salt you eat. May the most high Sri Pashpati and Sri Guhyeshwari who have in their mercy watched over you so long, continue to do so always."

§ 2

Gurkhas in the Indian Army.—The first suggestion that Gurkhas should be enlisted in special units in the Indian Army was made by General Ochterlony in 1814 during the first year of the Nepal war with England. It is impossible at this date to ascertain why this proposal should have been made at a time when it was less likely than at any other moment that the Gurkhas would respond. But in November 1814 a corps under Lieutenant Young was formed at Dehra Dun which, after the close of the

---

[1] At a parade of eight thousand troops at Katmandu the Prime Minister announced that the Nepal Government had allocated twenty-one lakhs of rupees (£140,000) to a fund for lowering the cost of food and grains. He also announced schemes started for improving Katmandu, including a light railway and ropeway.

The Prime Minister also stated that the British Government had offered four lakhs (£26,666) for distribution among the Nepalese troops who had served in India during the war.

war in 1816, became the Sirmoor, or 2nd, battalion.[1] Meanwhile the 1st Gurkhas, or Nassira regiment, had been raised at Subathu and the 3rd, or Kumaon levy, at Almora. In 1857 the 4th Gurkhas were raised at Pithoragarh and the 5th at Abbottabad.

Charters were granted to the first four regiments of Gurkha Rifles which secured them certain special privileges needed because their women and children would be without a natural home in India if a permanent habitation were not provided for the regiment. " Looking to the different circumstances in which recruits from Nepal entering our service find themselves as compared with other races, H.E. in Council considers it very desirable that each of the four Gurkha regiments should have a Station peculiarly its own " (Despatch from the Secretary to the Military Department to the Quartermaster-General, 18th March 1864). In conformity with this policy the 1st Gurkha Rifles were established at Dharmsala, the 2nd at Dehra Dun, the 3rd at Almora, and the 4th at Bakloh. The second battalion of the 3rd Regiment was later given quarters at Lansdowne.[2]

---

[1] By G.O.C.C. 379 of 1858 the Sirmoor Battalion (2nd Gurkhas) were granted a third colour in addition to the two in possession, and an extra Jemadar was appointed to carry it. This was a special reward for the battalion's extraordinarily gallant services at Delhi in the Mutiny.

Some idea of these services may be gathered when one realizes that it formed the main picquet on the Ridge (Hindoo Rao's House), assisted by the 6oth Rifles, the Guides, and detachments of other infantry regiments : that it was never once relieved during the whole siege : that it made two separate attacks on Kissenganj and sustained and defeated no less than twenty-six distinct attacks by the mutineers on the Ridge : that it was the only unit of the whole force which was exposed to constant fire, Hindoo Rao's House being within perfect range of nearly all the enemy's guns, and was riddled through and through with shot and shell : that for a period of three months and eight days the battalion was under fire morning, noon, and night : and, finally, that its losses, including the great assault on 14th September 1857, totalled 327 of all ranks out of the 490 with which it entered the siege ; of the nine British officers, eight were killed and wounded.

In 1863 the unit being a " Rifle" regiment, colours were discarded, but Queen Victoria designed and sent out to Dehra Dun a Truncheon to replace the old colours to which the Gurkhas had been extraordinarily attached. The extra Jemadar allowed for the third colour was retained for the Truncheon which is always paid the honours due to the Queen's Colour. When recruits are "sworn in" the Truncheon is brought on to parade as an additional ceremony and each recruit allowed to salute and then to touch it.

The Truncheon stands nearly six feet high, is of bronze and is surmounted by a crown in silver, supported by three Gurkha soldiers in bronze. On a silver ring below the figures the following words are inscribed in silver letters : " Main picquet, Hindoo Rao's House, Delhi, 1857." Below this ring is a representation in bronze of the Delhi Gate of the Palace of the Moguls with two kukhries (the Gurkha national weapon) in silver. Beneath the Gate comes another ring in silver on which is inscribed on three sides the words SIRMOOR RIFLES. On a third silver ring just below the upper end of the staff (which is of bronze) the words on the top silver ring are reproduced in the Nagri character. A fourth plain silver ring connects the bronze staff to the Truncheon.

[2] The later regiments have been associated with the following places, though they

On 29th June 1864 the following assurance was made by the Military Department: "It may be distinctly understood that the localities of the existing cantonment lines in which the corps are now located be given over to them in perpetuity as their homes." This, of course, referred only to the first four regiments; those added later are not regarded as "chartered."

The matter, however, aroused the criticism of the Commander-in-Chief

FIELD SERVICE, 1926   COLONEL, 1926

as early as August in the same year. But the Governor-General said that no variation could be made. In 1908, during the absence of the 2nd Gurkhas in Chitral, another battalion was ordered to occupy their quarters in Dehra Dun. But on 23rd September of that year the India Office cancelled these orders. The reasons were that for forty-eight years Dehra Dun had been the home of every soldier in the regiment. "He has brought his women there, assured of their protection during his absences. It is an enclave of Nepal. Moreover, many pensioners have bought small estates

could not be exclusively quartered there. The 5th Gurkha Rifles, Abbottabad; the 7th, Quetta; the 8th, Shillong and Lansdowne; the 9th, Dehra Dun; the 10th, Maymyo and Takdah.

near and expect that their heirs will enjoy them like themselves. Others stayed to be near old friends. Women expected the protection of the Regimental Funds in need." In short, these permanent homes were necessary because the Gurkhas had severed their connection with their own country. There is now no likelihood that the Gurkha regiments' charters will ever again be challenged. From the point of view of the War Office in India there are certain disadvantages in this special cantonment system, but the countervailing benefits are such that when in 1921 there was a proposal that the scheme should be modified, the matter was not pressed and nothing since has been heard about it.

Recruiting for the 9th Regiment is carried out among the Khas, and for the 7th and 10th among the Limbus and Rais.[1] For the others almost the only men enlisted are Magars and Gurungs. The special merits of the Gurkha as a soldier consist in his inextinguishable devotion to the art of fighting for its own sake, the readiness with which discipline and hardship are accepted, the curious ability that Gurkhas almost without exception possess to make friends with European—and especially Scottish—comrades in arms, and their astonishing hill work. Of the first no proof is needed, it is a characteristic that is recognized by all.[2] War is the only sport as well as the only work worthy of a man's attention, and though this unwillingness to deal with the commercial needs of the State has its obvious disadvantages it is not in this section of the book that reference need be made to it. In matters of discipline the Gurkha will put up with any regulations and will not complain however hard the life in war; but he looks for justice, and it is because the officers in the Gurkha regiments in the Indian Army are in most cases specially selected men that an excellent *esprit de corps* exists. The hill men possess the invaluable characteristic that they do not make trouble and respond at once to the welcome that they invariably meet with in the field. Of their hill work the fame is widely spread, and it is only necessary to quote again a story that is already a classic along the northern frontier of India.

§ 3

The Khud Race of the Gurkhas.—This is the story of the famous khud race between the 3rd Gurkhas and the 60th Rifles. Major-General Nigel Woodyatt, who was then in command of the 3rd Gurkhas, has given me personally an account of this contest, which took place at Ranikhet in 1907.[3] It appears that, owing to certain misunderstandings and mistakes in timing

---

[1] See Appendix XVII.

[2] I have myself watched from the windows of the Embassy in Constantinople a corporal's guard of Gurkhas whose sole idea of utilizing hours of recreation lay in assuming command in rotation and issuing words of command to willing companions.

[3] He has briefly noted it on p. 171 of his book *Under Ten Viceroys.*

which need not be detailed here, the 60th believed that in what in Britain is called a hill race, and is only known at Grasmere—a race straight uphill and back from and to given points—the Rifles would be able to hold their own against any Gurkha battalion. A challenge was issued which General Woodyatt promptly accepted on behalf of his own men. The matter was not to be decided at once, and a good deal of interest was taken in this competition. Both sides—each team consisting of a hundred men—went into training. As the day—the 20th September—approached, an intimation was sent from headquarters in India reminding Woodyatt that such inter-racial competitions were not encouraged by the Indian War Office. After some discussion with Colonel Wintringham, the Brigadier—who had himself been Adjutant-General in India—agreed to write to Simla and ask for a relaxation of the rule for a special occasion. Lord Kitchener was then Commander-in-Chief, and it may be that the matter reached his ears. In any case, permission was eventually given, not for a direct race, but for " a competition by time." So the contest took place.

So far as the climbing of the hill was concerned there was probably not much in it between the 60th Rifles and the 3rd Gurkhas. But, as General Woodyatt graphically described it to me, when it came to coming downhill the Rifles were simply not in it. The Gurkhas fell over the khud just as the raindrops collecting zigzag their way down a rain-beaten window. The result was that the first ninety-nine of the competitors belonged to the 3rd Gurkhas! One is inclined to wonder what happened to the hundredth on his return to his own camp. The General bears witness to the fine characteristics of the Gurkha soldier. " The temperament of the Gurkha reminds one of our public schoolboy. The same light-hearted cheerfulness, hatred of injustice, love of games, and veneration for superior ability or skill. There is the same mentality, with dogged affection (if well treated), and also, like the schoolboy, he works best and hardest with a firm controlling hand. No punishment, however severe, is ever resented if thoroughly deserved." But he cannot stand nagging. General Woodyatt notes the curious interest shown by Gurkhas in London. Apparently the most enormous structure of man has in itself some attractive power apart from the subtle beauties of atmosphere and sky-line which it certainly possesses for artists. The Great War gave many of them the chance of seeing it which they would not otherwise have had.

§ 4

The Police.—In old days the Nepalese village formed itself into a kind of watch committee to preserve law and order within its limits. To some extent this is still the case in India, and it will be remembered that a revival of the Panchayat formed one of the more interesting and possible parts of the reactionary changes advocated by Gandhi. In the towns and in some of the Tarai districts, where the nearness to the frontier invited the badmashes of both sides to assemble, some form of police has long been known, but it is only since the institution of the present regime that the police system has been efficient. Its members are now properly uniformed and fairly paid, and compose an active and loyal body. Constables are admitted only after previous training and a successful examination. A criminal investigation department has been created, and some young men of special ability have been sent to police training schools in India. These, on their return—having passed the standard of superintendents of police—have been placed in charge of districts in the Tarai where crime was specially frequent. They possess no judicial functions whatever, for the Maharaja has throughout recognized the necessity of keeping separate the judicial and the executive functions of the State.

The many different castes, which send their quota of criminals detained in prison, offer some problems, but these are overcome by a general application of the methods in force in India where the same care is necessary. Prison sentences for grave offences and to long terms of detention are received in the capital. Within the gaols attention is devoted to the cleanliness and the mental and physical well-being of the inmates. It is impossible to pretend that the comfort of the gaols of Western civilization is either possible or perhaps desirable, but that something remains to be done in this matter is recognized by the Nepal Government, which is now considering the erection of a new gaol at a little distance from Katmandu. The separation of civil and criminal offences will there be enforced, and reformatory treatment for the young will at least be given a trial. As far as is possible the internal organization of the prisons is in accordance with modern views, and such methods as the promotion to the post of warder of the best behaved; the registration of finger-prints; the teaching and encouragement of craftsmanship within the walls; the remission of part of the sentence to well behaved men; and—most remarkable of all—the grant of a small sum to discharged prisoners to enable them to tide over their first days of freedom and unemployment, are all illustrations of a similarity of the standards of Western and Eastern gaol methods. Crime is comparatively uncommon in Nepal, and a large number of those under detention are in gaol for inability or refusal to pay Government dues.

§ 5

Water.—Public spirit has always been characteristic of the inhabitants of Nepal. In old days it was chiefly manifested in the creation and upkeep of some of the most remarkable and beautiful religious buildings in all Asia. For to the Newari a holy shrine was a trust—and that it was a source of wealth also is no real diminution of the credit due to it. The offerings of the devout were chiefly spent upon the upkeep of the temple and its services. The pilgrimage routes that thread their way through the mountains of Nepal received some attention also, though more perhaps in the provision of rough shelters for the night than in any road-making or bridge-building in our modern sense. Less attention was paid to the domestic architecture of the country except in the case of edifices used by public officials or for official work. If it be true that a country is on the up-grade wherein the official and religious buildings far surpass the ordinary standard of private edifices in size and beauty, Nepal may fairly be conceded a prosperous future. The question of architecture will be dealt with in a special appendix. At present it is of interest to examine rather the practical modern improvements that have been introduced into Nepal.

The first provision which has to be made for any town, Eastern or Western, is that of a supply of fairly pure and abundant water. The three large towns of the Valley are each supplied with pure drinking water from independent sources. The most recent of these services is that which supplies Patan. This was completed in 1905 and was formally opened by the King in person. Patan has always suffered more than the other capitals from external and internal violence. It has been laid waste by war again and again, and it found what was almost its death blow in the sudden and overwhelming rivalry of its neighbour, Katmandu, only two miles away across the Bagmati. But it has been pointed out that, more than any other factor, the intolerably bad water supply and the consequent ravages of cholera were probably the cause of Patan's decline.

It is interesting to notice the connection that has existed between the wives of the Prime Ministers of Nepal and the provision of water for the town dweller and the wayfarer. It was the first wife of the present Prime Minister, Bada Maharani Chandra Loka Bhakta Lakshmi Devi, who interested herself in the lamentable hygienic condition of Patan. The water is drawn from springs to the south some four or five miles distant from the town.[1] The main pipe is carried across the Bagmati by a suspension bridge three hundred feet in span. This was the work of Colonel Kuma, and replaced the old structure which had been put up by General Bhim Sen Thapa nearly one hundred years before. The bridge, though no longer the most important lattice structure in the country, is six hundred and forty-five feet long between abutments, the width of the roadway being over twelve feet.

Elsewhere in Nepal pipe water has been provided, and it seems probable

---

[1] It is worth recording that this water supply was created by two Nepalese engineers, Colonel Kishore Narsingh and his brother, Colonel Kuma Narsingh, who had received a thorough course of instruction at Rurki.

that the inadequacy of the supply of pure water in the town of Jajarkot in western Nepal, her birthplace, was the cause of the activity displayed in this matter by the present wife of Maharaja Chandra, Bada Maharani Bala Kumari Devi. The water works were completed in 1924. In 1921 General Baber Sham Sher provided Pokhra, in western Nepal, with water in memory of his eldest son, Bala Sham Sher. So many are the instances of this new water conservation that it will only be possible to add that of Dhankuta in eastern Nepal, which has been blessed with a supply of pure pipe water.

§ 6

Roads.—It has long been recognized that the trade and prosperity of Nepal are greatly impaired by the absence of good roads. There are no railways in Nepal,[1] and the mountainous character of the country makes it necessary that all the transport in the hills should be carried on human shoulders. An obvious illustration of the difficulty is to be seen in the fact that it is impossible for laden and difficult for unladen ponies or mules or even elephants to climb the heights of Sisagarhi.[2] For this reason it is commercially impossible to develop much of the mineral wealth of the country. It is true that some of the more valuable minerals repay the heavy cost of freight to railheads on the Indian frontier, but the vast resources of coal and copper that Nepal is credibly reputed to possess cannot, at present, be advantageously worked. As they now exist the roads throughout Nepal—the Tarai should be excepted from this statement—are still mere mountain tracks fitted at the best for ponies and at their worst traversable by human beings only. This condition of things has been chiefly due to the vast difficulties presented by the mountainous character of the territory. Nepal lies along the Himalayas, and anything like a good road system has been in the past, and will probably long remain in the future, a practical impossibility. As it is, bad as they are, the greatest roads running east and west represent the labour of myriads of men and a constant drain upon the treasury of Nepal.[3] These tracks have to be carried across the natural drainage of the country which is from north to south. Consequently they consist of little else than a perpetual climb, a perpetual descent, and a perpetual river crossing. There is not so much difficulty in following the route, such as it is, over the spurs that sweep

[1] In 1923 a short stretch of narrow-gauge line was pushed into the Tarai by Mr. J. V. Collier for the purpose of transporting timber.
[2] Elephants cannot use the Sisagarhi and the Chandragiri tracks. They find their way slowly by special paths that are only available in the dry season.
[3] Jang Bahadur sanctioned the expenditure of three lakhs of rupees for broadening the two paths leading from Katmandu to Mechi and Doti. It will be seen that these two new tracks extended the entire length of the kingdom, from west-north-west to east-south-

down from the ice-bound spine of the Himalayas and bury themselves in the alluvial flats of India. It has been the crossing of the rivers that caused the almost intolerable delays that characterize internal transit in Nepal. A century ago the streams were spanned by mere rope bridges—

SUSPENSION BRIDGE OVER THE ANKHU KHOLA
NEAR AKANIA

the name " chaksam ",suggests that in Tibetanized localities iron chains were used at the more important crossings—which were always at the mercy of neglect, rot, and, in many cases, flood. The use of the curious timber cantilever bridges which are scarcely found elsewhere south of the Himalayas was an improvement, but though far more solid in structure,

east. The amount allotted for the reconstruction must not be judged by modern standards. From one end of the length to the other the actual labour was probably slave or unpaid. Material only was costly.

these bridges were necessarily almost at the level of the water and were consequently swept away or rendered useless by any unusual rise in its level. In bad weather, when the mountain rivers come down in spate, it was impossible either to ford the streams or to cross them by ferries. The recent policy of the Government of Nepal has been to replace fords, ferries, rope bridges, and cantilever bridges by suspension or lattice girder bridges. Only the most important of these structures can be here referred to. There have been constructed during the present Maharaja's term a fine iron girder bridge connecting Katmandu with Patan and one over the Nakhu river at Nakhu. Iron lattice girder bridges have been thrown over

CANTILEVER BRIDGE OVER THE BHARANG-BHURUNG STREAM

the Karra river at Karra, and over the Samari river at Samari, a mile or two south of Suparita; similar bridges exist over the Bhainsi, the Sirsiya (near Parwanipur and Raxaul—the latter being of plate girder) and the Kiyasod. In addition an iron plate girder bridge has been erected over the Dhobi Khola in Katmandu and at Dokaphedi, near Bhimphedi. Wire rope suspension bridges have been thrown across the Bagmati at Chobar; three over the Sunkosi; and others over the Indrani and the Budhi Gandak at Arhunghat and the Bagmati at Sundarighat, and Khokna; elsewhere the same work has been carried on across the Kali at Ridi on the main road from Palpa to Gulmi and at Ramdighat on the road from Palpa to the Valley; over the Gandak at Trisuli; across the Ankhu, the Rosi, the Likhu, and the Tamor at Dhankuta; over the Marsiangti, and at Dolkha over the Lisankhu. Similar bridges have also been constructed at Chapay, at Darandhay, at Tadi, at Palpa on the Dhobam road, and at Pangretar. Two stone bridges have been thrown across the Bagmati at Aryaghat and one at Gaurighat near Pashpati. A form of bridge with iron beams and brick walls and pillars has been used at Bhatgaon over the Kalimati near Bhimmukteswar, and at Bajra Gogini. New pile bridges stand across the waters of the Barhwa, the Sirsiya, and the Jhanjh near Hazmania, and at Dostea—three in all. They are also to be found between Hazmania and Patharghatta—the scene of Jang Bahadur's death where the road crosses the Chadi Samanpur—and at Sankhamul. Wooden bridges have been built at Kageshwari over the Betravati and over the Bharang-Bhurung. They may also be found on the main road to Piuthana at Balkhu; at Dakhinakali, over the Kalinadi, between Bhatgaon and Sanga; at Lamjang near Manabyasi; over the Labsay below Benighat; and between Taulihawa and Sohratganj over the Dhobi Khola. In some cases new wooden bridges of a stronger type have replaced an old-fashioned cantilever as over the Bridhaganga and the Kailas Khola in Achham.

§ 7

But the most important piece of road and bridge-making remains for special notice. Elsewhere the roads of Nepal have been improved rather by bridges than by a reconstruction of their surface. But there is one conspicuous exception, and it is worth while referring to it in some detail. It is the new road that traverses the larger part of the route from India to Katmandu. It runs from Birganj to Bhimphedi, and I take the following account of the road from a summary kindly written for me by Mr. A. C. Chattya and Captain T, Rayamajai, the executive engineers. The road actually starts at Raxaul bridge, which is the frontier between the two countries. There has been no serious attempt to deal with the surface of the existing flat avenue until a point about four miles north of Birganj is reached. The length of the section between Birganj and Simra is a little over fourteen and a half miles and the new road has been taken across open fields. The embankment and bridges are completed. The width is nowhere less than twenty feet. As has been suggested in chapter xi it is as yet *carrossable* for motor-cars and light vehicles only, though as the materials for metalling were ready in 1925 this work has probably been completed. In its course it crosses the Sirsiya at Pramanipur and Jitpur. There is also a minor steel bridge at Raxaul which is usable by six-ton loads.

From Simra the new road traverses the jungle. It is eight miles in length and has been metalled. The road has recently been rolled and is now fit for traffic. The same six-ton pressure has been provided for in the construction of all the wooden bridges (one major and eight minor) which have been found necessary.[1]

From Bichako the road runs for a little more than six and a half miles along the sides of the hills and the bank of the Churia river. It crosses the stream four times, maintaining its character and width throughout. The earthwork and the wooden bridges are for the most part complete. The four large steel bridges necessary for the crossing of the river have been ordered from the Continent, and before the publication of this book will probably have been set up in their places. The difficulties of this section may be understood from the fact that there are six major and thirty-two minor wooden bridges. These have been designed to carry ten tons live load. The steel bridges are of similar capacity.

The Churia pass itself presents some difficulty. The steep gradients of the existing road—some of which are as high as one in four—will be replaced by a tunnel seven hundred and eighty-five feet in length, which is practically completed. This tunnel is eight feet in width at the top, nine feet in width at the bottom, and ten feet high. The gradient, rising from south to north, is 1 in 31.9.

A comparatively flat stretch is now entered upon from the Churia Pass to the Samari bridge. In length it is about 7.7 miles and runs along the banks of the stream and through the jungle. All that remains to be done over this stretch is the distribution of the metal and its consolidation. There is one major steel bridge at the Karra river which is already in working order. Eight major and twenty-three minor wooden bridges facilitate the crossing of this heavily watered strip. From Samari the road runs along the sides of rocky hills and on the banks of mountain rivers for a length of 10.1 miles. Its minimum width is here decreased in a few places to twelve feet. The road has been in existence for many years and nothing has been done to it by the road department except remetalling and the preparation of schemes to improve the gradients and enlarge the width wherever possible. There are two major steel bridges already constructed at the Samari and Bhainsi rivers. Twenty-five wooden bridges are required

[1] Messrs. Martin and Co. of Calcutta surveyed these two sections in the winter of 1924 and have submitted a tender for the construction of a light railway from the frontier to Bichako. No decision has been made as yet as to the advisability of connecting up the Indian system with these advanced posts in Nepal. In the present attitude of the Nepal Government the railway would not be allowed to penetrate the country farther than Suparita. It is understood that the Maharaja himself is inclined to favour the scheme under proper safeguards, and it certainly would have the effect of largely reducing the cost of the freight of Nepal's exported mineral wealth and her imported rice. In connection with the proposal to construct this railway the Maharaja has always associated its advisability with the need for reducing the high rate of rice, the main sustenance of the inhabitants of the Valley of Katmandu. But Nepal thinks of other things than its material wealth.

and cart traffic is able to traverse this section only for six and a half months during the fair weather.

From Dhursing, the last station of the section just referred to, to Bhimphedi is a distance of about two miles. So far it has not been found necessary to do anything to this part of the route as, though rough, it is passable at all times. Of course, when the remainder of the road is completed the surface of the last section will be taken in hand. The whole of this Raxaul to Bhimphedi road is fifty-one and a half miles.

After Bhimphedi the road crosses the two passes Sisagarhi and Chandragiri, the steepness and roughness of which have been referred to more than once.[1] Any improvement of this road to correspond with the lower sections was found to be possible only at an immensely heavy outlay, and the Government did not leave out of account the fact that the severity of the track—road it is not in most places—was a traditional method of making access to the Valley from India less easy than it might otherwise be. After long consideration the Government decided that if possible an aerial ropeway should be constructed so as to facilitate the transit of goods over these passes to and from Katmandu, without in any way opening up for passenger traffic the new avenue into the capital. The Maharaja took up the question as far back as 1904. It was not at first considered a satisfactory expedient; and it was, perhaps, the very great improvement in this manner of transport which had been effected by the Italians during the Great War that induced the Maharaja to return to his original proposal. At this moment the ropeway is an accomplished fact between Katmandu and Bhimphedi.[2] The magnitude of this work, which is estimated to be about £100,000, will be seen from the details which Mr. R. S. Underhill, the engineer in charge, has been kind enough to give me.

"The Nepal Ropeway is 14 miles long as the crow flies, running from Dhursing near the head of the cart road which connects it with British India, to Kisipidi in the Valley of Nepal. It passes over mountains 4,500 feet higher than Dhursing, and its terminal at Kisipidi is 930 feet higher than that place.

"It carries general merchandise in average loads of 5 cwt., at the rate of 8 tons per hour in either direction, and the heaviest individual load permissible is 10 cwt.

"The Ropeway comprises seven sections, each being a complete unit in

[1] Mr. Underhill in his report of 1922 says that at both Bhimphedi and Thankot "the roads terminate abruptly at mountains which rise up like walls for some 900 metres so steeply that it is impracticable to make any cart road over them."

[2] The Ropeway was supplied by Messrs. Keymer, Son & Co., of London, with Messrs. R. Pearson and A. J. Knight as Consulting Engineers.

itself, driven by an electric motor. By the addition of further sections the Ropeway could be extended indefinitely.

" Each section comprises a single endless wire rope $\frac{7}{8}''$ thick and of 29 tons strength, which passes round a horizontal wheel 10 feet in diameter at each end of the section. An electric motor drives one of these wheels through suitable gearing, and thus causes the rope to travel continuously at $4\frac{1}{4}$ miles per hour. The loads are hung from clips on this rope at regular intervals 240 yards apart, and travel with the rope; loads going up to Kisipidi on one side, and travelling down to Dhursing on the other.

" The rope is supported by sheaves running on ball bearings carried on cross-arms at the tops of 106 steel trestles, which vary in height from 12 feet to 100 feet, to suit the configuration of the ground. The largest span between two trestles is 1,300 yards.

" At the end of each section the clips automatically disengage from the wire rope, run along an overhead rail through the station, and then engage with the rope of the next section; so that a load can travel continuously from end to end of the Ropeway.

" The power required to drive the Ropeway when fully loaded is about 80 horse power.

" The trestle foundations were commenced early in 1922. Railway strikes in India hindered deliveries of materials, so that trestle erection was not started until March 1923. The first $3\frac{1}{2}$ miles, comprising three sections of the steepest part of the line, have recently run a full load test satisfactorily, and the whole Ropeway is expected to be completed by midsummer 1925. Weather conditions permit of erection work being carried on for six months of the year only.

(Signed) R. S. UNDERHILL.[1]
11-6-24."

For travellers the route from India to Katmandu consists of a cart road for fifty-one and a half miles from the frontier to Bhimphedi; a mere track eighteen miles long over two steep and very difficult passes from Bhimphedi to Thankot, and thence by a fairly good cart road through the Valley from Thankot to Katmandu, a distance of about seven miles.

§ 8

Electric Supply.—The needs of the capital—and incidentally of the ropeway—are supplied by a fine installation near Pharping. This project

---

[1] Some difficulty was experienced by Mr. Underhill in constructing the supports for the ropeway. It was believed that the opening was to be celebrated by the immolation of children at the foot of the trestles, and in some cases he found villages emptied as he approached them. Mr. Underhill has also erected a short ropeway from the quarries behind Swayambhunath to the city of Katmandu. It is two and a half miles in length and carries road metal at a rate of four tons per hour.

was completed in 1911. The difficulties of the work may be understood from the statement of Mr. Bernard Pantet, the engineer in charge of the works, that eight and a half millions of cubic feet had to be removed and the Kati stream diverted. In the excavation of the reservoir a good deal of especially troublesome rock had to be cleared. The reservoir holds five hundred and twenty-eight thousand seven hundred and eighty-three cubic feet of water. The main pipe line is two thousand five hundred and thirty-eight feet in length, and the pressure of water at the power-house end is two hundred and eighty-eight pounds per square inch. The transmission line is seven miles in length, and it twice crosses the Bagmati by spans of nine hundred and six hundred feet respectively.

It is interesting to note that the power rate has been kept at a figure which London men may envy—two annas per unit. It need hardly be added that the supply of electricity at Katmandu has suggested and been the means of carrying through a large number of the reforms of the past fifteen years.

§ 9

Woods and Forests.—There will be found elsewhere in this volume [1] the report upon the working and the future of the greatest asset that Nepal possesses—her forest wealth. It is therefore necessary here, to say little more than that, except for certain woods and within certain districts, tradition sanctions that timber needed for public and private use may be taken, but only with the consent of the village headman, whose duty it is to see that there is no waste. It need not be said that such a method was disastrous to any settled policy of forest development and administration. A new regime has been begun, and under Mr. Collier's direction the present as well as the future revenues of the State have been and will be very greatly increased. The richness of these forests, even in their present undeveloped state, is astonishing. No doubt some difficulty will be found in the carrying out of a liberal policy which will involve the presence of a European supervisor in the Tarai—no one, of course, is allowed to cross the lower mountain barrier of the country—on account of the traditional dislike of the Nepalese to any novel method that is brought under their notice. But from the point of view of the Government there can be no question that a proper administration of these enormous tracts offers the best assurance that can be given for a wealthy future.

Famine has always been one of the enemies of Nepal. The country is almost entirely dependent upon a good monsoon for its supply of food, and though in general the mountainous nature of the State makes it difficult to find large areas of cultivation needing artificial irrigation, in the Tarai the water has been carefully and consistently conserved by a system that

[1] Appendix XIX.

finds its best illustration in the Saptarai district. After great difficulty and several failures, the present method was devised by Mr. Hanckell and by Mr. S. Athaim. Large granaries known as golas—from their circular shape—and bhakharis have been built in many parts of the country for the storage of surplus grain in years of plenty. The spectre of famine has practically been exorcised by these measures.

Among other improvements have been the reorganization and extension of the postal service. Nepal has not yet joined the postal union—a step which the Maharaja is probably considering at this moment; the stamps, therefore, are valid only for the national service. Any letters addressed to India or beyond have to be franked by Indian stamps.

A telephone line has been put up between Birganj on the frontier and Katmandu, and there is an extension from Birganj to Hajminia, about thirty miles distant, where the headquarters of the Maharaja are placed in the cold weather. The tariff adopted for the use of the telephone is one that many European listeners might wish adopted elsewhere. The charge is three Nepalese pice—which are equivalent to about three-eighths of a penny—per word.

In this rapid survey of the large reforms and improvements which have been carried out in recent years room must be found for a reference to the adoption of the Western calendar for all dates. Before the administration of the present Maharaja, the official practice was to record the day of the month according to its position in the dark or the bright fortnight of the lunar month. As this has been abandoned, only occasional reference has been made in this book to the discarded system of reckoning.

§ 10

Tenure of Land.—For purposes of tenure and assessment of land Nepal is divided into two regions. One is the flat, warm, and rich Tarai, the other contains the mountainous remainder of the State. The former is inhabited by a mixed population which has probably been obliterated and restocked many times from the adjoining lands. The *awal* itself is sufficient to account for this, for alone among the inhabitants the Tharus have the privilege of immunity from the devastating fever which reigns in the Tarai from March to September. The latter—by far the larger part of Nepal—provides a home for the Gurkhas, Newars, Rais, Limbus, Bhotias, Sharpas, and many others, to a description of whom a special appendix in this volume is dedicated.[1]

Between the hills and the Tarai is a narrow zone known as Bhitri Madesh, wherein the important districts of Makwanpur, Chitawan, and Dang-Deokhori-Sonar are separately administered. The rest of the terri-

[1] Appendix XVII.

tory is annexed for this purpose to the nearest Tarai or hill station, as the case may be.

The Tarai is divided into fourteen main zillas or counties—Morung, Saptarai, Mohotari, Sarlahi, Rautahat, Banra, Parsa, Butwal (Palhi-Majhakhand), Butwal (Khajahni-Seoraj), Deochori, Bankay, Bardia, Kailali, and Kanchanpur. In the mountainous regions there are twenty-five counties —tahsils, zillas, or ilakas—Ilam Dhankuta, No. 4 East (Bojpur), No. 3 East (Wakhaldhunga), No. 2 East (Lyanglyang), No. 1 East (Dhulikhel), No. 1 West (Nayakot), No. 2 West (Pokhra-Bandipur), Kaski, Lamjang, No. 4 West (Syangja), Palpa, No. 5 West (Gulmi), Piuthana, Salyana, Dullu (Dailekh), Doti, Baitadi, Jumla, Jajarkot, Bajhang, Achham,[1] Thalahra, together with the metropolitan districts of Katmandu, Patan, and Bhatgaon. These main divisions are subdivided into thums, daras, or garkhas which again are parcelled into gaons and mouzas.

A standard " ropni " of land has been created to get rid of the inextricable confusion of many different measurements of area according to the quality of the land. This ropni forms the unit for revenue assessment.[2] One traditional measurement for purposes of assessment has been allowed to remain. And it is interesting if only as indicating the kind of hereditary complication with which the present Maharaja has had to deal in standardizing the land revenue in Nepal as well as the difficulty caused by military jagirs. Maize lands, or lands situated on the hill-side, enjoy a special assessment. They are divided into three kinds, namely, " hal," " patay," and " kodalay." Hal is the area cultivated by a tenant with a pair or pairs of bullocks. This pays one nepali rupee only for the whole area thus cultivated. A tenant owning only one bullock and with the help of another bullock borrowed from his neighbour is a patay tenant and pays threefourths of a nepali rupee. The kodalay tenant uses the spade only and pays half a nepali rupee as rent for his land. The lightness of the rent for hill-side land has been a great factor in the extension of the cultivation of land of poor quality or of difficult access. It is a different thing with the rich rice-growing lowlands of Nepal. In some cases the rent therein is about half the actual produce of rice obtained from the land. In these lowlands in the Tarai and in Bhitri Madesh the " bigha," measuring ninety yards by ninety yards, is the standard unit.

No jagirs, or lands given as a reward for military service, are now granted in the Tarai. This custom lent itself to certain abuses which were partially put an end to by Jang Bahadur, but his reforms still admitted of hardship

---

[1] In the most recent map given to me by the Maharaja, Achham is joined with Doti.

[2] A chain for land measurement in the hills is six and one third cubits, or nine feet three inches in length. Sixteen square chains is termed a muri, and four muris make one ropni. Thus the measurement of the ropni is six hundred and eight and four-ninths square yards.

upon the tenants, for which, however, the middlemen between the original grantee and the worker on the actual land were chiefly responsible. The present Maharaja began to substitute cash payments for jagirs given for military service. The change has been carried out with great tact and under the direct guarantee of the Government. The rates are now fixed and reasonable, and the scheme has had the additional advantage of stabilizing the Government's annual revenue from the land.

All land in Nepal is ultimately the property of the State, but as in England there are freehold estates owned by private individuals, as well as the endowments for religious and charitable purposes, secured, as in the case of private property, by a "birta." Until recently, the tenants of these lands had no security of possession or fixity of the rent. This guarantee has been given by law and a special feature of the new enactment is that relief from damage caused by drought, floods, hail, landslips, etc., entitles the tenant to a proportionate remission of his rent. At the same time the register of land ownership has been regularized and the tenure of hill land in Nepal at this moment, for simplicity, justice, and security, compares not unfavourably with that controlled by the Government of India.

A similar classification of the rates of assessment has taken place in the Tarai. Here the land is divided into two classes: "dhanhar"—the fields where rice could be grown; "bhit," or fields capable of yielding dry crops only. Three longitudinal areas are recognized in the Tarai—"seir," the upper portion of the forest land; "majha," the middle; and "bhatha," the lowest strip. The depredations of the wild animals for which Nepal is famous are taken into consideration, and the assessment is easier in the upper zone than in that of the central strip which, in turn, is lighter than in that of the land adjoining the frontier.

The law dealing with the foreclosure of properties in areas with high tax has been modified and rendered more equitable. Other abuses, too, have been abolished by the present Nepalese Government. As already said, the carts, coolies, and supplies needed for the winter tours of the Prime Minister may no longer be requisitioned without a fair payment, the amount of which is settled by local competition. Buffaloes and goats needed for the sacrifices of the official Durga festival are in all cases paid for. A system of contractors over whose duties there is a strict supervision has been substituted. It is not without interest that the very large number of elephants maintained in Nepal and their notorious voracity have called for special legislation.

§ 11

Enough has been said to explain the high and sustained level of interior administration and foreign policy which the Maharaja has maintained throughout the long period of his government. Whether he has in his mind any purpose of broadening the basis of authority it is impossible to say. But his own experience has assured him of the danger that sometimes attends a rigid adherence to the existing regime. At present there is no other alternative but death or exile for a Prime Minister who either through weakness or wilfulness departs from the high standard that has been set up by Jang Bahadur and Chandra. It is unlikely that with the spread of civilization among all classes in Nepal these remedies for misrule should continue to be accepted as the only cure. That in his own lifetime Chandra would not do anything to limit his own absolute authority or that of his immediate successors is taken for granted. But lower down in the roll of succession there lurk certain dangers against which precautions should perhaps be taken—and with the present Prime Minister of Nepal conviction that action is necessary rarely long antedates action itself. The difficulties to which I refer will be apparent to anyone who carefully examines the list of succession contained in Appendix III in the first volume. It is to be hoped that the benignant autocracy which has raised Nepal to such a height of prosperity and power will not for many years be exchanged for yet another of the premature democracies which cause so much unhappiness in the Eastern hemisphere. At present there is no sign of any popular movement whatever. The Nepalese are content to be governed by their Maharaja in the absolute manner that he has proved to be best for his people at the present day. Abortive efforts, so the Maharaja told me, have been made to introduce across the border the dangerous virus of Indian sedition. As may be imagined, these attempts have been promptly and efficiently extinguished, No one who has made a long and careful study on the spot of the results of the introduction of Western parliamentary ideals among Orientals can have a doubt that our policy of encouraging Eastern peoples to run before they can walk, or wish to walk, has been one, so far, of disaster and retardation. It is not the most creditable side of the whole affair that these constitutions have been imposed rather through the weakness or the egoism of the British people than along the line of any clear or worked-out scheme, based upon knowledge of the Orient—and they have been abortive. What is true of other races of the East—with the possible exception of the Japanese— would be found even more true of the inhabitants of a kingdom who have hitherto found contentment, progress, and prosperity without the help of European methods.

One rises from a study of Nepalese affairs with a deeper conviction than ever that this mountain people are destined to play a more and more responsible and magnificent part in Indian affairs—the more responsible because the English are weakening in their willingness to shoulder the old burden of full responsibility—a burden which can only be taken up by a military race; the more magnificent because alone in Katmandu is the ancient tradition of Indian rule and Indian ritual maintained. And it is only by governing a people according to their natural tendencies that their future can be assured. Least of all should England wish that any change should be made in the capable and powerful administration of a State from which, more than from any other State in the world, she has just received so overwhelming a proof of its friendship and of its constant willingness to sacrifice itself in the service of its greater neighbour.

With this recognition of what is almost the only example in modern history of a personally affectionate bond between two States I bring this work to a close. The attempt has involved research in many fields and could never have been concluded without the generous assistance of all to whom I have applied for help. It has been my hope that a hitherto almost unknown territory and almost unrecorded history should be illustrated; that a gallant race which has long assumed the kinship of blood-brotherhood with ourselves on a score of fields of war should become better understood and appreciated wherever the English language is spoken; and that our debt to the master mind of Nepal should be paid before an already lengthy term of service and responsibility yields, as all things must yield, to the march of time.

From my windows in the Baber Palace in Katmandu I looked out across a view which seemed to sum up not unhappily the various eras of Nepalese history and the deeper currents of her life and character. There was no period missing. Far away to the south the ring of mountains, blue in the distance but clear-outlined in the pure air, was cleft sharply by the Kotbar, or sword-cut of Manjusri, by which, as legend tells, the Valley was first drained, and dry land appeared for the service of men: and when the evenings drew in the wavering ghosts of gods and heroes seemed still to people the amethyst mists. Nearer, were outstretched the fields that made the Valley a coveted land long before the days of walled towns—days in which the old tales of serpent gods and under-water treasures slowly gave way to stories of human labour and human piety. In the middle distance Patan stood out upon its fold of ground. Immediately in front was the swelling curve of the northern stupa built by Asoka, when history made its first entrance upon the stage of Nepal. Beside it and beyond it the gilded roofs of the most picturesque of all the royal squares of earth betrayed the long tale of this war-ravaged capital from those dark and little-known days in which England was as harassed and English history as hopelessly obscure. The sharp fall of the ground towards the sacred river Bagmati has another and a later interest still. For somewhere there—the site has been wholly lost and scarcely a tradition remains of more than its approximate position —lay the Christian burial ground of the missionaries who for a time, and

11   P

vainly, strove according to their lights and their prejudices to combat a faith of which they stood in horror and of which they knew nothing at all.

Then the Bagmati itself, the symbol of all that Hinduism stood and still stands for in this remotest Himalayan outpost of the faith, the one continual flowing link with an empire from which the new rulers of Nepal cut her off with no undetermined hand. On the hither bank the irregular outline of Thapathali, the palace of Jang Bahadur, the first maker of his country—a sign of the help that Nepal then for the first time gave in over-flowing measure to her great southern neighbour—and marked for English eyes by the low roof of the house in which the widow of Nana Sahib spent fifty years of a clouded and exiled existence. Then beneath me the trim, almost European gardens of the Baber Palace, a happy emblem of the great progress that the country has made, and its welcome of all that adds to the amenities of life. Thus in that one view Nepal was linked up from its dim origins with the full tide of modern life, and one turned away with the satisfaction that in much more than the mere luxuries of life the best standards that the East and the West together could present were maintained and would be continually maintained in this beautiful and mercifully still forbidden land of Nepal.

LOADING PLATFORM OF ROPEWAY STATION

APPENDIX XV

NOTES ON BUDDHISM IN NEPAL

§ 1

THE reader will remember that not long after Buddha's death the ecclesiastical differences common to all creeds arose in Buddhism also. The disintegration of primitive Buddhism, as was foreseen by Tathagata himself, was made certain by the extension of the theory of salvation from the Lesser to the Greater Vehicle, which may be said to have taken place about A.D. 250.

Before that time there had been no general re-interpretation of the doctrine of the Buddha, the Dharma, and the Sangha such as that implied by the teachings of the Greater Vehicle, but the Buddhist world was ready for a change. The pure and severe code taught by Sakyamuni had largely degenerated into a mere mass of confused ritual, little of which was understood, much of which became later an excuse for obscenity, and which in Tibet at least has resulted in a return to sheer animism, if not animalism, lightly veneered over by the claim to Buddhism by men whose creed Buddha himself would be the first to denounce. Dr. Oldfield, in a luminous passage, notes the chief services which Gautama rendered to mankind. " It was the great Teacher and Lawgiver of Buddhism who brought about the social and religious reformation by which his countrymen were freed from the tyranny of the Brahmans and emancipated from the degrading trammels of caste. It was his learning that dispelled their ignorance, his piety that rescued their creed from the profane absurdities of the grossest polytheism, and it was his humanity which purified their religion from the savage and sanguinary rites by which its worship had been disgraced." Except that blood sacrifice is still taboo, few of these reforms are to-day characteristic of Tibetan or Nepalese Buddhism.

If the Master himself visited the Valley of Nepal—a possibility which may almost be ranked as a probability—his teachings were of course promulgated there as early as the sixth century B.C. The erection of six stupas and a record of the establishment of a shrine and vihara at Deo Patan, which can be identified to-day, is a proof that the Emperor Asoka visited the Valley of Katmandu as well as Rummindei. He also permitted his daughter to marry a Buddhist devotee at Deo Patan. But in the Valley there developed a school of free-thinking Buddhism which was not unready to welcome the developments of the Greater Vehicle,[1] and in time accepted

---

[1] The important part played in the development of Northern Buddhism by early schools in Nepal is well shown in Mrs. Getty's masterly book, *The Gods of Northern Buddhism*, Oxford, Clarendon Press, 1914.

also the Tantric excesses which nowadays dominate the curious *mélange* in which it is sometimes difficult to say whether Hinduism or Buddhism is predominant.

It would be a mistake to suppose that in this duality there is necessarily any hostility. Hinduism and Buddhism have effected a condominium in Nepal, and greatly as the latter has been coloured by the association, it is not true to say that Hinduism is gradually ousting it. Most writers on Nepal assert that Buddhism is fading away there; and if by this is meant primitive and pure Buddhism, the statement is true—and has been true for a thousand years. But if Buddhism is meant in the sense in which Buddhism is regarded as the religion of Tibet, then the remark needs considerable modification. Deeply as Indian traditions and Indian superstition have affected the Buddhism of the Tibetans they would be scandalized at any charge of apostasy. In Nepal the Newars have accepted with Asiatic placidity a large number of embellishments to their earlier ritual and additions to their pantheon. This has been natural enough. The psychologist may recall that in general it is not in the nature of men living at high altitudes to develop the jealousy which at sea levels rends apart families as well as faiths. The newcomers are looked upon rather as captives than conquerors. The representatives of the earlier Mongol tribes that eventually trickled through the Himalayan barrier into Nepal during one or other of the great racial migrations of Central Asia are not greatly concerned with abstract theories of Buddhism. In Tibet local animism and a terror of topical and malign demons practically make up almost the entire religious equipment of the man in the field, over which the Blessed One presides from wall and altar and banner, a placid, meditative, and remote Master. But his personality, shadowy as it is, exists as the chief and almost the only connection that remains between the teachings of the historical Buddha and the practical religion of the Mongoloid peoples of Tibet.

While Buddhism was conducting this doomed struggle with polytheistic animism in and across the Himalayas, Hinduism in the plains below was reasserting its ancient authority against the simpler and austerer doctrine. In some parts of India, however, such as Bengal, the Buddhists were not driven away easily, and it was not until the eighth century that the followers of the Master gave up the struggle and either conformed to the older faith or, like the Huguenots of the seventeenth century, sought refuge in another country. Of those countries Nepal, Bhutan, and Tibet were the nearest and most obvious sanctuaries. In them Buddhism continued, but, as we have seen, it continued in a form which in Nepal made large concessions to Hinduism, and in the others capitulated to local superstition. The form of Buddhism which prevails in Nepal has not received the attention that it deserves, and although Dr. Oldfield has written a careful account of this mixture of two similar but antagonistic faiths, his description is coloured by his belief that Buddhism was a dying creed. It has, however, recently taken on a new lease of life. So long as the landmark of landmarks, the grave eyes of the Master—repainted and reconsecrated every few years—

THE SOUTH STUPA, PATAN

look out over the Valley from Swayambhunath, from Boddhnath, and a score of other torans, there will be a strong Nepalese-Buddhist community drawing inspiration from Lhasa but as loyally Nepalese as any Gurkha from the Kali to Kangchanjanga. Still there exists a tenacious belief that, however strange and foreign-born the rite, it is through the Master, the Law, and the Community, and through them alone that relief from reincarnation may be won.

§ 2

In this remote and mountainous state, where the influences of Mohammed and of Christ have never penetrated except as the creeds of a man's own rug or bed, Buddhism and Hinduism have carried on relations partly of hostility and partly of sympathy which are almost unparalleled in the history of comparative religion. Taking the country as a whole there is no sign that in the last seventy years the form of Buddhism which prevails there has lost much ground—in spite of the fact that the ruling class is not merely of the Hindu faith, but of the strictest persuasion of that faith. I do not mean by this that the Prime Minister does not attend annual ceremonies connected with Buddhism such as the Machendranath Jatra: it is indeed his practice to do so, and is only one more curious illustration of the harmony with which two faiths which elsewhere have found antagonism to the bitter end find here a common path to that peace which, after all, is the goal of both. Never has the Hindu Government of Nepal ever shown the least lack of respect for the Buddhist shrines of the Valley.[1] By tradition both Swayambhunath and Boddhnath are under the especial charge of the Dalai Lama in Lhasa, but local piety has always been necessary for the works of restoration; and in spite of its general disinclination to the presence of strangers, the Nepal Government has never hesitated to allow the Tibetan pilgrims full and free access to these peculiarly holy shrines.

Perhaps the simplest way of dealing with the state of Nepalese Buddhism at this moment is to use as a foundation the illuminating but all too brief notes of Sir Charles Eliot in his work, *Hinduism and Buddhism*. I do not entirely agree with his estimate of the decline of Buddhism in Nepal, but the summary is written by a man to whom the relations between the two faiths have been a life work, excellently and patiently pursued, so that a better estimate of the essential nature of Buddhism as a form of " exported Hinduism "—a truth that is the corner-stone of all useful study—could hardly be obtained.[2]

---

[1] I was in Katmandu in 1908 and noted the beginnings of decay in both Swayambhunath and Boddhnath. But every encouragement has been given by the Government to those who wish to restore, redecorate, and make additions to the Lamaic shrines of the Valley. An elaborate iron framework has recently been set up round the base of Swayambhunath, enshrining scores of prayer wheels. The upper structure has been entirely restored and re-gilt. The enormous dorje at the head of the flight of steps which had lost two of its arms has been restored: the plants that had sown themselves on the stupa itself and on the sentinel sikras have been rooted out and the surfaces re-whitened. At Boddhnath a similar work of reverent restoration has been carried through.

[2] Most of the recent writers upon the condition of Buddhism in Nepal have noted its

It is worth recalling here that before all others our debt to Hodgson as the pioneer is beyond all expression. Professor Max Müller remarks that before the time of Brian Hodgson "our information on Buddhism had been derived at random from China and other countries far from India, and no hope was entertained that the originals of the various translations existing in these countries could ever be recovered." In 1824 Hodgson announced that he had been able to discover in the monasteries and libraries of Nepal the original documents of the Buddhist canon, and from 1828 onwards a series of illuminating studies of northern Buddhism flowed from his pen. But even he did not and indeed could not fully note the peculiarities which in his time distinguished the contemporary Buddhism of Nepal from that of Tibet—then a totally unvisited country. He did, however, lay his finger on the three main distinctions; first, that Tibet has adhered to and Nepal has rejected the old monastic institutes of Buddhism. Secondly, that the former is still, as of old, wholly unperplexed by caste, while the latter is a good deal hampered by it; and that, lastly, Tibetan Buddhism has no concealments, while the Nepalese is sadly "prone to withhold many higher matters of the law from all but chosen vessels." Another dominating difference—which may indeed lie at the root of all the above distinctions—is that in Tibet the government is in the hands of the hierarchy, while in Nepal the final authority has long been exercised by rulers of Hindu faith. Hodgson also was the first to indicate the enormous extent of the ground which is common to Hinduism and to Buddhism.[1]

Briefly stated, Sir Charles Eliot's review of the position is this. A corrupt form of Buddhism, he says, still exists in Nepal. This country, when first heard of, was in the hands of the Newars, who have preserved some traditions of a migration from the north, and are akin to the Tibetans in face and language, though, like many non-Aryan tribes, they have endeavoured to invent for themselves a Hindu pedigree. That Hinduism crept in from the south we must accept, but of course its first advent cannot be traced. Buddhism, he says, was introduced under Asoka, but of its history there is little that can be known with any certainty. The country remained under the influence of both religions for many centuries.[2]

anomalous nature and then, in a manner more or less perceptible to their readers, have firmly passed it by on the other side.

In an otherwise well-documented review of contemporary Buddhism by M. Alfred Roussel, the references to Nepal are meagre indeed.

Even the manful Professor Rhys-Davids shrinks from the task of explaining what perhaps is as inexplicable as anything in all the chronicle of religion. In his invaluable work, *Buddhism*, he expresses, with a touch of satire, his sympathy with any man who sets before himself the task of disentangling the strands of Buddhism and Hinduism in Nepal.

[1] The practical identity of Nepalese Buddhism and the word of Shiva is put forward by Hodgson with some force. Perhaps the suggestion already made that—

"That which drew from out the mighty deep
Returns to the deep again."

may most probably explain the unique position which the intertwining of Hinduism and Buddhism in Nepal offers.

[2] M. Sylvain Lévi quotes from an inscription of the year 627, the joint and apparently friendly co-operation of eleven followers of the Hindu faith and six Buddhists.

KRISHNA-DEWAL TEMPLE IN PATAN

In 1324 the King of Tirhout, expelled by the Moslems from his own lands, seized Nepal and introduced a Brahman hierarchy. Later in the same century Jaya Sthiti Malla organized anew the society and religion of Nepal upon a strictly caste basis in consultation with this Brahman immigration. The followers of the two religions were codified in parallel divisions according to occupation, and ranked with similar Hindu castes. Rules and ceremonies were drawn up and, in its essentials, the status thus imposed is still in force. About the same time arose the Nathas, wandering ascetics revered by both creeds. The worship of Machendranath is probably an illustration of the influence of these people. In 1769, Sir Charles goes on to say, the Gurkhas, claiming Hindu descent, accelerated the Hinduizing of Nepal.

B. H. Hodgson has noted that the worship of an Adi Buddha, or Supreme God, was characteristic of Nepal.[1] Sir Charles Eliot observes that this dedication has parallels in India, where special gods of No-Matter are known. Indeed, the Buddhism of Nepal is less remarkable as a form of the extravagances of northern Buddhism than as a guide to, or at least a suggestion of, the last phases of the faith in Bengal before it was reabsorbed rather than reconquered by Brahmanism. Nepalese Brahmans do more than merely tolerate Buddhism. The Nepalamahatmya says: "To worship Buddha is to worship Shiva," and the Swayambhu Purana returns the compliment by recommending the worship of Pashpati. The official itinerary of a Vaishnavite Hindu pilgrim includes Swayambhunath, where without any sense of incongruity he adores Buddha under that name. It is true that more often the two religions adore the same image under different names—for example, what is Avalokiteswara to the one is Mahadeo to the other.[2]

The Nepalese pantheon contains three elements, often united in modern legends: firstly, aboriginal deities, such as Nagas and other nature spirits; secondly, definitely Buddhist deities or Boddhisatwas, of whom Manjusri receives the most honour; and thirdly, Hindu deities, such as Ganesha or Krishna.[3] The popular deity, Machendranath or Matsyendranath, appears to combine all these elements in his own person.

Modern accounts of Nepal, in Sir Charles's opinion, leave the impression

---

[1] The idea of the Adi Buddha goes back to the earliest ages of Nepalese Buddhism. Swayambhunath has probably stood for something like two thousand years as a symbol of "The Self-Existent One," who was not merely a First Cause, but a supreme and definitely conceived God.

[2] There is not this interchange of religious courtesy between the two faiths in India. The writer was present in 1908 when the present Tashi, or Panchan Lama, celebrated the famous mass beneath the Bo Tree at Buddhgaya. This concession was not obtained without difficulty. So completely Brahmanized had that place become that at one time there seemed likely to be some trouble, as protesting Hindus from Gaya attempted to obstruct the lustrations of the Grand Lama's attendants and followers round the temple.

[3] The temple of Ganesha at Deo Patan is said to have been built by Charumati, the daughter of Asoka. The priests of this Ganesha temple are Banhras. Kali is not often found, but it is remarkable that the Banhras are present at the bloody sacrifices to her at Devi ghat near Nayakot. The Banhras conducted the services. They wore red robes and their heads were clean shaven.

that even decadent Buddhism is in a bad way there; yet the number of religious establishments is considerable. Celibacy is not observed by their inmates, who are called Banhras, nor, it seems, are their other vows taken with great seriousness. The classes known as Bhikshus and Gubharjus officiate as priests, the latter being of the higher order. The principal ceremony is the offering of melted butter. The more learned Gubharjus receive the title of Vajracarya and have the sole right of officiating at marriages and funerals. There is little Buddhist learning in Nepal. The oldest Scriptures are the nine Dharmas.[1]

But all speculations upon origins can only be tentative. There is still an undiscovered world of Mahayana literature in Nepal, which it remains for the industry of the next two or three generations to translate, to collate, and to digest for the study of Western scholars. The royal library in Katmandu is a richer source of knowledge relating to the development of the Greater Vehicle than any other uncollated and almost uncatalogued collection of which we have information. But it need hardly be said that, important as these records are for the student of Buddhism, the man in the Nepalese street and field has very little use for comparative research.

For him there is the daily round and common task and, as everywhere else in the world, his interest in religion is entirely concerned with its application to his life and to the major and minor facts of his everyday existence. In the West there is still a strong prejudice in favour of the incorporation of some form of religious rite with birth, marriage, and death. In the East the identification of life and ritual is far more universal and intimate. From the hesitation of an Indian prince, better educated though he be than most Oxford graduates, to begin a journey or inaugurate a great work until the proposed day has been declared by the priests to be auspicious, to the half-anna charm against hail that the anxious Tibetan peasant buys confidently from the nearest Bon-pa magic-worker, there is no rank of life that is not priest-guided and in a measure priest-ridden; there is no action that does not need to be guarded by a special invocation, and there is no passage in the lives of Orientals which the jealous deities do not require them—of course through the priests, their vicegerents on earth—to safeguard by an outward act of deference. It is just as well to see that all the sources of good and, even more perhaps, all the sources of harm, are duly propitiated. Thus in Katmandu we find the Buddhist worshipping at the shrine of Sitala, the Hindu goddess of smallpox,[2] as cheerfully as the Hindu makes his offering to Machendra the Buddhist giver of rain in due season.

I have already referred to the universal popularity of the Machen-

---

[1] This, at least, was Hodgson's opinion, but M. Lévi has some doubt upon the subject. The Swayambhu Purana in its present form is not earlier than the sixteenth century. The Nepalamahatmya puts Buddha, Vishnu, and Shiva on the same footing, and identifies the first with Krishna. The Bagvatimahatmya is Shivaite, and ignores Buddha.

[2] Buddhists and Hindus alike worship Sitala. Being purely Hindu, the temple is arranged according to their creed. But the topmost roof has as its centre ornament a chaitya, by the side of which is a sword, indicating the worship of a female deity. This finial is set up to claim Buddhist affinity and authority over the temple, and the set of praying wheels round its base is intended for a like purpose.

dranath Jatra, which is attended with equal enthusiasm and reverence by men of either religion. The list of such doubled deities might be greatly extended,[1] and even in notes which have to be confined within strict li:nits, the temple of Mahankal should be again referred to here. This is a shrine of no great architectural pretensions lying on the western side of the Tundi Khel, immediately opposite the new hospital built by the present Maharaja. It is actually flush with the road, and up through the centre of the high plinth on which it is set runs a steep slope of steps, where all day long may be seen worshippers of both creeds. The Buddhist sees in the central shrine an image of Avalokiteswara: the Hindu worships in the statue the guardian deity of Nepal—Mahadeo: sometimes he finds in him

MAHANKAL

Hindu-Buddhist temple in Katmandu

his brother deity, Vishnu. Of *odium theologicum* there is little in Nepal and any differences between these two interwoven faiths would more probably be caused by a political than a religious issue.

The Brahmans in Nepal remain a close corporation and represent, though in practice it is never employed, the only authority that can in any sense of the word be said to exercise any influence upon the complete autocracy of the Maharaja. In the adjoining country of Tibet Lamaic prejudice has always denied access to foreigners. In the Valley of Katmandu

[1] Narayan equals Vishnu. Bhairab equals Shiva. Ganesha, Garuda, and Indra seem worshipped equally by both creeds. At Mahankal a small image of Akshobya rises out of the head of Mahadeo. Mahankal is identified by Hindus as Shiva or Vishnu and by Buddhists as Vajrapani.

this jealousy is more conspicuous in the case of Hindu shrines than in those of the Buddhists. Outside the Valley it is an interesting but difficult problem to solve whether the determination of Nepal not to be visited by Europeans is due chiefly to those of the northern or the southern faith. Of this hostility there is no question. Those who have been disappointed in their natural wish to visit the country are apt to put the refusal of the Nepal Government down to the Maharaja's personal unwillingness, and that he is reluctant for certain good reasons to allow this intrusion has been explained elsewhere. But wholly apart from his personal judgment, he would undoubtedly have to deal with serious opposition on the part of his people to any such visit by a European.

§ 3

It is impossible to take a proper interest in the treasures of the Valley without at least some knowledge of the symbolism of the statues, paintings, carvings, and general architectural characteristics of the shrines therein, so the following brief explanation may be justified. The expansion of that body of thought which has been referred to as the " Greater Vehicle " led to the creation of an overlapping and sometimes fortuitous pantheon. In this tangle it is, however, possible to distinguish certain main lines of doctrine and symbolism with which it is necessary to be in some degree acquainted.

According to the later and now dominant school there are five greater manifestations (Dhyani Buddhas) of the one Essential Buddha (Adi Buddha) to whom, as the Eternal and Self-Existent One, the temple of Swayambhunath is dedicated, but who is not himself knowable in any form.[1] The Dhyani Buddhas,[2] though propitiated and frequently represented in sculpture and painting, are scarcely more tangible. Another link is still needed with humanity. There is no real analogy between the Christian doctrine of the Trinity and the complexities of Buddhism, but it may perhaps give a line of understanding if the five Dhyani Buddhas, each of whom in his own period is supremely worshipped, are compared to God the Father who reigns in heaven and who has chosen certain means and certain divine persons through whom to create and control and teach the world of men.[3]

[1] Both the Red and Yellow sects in Tibet give him the name of Vajradhara, or the wielder of the thunderbolt.
[2] These Dhyani Buddhas are in theory very numerous, but in practice they are limited to five.
[3] There is much loose definition in the concepts of later Buddhism. Vairochana has at times been regarded as the unknowable Adi-Buddha, and there is reason to think that his invisible position in the central relic chamber of the stupa always places him somewhat higher than his four compeers. By others Vairochana's " son," Samantabhadra, and Vajrasattva, a disputed sixth Dhyani Buddha of late origin, are regarded as personifying the Adi Buddha. When recognized, as in Japan, his colour is that of the rainbow. It is remarkable that the doctrine of the Adi Buddha was originally taught in Nepal by the Aisvarika school about the eleventh century, according to Grünwedel. But it came to its full growth in China and Japan.

Now each of these five Celestial Essences is distinguished by symbols domains, and representations of his own.   He has his own special animal, used somewhat as supporters are used in heraldry, his own badge, his own special mudra or attitude, his own colour, his own consort,[1] his own celestial emanation or son, and—a matter which is of more importance than anything else to the wayfaring man—his own human manifestation or representative on earth.[2]   Each, too, has his own special badge, a special position for his shrine in or round the garbh of the stupa.   The following diagram will illustrate the meaning of the summaries I am about to make.[3]

	Dhyani Buddhas	Consorts	Celestial Emanation [or Dhyani-Boddhisatwa]	Human Manifestation	
Centre	Vairochana	Vajradhatisvari	Samantabhadra	Krakuchhanda	(Past Eras)
East	Akshobya[4]	Lochana	Vajrapani	Kanakamuni	
South	Ratnasambhava	Mamaki	Ratnapani	Kasyapa	
West	AMITABHA[4]	PANDARA	AVALOKITESWARA	SAKYAMUNI	(Present Era)
North	*Amoghasiddha*	*Tara*	*Visvapani*	*Maitreya*	(Coming Era)

THE FIVE DHYANI BUDDHAS

I

Vairochana, whose dominion is space, or possibly the universe, is white. His supporters are sarduls or mythical beasts, not unlike dragons.   He is always found in the mudra of teaching, hence the wheel is his badge. It has been noted that his shrine is assumed to be in the relic chamber in the centre of the stupa, a place of special significance and honour.   In order, however, that his shrine may not therefore lack worship he is also given one on the outside of the garbh at the right hand of Akshobya, *i.e.*, facing east by north.

His wife is Vajradhatisvari, who differs little from her sister goddesses. She is also called the White Tara, reincarnate in Princess Wen-cheng, the

---

[1] It may here be said that, although the name " Tara " is strictly applied to the White and Green female deities, it is sometimes used indiscriminately to indicate all the consorts of the Dhyani Buddhas.

[2] Still being careful to emphasize the danger of pretending to too close a parallel, the divine and human natures of Christ may be quoted as illustrative of the last two manifestations.

[3] Readers desirous of following up the symbolism of Northern Buddhism in Nepal and elsewhere are referred to George Roerich's *Tibetan Paintings* (1925) and Mrs. Getty's *The Gods of Northern Buddhism* (1914), as well as the earlier works of Waddell, Foucher, Grünwedel, and Oldenburg.

[4] Each Dhyani Buddha has, besides his conventional representation in the simple robe of a teacher, another in magnificent apparel with a crown and jewelled necklaces.   In the case of Akshobya this radiant version is known as Vajrasattva, and in that of Amitabha as Amitayus.   The other three Dhyani Buddhas retain their names when depicted in this royal fashion.

second wife of Srong-Tsan-Gambo of Tibet.[1] Sometimes she is given four arms, and in that case she bears as a head ornament the head of Amitabha, her husband's successor. The extra pair of arms and hands sometimes bear in front of her breast an object which it is difficult to identify, but which is in fact a large sapphire. In her right hand she bears a conventionally looped rosary of white beads.

Their son is Samantabhadra who, in the oldest sect of the Lamaic school unreformed by Tsongkapa, is elevated to the position of the Self-

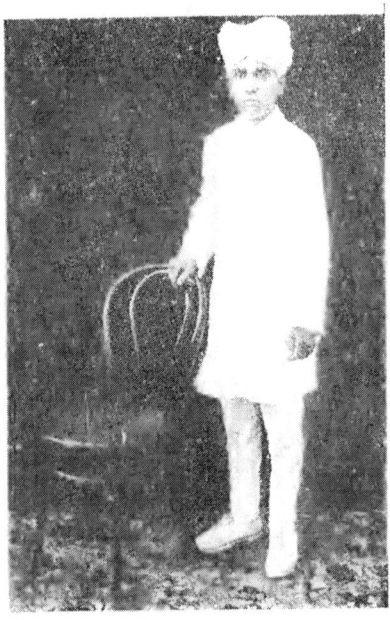

A NEPALESE IN MOURNING ATTIRE

Existent One, the Adi Buddha. In this case he is represented in the usual adamantine pose, but of a blue colour and naked. Their earthly representative was Krakuchhanda, whose place of sepulture was honoured in an undiscovered spot close to Kanakamuni's.

II

Akshobya. With him the colour blue is connected, the air, and the elephant and the East. He is represented in the attitude of Buddha calling

---

[1] The influence of this deified queen may have been responsible for the use of white by the Nepalese in mourning, in accordance with the Chinese custom.

the world to witness. His badge is the single Vajra, such as may be seen at the top of the steps in front of Swayambhunath.

His wife is named Lochana.[1] She, of course, is of the blue colour too, and, unlike her husband, who, except in the Yab-yum position[2] is unadorned, she wears a magnificently jewelled coronet. In her two hands she bears conventional long-stalked flowers, which are arranged to suit the composition of the horseshoe-shaped halo which enfolds her.

Akshobya's son is Vajrapani, who is represented as a rule in a standing position. He, too, bears a couple of conventionally modelled flowers, and is enshrouded by a vesica-shaped aureole.

Akshobya's earthly representative was Kanakamuni, at whose reputed birthplace close to Kapilavastu the Emperor Asoka set up a column—now shifted to Nigliva—on which the inscription, though damaged, may be read to this day. (See Appendix X.)

III

Ratnasambhava. This deity is connected with the element fire,[3] his colour is yellow, his supporter is the horse, his mudra is that of giving, his symbol is the Tri-ratna or triple jewel.[4]

His wife is Mamaki, who differs in no essential way from Lochana except that her colour is yellow. Their son is Ratnapani, and their earthly representative was Kasyapa.

IV

Amitabha.[5] This deity from most points of view is of greater importance than any other because he is directly connected with the one historical Buddha, Siddhartha Gautama of Kapilavastu. He is lord of the present cycle of time. His element is water, his colour is red, he represents light, and his throne is towards the west. His emblem is the lion. His attendant is the peacock, and he is represented in the attitude of meditation.[6]

[1] The five wives of these five beings are, as a matter of fact, allowed much licence in attitude and decoration, and even in limb and feature. The following descriptions are, therefore, true only of the more popular versions. Most of them have the seven eyes of Tara. It is often difficult, even when the breast is exposed, to deduce the sex of the deity represented. Females, however, rarely assume either of the poses which require both feet to rest upon the opposite thigh. In general they take up the "Lalita" pose, which is often assumed by Manjusri. Here the right leg is flexed at right angles and often supported by a floral bracket. The left foot, missing its support, lies horizontally between the legs.   [2] That is, the position of sexual intercourse.
[3] So Getty, *The Gods of Northern Buddhism*, p. 35. Waddell attributes to Ratnasambhava the element of earth.
[4] These jewels are conventionally represented somewhat in the shape of a cluster of three circular knobs arranged in a pyramid and often continued carrotwise a little distance below.
[5] The two Grand Lamas of Lhasa and Tashi-lhunpo are reincarnations respectively of Avalokiteswara and Amitabha. Now Avalokiteswara, though one of the best known deities in Northern Buddhism, is an emanation of Amitabha, and therefore, though the fact is little known, the Tashi Lama is spiritually the superior of the Dalai Lama of Lhasa. The former, whose estates lie to the north of the Nepal frontier, has now almost no political power, and therefore Nepal, in dealing with Tibet, is concerned only with Lhasa.
[6] In his radiant manifestation, Amitabha appears as Amitayus the Lord and Giver of Life. He is never found in the Yab-yum pose.

His wife is Pandara, who has become identified, by the curious mixture of religions of Nepal, with Sita, the wife of Rama, the last incarnation but one of Vishnu.[1] She has lotus plants in her fingers, though these occasionally give place to small golden sacrificial pots. Their son is Avalokiteswara, or Padmapani, who plays a considerable part in the theological representations of the Valley.

V

Amoghasiddha. He is the Dhyani Buddha to come. His colour is green; he represents earth;[2] his badge is the double Vajra and his seat is to the north; his attendants are garudas or winged sprites, generally represented with birds' heads. His attitude is that of reassuring or fearlessness, and his haloes are curiously decorated, though in habit he is as ascetically dressed as his predecessors.

His wife is the Green Tara, the Nepalese goddess *par excellence.*[3] She carries in her hands representations of the blue lotus, but except by her colour is not distinguished from her predecessors. Their son is Visvapani, and their earthly representative is Maitreya, the Merciful One, whose coming on earth will close the present era and inaugurate the period under the direction of Amoghasiddha.[4]

With the exception of Gautama Buddha himself, and perhaps of Avalokiteswara, the Word or Creator of the World, the most popular in Nepalese eyes of all the foregoing deities are no doubt the Green and the White Taras. One reason is, of course, that these two deities were reincarnated in two actual women, of whom one at least was a princess of Nepal.

Mention must also be made of Manjusri, who, though only a detached Boddhisatwa and therefore not included in the table, is exceedingly popular as the celestial visitor who created the Valley and introduced Buddhism into Nepal from his home in the sacred Wu-t'ai-shan in Shansi—the Hill of the Five Peaks. At Wu-t'ai-shan there is still a structure remotely resembling the shrines of Boddhnath and Swayambhunath, and it does not appear that any other similar shrine is to be found in China proper. Manjusri is a guardian deity of China, and is almost unknown among Indians, though M. Lévi points out that it is there that a historical basis for his personality may be found. His prototype was born in Orissa about the time of Alexander's invasion. It is commonly said that the Hindus in

[1] There is, however, a certain tendency among Hindu pandits to teach that, after his life as Krishna, Vishnu was again reincarnated in the person of the historical Buddha.

[2] Waddell gives water as his element.

[3] See vol. i, p. 29. The Green Tara was also the sakti of Avalokiteswara.

[4] It is remarkable that while Maitreya is comparatively seldom found among the statues and paintings of Nepal, he has been specially chosen as the Lamaic deity of China. He presides, a huge standing figure seventy feet high, in the Holy of Holies of the Lama Temple in Peking. Representations of the same god, either standing or seated in the European fashion, are to be found from one end of China to the other. He has also had his political uses, for it is credibly believed that the Buriat Dorjieff actually tried to win the late Tsar of Russia to the cause of the Dalai Lama by assuring him that His Majesty was the re-born Buddha upon earth, for whose coming the faith had looked for 2,500 years.

Nepal have recognized in him the female divinity of its own pantheon, Sarasvati, the wife of Brahma; but, though the distinction may be fully understood only by the initiated, it is probably as the sakti or consort of Manjusri that Sarasvati is worshipped.

Machendranath is identified with Avalokiteswara or Padmapani, the celestial emanation of the Dhyani Buddha of the present manifestation, which accounts for his rufous colour. His association with the rainfall is connected with his legendary redemption of the starving Valley after a period of unexampled drought, for he made Gorakhnath rise from his seat of Nagas and give the Valley the much desired rain. The credit is claimed by both Buddhists and Brahmans. The Buddhist account contains a curious description of the honours paid by the Brahmanic pantheon to Avalokiteswara : the latter version admits that Machendranath was the tutor of Gorakhnath, but makes the interest of the story centre round the latter.

The Maypole-like structure of his car is crowned with an image of the curious and somewhat doubtfully accepted sixth Dhyani Buddha, Vajrasattva. He is an addition of comparatively recent date and is connected with the intrusion of Tantric worship into the already enlarged pantheon of the Mahayana or Greater Vehicle.

Kuvera or Jambhala is the god of wealth, and may be identified by the stoat or ferret which rests upon his left forearm and by means of which he fetches up his treasures from the lower world. In his right hand he bears a sword and his attitude is generally that adopted by the " consorts " just referred to.

The dragon-heads which are used throughout Nepal as gargoyles and waterspouts are practically identical with the " makaras," well known as terminals at the corner of gilt copper roofs in Tibet. They are found, indeed, over the whole of Buddhist Eastern Asia.

§ 4

The arrangement of the shrines round the stupa is to be noted. As we have seen, Amoghasiddha faces the north; Akshobya the east; Ratnasambhava the south; Amitabha the west. The consorts of these deities have smaller shrines, generally placed at the right hand of their lords, half-way between the cardinal points. Vairochana is supposed to inhabit the centre of the stupa, but the Nepalese have not been satisfied with this concealment, so in almost every case· there will be found a shrine immediately north of Akshobya's which commemorates the White Deity. In some places, as at Kirtipur, the curious tradition is maintained of representing him by an almost shapeless block of stone. Those who have been to Borobodoer in Java will remember a similar lack of finish which, it is asserted by some students, was intended to represent the inability of the human mind to grasp the infinite.[1]

---

[1] It may, however, be merely a copy of the unfinished state of the Buddha upon the Diamond Throne of Buddhgaya. This may have been due to the impossibility of man to represent the Supreme God by brush or chisel.

CAR OF MACHENDRA

The parts of the stupa itself are generally known by names which are more suggestive than accurate. The round hemispherical mass is known as the " garbh," though that name should strictly be applied to the relic chamber in the centre and to the small shrines of the Dhyani Buddhas round its base at the cardinal points of the compass. The square brick-built erection on the top of the " garbh " is called the " toran." This again is a misnomer, as the word should strictly be applied to the gilt shrines which are set in the middle of each side of the top. Above them come the thirteen gilt rings, " churamani," which taper until they are crowned by the " kalsa," or ornamental finial—known in Burma as a " hti." The sides of the " toran " are generally plated with gilt copper, and the eyes which form the most remarkable feature of the entire temple are painted upon these plates: at Boddhnath the nose is shaped like a mark of interrogation. There is a curious tradition by which the centre of the upper lid possesses a downward curve in the middle, which lends to the eyes a fascinating aspect of mingled meditation and detached watchfulness.

§ 5

A few of the symbols connected with Nepalese Buddhism may be mentioned. The circular bump on the forehead of a Buddha is called the " urna," and, strictly speaking, should distinguish those alone who have received enlightenment. It is, however, sometimes used in representations of Boddhisatwas or those who, by their saintliness and learning, have quali-fied for the highest rank of Buddha.

The knob at the top of the hair of the head of Buddha is known as the " usnisa." The legend goes that Buddha was so frequently distracted from meditation and teaching by the necessity of having his hair cut that he murmured some quiet expostulation. At once his hair all over his head became tightly curled and of a rich blue colour. Thenceforth he apparently had no need of the barber. The " usnisa " is not infrequently used as a support for some symbol denoting a peculiar manifestation of the Great One who is represented.

The representation of three jewels upon a lotus symbolizes the whole of essential Buddhism. The three jewels represent the Buddha, his Law, the Church, or his followers; and their setting upon the lotus is a declaration in paint or stone that the triune God resides in him of the jewel and the lotus. This will be recognized at once as the basis of the one eternal ascription of all Buddhism—" Om mani padme hum."

Mortal Buddhas are, as a rule, represented as of a golden colour, and the following list, though without historical foundation with the exception of the last, may be useful as giving the chronological order of their reputed appearances on earth. After a long succession of other earthly manifesta-tions, among whom the Dipankara Buddha is by far the most distinguished, we come to the last seven that have appeared on earth:

1. Vipasya. He is specially connected with the Valley of Katmandu.

2. Sikhi.

3. Visvabhu.

(Here we enter the range of the five deities that I have already described.)

4. Krakuchhanda.

5. Kanakamuni.

6. Kasyapa.

7. Sakyasingha, who, of course, is the same as Sakyamuni or Prince Gautama.

Buddha is said to have accepted the existence before himself of Krakuchhanda, Kanakamuni, and Kasyapa.

A form of plinth was probably always used originally to support the vajra or double dorje, which is the especial and jealously guarded symbol of the Lamaic priesthood. Of its best shape, known as the Dharma-dhatu-mandal, an example is to be found at the top of the steps leading to Swayambhunath. It consists of a small circular and drum-like building of stone, the circumference of which is generally charged with the symbols of the year under the Lamaic code. These are, in succession :

(1) The rat; (2) the bull; (3) the tiger; (4) the hare; (5) the dragon; (6) the serpent; (7) the horse; (8) the sheep; (9) the monkey; (10) the goose; (11) the dog; and (12) the pig.

Double footprints not only appear in the armorial bearings of the State of Nepal, but are to be found carved in a thousand places throughout the Valley. The name they bear is " paduka," and they differ according to the personage indicated. Manjusri has an eye on the sole of each foot. Vishnu can be recognized by an incised text, and Buddha's own footmarks are indicated by a circle.[1]

§ 6

The outstanding characteristic of original Buddhism was that it was strong for the strong and weak for the weak. Buddha himself seems to have paid scant attention to the weaker brethren of the flock and their need for simple doctrine, regular worship, and a personal and anthropomorphic symbolism of the principles of the faith. Human as his outlook was, he seems hardly to have realized one of the great truths that dominate the relations between a plain man and his faith. Perhaps it may be said that Christ himself needed a St. Paul to add to the abstract magnificence of his teaching the practical but sometimes chilling ordinances and interpretations of the Epistles. And even the dogmatism of St. Paul had to be amplified, glossed, and gilded in succeeding generations of Christians —at the cost, perhaps, that the added ritual often became the rule of life for the ordinary man, rather than the great verities which that ritual was intended to enshrine.

---

[1] Like other creeds Buddhism was compelled to make concessions to the faith it found already reigning in the land. After all, do we not ourselves borrow some of our customs from sun worship, our days of the week from Scandinavian gods, and Christmas itself from the anniversary of Mithras?

The same process may be observed in the degeneration of Buddhism. Probably never more than two per cent. of any people in the world have ever been content to guide their lives by the abstract principles of even'the noblest code of ethics. Colour, warmth, and harmony must be associated with these principles before they can be assimilated by the masses that have most need of them. Nor is this all. In Nepal, as in Tibet, the new gospel of Buddha could not—and naturally could not—dethrone the local animistic superstitions which had for so long served the common people as a religion, and in the long run Buddhism was compelled to capitulate—as Buddhism has always been obliged to capitulate to the local preferences and prejudices of every country in which it has obtained a footing. In Nepal this process of assimilation with mere animism never assumed the proportions which it did in Tibet. On the south slope of the Himalayas, instead of a concession to Shamanism the tendency has been rather to a compromise between Tantric extravagance and the steady influence of Hinduism.

APPENDIX XVI

AUTHORITIES

§ 1

THE source to which a student of Nepalese history would naturally go for a responsible narrative is the Vamshavali, or Chronicle of Nepal. Though, in its present shape, it does not date from a more remote period than the sixteenth century, it contains the traditions of a very much older period. As the name implies, it professes to be a genealogical table rather than a record of incidents, but, as a matter of fact, although an occasionally true and more often a fanciful genealogical descent of the princes of Nepal is herein recorded, its real interest lies in the notes which accompany these data. The work itself is known in more than one form, but the Buddhist edition that Dr. Daniel Wright caused to be translated about the year 1876 is perhaps the safest guide. In spite of earlier evangelization the real tide of Hindu influence dates from the time of the Gurkha invasion; before that time the record of the chief events of the kingdom was compiled by Buddhists, and later Hindu chronicles had only the story of their rivals as a basis for their own work before Jaya Sthiti Malla.

But it must be said at once that though this Chronicle is almost the only source of information about the earlier age of Nepal, it scarcely presents more than a series of unhistorical legends and impossible genealogies until the reign of the Malla dynasty. There is no more difficult problem in Oriental history than the precise meaning which is to be attached to legends of the appearance of deities and other unscientific records. It would be unwise wholly to dismiss them. They often contain in an Oriental guise a hint which may usefully be followed up, and even in their most extravagant form these legends are of importance if only from the fact that they still form the basis of common belief and still influence the life of the inhabitants.

As an instance of the unwisdom of applying Western scientific tests to the statements of such a chronicle as the Vamshavali, it is enough to quote a couple of passages from Wright's translation :

"Dwapar Yuga lasted 834,000 years. . . . The Kiratis came into Nepal at the 15,000th year of the Dwapar Yuga, and they ruled over the country for 10,000 years. The gods came into the country after the Kiratis. Dharmadatta Raja reigned one thousand years. After this the country remained without a king for one thousand years. Bisalnagara existed for two thousand years. Pingala's adventures extended over fifty years. When 950 years of the Dwapar Yuga still remained, the gods came to the decision that it was necessary to appoint a Raja. After this the Kali Yuga commenced."

Now from a modern point of view it would be difficult to quote any less serious attempt—and the Vamshavali is a most serious attempt—to write history. But no one who has lived in the East will fail to see in these exaggerated and inconsistent notes a general statement which is probably true. They may be reduced to modern phraseology as follows. At some time to which the memory of man runneth not to the contrary, certain barbarous Eastern tribes, called Kirantis, overran the central fertile Valley of Nepal. We have references to these Kirantis in Hindu literature, and their descendants under the same name, no longer stirred by the lust of conquest, may be found to-day in the mountainous basin of the River Arun. The Kirantis evidently dominated the centre of Nepal for some time, and it was not until they had been pressed back to their original eastern haunts that religion was able to obtain a hold upon the country. From this time onwards there was alternating monarchy and anarchy, or, if not anarchy, at least a state of tribal warfare which set every man's hand against the inhabitants of the next village. Such a state of things soon rendered it again impossible that any faith should burgeon in this distracted soil. Therefore by the direct interposition of heaven, the Valley was again united under the control of a single prince and there was peace over Nepal. But the evil days had only been staved off for a while.

To take another illustration :

"Jitedasti. This Raja by the order of Arjuna went to Kurukshetra to fight against his enemies, the Kauravas mentioned in the Mahabharata. During this reign Sakya Sinha Buddha came into Nepal from a city named Kapilavastu, and having visited Swayambhu chaitya and Manjusri chaitya, fixed his abode at Puchhagra chaitya. While there he accepted the worship and offerings of Chuda, a female Bhikshu, and made 1350 proselytes, viz., Saliputra, Maudgalyayana, Ananda, etc., from the Brahman and Chhetri castes. To several Boddhisatwas such as Maitreya, and gods such as Brahma, who came to Nepal expressly to see him, Sakya described the glory of Swayambhu. . . . He next ascended into heaven and returned, after visiting his mother, who had died on the seventh day after his birth. Then, after preaching his doctrines to the people, he saw that the time of his death was approaching and went to a city called Kusi.[1] Here, while he was preaching to an assembly of gods (such as Brahma) and Bhikshus (such as Ananda), he disappeared. Some of his followers remained in Nepal and professed his religion. Raja Jitedasti did not return from the wars recounted in the Mahabharata."

Now this is, of course, a rambling and irreconcilable story from many points of view. It is interesting, however, to trace in it the ambitions of the early Nepalese princes, and an earnest if ill-informed attempt to credit Nepal with the later phases of the Buddha's life. It was not long before the presence or absence of ancestors at the great struggle of Kurukshetra became, among Indian princely families, a kind of hall-mark or test of long descent, exactly as the Roll of Battle Abbey continued for many unscholarly generations in England to be appealed to by ambitious families as a final proof of long ancestral nobility or knighthood. What happened in India was that a family which won a principality took care that the claim of some ancestor to have fought at the battle of Kurukshetra was duly included in its archives.

If the battle had any real existence, that is if it represents a crisis in a long struggle on the part of the early reigning families in the district of Delhi against the invasion of foreigners, it must be placed between 1500 and 1100 B.C. It is absurd to assert that the visit of the Buddha Sakyamuni to Nepal took place even about the latter year; it is scarcely less uncritical to suggest that it was in Nepal that the three famous disciples whose names are mentioned in the Chronicle accepted the new gospel.

But we may discover in this fanciful account a vein of truth. That Sakyamuni at some time during his long life made his way to the Valley is on the whole probable. It is a comparatively short distance from his birthplace and the scenes of his teaching, and it is evident from the visit of the Emperor Asoka and the important monuments erected by him at Patan and at Kirtipur, that the legend of this visit must have been accepted as true by the highest Buddhist authorities only about 250 years later. In this wayward account we may notice the reconciliation of Buddhism with the full pantheon of the gods of India. As has been said above, the present intermingling of the two faiths in Nepal is one of the most interesting features of that country.

The manner in which the Nepalese Chronicle was written even in the seventeenth century is an indication of its critical value. The following is an extract from the Vamshavali: "While this kazi was in Bhot (Tibet), some mischief-maker told the Raja that Nityananda-swami (who had been

---

[1] Kusinara, the modern Kasia.

appointed Chief Priest of Pashpati by his mother) never bowed to Pash-patinath, and the Raja went to see if this were the case. Nityananda-swami guessed his purpose in coming there, and after the ceremony of worship had been finished, and Chandeswari had been worshipped, he bowed to Kama-devatá, whose foot broke and fell off. He then bowed to the Dharma-sila, and it cracked in two. Next he bowed to a stone inside the southern door, which also fell in pieces. After this, he was on the point of rushing inside to bow to Pashpatinath, when he was forcibly stopped by the Rajá. . . . He died shortly after this."

It is a matter of importance that this fantastic Chronicle should be approached from the right point of view. It can neither be dismissed nor, except in some of its latest chapters, can it be accepted in any literal sense. The gradual abandonment of the figurative language of the early part, and a genuine attempt towards the close to render justice to the passing inci-dents of each year, are remarkable and deserve attention. It is true, of course, that when the national pride, or rather the pride of the reigning king, demanded an adjustment of facts, those facts were generally adjusted. I may quote, in illustration of this point, the account in the Chronicle of the invasions of Nepal by the Chinese in 1792 and by the English in 1814-16.

" The Chinese Emperor sent a large army under the command of Kazi Dhurin and Minister Thumtham. This army reached Dhebun when the Raja employed one Lakhya Banda of Bhinkshe Bahal to perform puras-charan, while Mantrinayak Damodar Pande cut the Chinese army to pieces and obtained great glory. Afterwards the Chinese Emperor, thinking it better to live in friendship with the Gorkhalis, made peace with them." As a matter of fact, the Chinese victory was complete, though perhaps not so overwhelming as it was represented to be on the stone pillar below the Potala in Lhasa.[1]

As to the war with the English, the following brief record speaks for itself. " In the reign of Girban-Juddha Vikram Sah a war broke out with the British in the Taryani, but, depriving them of wisdom, the Raja saved his country. Then, calling the British gentlemen, he made peace with them, and allowed them to live near Thambahil." This, however, is by no means so inaccurate; the behaviour of the Nepalese during the early months of the war reflects high credit upon their military efficiency. But the statement as it stands leaves something to be desired as a record of the issue of a war by which, as has been seen, the Nepalese surrendered a part of the territory they were occupying in the Tarai and elsewhere, and accepted the presence of a permanent Resident in Katmandu.

It will be seen, therefore, that the Vamshavali is a book that must be read with healthy scepticism, with perpetual sympathy, and with an under-standing of local credulity and local prejudices. As an historical record it cannot for a moment compare with the Chinese chronicles, and it is indeed uncertain from what materials the Vamshavali was originally composed. No doubt its sources will be traced when the invaluable but hitherto

[1] This record, by permission of Sir Charles Bell, I add to this volume as an appendix, No. XXI.

scarcely opened library of Katmandu is at last thoroughly examined. There is in this little known collection material for a valuable history of the place and importance that Nepal occupied in other days from a political and a religious point of view, and it cannot be doubted that there will also be found a great deal of historical material which will throw light upon the hazardous chronology of the earlier Nepalese dynasties. Although Brian Hodgson was presented with a certain number of volumes all of which, together with a large selection of Nepalese manuscripts bought by himself, he gave to various public libraries in Europe, the mass of material that still remains on these shelves is very great. A catalogue of some part of this collection, presented by Dr. Wright, is in the University Library of Cambridge (Add. MSS. 912), and M. Lévi, during the course of a recent visit (1923) to Katmandu, devoted much of his time to the Royal Library.[1]

§ 2

Grueber.—So far as other records exist it is as well to remember that few documents of European origin are extant which deal with the history of the country before the nineteenth century. Two or three Jesuit fathers had visited the country but they left little record. The partial downfall of the Jesuit order created a difficulty which the Pope solved by allotting the district of Nepal to the Capuchins. Sixty years later, the Gurkhas in 1769 expelled them, and they retired to India where for a short time they endeavoured to maintain some communication with Nepal from Bettia.

One of the Jesuits to whom reference has just been made was Father D'Andrada, who went up to Tibet from Agra in 1624. He did not then visit Nepal, but at Chaprang he met some of the colony of Nepalese workmen who had established themselves in Tibet. In 1661 Father Grueber and Father Dorville, Jesuit priests in Peking, were ordered to return to Europe. They left in the month of June of that year, and after a stay in Lhasa of two months they reached India through Nepal. Father Dorville died soon after his arrival in India; but Father Grueber continued his journey by the regular trade route through the Persian Gulf and Asia Minor. He remained in Rome but a short time, and then again set out to the East. But in attempting to follow the road to China that had been pursued by the elder Polos he met with a check and died three years later. It is to be regretted that Father Grueber was not allowed, or at

---

[1] One of the few outstanding experts in Sanskrit and kindred tongues and customs, Mr. Cecil Bendall, afterwards Professor of Sanskrit at Cambridge, was permitted in 1884 to visit Katmandu. After some delay the Maharaja gave orders that the entire contents of the library were to be submitted to him. He set to work at once. That evening, however, he was informed that the rest house where he was staying would be required in its entirety by a visitor from India representing the Public Works Department. It is not added that the Resident offered him hospitality, so we must assume that a unique opportunity of obtaining expert information about the Katmandu MSS. was thrown away by the Resident and the chief of the P.W.D. in order that one of the latter department should not be asked to sleep under the same roof as a scholar. Mr. Bendall's account of the incident is a model of irony and good nature.

least did not give himself sufficient time, to write a connected story of his travels; but his letters have been edited by Father Kircher, and in them we find the first European reference to Nepal and its cities under names that are known to-day.

Describing the terrors of the journey to Kuti, which he rightly termed the northernmost city of the kingdom of Nepal, he said: " From Lassa or Barantola in latitude 29° 6' they came in four days' journey to the foot of the Mount Langur. This hill is of unsurpassed altitude, so high that travellers can scarcely breathe when they reach the top, so attenuated is the air. In summer no one can cross it without gravely risking his life because of the poisonous exhalations of certain herbs.[1] Neither carts nor horses can pass this way because of the terrible precipices and the stretches of rocky path. The whole journey has to be done on foot, and from Langur it takes a month to get to Cuthi, the first town in Necbal. . . .

" From Cuthi one reaches in five days the town of Nesti, where the inhabitants live in the darkness of idolatry. There was no sign of the Christian faith. However, all the things which are necessary for human life were abundant, and one could there, as a matter of course, buy thirty or forty chickens for a crown.

" From Nesti the traveller reaches Cadmendu, the capital of Necbal, in six days. This city is situated in 27° 5'. The king there is a powerful monarch. He is a pagan, but he is not an opponent of the gospel of Christ. From Cadmendu half a day's journey brings one to the town of Baddan which is the seat of the government of all the kingdom. From Necbal five days' journey brings one to Hedonda, a small town of the kingdom of Maranga. . . .

" These are some of the customs of Necbal. Whenever a man drinks from the same cup as a woman to do her honour, others, men and women alike, three times pour them out cups of tea or wine, and while they drink them, stick on the edge of the cup three lumps of butter. The drinkers take them and smear them on their foreheads.

" There is another custom in this country of monstrous cruelty. If a sick man is near to death and no further hope of his life is entertained, they take him outside away from his house into the fields, and there throw him into a ditch already full of dying men.[2] He there remains exposed to the inclemencies of the weather, without consolations of religion nor pity they leave him to die; afterwards his corpse is given to birds of prey, wolves, dogs, and other similar beasts to eat. They are convinced that the only monument of a glorious death is to find a resting-place in the belly of living animals. The women of this country are so ugly that they resemble rather devils than human beings. It is actually true that from a religious

---

[1] Mountain sickness affects certain passes and although it is due to the rarefication of the air, it is always put down by the Tibetans to the existence of maleficent dragons and things which breathe out foul odours and miasmas.

[2] The Father is here mixing up the custom of exposing the dead of Tibet to vultures, dogs, and pigs, with the Nepalese rite of steeping the limbs of a dying man in the water of the Bagmati at Pashpati. Neither habit has been altered since his time.

scruple they never wash themselves with water but with an oil of a very unpleasant smell. Let us add that they themselves are no pleasanter, and with the addition of this oil one would not say that they were human beings but ghouls.

" The king [of Cadmendu] welcomed the fathers very warmly, perhaps because of a telescope, which was up to that time unknown in Nechal, and other mathematical instruments which roused the royal curiosity to such an extent that he wished to keep the fathers with him, and he only allowed them to go after having exacted from them a promise to return. He promised them that when they came back he would build a house for the use of our Order and provide a large annual subsidy, and above all, would permit them to preach the gospel in his State." [1]

From the Valley Grueber went down into the Tarai to Hetaura, which he described as possessing no permanent buildings, though there were many straw-built huts and the office of the tax-gatherer. To this account is added the curious note that the king of Moranga pays to the Mogul Emperors every year a tribute of 250,000 rix dollars and seven elephants. This kingdom of Moranga, according to another note by Kircher, protrudes into the kingdom of Tibet. Its capital, Radoc (Rudok) is the last place reached in other days by Father D'Andrada in his voyage to Tibet. He found many proofs of the Christian faith, which had been established there, in the baptismal names still in use—Dominique, François, Antoine.

M. Lévi writes an interesting note upon the geography of Father Grueber's journey and the identification of his names. He suggests that Langur represents the hilly region west of Khamba Jong. In his view the word " Langur "—which is a generic term for a hill or a mountain—indicates the steep height of the Katambala which one crosses between Kamba Partsi on the Tsangpo and the shores of the Yamdok-tso.[2] This corresponds very well with his statement that the hill is four days' journey from Lhasa. The actual distance is perhaps fifty-seven miles, and Georgi is more accurate in estimating the time at three days. I have done the journey myself in one day, but a special dak was laid for me and three stages compressed into one.

§ 3

Tavernier.—After Grueber comes Tavernier, the famous Grand Jeweller

[1] The worthy Father was interviewed in Rome upon his amazing journey, and in the course of his remarks he explained the incident of the telescope. He says that the king of Katmandu, whose name was Partasmal (Pratapa Malla), was carrying on a war with a small king named Varcam of Bhatgaon. The latter had perpetually raided the territory of Pratapa, and the Father rendered a signal service to the troops of Katmandu by lending this eyeglass to the King. But not understanding the effect of the lens, Pratapa, seeing his enemy apparently so close to him, gave orders that his soldiers should march at once against them.

[2] Although M. Lévi's description is accurate, it is necessary not to confuse it with the more common use of the word " Langur " as applying to the enormous massif which extends from Jongsong la, where three countries meet, to the Kuti Pass. It really refers to the most magnificent group of mountains known on this planet. But that this hyperbolic phrase may have been used by local pride for lesser massifs may well be believed.

to the Indian Emperor. He reports that, five or six leagues beyond Gorakh-pur one enters the territory of the Raja of " Nupal." This prince is a vassal of the Great Mogul and sends him every year one elephant as tribute. He resides in the city of Nupal, from which he takes his name, and there is very little either trade or money in his country, which consists only of forests and mountains. As M. Lévi notes, Tavernier was obliged to trust to inadequate and partial information for the religion of the country. But he records the state of trade between India and Tibet through Nepal. He says that the kingdom of "Boutan"¹ is of great extent, but no exact knowledge of it is possessed by any one. Musk would be a profitable merchandise were it not for the taxes levied upon it on the way to Europe and the evaporation which is suffered during the hot weather. Tavernier describes a trick practisèd upon the customs house of Gorakhpur by merchants proceeding to Tibet for musk or rhubarb. If they fail to come to an arrangement with the *douane*, they take another road which is very much longer and more difficult because of the ranges of snowy mountains and the wide deserts on the other-side. This alternative road is of interest because it indicates the only other avenue to Tibet which was known to the Indians even in the days of Tavernier. He explains that it lay over the Khaibar Pass to Kabul. A part of the merchants, who come from " Boutan " and Kabul, go to Kandahar and from there to Ispahan, and these generally bring back coral in lumps, yellow amber, and lapis lazuli. Other merchants who come from Multan, Lahore, and Agra, deal in woven stuffs, in indigo, and in pieces of cornelian and crystal. The contribution of the Gorakhpur merchants, who have made their arrangements with the *douane*, is coral, yellow amber, bracelets of tortoiseshell and others of sea shells with a large number of round and square pieces about the size of French fifteen sous pieces—which are also of the same materials.

" When I was at Patna," says Tavernier, " four Armenians had already made a journey to Boutan from Dantzic where they had made a large number of figures in yellow amber representing every kind of animal and monster, which they were going to carry to the king of Boutan for idolatrous use in his pagodas. The Armenians have few scruples wherever they find any possibility of making money; they do not hesitate to supply the materials for idolatry, and they told me if they had only been able to make the idol for which the king had given them a commission, they would have been rich men. He had ordered them to make for him a figure in the form of a monster with six horns, four ears, and four arms with six fingers on each hand, all of yellow amber. They had not, however, been able to find sufficiently large pieces for the work."

Tavernier goes on to describe the road from Patna to Tibet. Seven days are taken for the journey to Gorakhpur. From thence to the foot of the Himalayas was only eight or nine days' journey, during which the caravan suffered much from the overgrown nature of the track and the large numbers

¹ This is interpreted by M. Lévi to mean Tibet, but it was probably used as a general term describing all the Mongolian districts hemming in Nepal to the north, north-east, and east.

of wild elephants. The merchants got little sleep at night and were obliged to surround themselves with fires and to frighten off wild beasts by loosing off their muskets at times. An amusing description is given of the elephant which marches noiselessly upon the caravan, not for the purpose of doing any harm to men but to carry off the stores, such as bags of rice or flour or pots of butter. After a reference to the hardy nature of the little horses of this district, which were useful for transport up to a certain point, Tavernier seems to refer to a characteristic which is remarkable to this day—the necessity for the use of palkis for the rest of the journey to Tibet. He adds, however, that for some of the steeper parts of the Himalayan passes it is necessary to employ women as carriers. Three of them take it in turns to carry him. The horses have to be led by ropes. Baggage and provisions are placed upon goats. He goes on to say that the women who carry the men over the passes are only paid two rupees for ten days' work, and that as much is paid for each hundredweight carried by the goats. After the passage of the Himalayas, oxen, camels, horses, and palkis were available for those who wished to travel comfortably.

§ 4

According to Markham, Father Desideri, a Jesuit missionary in Lhasa, returned to India through Nepal. At Lhasa he had made converts of a small number of Nepalese merchants, but the traditional hostility between the Jesuits and the Regular missionaries brought about their recall. The Capuchins, however, remained on in Lhasa until 1745. They had established at Katmandu in 1715 a branch of the mission, but the hostility of the Brahmans drove them to seek shelter in Bhatgaon a week later. Father Horace della Penna was at the head of this *succursale*, and he fought valiantly for the faith to which he ultimately became a martyr as surely as many who have won that name in other fields. He demanded help from Rome, but received little. He then took what must have seemed to him the extreme step of returning to Rome and making a personal appeal on behalf of his lonely mission. This time, on his return, he brought seven Capuchin Fathers with him. They reached Bhatgaon on the 6th February 1740, and, after waiting for Tibetan passports, they set out on the last stretch of their long journey, and entered Lhasa on the 6th January 1741.

Perhaps from a sense that all was not well, Father de Recanati, who had been left in charge of the Nepalese mission during the absence of Father della Penna, established outside Nepal yet another branch of the mission. A certain amount of caution is required in accepting the terms in which any missionary records his spiritual successes, and it may not have been so much for the spiritual advantages as for more material reasons that the Raja of Bettia asked for the establishment of this mission. It is clear, however, that in the middle of the eighteenth century the earnest and probably untactful energy of Christian missionaries was accepted both in Nepal and along the Indian border. But this tolerance was of no long duration. At the expulsion of the Christian missionaries from Lhasa,

Father della Penna, a veteran evangelist, broken in spirit by this failure, arrived in Patan in the summer of 1745, and died there two years later. He was buried in the little Christian cemetery with an inscription in two languages, Latin and Newari, testifying to his constancy and his virtues. The Latin inscription is as follows:

A.R.P. FRANCISCVS HORATIVS A PINNA BILLORVM
PICENAE PROVINCIAE CAPVCCINORVM ALVMNVS
MDCLXXX NATVS
INFIDELIVM CONVERSIONES OPTANS
A.S.C.D.P.F. AD TIBETI MISSIONES MISSVS
XXXIII. AN. INTER INFIDELES VERSATVS
XX. EISDEM MISSIONIBVS PRAEFUIT
TANDEM
SENIO AC MORBO CONFECTVS ET MERITIS CVMVLATVS
LXV. AN. AGENS SECESSIT E VIVIS
XX. JULII MDCCXLVII [1]
SUPERSTITES MISSIONARII
M. H. P.
A. M. D. G.

The fate of the Capuchins in Nepal also was not long delayed. Three or four of them were still in the mission at Katmandu in 1768. The branch which had been established in Patan had been abandoned. One of the Fathers, Michel Ange, was instrumental in saving the life of a brother of Prithwi Narayan who, as already mentioned, had been wounded in the attack on Kirtipur. There was therefore at the outset of the Gurkha regime some friendliness between the Fathers and the conquerors. But, as has always happened throughout the East—and as the universal use of the word " firinghi " or its equivalent for all classes of Europeans testifies—Prithwi Narayan made no distinction between Europeans, and, angered by the action of the East India Company in sending up a detachment from India in 1769 announced that the missionaries represented European policy rather than the Christian religion, and a year later he abruptly ordered them and their converts to leave what was now his country. The luckless mission therefore made its way down to the cold weather station which had been established at Bettia.

From that moment the door has been shut to Christian missionary effort in Nepal. Perhaps, considering the spirit in which the doctrines of Christianity are often received by the Asiatic, this is not the disadvantage that it might be deemed in some quarters. It is true that at this moment Christianity is accepted in China by a large number of its inhabitants. There is indeed no small hope that the doctrines of Christ will in the not distant future play a considerable part in the ethical development of some

[1] M. Lévi insists that the date of the inscription on Father Horace della Penna's grave should be 1745 and not 1747.

portion of that country. But no more prevalent mistake is made than the haphazard manner in which all missionary effort is considered and judged by stay-at-homes who contribute to that effort only a pecuniary support. In China there is a mass of 480,000,000 to whom religion in the sense of a code of morals or an observance of ritual is alike unknown. They have been accustomed to the large generalizations of thinkers such as Confucius or Lao-tzu, and this spacious attitude towards ethics, while it has deprived them of the moral support that may or may not attend the adoption of a stricter creed, has left a tradition of open-mindedness in these matters. To no thinking Chinese could the story of Christ's personal doctrine fail to appeal, and as there has been no official opposition to the spread of Christianity from any hierarchy in China, the success of missionaries has been indisputable, especially in the southern provinces of China.

The case is very different in Nepal. The Gurkha dynasty has always been celebrated for the careful manner in which it has fulfilled its religious obligations. In doing so it has reflected the general spirit of obedience, if not devotion, which runs through all sections of the Gurkha people. There is no bigotry, and sometimes the Gurkha soldier will seem to his envious Brahman colleague in the plains of India to allow himself a licence which the Brahman would fain be able to enjoy himself. But his essential fidelity to even the minor details of his creed is one of the characteristics of every member of the ruling races in Nepal. Almost as much might be said for the Newars and others of the earlier inhabitants of the country. Their Buddhism has been largely tinctured by Hinduism, but of their personal piety there can be no doubt. No one who has seen one of the greater festivals of the Nepalese, such as the exhibition of the image of Machendra from his car at Patan, can doubt the strange and even passionate devotion that inspires those who follow one or other of the creeds in the Valley.

Nepal has definitely refused to entertain within her borders any man or woman whose mission in life it is to upset the existing faith of the people, and this policy has been deliberately adopted by the Nepalese Government because it sees in the mission and the missionary a political rather than a religious embassage.

In Lhasa the expeditionary force of 1904 discovered a bell with the inscription: "Miserere mei Domine." It was a surviving relic of the Christian mission there. So far as I know, nothing whatever remains in Nepal to mark the devotion and the temporary influence of the Capuchins. No trace remains of the little cemetery between the north side of Patan and the Bagmati. Not even a tradition of a site recalls the work of these men. They were permitted to remove all their possessions to Bettia, and only an empty episcopal title still exists to commemorate their effort. Perhaps diligent research may yet find, built into a wall, some gravestone from that lost cemetery or some service book in a hitherto unrecorded collection, but at no time would the inventory of a Capuchin body have shown much beyond the bare necessities of its life and precious vessels of its ritual. The latter they had full time and opportunity to bring away, and if there ever were a bell in Patan like that which was found in Lhasa, we may be sure that Prithwi Narayan allowed them ample means of bringing it down with them to India. Not without justice M. Lévi notes that the historical results of this mission were deplorably inadequate. " Considering the sixty years of preaching, of expenses, of voyages between Rome and the Himalayas, the result was at least mediocre. Moreover, science gained almost as little as religion. The Capuchins had found, under the Malla dynasty, a situation exceptionally favourable. The road to Lhasa was open; Nepal welcomed them; Buddhism was at its height; the country was prosperous; science and art were held in honour, and literature at least in favour. But all these advantages produced nothing. Let us compare the loss to science of the slackness or dullness of the Capuchins with the fruitful work that the Englishman, Hodgson, did in Nepal in different circumstances about the year 1820. The country, conquered by the Gurkhas, was then strictly shut up; Buddhism was under a ban and decaying; suspicion, violence, brutality, characterized the princes. The towns were encumbered with the ruins caused by war and pillage. Nevertheless, the persevering work of one man, undertaken and carried through under such unfortunate conditions, revealed to Europe not only a literature and a religion, but no inconsiderable chapter of human history."

Perhaps this futility was due rather to the traditions of an unlearned Order than to any actual laziness on the part of individuals. Thus several important works by Father della Penna have been simply lost. The same fate has been suffered by the treatise upon the religion and customs of Nepal written by Father Constantine d'Ascoli in 1747. Forty-five years later this manuscript was still lying neglected and unpublished in the library of the Propaganda in Rome. It is there no longer. Nor has the fate of the work of Father Cassian da Macerata been much happier. Except for a rough map of the position of the three capitals of the Valley, all the notes made by Father Cassian about Nepal have been lost. But this is not a matter for wonder. Of the general attitude of the Fathers towards history and literature, towards the things that widen man's knowledge or tell of his inner life, we have a terrible record in the diary of a Captain Rose: " By chance I met some of the Italian missionaries who had recently been thrown out of Nepal. I was very hopeful of getting some useful information from them, but I was seriously dissatisfied. The head of their mission, who seemed to be the most intelligent of them, could not give me the least information about any place or any object which was not within the actual circuit of the city in which he dwelt; and he had been living twelve years in the country! But to show me his missionary zeal, he proudly said that he had burned three thousand manuscripts during his stay there."

APPENDIX XVII

THE RACES OF NEPAL

§ 1

THERE are few more complicated questions in the ethnology of any nation than that presented by the races of Nepal. The problem has been approached from several sides; attempts have been made to distinguish the various groups by their physical features, their language, their religion, their domestic customs, and their fighting qualities, but much remains to be done before any certainty can be arrived at. To history there is almost no appeal.

It may simplify the examination of these groups if we at once set apart the Newars of the Valley and the pure-blooded Thakurs, a Rajput people, the clans of which not only provide the two pre-eminent families in Nepal—that of the King and of the Prime Minister—but have kept their descent comparatively speaking pure from the admixture which is the chief source of difficulty in classifying all other tribes, from the Khas to the frankly Mongoloid Murmis.[1]

A NEWAR IN HIS NATIONAL DRESS

§ 2

The Newars.—The Newars are the most important of the quasi-aboriginal races of Nepal. In spite of the industry of Colonel Vansittart, so little is known about the origins of Nepalese

[1] The following extract from Abbé Huc's *Recollections of a Journey through Tartary, Tibet and China*, written in 1846, will be of interest because there can be no doubt that by the word "Peboun" the traveller intended to indicate the Nepalese. It would be interesting if any student could suggest the origin of this curious name.

"Among the foreigners who form part of the permanent population of Lhasa, the Pebouns are the most numerous. They are Indians from Bhutan, small in stature but vigorous and full of life and spirit; their colour is deep olive brown, their eyes small, black and keen; and on their foreheads they bear a deep red mark which is renewed every morning. They are the only workers in metal in Tibet. They place a red globe with a white crescent underneath on the doors of their houses. The Pebouns fabricate vases of gold and silver ornaments for the use of the Lamaic monasteries which would not disgrace European artists . . . These people are extremely jovial and childlike in temper, like children laughing and frolicking in their leisure hours; and singing continually over their work. Their religion is Indian Buddhism but they show great respect for the reforms of Tsong-kapa."

races that it would be rash to assert of any tribe that it was not a migrant into the country within historic times. In most cases all that is known merely suggests the arrival of the tribe at an earlier or later period, and the closing of the country to palaeological exploration makes any theory of a pre-Mongolian population in the hill districts a hazardous project. However, the Newars claim to be the original inhabitants of the Nepal Valley—which is still their centre and beyond which they do not penetrate far in any direction, with the notable exception of Lhasa, where there is an important colony of Newar art-workers in gold, silver, bronze, and copper.[1] The language test, according to Hodgson, shows their relationship to the Tibetans. The continual pilgrimages and trading that have gone on from the earliest days between India and the Valley have naturally affected not merely their language, but their blood, though Hamilton is of the opinion that no real departure from type took place until after the advent of the Gurkha conquerors. To this Vansittart demurs, and the almost impartial balance between Buddhism and Hinduism which prevails among nearly all classes of the Valley probably indicates fairly well the proportions of the two bloods as well as of the two faiths. The Newars are enlisted in the Nepalese army, though in no great numbers and were never drawn upon as recruits for the Gurkha regiments in India until the emergency created by the 1914-1918 War, but they hold the palm in all Nepal for their industry, their art, and their agriculture. Of their domestic customs it may be interesting to record that every Newar girl while a child is married to a bel fruit, which, after the ceremony, is thrown into a sacred river. This fictitious marriage is of great use to the Newar women. The bel fruit is presumed to be always in existence and therefore she can never become a widow. Remarriage—continual remarriage—is therefore possible for her. Divorce is easy, though the ancient custom whereby a dissatisfied wife had merely to place two betel nuts in her husband's bed and go away a free woman is yielding to modern standards. The morals ·of the Newar women are not of a strict order, but this is largely to be attributed to the fact that they live in the governing centre of Nepal where some even of the more highly placed officials still regard irregular marriages as one of the privileges of their sex.

Reference has already been made to the Tharus, who are immune from the ravages of awal in the Tarai. They are the poor relations of the Newars of the Valley and are undersized and scraggy, but they are capable of great efforts of endurance. Vansittart notes that this section of the tribe, of which the members in general are merely carters, peasants, and fisher-men, are chosen for the dangerous and difficult business of catching wild elephants. They seem to combine the activity of an animal with the cunning and craftiness characteristic of the less developed races of humanity.

[1] It is believed by many that the best work in these materials that Tibet possesses was actually made by Newars. The Tibetan standard of workmanship is higher than that of Nepal, but this may be accounted for by the far greater demand there for objects con-nected with religion, and the more exacting standards set up in Tibet by the presence of much good Chinese work.

§ 3

Thakurs and Khas.—The Thakurs claim royal descent, and the head of the purest blooded tribe of all, the Sahs, is the King of Nepal himself. At first sight it would seem certain that these tribes are in fact due to an emigration from India caused by the ravages of Mohammedan conquerors. It is only right, however, to notice that the existence in Nepal of a pure Hindu race called the Khas is mentioned in ancient chronicles as early as the year A.D. 1000. They are recorded as living at a lower level than the Magars, who, it will be seen, cultivated the middle zone of Nepal below the Gurungs. This Rajput immigration into Nepal is an undoubted fact, and of the comparative purity of the blood in some at least of the leading families there can be little question.[1] Finding in Nepal a race that claimed to be not merely of Indian but of Rajput descent, the newcomers were content to allow the name Khas to cover the old inhabitants and themselves alike. It is said that a Khas who left Nepal and settled in the plains was accorded both the name and the privileges attaching to Kshatriya birth.

To the already existing confusion of races, castes, and classes in Nepal the Brahmans contributed much by the lax manner in which they accorded the rights of caste to the new arrivals, to their own progeny, and even to the natives of the hills who were content to embrace Hinduism. It may perhaps be said that they granted the Vaisya caste to the rank and file of the converts. To the chieftains, however, the Brahmans attributed pedigrees of marvellous length and complexity, basing them upon the ultimate paternity of the sun or of the moon. Nor did they deal less valiantly with their own illegitimate offspring. Children of unions between Brahmans and Rajputs were given a higher social standing than the Magars and Gurungs. Hodgson remarks, " The natural pride that characterizes all mountain races throughout the world was highly developed in Nepal. The women did not refuse union with Brahmans, but insisted that the children should be granted the high military caste of Kshatriya—the caste best known by its most distinguished representatives the blue-blooded Rajputs of Rajputana," and he adds a curious and illuminating note that the " offspring of the original Khas females and Brahmans with the honours and rank of the second order of Hinduism got the patronymic titles of the first order; and hence the key to the nomenclature of so many branches of the military tribes of Nepal is to be sought in the nomenclature of the sacred order." The Khas, drawn from this mixed source, have produced many of the greatest men of Nepal; perhaps it was from their origin and association that they were used as administrators over a large part of the state. Brian Hodgson noted that the language of the Khas—commonly

---

[1] It is interesting to recall the legend that when the Emperor Asoka came to Nepal in 250 B.C., he found living at Patan a man of such pure Chattri descent that he gave his daughter Charumati to him in marriage. Moreover, the Sakyas from whom Buddha sprang in the sixth century were Kshatriyas living within the present territory of Nepal. The presence of pure Rajput families with whom the refugees from Islam were able to intermarry may be accepted.

II   R

called Khaskura [1]—had ousted several vernacular tongues, and Colonel Vansittart asserts that it is understood more or less all over Nepal from the Kali to the Mechi. To this statement the present Maharaja demurs, and there can be no doubt that the vernaculars of Nepal have maintained much of their old importance, though for official purposes many Nepalese have become bi-lingual. Philologically the language is in substance Hindi.

It is impossible to trace in detail the infinite complications of caste and consequent nomenclature that can be caused by intermarriage in Nepal. In this meticulous enquiry the Nepalese excel, and the minute human subdivision in which they take such pride may be illustrated by the fact that the Nepalese, like the Tibetans, have no less than sixteen different words by which to describe the varying proportions of pure blood caused by the cross-breeding and in-breeding of the yak and the humped cattle of the Indian plains. It is to be noted, however, that so far as the army is concerned, the tendency towards an acceptance of Brahmanic prohibitions and prejudices is greatly on the increase. Few things are more disliked in Katmandu than the suggestion which has been made too freely that during the late war the higher classes of Gurkha soldier permitted themselves to break the rules of their caste. They seem indeed to have observed them with a strictness that the statements of previous writers upon the subject did not lead one to expect.

§ 4

Gurungs.—Of the other tribes in Nepal it may be said that the majority are clearly of Mongolian and even recent Mongolian descent. It is possible that during one or more of the historical Mongolian migrations to the west in search of food, peace, and wi at is called nowadays a place in the sun, a small number were bold enough to find their way over the terrible ice wall of the Himalayas down to the temperate valleys of Nepal. Of these the most important are the Gurungs and the Magars. These tribes have long been used by the dominant Gurkhas as soldiers, and for that reason they have spread more widely than others of the Mongoloid races. The original homes of the Gurungs lay in the west of Nepal, and it may be said that in general the Magars descended lower down the valley of the Himalayas than the Gurungs. . They retain to a greater measure than is always recognized, a sympathy with the Buddhism which they practised before the arrival of the Indian conquerors. They have always been greatly influenced not only by the faith of their overlords, but by the inevitable blood mixture which followed the invasion of Nepal by Indian soldiery who were unable to bring their own women with them, and perhaps felt also that among these remote mountains infractions of the laws

---

[1] Sir Charles Bell noted with interest in Katmandu that the name naturally used by writers to denote the *lingua franca* of Nepal, Khaskura, was not recognized, even by the most intelligent of those with whom he came in contact.

of caste were less important than in the priest-ridden plains below. Brian Hodgson asserts that though the Gurungs have been accepted as a Hindu tribe, they are denied the sacred thread " and constitute a doubtful order below it." Like the Magars, their appearance is that which the outer world specially associates with the word Gurkha. They are short, strongly built men capable of extreme hardihood and endurance, and born fighters. Their good spirits are proverbial, and they have a personal charm which can best be understood by asking the opinion of any British officer of any Gurkha battalion in India. The following happy description of Colonel Vansittart cannot be bettered: " They are kind hearted, generous, and, as recruits, absolutely truthful. They are very proud and sensitive, and they deeply feel abuse or undeserved censure. They are very obstinate, very independent, very vain, and in their plain clothes inclined to be dirty. They are intensely loyal to each other and to their officers in time of trouble or danger." There are two crack regiments of Gurungs in the Nepalese army chosen for their height as well as for other qualities. The Gurungs in Eastern Nepal have been almost entirely merged by intermarriage with the other races, and as soldiers may be said to have sunk below their level.

The senior Gurung clan is that of the Ghalis, whose chief once reigned over the territory of Lamjang.[2]

A MAGAR IN HIS NATIONAL DRESS

§ 5

Magars.—The Magars originally occupied the Tarai and lower mountain districts near Butwal and Palpa, and are still found chiefly west of the Valley. Although they were of Mongolian descent, their propinquity to India had diluted the northern blood, and had undermined their Buddhist tendencies, for they accepted at least a nominal conversion at the time of the Rajput invasion. After surrendering Palpa to the invaders, the Magars seem to have spread widely both east and west.

[1] Among the Gurungs, and often among the Magars as well, divorce can be very easily obtained. The husband has to pay forty rupees for his divorce, and the wife one hundred and sixty rupees. Two pieces of split bamboo are tied together, placed on two mud balls, and the money is put close by. If one party takes up the money, the other party can go his or her way and marry again legally.

[2] Maharaja Chandra, in answer to my question why the titles of Kaski and Lamjang were taken for those of the principality which is an appanage of the office of Prime Minister, told me that probably Jang Bahadur was anxious to identify the office with that of a famous fighting people.

The four chief classes of Gurungs are the Ghali, Gotani, Lama, and Lamachine; the Solahjat Gurungs are supposed to be socially inferior. Of the Magars there are six chief tribes, Ale, Pun, Rana, Burathoki, Gharti, and Thapa. Of these Vansittart says: " Of all Magars there is no better man than the Rana of good clan. In former days any Thapa who had lost three generations of ancestors in battle became a Rana, but with the prefix of his Thapa clan." This tribe claims direct descent from the original Rajput invaders of the country, as such classes among them as the Suraj-bansi and the Chitor suggest. The Thapa tribe has so high a reputation that many claim to be Thapas who have no right to the name. There is among the crack regiments of Nepal a Magar battalion of men physically as fine as the Gurung detachments to which reference has just been made.

§ 6

Eastern Races.—In the east of Nepal by far the most important group is that of the Kirantis. As Colonel Vansittart explains, this name should apply to the Khambus or Rais only, but the intermarriage between the Yakkas and Yakthumbas and the Khambus has been so indiscriminate that their appearance, their customs, and their religion are practically identical. But he notes that in spite of this interchange of blood, each tribe has retained in a great degree its own language. It will be remembered that the Kirantis have played a great part on the stage of Nepal. For a number of generations, which it is impossible to define with any certainty, the Kirantis were the predominant race in Nepal and reigned over it from the Valley of Katmandu. Reference has repeatedly been made to these Kirantis in early Indian history.[1] Although they have lost to some extent their Mongoloid appearance, it is worth noting that the occasional Mongol migrations through the ice wall of the Himalayas is described by Sarat Chandra Das in connection with these Nepalese people. He notes that the village of Yangma was founded by Tibetans from Tashirabka, one of them having discovered the valley and its comparative fertility while hunting for a lost yak calf.

The Kirantis occupied a semi-independent position for some time after Prithwi Narayan had established himself in Katmandu, and it seems that when it became necessary to assert Gurkha authority over the eastern end of Nepal, the excuse for action was the insistence of the Kirantis upon maintaining their ancient custom of eating beef.

Until recently they represented the animistic superstitions of the aboriginal tribes of Tibet.[2]

---

[1] Arrian refers to these people as the Kirhoedi.

[2] The Buddhists, with all the official strength that they possess, have never been able to exterminate in Tibet either its indigenous pantheism—if such a word may fairly be used of a faith that discovers in everything a devil rather than a god—or the Bun-po— the Black Monks, who are its ministers. Paganism, Hinduism, and Buddhism here in Eastern Nepal make up a *mélange* of faith of which the first is still the only factor of any importance. Colonel Vansittart notes that their " religion " is a mixture of whatever gives the least trouble to its devotees of these three creeds. With a large toleration worthy of

Sir H. Risley notes that the Kirantis seem to have intermingled largely with the Lepchas from Sikkim and little with the Hindus.

He describes the Limbus as centred in the mountains between the Dudh-kosi and the Kanti, though Hodgson locates them between the Arunkosi and the Mechi.[1] They are among the oldest recorded populations of the country and their features indicate that they are descendants of early Tibetan settlers in Nepal. They are scarcely taller than the Lepchas, more wiry, as fair in complexion, and as beardless. Risley combats the usual military theory that the Limbus are inferior in soldierly qualities to the Khas, Magar, and Gurung tribes. To this day they are used only to a small extent in the personnel of the Gurkha regiments of India, but they make excellent policemen, and Colonel Vansittart remarks that the prejudice against them as soldiers seems rightly to be dying out rapidly.[2]

The Kirantis are as lax in their domestic habits as in their religious observances, but in the middle of this somewhat casual slackness a curious and fiercely sanctioned law is to be found. Intermarriage between cousins is prohibited for three generations or, as some say, for seven. Within the clan itself marriage is absolutely forbidden, and the same veto is imposed upon any intermarriage between the descendants of two men who have contracted a formal brotherhood. This is a curious custom which is found throughout nearly the whole length of the Himalayas. A rite performed by a Brahman or a Lama confirms and establishes irrevocably a fictitious blood brotherhood between the two friends, of which one of the results was that their descendants, until lately, were forbidden on pain of death to intermarry.[3]

The customs of the Rais, the other great section of the Kiranti race, are practically identical with those of the Limbus. There is a touch of satire in Risley's comment upon the divorce laws in force among the Rais. " Women are faithful to the men they live with while they live with them, but they think very little of running away with any man of their own or a cognate tribe who takes their fancy, and the state of things which prevails approaches closely to the ideal regime of temporary unions advocated by would-be marriage reformers in Europe."

Of other tribes in Nepal reference must be made to the Sunwars and Sunpars. These are of the same race and are distinguished only because the former live to the west of the Sunkosi and the Sunpars to the east.

Akbar or Kublai Khan " for the celebration of a religious ceremony a Lama is called in, but if no Lama is available, a Brahman will do, and if neither can be got then any religious mendicant or none at all will do equally well." Colonel Vansittart has published a translation of a Limbu History of which a significant point is that the original inhabitants claimed to be men from Benares. Reference is made to the semblance of autonomy conceded to the Kirantis by the Gurkhas after the subjugation of the country.

[1] S. C. Das says that the country between the Arun and the Tamor is known as Limbuana.

[2] In the Nepalese army there is one regiment recruited exclusively from Limbus. They are good soldiers, but so quarrelsome that it has been found impossible to quarter them in any town containing troops drawn from other Nepalese races.

[3] The punishment to-day is a fine, and possibly banishment from Nepal also. Neither death nor slavery is now imposed.

The Sunwars live chiefly in the mountainous district north of the Valley, between the Gurungs in the west and the Rais in the east. Of these two Colonel Vansittart notes the laxness in all religious matters. They are of Mongolian descent and nominally at least are Buddhists, but in deference to the religion of the ruling and governing races of Nepal there is an outward veneer of Hinduism.

The Murmis are the hewers of wood and drawers of water, coolies by heritage and ready to merge their individuality in almost any adjacent tribe. They have accepted as Murmis many Tibetans and Lepchas. They eat beef freely and have earned the title of carrion eaters from Tibet from their traditional descent from Mahesur, a younger brother of Brahma and Vishnu, whom his seniors, by a trick, induced to eat cow's tripe. It is a curious local belief that the wearing of the sacred thread by Brahmans is due to Mahesur's anger at being thus trapped. He struck his brothers with the tripe, some of which clung round their shoulders and originated the custom referred to.

The Murmis do much of the menial work in the Valley of Katmandu.

§ 7

Caste in Nepal.—Respect for caste regulations is everywhere on the increase rather than the decline in Nepal, though it is not to be wondered at if some of the lower tribes who still retain their Mongolian Gallionicism, if not a very deep veneration for their paternal Buddhist faith, allow themselves concessions when far from their homes. Years ago the Nepalese soldiers had no doubt fairly easy consciences. Hodgson, in his direct and sometimes whimsical manner, describes the advantages to the British Raj of having under its command " these highland soldiers who despatch their meal in half an hour, and satisfy the ceremonial law by merely washing their hands and faces and taking off their turbans before cooking, [and] laugh at the pharisaical rigour of the Sipahis who must bathe from head to foot and make puja ere they can begin to dress their dinners, must eat nearly naked in the coldest weather, and cannot be in marching trim again in less than three hours." The rest of this recommendation will be found in chapter v. It is worth reading carefully as a proof of Hodgson's curious ability to estimate not only the men among whom he was working, but the political development of India. The conduct and gallantry of the Gurkhas in the Great War fully justify this warm-hearted eulogy written in 1832.

It is pleasant to conclude these notes upon the manners and characteristics of the Gurkhas by the plain statement that never has any Nepal chief taken bribes from, or sold his services for money to, any other State whatever.

APPENDIX XVIII

A MARRIAGE CEREMONY

THE following extract from a letter referring to the ceremonies that attend the wedding of a member of the families of the King and the Prime Minister may be of some interest.

" May 22nd, 1924.

" At four o'clock a carriage was sent for me from the Singha Darbar, the Maharaja's palace, where I met the Commander-in-Chief, Bhim Sham Sher, the Prime Minister's brother, a man who conveys authority in every gesture. He is grey-bearded, and has something of the penetrating glance of his brother. His position is scarcely sufficiently described as Commander-in-Chief: indeed, the title of Jang-i-lat, which in India translates that title, is borne by his younger brother, Judha Sham Sher, the first Commanding General. . . . The Commander-in-Chief is the Prime Minister's right hand, and takes a good deal of the practical work of administration off his hands. . . .

" Nearly the whole of the Prime Ministerial family were present at the Maharaja's palace, and the splendour of their official head-dresses added very greatly to the beauty of the *mise-en-scène*. With the Commander-in-Chief was his son, General Padma Sham Sher, a commanding figure and a man to whom the British Empire owes no small debt of gratitude. General Judha was with his sons Bahadur Sham Sher, Agni Sham Sher, Hari Sham Sher, Surya Sham Sher, and Narayan Sham Sher. All of the sons of the Maharaja were present—General Mohan Sham Sher, General Baber Sham Sher, General Kaiser Sham Sher, General Singha Sham Sher, General Krishna Sham Sher, General Vishnu Sham Sher, and the youngest, General Madan Sham Sher, a small boy who was delightfully conscious of the full uniform in which he was dressed for the day. The only one missing at first was the bridegroom, General Shanker Sham Sher. The Envoy, Mr. Wilkinson, Colonel and Mrs. Hunter, the Legation Surgeon and his wife, Mr. and Mrs. R. S. Underhill, and Mr. and Mrs. Bruford arrived shortly afterwards.

" It was a very hot day, and the coolest place was on the deep verandah outside the State hall of the Maharaja's palace.¹ Soon afterwards the Prime Minister entered with the bridegroom. He then returned to the main entrance to receive the King. Many generals and persons of civil distinction meanwhile joined the crowd that was gathering on the verandah, but most of them had their official work and position in the reception of the King or in the elephant procession which was to follow, and remained only a few minutes. The King of Nepal was then led to his seat by the

---

¹ A photograph of this marble hall will be found on p. 189, vol. i, and will give a better impression of the opulence of these Nepalese palaces than the most detailed description.

Prime Minister. He is a man of about eighteen years of age and remarkably handsome; his life of seclusion is perhaps responsible for his paleness. He sat silent and motionless on his chair unless someone was being actually presented to him. He was dressed in a dark blue frock coat and white Jodhpur breeches, and wore a well-shaped yachting cap with a large device in diamonds. In his right ear was an enormous single ruby, and in his left a correspondingly large diamond; in the buttonhole of his coat he wore a large crescent composed of huge precious stones, of which I remember a diamond, a ruby, a sapphire, and either a yellow sapphire or a topaz, each of them being about the size of the forefinger nail. He had damaged his hand by a fall from his bicycle, and wore a black and white bandage.

" After a formal military ceremony, the elephant procession started from the Palace to the house where the bride was awaiting her fiancé. The King's elephant came first, draped in a magnificent ' jule ' of rose velvet and gold lace. The Maharaja followed on a beast draped with green velvet. The howdah was scarlet, and the colours of Nepal were thus displayed by him. The mahout bore a kalasa of gold with a handful of peacock feathers closely interwoven. There were many minutes of waiting before the procession started. Guns went off in interminable salutes, and troops marched and counter-marched in accordance with a ritual which has probably long been lost except in this remote mountain kingdom. Candles of brown wax burnt themselves out in guttering tears and smoke. One hundred bridesmaids, dressed in rose and red and purple and mauve, obeyed the orders of a strict directress. The troops at last began to march off, and were followed at no long interval by these bridesmaids who, for the most part, drove in brakes of a distinction that betrayed St. James's Street. Then at last came the bridegroom, dressed in russet, crimson, and gold, who, according to immemorial tradition, was carried on the back of a servant in old rose. Immediately afterwards followed the ' Mistress of the Robes,' a dignified woman of middle age in a gown of such a rose colour as you might search London in vain to find, before whom was borne the kalasa, the mystic flagon of union, covered with flowers. Then followed the King who, with due ceremonial, mounted his elephant with his Lord-in-Waiting, Padma Sham Sher, the Commander-in-Chief's son. The Maharaja then took his place upon his own elephant. He wore a dark blue frock coat with black velvet cuffs and gold embroidered shoulder straps. He wore a sword hanging from a red silk and gold belt, and the large red cap, somewhat similar to the King's, which he wears in preference to his diamond-covered head-piece. We set off at a slow pace across the bridge that spans the Tukhucha, and mounted to the Tundi Khel, or great parade-ground. Here the first of the triumphal arches greeted us. It was an elaborate construction built of gaily painted wood adorned with flags and panelled with elaborately devised scenes, many of which must have been taken from the quasi-amorous picture postcards that may be bought from the window in many shops in outer London. Others, of greater interest, were traditional representations of the deities of Nepal, or portraits of the Maharaja. Our route led across the Tundi Khel and then, turning to the right, we skirted the road that borders it on the west. There were two or three more triumphal arches, of which the most magnificent was undoubtedly that under which we passed from the Tundi Khel to the lane running north between the palace gardens of the royal quarter.

" Along the whole of this route the inhabitants of the Valley had gathered themselves in their hundreds of thousands. They were a perfectly orderly crowd, and scarcely needed the authority of the Katmandu police and the troops which had been called in to line the road. Everyone was in gala dress, and I doubt whether anywhere else, except in Burma, so much sheer colour could have been collected beside a mile and a half of open road and plain. As the King passed there was a silence, due no doubt to respect for his semi-divine position. But the sight of the Maharaja stirred the entire plain to enthusiasm, and Chandra Sham Sher, half smiling at this exhibition of his popularity, duly and gravely saluted it. On arrival at the palace which had been lent to the bride for the purposes of the day's ritual, we all alighted, and for some time there was the usual buzz of conversation which in every country under the sun relaxes the tension of waiting for a notable ceremony.

" After keeping the bridegroom waiting for a decent period, the bride's young brother appeared, and with timid solemnity affixed the *tika*, or scarlet caste-spot, upon the forehead of Shanker Sham Sher. This implied the full acceptance by the bride's family of the bridegroom, and was the most important of the day's ceremonies to which any but members of the two families themselves were admitted. Meanwhile bands were playing, guns were going off in all directions inside the garden, and much vigour was shown by the various officers in charge of arrangements. Shortly after we were driven to our respective homes, while the remaining ceremonies took place in private.

" Next day there was another ceremony, of equal importance, which on this occasion took place at the Singha Darbar. The King was again present. This time with full ceremony the bridegroom brought home the bride to the house which was to be her home. She looked about fifteen years of age, but wore a heavily embroidered veil, and studiously kept her head bowed down and her eyes fixed upon the floor of the howdah. She remained outside the main entrance while her bridegroom was again carried on the back of a porter dressed in almost the same old-rose velvet in which the bearers of the Sedia Gestatoria of the Pope are habited. Then, amid a final crash from the many bands and a multitudinous salute of guns, the bride and bridegroom were enthroned in a structure which had been erected in the great courtyard of the Singha Darbar. Here, as a counterpart to the ritual of the previous day, it was the young sister of the bridegroom who affixed the *tika* to the forehead of the bride. Formal congratulations then took place, and the young couple eventually retired within the palace. After that there was a final procession of the richly dressed bridesmaids on the drive outside the main entrance. These bridesmaids form one of the most curious features of any important Rajput wedding, though in Rajputana itself they are rarely as numerous as in Katmandu. They are not all in their early youth, and the first thing that strikes one is the amazing resemblance to each other which has been achieved by a most careful make-up and identical hairdressing. The face is of an even Egyptian pallor, and the suggestion of that country is increased by the extension of the strictly and sharply curved eyebrow of great length, and the heavily antimonied eyes. Not all of the bridesmaids have consented thus to sink their personal charms in a conventional mould, but the senior members of this long cortège were strict in observing the tradition. As for their dress it was, as has been said, in tints of fuchsia, crushed strawberry, and rose, shot through with golden tinsel. Their head-dresses conformed to an ancient pattern of gold and white; and a strictly plastered down whisker, three inches long, added a curious sense of sexlessness. It was evident that they belonged rather to the earlier than the later races of the Valley.

"There remains one more feature in the ceremony which must be mentioned. A march past of all the guards of honour and of the troops lining the route took place before His Majesty, who stood with impassive dignity in the centre bay of the great verandah of the Singha Darbar. Beside him stood the genial but commanding figure of the Prime Minister. In addition to the troops and the beasts that had already taken part in the processions, there passed by also endless bands and endless Gurkha companies, all of them well set up and businesslike. Then followed roughly made figures of camels, elephants, and tigers on wooden platforms on wheels which rattled noisily along the hard drive in front of the palace. A rhinoceros followed, and many curious automatic figures—two Hindu women quarrelling, two men boxing, some men in grey fur suits, intended to represent bears, and some Nepalese devil dancers, resembling those of Tibet but less gaudily painted and therefore more impressive.

"These were spaced by pairs and groups of men, who fought theatrical contests with each other as they passed. To the half-dozen Europeans present perhaps the most remarkable thing was a kind of a cardboard scarecrow on horseback intended to represent an Englishman. He was dressed in an almost phosphorescent lavender suit, and in his face and figure he embodied all the forms of caricature that the appearance and habits of Englishmen have suggested to other races, European as well as Eastern. There was not a trace of malice in this exhibition, which was almost the best received item of the long programme.

"At last the brakes and the omnibuses were filled by the cheery robes of the bridesmaids, and a State elephant carried away to their married life the recently wedded couple, the bridegroom, for the last time, enjoying his curious rose-coloured mount."

APPENDIX XIX

FORESTRY IN NEPAL

By J. V. Collier

WHILE it is the quality of her Gurkha soldiers that has made the name of Nepal famous throughout the world, yet Nepal is almost equally renowned for the extent and quality of her forests. These forests form the most important part of the great Himalayan timber belt stretching from the Indus to Sikkim. The length of this belt is not less than one thousand miles, of which at least five hundred are in the territory of Nepal. Not only are these Nepalese forests important on account of their extent, but it is within the eastern and western limits of that kingdom that conditions of climate and rainfall are most favourable to the vigorous growth of forest vegetation—and those favourable conditions are reflected in the very high reputation the Nepal forests enjoy for the size and quality of their timber.

The forests belong to what is generally known as the Eastern Himalayan region which terminates westwards at the Kali river which forms the boundary between Nepal and Kumaon. But whereas the flora of the Western Himalayan region has been studied for many years and by a multitude of observers, the flora of Nepal is still almost a closed book, and there is little doubt that its study will eventually throw light on many existing botanical uncertainties. An instance of the errors into which botanists and foresters may be led owing to this gap in the knowledge available to them has occurred recently. Any botanical or forest text-book places the eastern natural limit of the deodar (*Cedrus deodara*)—perhaps the most important timber tree of the Himalayas—at the Niti pass in the Garhwal district of Kumaon. But a recent and accidental discovery has placed it beyond doubt that extensive deodar forests exist in the basin of the Karnali river of Nepal. To a botanist or forester this fact is of great interest and importance, as it raises the question of why the tract between the Niti pass and the Karnali river, a distance of not less than one hundred and fifty miles, should contain not a single natural deodar tree; and in turn this question raises the interesting speculation as to the means by which this wide gap was bridged. This is only one instance of the discoveries which must be awaiting research into the flora of Nepal.

Like the western regions of the Himalayan forest, the Nepal forests can be roughly classified into three main altitude zones: (1) the tropical zone, up to about 4,000 feet; (2) the temperate zone, from 4,000 feet to 10,000 feet; and (3) the Alpine zone, from 10,000 feet to the limit of tree level at about 16,000 feet.

(1) The tropical zone is commercially the only zone of real importance. It begins with a belt of forest stretching out into the Tarai plains, and

consisting of four very distinct types of forest, which are: (i) forests of Sal (*Shorea robusta*), the most important timber tree of the country; (ii) riverain forests of Shisham (*Dalbergia Sissoo*) and Khair (*Acacia Catechu*) and other less important species; (iii) mixed deciduous forests in which the predominant or important trees are the Asna (*Terminalia tomentosa*), the Semal (*Bombax malabaricum*), the Toon (*Cedrela Toona*), and a great number of less important species; and (iv) moist savannah forests, largely consisting of areas of tall grasses, the haunt of rhinoceros and tiger.

(2) The temperate zone may be divided into two zones: (i) a belt between 4,000 feet and 8,500 feet, containing as characteristic trees, the Oaks, Maples, and Pines; and (ii) the forests above 8,500 feet, in which the Spruces, Firs, Cypresses, and Larches are the chief species. Although this temperate zone is of comparatively little commercial importance, it fulfils a purpose even more important to Nepal than that of a source of revenue, by supplying the dense population of these middle altitude tracts with their fuel, timber, and grazing requirements.

(3) The Alpine zone, above 10,000 feet, is commercially and economically of little importance. Its characteristic trees are Rhododendrons and Junipers.

The history of mankind in Nepal has been, and still is, in many places a story of struggle against the forests and their wild denizens. The original form which this struggle took was that of shifting cultivation. A family would clear a few acres, burn the debris, and cultivate the enriched virgin soil for a few years, shifting on to another site when the soil showed signs of losing its first richness. But it was soon learned that, unless the cultivated areas were wide in extent, the labour of the cultivator was largely lost through the depredations of wild animals, and consequently men began to clear the forests more systematically, and to create large clearings of which the edges only might be at the mercy of pig and deer. This replacement of forest area by cultivation is still being carried out all over Nepal, but there is now a new factor to consider. For whereas the early cultivators were clearing and burning worthless material, the cultivator of the present day is often felling forest of great commercial value, and one of the most urgent and difficult problems of the Government is the control of this substitution of crops for forests. There is no doubt that Nepal, with her growing population and with the tendency of her landless surplus manhood to emigrate into India, must adopt and press forward a policy of tree felling in all localities where crops can grow and men live happily. But there are economical and there are wasteful methods of carrying out such a policy, and the methods of the past have not always been the best.

The present policy of the Government is:

(i) To replace forest by cultivation wherever conditions for cultivation and human habitation are favourable;

(ii) To prohibit the removal of forests where the climate is too unhealthy, and where crops can only be grown with the risk of loss of the life or vigour of the cultivators;

(iii) To insist on large extensive clearings, so that the depredations of wild animals are reduced and the climate improved;

(iv) To realize in full the value of the forests cut and replaced by crops.

There is no doubt that this is a wise policy. If it is carried out faithfully it will increase the area of crops, and render the country more dependent on its own food supplies; while it will lessen or completely stop the present drain of the country's manhood into India. This policy must be pursued for many years before there need be the slightest grounds for fearing that sufficient forest will not remain. For in the temperate zone it is certain that cultivation can never occupy more than one-third of the total area, the remainder being too steep or rocky to admit of the growth of crops. Perhaps in the Valley of Katmandu and its vicinity a condition has been reached in which it would be wise to call a halt to the increase of cultivation, for in this valley civilization dates back so many hundreds of years that there are now signs of an insufficiency of forests and the fuel which they supply. But elsewhere the day on which the restriction of cultivation need become a question for consideration is still far off.

If, in the past, mistakes have been made in the carrying out of this policy of the increase of cultivation, they have taken the form of allowing the clearances to be made in a haphazard manner, and without sufficient forethought. Small islands have been cleared in seas of forest, with the inevitable result that the forest has within a short time reconquered its territory. Thousands of these deserted clearings are to be seen throughout the whole extent of the forests. They have taught the lesson that clearances are useless and wasteful unless they eventually coalesce so as to form one great cleared area, which wild animals cannot invade, and which exposure to sun and the free circulation of winds will render more healthy.

A second mistake of the past has been the failure to realize the value of the felled timber, which has often been burned or left to rot. While in the temperate zone the material may be of very little value, in the tropical zone it is almost always valuable and able to repay the cost of extraction. It is in the forests of this zone that the Government possesses a real commercial asset. It is here that the most valuable timber is found, and it is within this zone that the climate is in many places so deadly for half of the year, that the replacement of the forest by a permanent and prosperous cultivating population is probably for ever impossible. In these forests the chief timber trees are the Sal (*Shorea robusta*), the Shisham (*Dalbergia Sissoo*), and the Asna (*Terminalia tomentosa*), and it is the policy of the Government to conserve and improve and to treat them as a valuable State property. They have been worked for revenue purposes for many years, and on several different systems. The chief method has been to issue permits to Indian merchants for the removal of logs—to be sawn elsewhere—on payment of a fixed royalty levied per cubic foot of timber. This method, while apparently sound in theory, has in practice often proved very wasteful. For the Indian merchant is naturally thinking of his maximum profit, which depends on his extracting, and paying the royalty on, nothing but the most perfect logs. It is characteristic of all Himalayan broad-leaved timber trees that, with no exterior sign of defect, their logs often exhibit on felling certain defects which may, indeed, be of slight consequence, but may, on the other hand, be so serious as to render the extraction of the log unremunerative. The practice of the merchant has naturally been to reject and to leave to rot in the forest all logs which, on being felled, exhibit the slightest defect, and to export only the most perfect timber. It would be no exaggeration to state that in many cases the value of the logs extracted under this system of sale is less than the value of the logs cut, found defective, and left behind in the forest. The Government is aware of the disadvantages of this system and is adopting the obvious remedy. It now allows selected merchants to saw the felled logs *in situ*. The advantages of this method are clear. For the problem of forest exploitation is one of transportation, and while the whole of a defective log may not repay the cost and labour of extraction, it is often the case that if the defective parts are removed at the felling site by means of the saw, the remaining sound timber can be transported and marketed with profit. If merchants of the best type can be found to work this system it will prove successful and profitable, but the chief difficulty is to induce reliable and honest contractors to invest their capital in a country and under conditions of which they may have no experience or knowledge. It was with the object of creating this necessary confidence that the Government has recently enlisted for a short term of years the services of a British forest officer who, with some fifteen years of experience of the working of forests in India, may be able to induce the best class of Indian contractor to work in the far richer forests of Nepal. For their development depends solely upon the solution of this difficulty. Of the worst class of contractor hundreds can always be found—men who will regard their engagements with the Government as opportunities for fraud and theft; but it is the present policy of Nepal to discourage this class, and to encourage by every possible and reasonable means the introduction of merchants possessing both capital and integrity. Such are very rare, but there are already signs that the difficulty is not insoluble.

An impetus was given in the direction of forest development on the best lines during the War when His Highness the Maharaja added to his many acts of generous friendship by offering to the British Government 200,000 broad-gauge sleepers free of all royalty charges. The extraction was carried out by an officer of the Imperial Forest Service, and the contractors employed by him; and the most reliable men of this class to be found in Northern India are still working in Nepal.

The question of exploitation cannot be separated from that of conservation. It is the policy of the Government to treat as a permanent national asset those forests which for climatic or other reasons can never give way to prosperous cultivation. The chief measure at present adopted to ensure the woods of Nepal against destruction is the fixing of the minimum age at which the most important timber trees may be felled at one hundred years. This rule, if not relaxed, is an absolute insurance against deforestation, and the forest staff in Nepal is at present too small to admit of the adoption of other safeguards which may be more scientific but which will not be so certain in their effect. In imposing the one hundred years' age limit the Government is doing its duty to its successors, and with this age limit there can at any rate be no destruction. The question of fire protection is still left unsettled. While it is true that the forests of India are fire-protected, there are many signs that the Indian foresters are beginning to doubt the benefits of complete fire protection, which is alleged by many observers to be favouring the less valuable kinds at the expense of the more valuable timber-yielding species. It is probably true that the natural regeneration of these valuable trees is more general and more prolific in Nepal than in the Indian forests. Expert opinion in India has already gone so far as to pronounce in favour of partial protection only. The policy of the Nepal Government is to wait until a definite conclusion is reached on this very important question. For complete fire protection cannot be introduced except at great expense, while its introduction must inflict irksome restrictions and considerable hardship on the cultivators in the vicinity of the protected areas. Unless therefore fire protection can be proved to be absolutely necessary to the maintenance of the forests, the Government of Nepal is wise in not attempting it.

APPENDIX XX

NOTES ON THE ARCHITECTURE OF NEPAL

EARLIER than Purana Swayambhunath and the stupas erected by the Emperor Asoka in the year 250 B.C., it is probably useless to seek for any remains of architecture in Nepal proper. More and perhaps older traces of very early Buddhist construction will no doubt be discovered when the country near Rummindei or Tilaura is thoroughly examined and excavated. A mile from the frontier of Nepal, though across it, is the little stupa at Piprawa which yielded so magnificent a treasure when opened by M. Peppé. This is certainly pre-Asokan, and whether Piprawa—according to the Chinese traveller Fa-hsien—or Tilaura—according to his successor, Hsüan Tsang—represents the original Kapilavastu, there can hardly be a doubt that this part of the Tarai on both sides of the boundary pillars would return a harvest of knowledge of fifth century building were it properly investigated.

But in neither case would the remains, though on soil that is to-day Nepalese, be in any sense representative of Nepalese architecture. They were built by Indians on what was then Indian soil, and their principles, design, and symbolism were derived from Indian tradition. In setting up his six stupas in the Valley, Asoka copied the form which he had already encountered at Piprawa and elsewhere. To this design he was faithful, and the original stupa at Sanchi did not differ materially from the Patan model, though it is doubtful whether any of his erections in India were equal in size to the Laghan or southern stupa at that place. The smaller memorials that he set up in the centre of Patan and at Kirtipur have been so entirely altered by the accumulation of ornament during two thousand years, that it is now impossible to conjecture what the nature of Asoka's original structure was. In all probability it resembled on a small scale those which are mercifully left intact. We are not much helped by the existing shrines of Swayambhunath and Boddhnath, for the additions that have been made—though they do not essentially alter the original conception of their builders—are due rather to general Tibetan tradition than to anything peculiar to Nepal.[1] Later modifications of the original Buddhist doctrines

[1] As we see at Sanchi, Asoka recognized the value of a hill as a plinth for his work. It may be perhaps assumed that so obvious and outstanding a hill as Swayambhunath

256

led to the addition of the four gods in their niches at the compass-quarters of each shrine. The gilding of the toran and its ornamentation with eyes and the subsequent erection above it of the thirteen-fold " churamani " of gilded rings with their magnificent finial or " khalsa " are probably of genuine Nepalese development, though their resemblance to Buddhist decoration in Burma offers some food for thought.

The most interesting and perhaps the earliest record of Nepalese architecture of a character similar to that which is its peculiar pride to-day, is to be found in the account of a Chinese travel book dating back to the days of the T'ang dynasty. It cannot be later than the earliest years of the

CARVED WINDOWS IN THE DARBAR AT BHATGAON

tenth century A.D., and is almost certainly earlier than the middle of the eighth. This narrative is probably based upon the records left by Wang Hiuen-t se about the year 657. It states that the houses of the Nepalese were made of wood and the walls were carved and painted. They were artists in sculpture work and had decorated with extraordinary richness the palaces of their kings. It cannot be doubted that the following description is of a structure which in no important sense differed from that of the pagoda which is found alike in Nepal and in China, but of which it is apparently impossible to find any example or even a reference in China of equal antiquity. " In the middle of the palace there is a tower of seven storeys roofed with copper tiles. Its balustrade, grilles, columns, beams, and

would have been used by him in preference to the far less impressive fold of ground' at Kirtipur had it not been already dedicated by an existing shrine.

II   S

everything therein are set about with fine and even precious stones. At each of the four corners of the tower there projects a water-pipe of copper. At the base there are golden dragons which spout forth water. From the summit of the tower water is poured through runnels which finds its way down below streaming like a fountain from the mouths of golden Makara."

It is a piece of good fortune to find so accurate and early a description of the form, the richness, and some of the existing features of Nepalese architecture in a Chinese record. It is the more impressive because its author was not concerned to prove anything but to record a marvel.[1]

GOLDEN GATE AND CARVING, MULCHOK, HANUMANDHOKA, KATMANDU

At a later date we have the evidence of more than one Chinese traveller that the Palace of the King of Nepal was an immense structure. We have the testimony of the Chinese chronicles that it had many roofs, a point which was made because in China there were not then any of the " pagodas " which are now one of the chief characteristics of Chinese architecture. Reference is also made to two edifices accompanying the Swayambhunath

---

[1] General L. de Beylié, recalling the parallel offered by the Bronze Monastery of a Thousand Cells which, in the second century A.D., was ornamented with precious stones by King Dutthagamani at Anuradhapura, finds that the influence of Nepalese structure and ornament can be traced far beyond the limits of the country. He discovers them in eleventh-century work in the great Ananda Monastery at Pagan, and he also says that " les pyramids talaines ronds avec des cercles superposés derivent necessairement en principe des stûpes du nord de l'Inde et du Népal." He considers that the concentric circles of the " hti " in Burma and Assam also are taken from Nepal as well as the square entablature of the top of the dome (toran).

stupa which, though now replaced by the more Indian type of " sikra," seem to have been remarkable in the eyes of the travellers.

A WINDOW OF CARVED WOOD, BHATGAON

It is impossible to accept as proved the statement which is occasionally made that there were no superimposed roofs in China before the seventh century, but no record of them remains in the paintings or the early sculptures which still exist, and it is a wild conjecture that the King of Nepal, in the middle of the seventh century, had invited Chinese builders to visit him at a time when no one but those impelled by religious fervour or urgent state business undertook the circuitous and extremely dangerous journey.[1] On the whole, we may with some caution credit Nepal, the land of timber and piety, with the conception of a style of architecture clearly

A WINDOW OF CARVED WOOD, BHATGAON

based upon " wooden " principles and necessities, which has too lightly been regarded as the invention of the Chinese. It cannot even be said that the latter improved upon their model. As I write I look down upon the

[1] It will occur to a visitor to Peking that in the T'ien Ning szu, just outside the western wall of the Chinese city, there remains a temple of pagoda form which was certainly founded before the close of the Sui period in A.D. 617. But venerable as the existing structure is, it is impossible to attribute it in its present form to a date earlier than A.D. 1000.

yellow roofs of the Forbidden City of Peking. In number and size these naturally eclipse the similar structures of Nepal. But magnificent as they are, they offer no instance of more than a triple roof, and in all that historic expanse there is nothing which can for a moment compare in beauty and richness with Changu Narayan or with the royal square of Patan. Another building is described from the store of material that Wang Hiuen-t'se collected in the following way. " In the capital of Nepal there is a building of many stages which is more than 200 chih in height.[1] It is 400 feet in circumference. Ten thousand men can be drawn up upon it. It is divided

A NEPALESE TEMPLE

into three terraces and each terrace is divided into seven stages." The fineness of the sculpture in the four pavilions which attend this tower, and the wealth of the decoration in precious stones and pearls is referred to.[2]

M. François Benoit has dealt with the problems presented by Nepalese architecture in his admirable summary, *L'Architecture: l'Orient Medieval et Moderne* (H. Laurens, Paris, 1912). He notes that the cathedral in Lhasa—it bears different names, the Jo-kang, the Lhabrang, and, in a

---

[1] The chih varied from 11.5 to 15 in., with an average of 12. The height may therefore be taken to have been about 200 feet.

[2] It is difficult to form a conception of the shape of this building. Allowing for some exaggeration, it might have taken the form of a square Altar of Heaven surmounted by a very much larger Temple of Heaven. In any case the mere size of the building suggests that many storeyed work had long been known in Nepal.

stricter sense still, Lha-sa, or the place of God—was built by Srong-Tsan-Gambo to shelter the holy images which his Nepalese and Chinese brides had brought with them to his capital. It is impossible to guess what the original architecture may have been; but in the existing eastern cell where the famous " golden idol " is enshrined, the arrangement, though on a very much larger scale is similar to that of the external shrine at the cardinal points of the Patan stupas. It may also be added that a custom found more largely in Nepal than in China is here adopted. I refer to the barring of the entrance by a flexible wrought-iron grille. The iron curtain in front of the golden shrine of the cathedral in Lhasa is of peculiar con-

TEMPLE OF AKAS BHAIRAB, KATMANDU

struction. It suggests the linking together of a large number of snaffles, a design which may be seen in a modified form in the screens protecting the eastern shrines of Swayambhunath. M. Benoit also finds the influence of Nepal in Burma, in China, and possibly even in India. Perhaps the modern tendency to derive similar architectural formulas that exist in different countries from a single source has not sufficiently taken into consideration similar climatic or economic conditions. But of the unquestionable influence of India upon Nepal in its later architecture, a better illustration cannot be given than that which the temple of Radha Krishna at Patan offers. Its resemblance to some of the work at Fatehpur Sikri must be obvious to anyone who has visited Agra.

The four most typical temples of purely Nepalese construction are the

Taleju close to the Royal Palace inside Katmandu, the shrines of Machendranath in Patan and of Changu Narayan to the north of Bhatgaon, and the Nyatpola or "five-roofed temple" in that city. Except one small shrine near the bridge, there is scarcely anything of the first rank in Pash-

GATEWAY SHOWING WOOD CARVING IN THE TEMPLE OF BARAHI

pati. In general the Nyatpola of Bhatgaon may be taken as an illustration of the usual design of Nepalese religious architecture. It is not as beautifully carved as Changu Narayan, but it offers the characteristic feature of a five-fold base composed of rectangular terraces threaded by a steep ascent guarded by five pairs of conventional figures. At the top a square chamber within a colonnade of wooden pillars supports the lowest and heaviest roof. This again is surmounted by another much lower chamber with its roof, and so in diminishing proportion until the fifth or uppermost roof crowns the structure and is itself ensigned by a gold finial.

KURWABAT, BUDDHA-BHAGAWAN TEMPLE, PATAN

Each of these roofs is supported by struts projecting at an angle of 45 degrees or more from the entablature which crowns the pillar work of the lower storey. It is in this work that Nepalese art has had its especial triumph. It is not necessary to describe in detail the vigorous and graceful sculptures

which may be seen in many of the plates of this book ornamenting these
struts. Elsewhere the Newar craftsman betrays an equal capacity to
carve in relief or in the round. But these ornamental brackets are probably
the most striking characteristic that Nepalese architecture possesses.

Apart from the temples, the viharas or monastic settlements exhibit
a style which is also peculiar to this country. In the centre of a square
courtyard, two storeys in height, there will generally be found a closely

HOUSE FRONT, KATMANDU

slatted cage containing an image. This structure is presumably
intended solely to protect the figure from defilement, like the stone lattice-
work that shelters each of the upper images at Borobodoer. Smaller
grilles admit light but defeat the curiosity of strangers wherever a window
is pierced in the wall of the vihara. The roof of the domestic, as well as
the religious structure, projects considerably. This is perhaps intended
to protect the inmates from the sun as well as the rain.

Houses are mostly of three storeys and the projecting penthouse—eaves
they can hardly be called—in which each roof ends, is stayed by a dozen
props, each of which may be material for exquisite carving and in every

case receives a conventional ornament. In general the houses are built of plain red brick of a singularly rich cardinal maroon colour. The lowest stage is as a rule open in front whether it is used as a shop or as a lounge.

A CORNER AT BHATGAON

The entablature is supported by four pillars, each of which may be the object of good conventional ornament. The spandrels formed by low arches over the three bays are also generally well ornamented. In the distance the steep ladder which serves as a staircase may be seen. The first floor is generally lighted by a broad low window of which the sill and the lintel are carried horizontally into the brickwork beyond the breadth of the window. These are often beautifully decorated. The second and third storeys are usually lighted by a three-bayed window considerably larger than that of the first floor. The third storey, however, is of much less height than the second, while the attic—which is lighted by a single dormer-window—is of insignificant height. Such a house as this in a town has generally two superimposed roofs. The first floor has, as a rule, no such protection from the sun and rain, which may be the reason why its window is generally smaller than those of the upper floors. The characteristic Nepalese effect is maintained by a series of struts which support the two

A RICHLY CARVED WOODEN DOOR AT KATMANDU

roofs at intervals of perhaps three feet. In the country the roof often presents the characteristic "jerked head" of a Sussex farmhouse, and sometimes by a reverse process the ridge pole is cut between the two ends and a flat roof created, terminated at each end by pyramidal gables.

The domestic architecture of Nepal is picturesque beyond that of any other country. A fine tradition has been built up out of the possibilities and necessities of this wooded, rainy, and sunlit Himalayan State, not the least effective characteristic of which is a beautiful alternation of light and shade that modern European architecture seems unable or unwilling to secure. The shadows beneath the long eaves and the open structure of the ground floor contrast beautifully with the rich sunlit expanse of the crimson walls. Ornament has been kept strictly to its proper place. No doubt a practical reason could be found for the Nepalese habit of prolonging

BRASS WORK AT THE TEMPLE OF MACHENDRA

the lintels and sills of doors and windows, but they need no further justification for the artist than the beautiful arabesques for which they offer a field. and the foliated volutes which in. the finer examples lend an apparent

BRASS FIGURE OF TARA, SWAYAMBHUNATH

support to the windows they accompany. The gadrooned and tapered pillars of the old palace in Katmandu have a quality that is rare even in the marbles of Shah Jehan, and the curiously engrailed and invecked shallow cusps of the low arches have no counterpart anywhere that I can

35

NEPALESE BRASS WARE

remember. It is not impossible that the cantilever timber bridge, which is still the regular type for medium sized crossings in Nepal, had its influence upon these long flattened brackets.

The spandrels of the doorways are often deeply carved, though in most cases clogged with alternate coatings of paint and dirt. The arch of the door is in some cases ornamented in a way that is probably not found elsewhere. Slung in the corners of the arch are sometimes to be found beautifully modelled pieces of wood carvings à jour, in a form either geometrical or arabesque. In special cases it may take the form of an animal. Inside, in the case of the larger houses, there is a courtyard in the centre of which may be found, as a rule, a neglected statue or the stub of a pillar. Glass is now used in all but the poorer buildings.

The excellence of the Nepalese copper and bronze craftsmen—which has led to a permanent colony in Lhasa where much of the best Tibetan work is made by them—has contributed greatly to the decoration of the architecture. Of this the golden door of Bhatgaon is the most prominent illustration, but there is scarcely an important structure which does not boast some of this handiwork. Especially admirable are the demi-lunes, or escutcheons of gilded copper, which crown the principal doors and enshrine veranda openings. More magnificent than any other examples of work in the round are the figures of human beings, gods, garudas, and deified characters, peacocks, and cobras which surmount the tall graceful shafts in the Darbar Squares and the forecourts of the chief temples. Of statues in the round the finest is without doubt the bronze Tara which faces the western side of Swayambhunath.

Of lesser work in bronze much has already been written, and in addition to the plates given here reference should be made to the exceptionally good photographs of Nepalese brass work that are contained in Mr. Percy Brown's *Picturesque Nepal*. Of " natural " pictorial work there is nothing better than the copies of European portraits that illustrate the Darbar Hall in the Hanuman-Dhoka. Exception may be made of the curious portrait of Prithwi Narayan, which hangs in the old Diwan-i-Am of the Palace. I failed to get a good photograph of it, and so made a sketch which is reproduced in the first volume of this book.[1] The style is, of course, purely Indo-Persian, but there is no reason to doubt that it was painted by a Nepalese artist.

There is a school of Nepalese religious painting which is closely modelled upon, or rather allied to, that of Tibet. The Nepalese work is not so fine, but in colour it is as good as that of Tibet. As to the drawing and composition.it must be remembered that no scope or latitude is permitted by Buddhist tradition. It is therefore difficult to be certain, except after considerable acquaintance with both schools, to which any given painting should be attributed.

---

[1] Page 60, vol. i.

APPENDIX XXI

TWO RECORDS OF THE INVASION OF NEPAL BY THE CHINESE
IN 1792

I

Written by the King, and engraved upon a stone slab below the Potala, Lhasa [1]

THE monument of the deeds fully accomplished ten times.
    Now that the Gurkhas have submitted to me, the Imperial army
has been withdrawn, and the completion of this brilliant tenth achievement has been set out in the Letter. Though the fame of this matter was
great, it has not been fully manifested. Therefore the proclamation has
been inscribed on this monument, that the monument may serve as a moral
for the minds of men.
    It comes to my mind that my mind was formerly attached to the
Yü-kur writing. According to the writing of Che-u-kur the acts of the
respectful and sympathetic Amban, and of the Owner of the country, able
to perform all things, are set down here. It is written in a chapter of the
Lü A-u that, when the mind is in a good state, the mind and the deeds
are joined together. However, he who acts in accordance with the above
precepts will obtain the approval of the Heavenly Protector [2] and will gain
reward. As my conduct was on those lines, I gained all the merits necessary
for carrying out the ten wars to a successful conclusion. It is fitting that
they should be carved on this monument.
    The merits of the ten times are as follows:

> Two victories over the Chung-kar.
> One victory over Hu-i Se.
> Two victories over Tsa-la and Chu-chen.
> One victory over Ta-i Wan.
> Two victories over Mi-han-tan and An-tan.

    Now I have fought twice with the Gurkhas. I have made an end of
them, and they have tendered their submission to me. This completes
the ten times. Three of the internal victories are of lesser importance.
    Now as regards the submission of the Gurkhas in the Female Earth-
Bird year. Although they brought troops for looting Ü and Tsang,[3] the
A-u Hu-i not daring, Pa-chung did not go into the matter thoroughly,
but arranged it in a hurry. So the Gurkhas were not frightened.
    Again, having obtained loot last year, they came back. The wicked
Minister was degraded, and the famous Chang-chun was sent. The latter

---

[1] I am indebted to Sir Charles Bell, K.C.I.E., for his kind permission to take this
record from his book, *Tibet, Past and Present*, 1924.
[2] *I.e.*, the Emperor of China.
[3] The two main provinces of Central Tibet. Lhasa is in Ü ; Shigatse in Tsang.

arranged on a large scale for provisions and wages. Fu-kang men appreciated my gifts highly, and did not consider fatigue or fear.

During the winter of last year additional soldiers of Solon [1] and Szechuan came quickly, batch by batch, along the Sining road, and arrived in the country of the thieves [2] during the fifth month of this year. Immediately on their arrival they retook the country of Ü and Tsang, and captured the territory of the thieves. They traversed the mountains, so difficult to push through, as though they were moving over a level plain. They crossed rivers with great waves and narrow gorges as though they were small streams. They climbed up the peaks of mountains and descended again in the pursuit. They captured the important places and at the same time captured the roads in the gorges. Not considering injuries to hands or feet, they fought seven battles and gained seven victories. The thieves were panic-stricken.

After that, when the troops arrived close to Yam-bu, [3] the chief leaders of the thieves were sent. They submitted respectfully and represented that they would conduct themselves according to our orders. Although they carried out the orders of the great Commander-in-Chief, they were not allowed to enter our encampment. The reason for this was that last year they seized Ten-dzin Pal-jor [4] and those with him by means of a falsehood; and so they were not allowed to enter.

Owing to the great heroism of the mighty army the thieves were helpless. He could have had them removed from his presence, and could have made an end of them, letting not even one of them escape. However, that was not the wish of the Heavenly Protector. Even if all those territories had been obtained, as they are more than a thousand distances from the frontiers of Ü and Tsang, it would have been difficult to cultivate them and to guard them. As for ordinary, simple people, even if they obtain a thing, the end will not be gained. [5] Therefore orders were given, the respectful submission was noted, and the army was withdrawn. Thereby the work was completed. [6]

---

[1] Sir Charles Bell makes the following note: "A district in the upper part of the Tibetan province of Gyarong, annexed by China in 1863. It is therefore evident that there were Tibetan troops in this army that conquered the Gurkhas. It appears also that several Tibetan officers took part, including Do-ring Shap-pe, Yu-to Shap-pe, and Chang-lo-chen De-pön (Colonel)." This latter statement is perfectly true; but the troops from "Solon" were actually a well-known contingent from a district in the north of China. It appears that the Solon men were in especial request for distant or dangerous enterprises. I am indebted to Baron A. Staël Holstein, of Peking, for this observation and for calling my attention to the following extract from the Peking Chronicles.

[2] I.e., the Gurkhas.　　　[3] I.e., Katmandu, the capital of Nepal.

[4] The Do-ring Shap-pe. It is said that the Chinese sent him with the Yu-to Shap-pe and Chang-lo-chen De-pön as peace envoys to the Gurkhas, and that the Gurkhas seized them and carried them off to Nepal.

[5] I.e., "even if Nepal be annexed to Tibet, the Tibetans will not be able to hold it."

[6] European writers, following Chinese authorities, put the Gurkha army at eighteen thousand men and the Chinese at seventy thousand. Tibetans in general put the Gurkha army at about four thousand, and the Chinese army at about nine thousand, of whom half or rather more were Tibetans.

II　　　　　　　　　　　　　　　　　　T

Formerly, in the time of King Thang Tha-ï Tsung, there was a conference with the Chi-li.[1] As it was shown that they [the Gurkhas] were conquered and powerless, he [the Chi-li] said[2] that they would always remain on good terms [with China]. It is not fitting to take the Chi-li as an example.[3] The frontiers of Ü and Tsang are not near to China. They [the Gurkhas] fearing to lose their lives, were compelled to submit respectfully. A pretended submission, made in order to obtain peace, will not suffice. A great victory has now been obtained. The thieves have offered a heart-felt submission, and this is believed and accepted. Affairs have been arranged in accordance with the three points of King Tha-ï Tsung of Thang-gur.

Need I write the former affairs of the Tor-gö,[4] how they became afraid of us and followed us? How they came to agree with us and to follow us, this has all been written already. Now the Gurkhas having admitted their fault, and wishing to save their lives, fear us and follow us. Thus agreeing with us and following, the two qualities are complete. The failing was theirs, and they have admitted their fault: that is how the matter stands. If this matter be considered, it will be seen that the people of Ü, abandoning military pursuits, devote themselves solely to literature. Thus they have become like a body bereft of vigour. This is unfitting. If a people abandon military pursuits and make literature their chief object, they become unable to safeguard their former position. This should be known.

The manner of going and the manner of returning[5] are clearly written in the book entitled *The Planets and Stars*. Now understand this and do not forget it.[6] It is to be considered again and again at the time of making war, that it may be of advantage.

Owing to the knowledge gained during fifty-seven years of warfare these ten deeds have been fully completed. This is the gift of the Heavenly Protector. Thus the kindness of the Heavenly Protector is exceedingly deep. I also have faith in it. They [the Gurkhas] thought they could achieve a great deal by violence, but the favour of the Heavenly Protector remained. It is hoped that this will tend to turn- people into men of complete justice. Besides this, there is nothing to be said.

This has been written by the King on an upper date[7] in the first month of winter in the fifty-seventh year of the reign of the Heavenly Protector, that is to say, in the Male Water Rat year.

---

[1] Apparently the British. The Tibetan word for foreigners of European extraction is "Chi-ling."

[2] The non-honorific word for "said" is used here—the word applied to the common people to indicate contempt for the representative of the Chi-li.

[3] *Semble,* in keeping Indian territory for themselves, after conquering it.

[4] A Mongolian tribe conquered by the Chinese.

[5] *I.e.,* the rules of human conduct.

[6] As a matter of fact the Tibetans, with but few exceptions, do not even know that this inscription relates to the campaign against the Gurkhas. They know only that it was erected by a former Amban.

[7] *I.e.,* during the first half of the month.

II

A Descriptive Account of the Military Operations of the Sacred [Manchu] Dynasty [Shêng-wu-chi]. Compiled by Wei Yüan, native of Shao-yang [Hunan province]. The Expedition against the Ghorkhas [Nepal] in the Ch'ien-lung reign.[1] Literally translated (1926) by Mr. H. S. Brunnert.

Wei Yüan [T. Mo-shên] died A.D. 1856. He served as a magistrate in the provinces. He wrote the " Shêng-wu-chi," a descriptive account of the military operations of the Manchu dynasty, and also the " Hai-kuo t'u-chih," a record of foreign nations, founded on the notes of Lin Tsê-ksu.[2]

To the west of the provinces of Ssŭch'uan and Yünnan lies Wu-ssŭ Tsang[3]—Tibet; to the south-west of the latter—Ghorkha [Nepal], and to the south-west of Nepal—" The Five Indies."

India is the Ancient Buddhist Kingdom. It lies to the west of Onion Range,[4] [Ts'ung-ling shan] and, on the south, is bounded by a big sea and the distance between India and Tibet is fully equal to 2000 *li*. The opinion hazarded by some persons that Tibet is the Ancient Buddhist Kingdom is not true.

If one is journeying from Ta-chien-lu, in Ssŭch'uan, westwards, there are more than 20 stations to Anterior Tibet, 12 stations more to Central Tibet, another 12 stations to Ulterior Tibet; after 20 stations more is situated the iron suspension bridge at Chi-lung,[5] which is the remotest frontier place in Ulterior Tibet; to the west of this bridge lies the land of Ghorkas [Nepal].

The original name of Ghorkha is Pa-lê-pu[6] country. In old times it was divided into three parts or tribes: Yeh-lêng-pu, Pu-yen-pu, and K'u-mu-pu.[7] In the 9th year of the Yung-chêng reign (1731) each tribe presented to the Throne memorials written in golden characters, also native products, in token of tribute, but afterwards the three tribes were amalgamated[8] into one, and this country then became the neighbour of Ulterior Tibet. Its dimensions are: from East to West—several thousand *li*; from South to North—more than one thousand *li*. The Capital is called Yang-pu; it lies approximately at 11-12 days' journey from the frontier. This country also has some Buddhist monuments; therefore, the Tanguts[9] yearly came in pilgrimage to worship at the pagodas and whitewash them.

From ancient times Nepal had no relations with China; the beginning

---

[1] This is contained in chapter v of the Account, and has been translated by C. Imbault-Huart, *Histoire de la conquête du Népal.*
[2] *A Chinese Biographical Dictionary*, by Herbert A. Giles, p. 871, no. 2300.
[3] Signifying "central" and "pure."
[4] The Belurtagh Mountains in Turkestan.
[5] Name of a place: *Kirong.*   [6] Parbatiya.
[7] These are Patan, Bhatgaon, and Katmandu respectively.
[8] By the Ghorkhas.   [9] The Tibetans.

of the hostilities between them dated from the 55th year[1] of the Ch'ien-lung reign, when Nepal invaded Tibet.

In the 46th year[2] of the Ch'ien-lung reign the Panch'ên Lama of Ulterior Tibet came to the Capital of China to congratulate the Emperor on the occasion of his 70th anniversary; donations to the Pontiff came from "inside and outside,"[3] like seas overflowing and mountains "heaping." When the Panch'ên Lama passed away in the Capital, his remains were escorted back to Tibet. As to his treasures, they all became the property of his elder brother Chung-pa Hutukhtu. But the latter gave no donations either to the Monasteries or to the Tangut soldiery; besides, he declined the claim of his younger brother Shê-ma-rh-pa to have his share in the division of treasures, on the ground that he [Shê-ma-rh-pa] had embraced "the Red Religion." Angered by this refusal, Shê-ma-rh-pa brought his complaints to the Ghorkhas, and used the hoarded treasures of Ulterior Tibet and the Chung-pa's arrogance as incitements to them to invade this country.

In the 3rd month of the 55th year[4] of the Ch'ien-lung reign, the Ghorkhas, using as the pretext the increase of taxes on merchandise and the admixture of dust in the table-salt, sent troops and invaded the frontier area. The Tangut soldiers were not able to make any resistance. As for the officers whom the Government appointed, in order to help in the extermination of invaders—e.g., Officer of the Guards Pa-chung, Tartar Generals Ao-Hui, Ch'êng-tê, and others—they tried to settle the matter amicably and to get peace through bribery. So they secretly advised to the Tibetan Abbots[5] and other ecclesiastics privately to pay the Ghorkhas a yearly subsidy of 15,000 in gold in order to stop the military operations.

At that time the Dalai Lama could not agree to the suggestion. Nevertheless, Pa-chung ventured to deceive the Emperor by presenting a memorial to the effect that the rebels had surrendered. So far was this from being the case that he actually persuaded the Ghorkha chieftain to bring tribute, in order to be appointed Prince[6] of the country [Kuo-wang]. In this "War" not a single soldier was lost, but a million was spent on soldiers' rations.

In the 7th month the Ghorkhas sent an Envoy to Tibet to bring the tribute and to present a letter to the Imperial Resident there, requesting that the stipulations of the Treaty [with Pa-chung] be complied with. But General Ao-Hui, fearing the disclosure of the above mentioned facts, put this letter aside and did not memorialize the Throne.

Next year[7] Tibet again did not observe the Treaty, as regards [? in spite of the receipt of] the yearly subsidy. In consequence, the Ghorkhas again raised troops and penetrated deeply into Tibet, under the pretext of punishing the country for the breach of the Treaty.

To the south west of Tashilumpo, in Ulterior Tibet, are situated: Ch'ü-to-chiang-kung[8]—to the East, and a mountain range, bearing the

---

[1] 1790.　[2] 1781.　[3] From the capital and from the provinces.　[4] 1790.
[5] K'ar-pu.　[6] Ruler.　[7] 1791.　[8] Name of a place.

name of P'êng-ts'o-ling—to the West, both possessing important strategical positions, consisting of sheer precipices, successive ridges and defiles. The rebels' infantry, to the number of several thousands, debouched from a place, named Nieh-la-mu.[1] At that time, the Government troops, both Tibetan and Chinese, had only to divide themselves into two detachments, the one defending Ch'ü-to-chiang-kung, to prevent the enemy from advancing; the other making a detour to the P'êng-ts'o-ling mountain range, in order to cut off the enemy's retreat. In that case, the Ghorkhas, who had invaded the country very deeply, but were unable to get reinforcements, would be forced to disperse without a combat.

But Pao-t'ai, the Imperial Resident in Tibet, on learning about the rebels' advance, in the first place had the Panch'ên Lama removed to Anterior Tibet; then, panic-stricken by the rebels' movements, he memorialized the Emperor, supplicating to have both Pontiffs removed out of Tibet: Dalai Lama—to Hsi-ning,[2] and Panch'ên Lama—to T'ai-ning respectively, being ready to abandon the Tibetan territory to the rebels.

As the city of Tashilumpo is situated on a mountain and has a river in front of it, thus possessing a strong strategical position, the Lamas, to the number of several thousands, had only to occupy the city walls and guard them, waiting for the reinforcements to arrive. But Chung-pa Hutukhtu had already fled, taking with him all his treasures. As for Chi-lung Lama[3] and other ecclesiastics, they all alleged that, as their divinations had showed, the Heavenly Mother was against fighting. In consequence, the population became quite downhearted, and the rebels succeeded in plundering the city of Tashilumpo mercilessly. This caused great consternation throughout the whole of Tibet, and both Pontiffs urgently memorialized the Throne about the critical state of affairs.

The Officer of the Guards, Pa-chung, was just then accompanying the Emperor to Yehol, and hearing that the rebels had invaded Tibet, he committed suicide by throwing himself into a river. At that time Ao-Hui held the post of Governor General of the province of Ssŭch'uan and Ch'êngtê that of Tartar General there. Both shifted all the guilt on Pa-chung, saying that, being master of the Tangut language, he had conducted privately all the negotiations, so that he alone was responsible, and that they had had no knowledge of them at all.

When the Emperor ordered them to proceed to Tibet to exterminate the invaders, they advanced by easy stages and were in no hurry to enter the Tibetan territory. But His Majesty knew that both were quite unreliable. So he commanded Duke Fu-k'ang-an to assume the post of Tartar General and Duke Hai-lan-ch'a to be his Military Assistant; also, to mobilize the Manchu troops of the Solon[4] tribe and the native drilled forces for the extermination of rebels. As for the supplies of the army the Emperor ordered them to be provided: by Sun Shih-i, the Governor General of the Ssŭch'uan province;[5] for the Eastern region of Tibet, by

---

[1] *Nilam.*   [2] In Kansu.   [3] Chief councillor.
[4] From the region of the Amur.   [5] A.D. 1720-96.

the Imperial Resident in Tibet, Ho-Lin; for the Western region of Tibet, *i.e.*, for the area lying outside the frontier place of Chi-lung, by the former Governor General of the Ssüch'uan province, Hui-Ling. Pao-t'ai was ordered to wear the cangue¹ in front of the army. Moreover, the main forces were to enter Tibet by way of Kokonor steppes, thus shortening the journey by 30 stages, in comparison with the advance *via* Ta-chien-lu in Ssüch'uan.

The rebels, relying on the precedent of the last year's war, when peace had been obtained through bribery, returned to their country, taking with them all the booty and leaving one thousand men to guard the frontier.

Ao-Hui, Ch'êng-tê, and others, though at the head of 4,000 soldiers, neither attacked the enemy's forces laden with booty, nor routed the rebels left for the defence of the frontier; they only reduced the small fortified place of Nieh-la-mu, held by about a hundred rebels, and then memorialized the Throne to the effect that the enemy had retreated. They intended that the matter should be regarded as closed, and did not mention the presence of the rebel forces at such two places as Chi-lung and Yung-hsia. But the Emperor rebuked them and refused to act upon their suggestion.

In the 2nd month of the next year² the Tartar General and his Military Assistant, advancing through Kokonor entered the territory of Ulterior Tibet.

In the 4th intercalary month 2,000 Solon soldiers also 5,000 soldiers quartered in Chin-ch'uan,³ all assembled on Tibetan territory. To these numbers are to be added 3,000 Government troops from Tibet itself; 70,000 piculs of wheat, and more than 20,000 cows and sheep were bought on the spot to secure, for one year, the provisioning necessary for 10,000-15,000 soldiers, so as to avoid any uncertainty about the transportation of supplies from the interior of China.

During the 5th month the rebels, who had been left to guard the frontier, were several times defeated, and the Government troops completely recovered the Tibetan territory. In the beginning of the 6th month the main forces penetrated deeply into the enemy's territory.

Out of fear that the rebels might make an encircling movement and attack our troops in the rear, the Commandants of Forces Ch'êng-tê and Tai-sên-pao and Brigadier-General Chu-shên-pao began to advance by the eastern and western roads respectively, in order to divide the enemy's forces; while the main army began its advance by the central road. Hai-lan-ch'a formed the vanguard from 3 detachments of troops; Fu-k'ang-an followed him with 2 detachments.

At the iron suspension bridge, 80 *li* distance from Chi-lung, they approached the enemy's first mountain pass. The rebels broke the bridge and made a resistance, using the natural advantages of the place. While Fu-k'ang-an, with the main force, was standing in front of the enemy, Hai-lan-ch'a, using bamboo rafts, crossed the river up-stream and, mak-

---

¹ A heavy square wooden collar worn as a humiliating punishment.
² 1792.   ³ Ssüch'uan.

ing a detour through the mountains, appeared above the rebels' camp. Fu-k'ang-an, on his side, immediately took advantage of the situation thus created to construct a bridge. Then, having captured the enemy's post, they made a joint attack on the rebels' camp and pursued them for a distance of 160 *li* to the place named Hsieh-pu-lu. As on the road there existed no place suitable for a camp, they did not meet a single enemy.

After pursuing the rebels another stretch of 100 and a few score *li* they reached the mountain-range Tung-chüeh-ling, where two cliffs, "standing like walls," were separated by a river, with deep water and a swift current. Our soldiers climbed them by by-paths, braving dangers equal to those presented by the iron suspension bridge. Then, taking advantage of a dark and rainy night, they divided their forces into two parts and both up and down stream threw bridges across the river made out of dead trees, which enabled our troops to cross and capture an important strategical position.

On the 9th day of the 6th month our troops reached the Yung-ya mountain. The Ghorkha barbarians, stricken with consternation, then despatched envoys to our camp, offering submission, but the Tartar General and h's Military Assistant sternly rejected this offer and for several days did not send any answer.

Afterwards our troops again attacked the rebels from three directions, routing them in six engagements, and then passed over the big mountain. Successively they killed 4,000 rebels and invaded more than 700 *li* of their territory. Our troops were by this time nearing the enemy's capital city, Yang-pu.

Up to this moment they had had the mountains on their eastern and western sides, these mountains being separated by a river; but after they had reached the Yung-ya mountain, they had now mountains on their southern and northern sides, these mountains also being separated by a river. The rebels were holding both mountains, and in the centre there was a bridge.[1]

In the beginning of the 8th month our troops made an attack from three directions, took the mountain on the northern side of the river, and routed the rebels to the north of the bridge. The enemy's capital was then situated beyond the big mountain on the southern shore of the river forty or fifty *li* away.

The rebels, numbering ten battalions, were holding the mountain very strongly. Hai-lan-ch'a proposed to guard the river and make a camp there, but Fu-k'ang-an did not consent to this plan. He crossed over the bridge and attacked the enemy; then, in spite of rain, he climbed the mountain to 20 *li* distance and reached a very steep place. The enemy, taking advantage of his position on the summit of the mountain, poured down trees and stones "like rain," and at the same time those rebels who were separated by river and mountain made an attack from three directions.

Our troops sometimes fought and sometimes retreated. The number of

---

[1] See account of this fight, vol. i, pp. 68-69.

killed and wounded was very great. Hai-lan-ch'a, from across the river, came then to the assistance, and O-lê-têng-pao, holding the bridge, fought stubbornly; and succeeded to repel the enemy.

At that time the enemy's country bordered, on the southern side, upon an Indian land named " P'i-lêng "[1]; this land had long ago become Britain's dependency and repeatedly had had quarrels with the Ghorkhas. When Fu-k'ang-an, at the head of his troops, had entered the enemy's territory, he sent to all the countries bordering upon the Ghorkhas, *i.e.*, Chê-mêng-hsiung[2] and Tsung-mu-pu-lu-k'ê—on the south-east, Pa-tso-mu-lang—on the west, Chia-ka-rh and P'i-lêng—on the south—the intimation to attack the Ghorkhas simultaneously, promising to divide between them the Ghorkhas' lands, after peace had been restored.

About this time the Ghorkhas also had addressed themselves to P'i-lêng, asking to help them in their critical situation. But P'i-lêng, pretending that they would come to the assistance with their soldiers, in reality invaded secretly the Ghorkhas' frontier.

The Ghorkha barbarians, being forced to withstand two powerful enemies, were afraid that they could not succeed in it; moreover, they apprehended that this news would rouse our troops' energy. Therefore, they again sent envoys to our camp to ask humbly for mercy.

At that moment our troops had just suffered a reverse, whereas the enemy's country presented more and more dangers to them; besides, after the 8th month, the big snow in the mountains would make the return most difficult. Therefore, the rebels' request for surrender was granted.

They gave back the former treaty; restored all the treasures, plundered in Tibet: the golden spires of pagodas and the golden tablets, seals, etc.; released Tan-chin, Pan-chu-rh,[3] and others, formerly held by them; gave back the corpse of Shê-ma-rh-pa and promised to present, as tribute, tame elephants, horses, and musicians, asking the eternal observance of the stipulations and the withdrawal of our troops.

Originally our Emperor had intended to divide the Ghorkha country between the chieftains of various native tribes and to bestow the title of Prince of the 2nd degree on Fu-k'ang-an, but on hearing that the rebels' request for surrender had been granted he gave his sanction to this settlement [and withdrew his army], leaving behind 3,000 Tibetan soldiers and 1,000 Chinese and Mongol soldiers to guard the Tibetan frontier. From that time began the garrisoning of Tibet by the Government troops.

There is a big road leading from Ulterior Tibet to Ghorkha, *via* Ting-chieh,[4] but persons using this road must make a detour through Pu-lu-k'ê-pa[5] and other tribes, and it takes more than a month's time. Therefore our troops, advancing from Chi-lung, took the nearer road, along which there were precipices on the left and torrents on the right; it was impossible,

---

[1] " P'i-lêng " is the Chinese form of " Feringhi " or " Frank," by which name most of Asia describes the European.
[2] Sikkim.   [3] Kalon : Councillor of State.   [4] Tingri.
[5] This is an astonishing misstatement, unless by Brukpa (Pu-lu-k'ê-pa) all semi-Tibetan tribes along the Central Himalayas is meant.

even for a single person, to ride: the Tartar General himself and his Military Assistant also were walking on foot all the time. As the tame elephants which had been sent as tribute used the big road, they arrived in Ulterior Tibet in the spring only of the next year.

As for the Wu-la-ling mountain-range, one must spend a whole day's time to cover the distance of 120 *li* in order to ascend and descend it; as soon as it is getting slightly dark, instantly it is impossible to find the right road; moreover, the accumulated snow forms walls, "like the covered way through a city gate," to the depth of several tens of chang.[1] Men going to and fro do not dare to utter a word, otherwise an avalanche " as big as a house " would crush them to death. When the Ghorkhas, after having plundered Tibet, were returning to their country, nearly all 2,000 persons, who had passed over this mountain-range were frozen to death; indeed, to the south of the Onion Range[2] Merciful Heaven has put a boundary between the centre and the west. The dangers are doubled as compared with those of Chin-ch'uan, and surpass by far the dangers presented by Turkestan. The military forces of the Han and T'ang dynasties had not reached this region. Fortunately their [Ghorkha] officers and men were going barefooted; they had the habit previously to agree upon a date and then to retreat after a slight engagement, whereas our troops, regardless of this usage, were first in making surprise attacks on the enemy and, in the long run, came out victorious in several engagements.

Beginning from that big punitive expedition and till now the Ghorkhas have been bringing us tribute uninterruptedly.

Their [Ghorkha] country borders: on the west—upon Cashmere [Kashmir] of Northern India and to the south—upon Chia-ka-rh of the Eastern India, named in the Annals of the Ming Dynasty " Pang-ka-la," alias " Mêng-chia-la "[3]—an old dependency of England, with a capital city named " P'i-lêng " [author's note: alias " Ka-li-kê-ta "[4]].

In the 6oth year of the Ch'ien-lung reign,[5] the English Ambassador,[6] who was bringing tribute, himself made the following declaration: " Two years ago, when your Tartar-General, leading the troops, had reached the land of Ti-mi tribe, situated to the south-west of Tibet, our country's soldiers also rendered assistance. If, in future, you again stand in need of employing foreign troops, we are willing to exert our strength."[7] Then for the first time did our Government learn that, during the previous punitive expedition against the Ghorkhas, they also had had troubles from foreigners on their southern frontier.

When, in the 2oth year of the Tao-kuang reign,[8] the English barbarians had invaded the provinces of Kuang-tung and Chekiang, the Ghorkhas, on their side, also sent Envoys to the Imperial Resident in Tibet, to make the following declaration: " Our country borders upon the land of P'i-lêng,

---

[1] A measure of ten Chinese feet. [2] Ts'ung-ling : see *supra.*
[3] Bengal.   [4] Calcutta.   [5] 1795.   [6] Earl Macartney.
[7] No record of any such statement by Lord Macartney can now be traced.
[8] 1840.

which is a dependency of Li-ti, and at the hands of which it repeatedly suffered insults. Now, upon learning that hostilities have commenced between Li-ti and the Metropolitan Dependency, and that the latter has gained several victories, we are willing to lead our troops to make an attack on the Dependency of Li-ti, in order to render assistance in the punitive expedition undertaken by your Emperor." At that time the Imperial Resident in Tibet did not know that " Li-ti " meant " England "; or that "the Metropolitan Dependency" meant "the Kuang-tung province of China "; or that, in consequence, "A Dependency of Li-ti " meant " Bengal [Mêng-Chia-La] of Eastern India." Therefore, he rejected their offer, answering that " the barbarians were attacking one another, and that the Heavenly Dynasty [1] never interfered in such a matter."

The capital city of England is situated beyond a great western ocean, but England's Dependency—India—borders upon the land of Ghorkhas. As there was a hereditary enmity between these two countries, and the English barbarians did not fail to seize their opportunity when China attacked the Ghorkhas—the Ghorkhas, on their side also, were willing to assist China when this country attacked the English barbarians.

PEKING: 16.1.1926.

APPENDIX XXII

TREATY OF PEACE BETWEEN NEPAL AND TIBET, 1856

A

THE following is a translation of the Nepalese text. There are three other translations, one from the Tibetan text, one by Sir Charles Bell, and the third by C. U. Aitchison, which differ slightly from the Nepalese in some particulars.

We, the undermentioned Nobles, Bharadars, and Lamas representing the Gorkha Government and the Tibetan Government [2] have mutually settled a Treaty of the following ten Articles, and with Supreme Being as witness we have affixed our seals unto it of our own free will and choice.[3] The Emperor of China shall continue to be regarded with respect [4] as heretofore. So long as the two Governments continue to abide by the terms set forth herein, they shall live in amity like two brothers. May

[1] China.

[2] The Tibetan text here inserts "having assembled together" and Sir Charles Bell has "held a conference."

[3] The Tibetan text omits "of our own free will and choice." Instead it inserts "being satisfied."

[4] Aitchison here has "We further agree that the Emperor of China shall be *obeyed* by both States as before."

the Supreme Being not allow that side to prosper which may make war upon the other; and may the side be exempt from all sin in making war upon the other side which violates the terms contained in this agreement [Treaty].

(Here follow the names and seals of the signatories.)

SCHEDULE OF THE ARTICLES OF THE TREATY

Article I

Tibet shall pay a sum of Rupees ten thousand annually to the Gorkha Government.[1]

Article II

Gorkha and Tibet have both been regarding the Emperor of China with respect.[2] Tibet being merely a country of Monasteries of Lamas and a place for recitation of prayers and practice of religious austerities, should troops of any other Raja invade Tibet in future,[3] Gorkha will afford such assistance and protection as it can.

Article III

Tibet shall not levy any taxes (on routes), duties (on merchandise), and rates (of any other kind) leviable by Tibet on the merchants and subjects of the country of Gorkha.[4]

Article IV

Tibet shall return to the Gorkha Government all Sikh soldiers held as prisoners and also all officers, soldiers, women, and guns[5] of Gorkha that were captured and taken during the war; and the Gorkha Government shall return to Tibet all the soldiers of Tibet captured in the war, as also the arms, the yaks whatever there may be belonging to the Rayats of Kirong, Kuti, Jhunga, Taklakhar, and Chhewar-Gumbha,[6] and on the completion of this Treaty all the Gorkha troops that are in Taklakhar, Chhewar-Gumbha, Kerong, Jhunga, Kuti, Dhyaklang; and up to[7] Bhairab Langur range shall be withdrawn and the places evacuated.

[1] The Tibetan text inserts the words "in cash"; but Aitchison has the words "as a tribute"; and Sir Charles Bell "as a present."

[2] Aitchison here has "borne allegiance"

[3] The Tibetan text has "should any other Government invade" while Sir Charles Bell says "if any foreign country attacks."

[4] Aitchison adds "and others trading with its country."

[5] The Tibetan text and Sir Charles Bell both add "servants."

[6] Aitchison follows the Nepalese text here in the names of places, but the Tibetan has "Pu-rang and Rong-Shar" instead of "Taklakhar and Chhewar-Gumbha," while Sir Charles Bell for the first three has "Kyi-rong, Nya-nang, Dzong-ga," and follows the Tibetan text for the last two. Aitchison renders "Dhyaklang" (of the Nepalese and Tibetan texts) "Dhakling," while Sir Charles Bell calls it "Tarling" and adds another place, "Latse," which is not recorded in any other text.

[7] Aitchison has "this side of" instead of "up to," while Sir Charles Bell does not mention the Bhairab Langur range at all.

Article V

Henceforth not a Naikya [Headman] [1] but a Bharadar shall be posted by the Gorkha Government at Lhassa.

Article VI

The Gorkha Government [2] will establish its own trade factory [3] at Lhassa which will be allowed to trade freely in all kinds of merchandise from gems and ornaments to articles of clothing and food.

Article VII

The Gorkha Bharadar at Lhassa shall not try and determine suits and cases amongst subjects and merchants of Tibet; [4] and Tibet shall not try and determine suits and cases amongst Gorkha subjects, merchants, the Kasmeries of Nepal, [5] residing within the jurisdiction of Lhassa. In the event of dispute between the subjects and merchants of Gorkha and those of Tibet, the Bharadars of both Gorkha and Tibet shall sit together and jointly adjudicate the cases. All incomes (fines, etc.) [6] from such adjudications realized from the subjects and merchants of Tibet shall be taken by Tibet, and those realized from the Gorkha subjects and merchants and Kasmeries shall be taken by Gorkha.

Article VIII

A Gorkha subject who goes to the country of Tibet after committing murder of any person of Gorkha [7] shall be surrendered by Tibet to Gorkha; and a Tibetan subject who goes to the country of Gorkha after committing murder of any person of Tibet [8] shall be surrendered by Gorkha to Tibet.

Article IX

If the property of Gorkha subjects and merchants be plundered by any person of Tibet, the Bharadars of Tibet shall compel the restoration of such property to the Gorkha subjects and merchants; should the property be not forthcoming from the plunderer, Tibet shall [9] compel him to enter into arrangement for restitution [of such property]. [10] If the property of Tibetan subjects and merchants be plundered by any person of Gorkha, Gorkha shall [9] compel the restoration of such property to the

---

[1] The Tibetan text has "Newar Naikya," while Aitchison has a note added by Col. Ramsay that a Naik meant a person of inferior rank.

[2] Aitchison adds "with the free consent of the Government of Tibet."

[3] Sir Charles Bell has "will open shop."

[4] Aitchison has "will not interfere in the dispute," etc.

[5] The Tibetan text has "Mussulmans" for "Kasmeris," while Sir Charles Bell has "Mahomedans of Katmandu." Aitchison has "Kashmiris" but omits "of Nepal."

[6] Aitchison has "aindani."

[7] The other texts all omit "of any person of Gorkha."

[8] The other texts all omit "of any person of Tibet."

[9] The Tibetan text and Sir Charles Bell here insert "after making enquiries" and "after enquiry."

[10] The Tibetan text and Sir Charles Bell add "within an extended time," while Aitchison has "and will be allowed a reasonable time to make it good."

Tibetan subjects and merchants. Should the property be not forthcoming from the plunderer, Gorkha shall compel him to enter into an agreement for the restitution [of such property].¹

Article X

After the completion of the Treaty neither side shall act vindictively against the person or property of the subjects of Tibet who may have joined the Gorkha Durbar during the war, or of the subjects of Gorkha who may have so joined the Tibetan Durbar.²

This the third day of Light fortnight of Chaitra in the year of Sumbat 1912.³

N.B.—Bharadars are the high Civil or Military officers under the Government of Nepal or of Tibet.

In this translation " Tibet " is used for " Bhote."

B

As the matter is of some importance I add here another translation from the Tibetan text recently given to me by the Maharaja of Nepal in order that any discrepancies may be recognized. It is followed by a few notes from the same source.

SVASTI

Document setting forth the alliance and agreement under ten heads between Gurkha and Tibet, agreed to at the meeting of Nobles, Priests, and Laymen, duly signed severally and jointly by the Shri Gurkha Court and the Shri Tibetan Court.

Taking the Precious Rarity as Witness we have jointly and severally affixed our seals in sign of faithful promise.

Whilst conforming to what has been written concerning the continued respect as before towards Shri the Great Emperor, the Courts jointly and severally continue in mutual agreement like brother-children.

May from whatever individual of each Court who, not observing this, makes war-trouble, Shri Rarity withhold its Blessing.

If any one of both does not abide by what is stipulated in this document and violates it, he who makes war against him is without sin.

The authorized bearer of Shri the Gurkha Maharaja's intention, His

¹ The Tibetan text and Sir Charles Bell add " within an extended time," while Aitchison has " and will be allowed a reasonable time to make it good."

² Aitchison enlarges somewhat on this version and has : "all subjects of Tibet," etc., "shall be respected both in person and in property, and shall not be injured by either Government."

³ Aitchison has : " Dated Sambat [1912] Chaitra Badi 3rd [2nd day] Sombar. Corresponding with the 24th of March 1856." The Tibetan text reads : " This the 10th day of the Second Month of the Medhuk year"; while Sir Charles Bell states : " Dated the 18th day of the 2nd month of the Fire-Dragon year."

Honour Shri Madhara Jang Kumar Kumar Tamaja Shri Tayim Minitar Yen Kamanda Incib Janarala Janka Bhadur Kuwar Radna (seal).

His Honour Shri Madar Jang Kumara Kumarangta Maja Shri Minitar Janarala Bam Bhadur Kuwarra Rana (seal).

Seal of His Honour the Shri Gururaja Pandita Dharmadikara Shri Bijai Pandita.

His Honour Shri Madhara Jang Kumara Kumarangta Maja Shri Kamengdhar Incib Janarala Kisina Bhadur Kuwar Rana (seal).

His Honour Shri Madhar Jang Kumara Kumarangta Maja Shri Kamendhar Incib Janarala Rana Utip Shingha Kuwar Rana (seal).

His Honour Shri Madhar Ja Kumara Kumarangta Maja Shri Janarala Jagta Samsher Jang Kuwar Rana (seal).

Shri Madhar Ja Kumara Kumarangta Maja Shri Janarala Dhir Samsher Jang Kuwar Rana (seal).

His Honour Shri Madhar Ja Kumara Kumarangta Maja Shri Janarala Bhagtabir Kuwar Rana (seal).

His Honour Madhara Jang Kumara Kumarangta Maja Shri Leptenta Janarala Bhakhata Jang Kuwar Rana (seal).

Seal of Shri Metsau Hariya Rana Sher Saha.

Seal of Shri Karnel Tilipi Karma Shingha Tharpa.

Seal of Shri Karnel Dili Shingha Bhasa Nyeta.

Seal of Shri Karnel Kulman Shingha Bhasa Myeta.

The Tibetan Lamas and Nobles who have come to Nepal.

Seal of Private Secretary Ngagwang Gyal Tshan, representative of the Shri Potola Lama.

Seal of Ngagwang Samdub, Abbot of Shri Depung Monastery.

Seal of Lozang Rabgyang, Chairman of the collected houses of Shri Depung Monastery.

Seal of Lozang Thuchen, Abbot of Shri Sera Monastery.

Seal of Lozang Jamyang, Chairman of the collected houses of Sera Monastery.

Seal of Ngagwang Nyima, Abbot of Shri Gaden Monastery.

Seal of Rabgyay Nyima, Chairman of the collected houses of Shri Gaden Monastery.

Seal of Lozang Gyaltshan, Abbot of Shri Tashilhumpo Monastery.

Seal of Gile tagsa, Chairman of the collected houses of Shri Tashilhumpo Monastery.

Seal of Jamyang Monlam, representative of the Precious Great Chair Lama of Shri Sakya Monastery.

Seal of Gyaltshan Tondub, representative of the Incarnation-Lama of Shri Tshecholing.

Seal of Duke She-tag, executive Minister of the Shri Lhasa Palace.

Seal of Shri Minister Pallhun.

Seal of Shri Minister Taiji of the Samdub Podang.

Seal of Shri Minister Taiji of the Tashikhangsar.

Seal of Nyima Tondub, Treasurer of Shri Tashilhumpo.

Seal of Chief Secretary Dumpa-se, the nephew of Minister Shri Duke Shetag.

Setting forth the alliance and agreement:

First. Tibet to pay annually to the Gurkha Court ten thousand silver ales.

Second. Whilst the Gurkha Country and Tibet are both respecters of Shri the Great Emperor, as this Tibet especially has become solely a dwelling place of Lama-monasteries and celibate religious hermits, therefore from now onwards, when a war-maker of another Court arises in Tibetan territory, the Gurkha Court to protect and bind as far as possible.

Third. Declaration that from now onwards Tibet will not take from Gurkha subjects and traders, trading taxes, road taxes, or any kind of tax.

Fourth. The remaining Singpa soldiers who have been taken prisoners by Tibet, and the Gurkha soldiers who have been taken prisoners in the present war, officers and men, with women, of all descriptions, to be sent back by Tibet to the Gurkha Court. All Tibetan soldiers, and all arms and yaks of the people left behind at Kyitong, Nyanang, Dzongka, Puring, and Rongshar to be sent back by the Gurkha Court. After the conclusion of this alliance and agreement, the Gurkha troops to give up the territories of Puring,[1] Rongshar, Kyitong, Dzongka, Nyanang, to withdraw to this side of the Darling pass and to be called back.

Fifth. In Lhasa from now onwards the Gurkha Court not to appoint a Nepali Head but a Nobleman.

Sixth. In Lhasa from now onwards the Gurkha Court to have shops. Trade in jewelry, ornaments, textiles, food of all kinds, to be permitted as much as desired.

Seventh. If trouble arises amongst Lhasa subjects or traders, the Gurkha Head not to be permitted to judge. When trouble arises amongst Gurkha subjects, traders, or Kaches from Yambu, the Tibetan Court not to be permitted to judge. When trouble arises amongst Gurkha and Tibetan subjects together, this to be judged in a meeting of Gurkhas and Tibetan Noblemen together. At the occasion of the judgment the fine of the Tibetan subjects to be received by the Tibetan Noble. The fine of Gurkha subjects, traders or Kaches, to be received by the Gurkha Noble.

Eighth. If a Gurkha subject having committed murder goes to Tibetan territory, he is to be handed over to Gurkha by Tibet. If a Tibetan subject having committed murder goes to Gurkha territory, he is to be handed over to Tibet by Gurkha.

Ninth. When property or treasure of a Gurkha subject or trader is robbed by a Tibetan subject the various Tibetan Official Nobles to order search to be made in order to restitute them to the Gurkha subject who is

---

[1] According to Aitchison's version of the Nepalese treaty the names should read as follows: Taklakhar, Chhewar-gumbha, Kyirong, Jhunga, Kuti, Dhyaklang, Bhairab Langur. Thus the meaning of the last stipulation of Clause 4 is "give up . . . Jungha (?), Kuti, and retire to the Nepalese side of the Bhairab Langur or watershed forming part of the north-eastern frontier of Nepal."—P.L.

the owner of the property and treasure. When the robber cannot restitute the property or treasure, the Tibetan Noble to fix a date for the later restitution of the items to be received. When property or treasure of a Tibetan subject or trader is robbed by a Gurkha subject the various Gurkha Official Nobles to order search to be made in order to restitute them to the Tibetan subject who is the owner of the property and treasure. When the robber cannot restitute the property or treasure the Gurkha Noble to fix a date for the later restitution of the items to be received.

Tenth. The two Courts, jointly and severally, not to show anger after the conclusion of the treaty and agreement, towards property or life of Tibetan subjects who at the occasion of the present war have come siding with the Gurkha Court, and of Gurkha subjects who have come siding with the Tibetan Court.

Fire-Dragon year, second month, eighteenth day.

NOTES

1. Preamble.
"The Precious Rarity" is the Tibetan word for God.

2. Gurkha Signatures.
All the Gurkha names of signatories have been transcribed from the Tibetan text in which they are written very freely.

3. Tibetan Signatures.
The Tibetan names and titles are all correctly written.

4. First clause.
"Ale," the name of a silver coin.

5. Second clause.
"Respecters." This word means only that, and not "subject" or "worshipper."

6. Third clause.
Here and elsewhere the text may be understood as "subjects *who are* traders," or "(ordinary) subjects *and* traders." The context is in favour of the second rendering. In Tibetan there is no marked difference between the two expressions.

7. Fourth clause.
"Singpa," probably Sikhs. That is the modern meaning of the word.

8. Fourth clause.
"The Darling pass." From the Tibetan text it may be understood that Darling is one of the districts from which the Gurkha troops have to withdraw, like the previously mentioned districts. If this is meant, the last part should run "give up Dzongka, Nyanang and Darling, and withdraw to this side of the [unnamed] pass or passes."

9. Fifth clause.
Nepali, here evidently used in the sense of Newari. The Gurkhas are Nobles and the Nepalis not, in this use of the term.

10. Sixth clause.
"Have" shops. Literally, "put" or "keep" shops. The meaning is that Gurkha subjects may trade.

11. Seventh clause.
"Subjects *or* traders," as in No. 3, might also mean "Subjects *who are* traders." The name "Kache" means in Tibet both a Kashmiri and a Mohammedan. It is likely that the latter meaning applies here. Yambu, probably Katmandu, or the whole Valley of Nepal, or even the whole country.

12. Ninth clause.
"Robbed" is, technically, taken with violence, not merely "stolen."

APPENDIX XXIII

THE TREATY OF 1923

THE text of the Treaty concluded between the British Government and Nepal is here given, together with the speeches delivered on the occasions of its signature on 21st December 1923. The ceremony of signature took place in the Singha Darbar in full state. The British Envoy, Colonel W. F. T. O'Connor, was escorted in a carriage and four from the Legation to the Singha Darbar by a Nepalese officer, the Nepal Government Mir Munshi, and ten sowars, a royal salute of thirty-one guns being fired from the Tundi Khel as the procession left the Legation grounds. Arms were presented by a guard of honour at the Singha Darbar, and the Envoy was received by His Highness the Maharaja at the steps of the Grand Council Hall and conducted to his seat.

The whole assembly rose to its feet for a moment as a mark of respect before the Treaty was read aloud by Bada Kaji Marichi Man Singh. Then followed the signature by the Maharaja and Colonel W. F. T. O'Connor and the delivery of congratulatory speeches by the latter and His Highness, the assembly remaining standing until the conclusion. A salute of nineteen guns was then fired and the entire body of troops outside presented arms. " Attar and pan " were then presented by His Highness to the Envoy, and after a few minutes' conversation Colonel O'Connor was escorted back to the Legation.

Two days' general holiday, illuminations at night, the distribution of food and clothes to the poor, and a remission of three months from all except life sentences, were then announced in honour of the event.

TEXT OF TREATY OF 1923 BETWEEN NEPAL AND GREAT BRITAIN

WHEREAS peace and friendship have now existed between the British Government and the Government of Nepal since the signing of the Treaty of Segowlie on the 2nd day of December One Thousand Eight Hundred and Fifteen; and whereas since that date the Government of Nepal has ever displayed its true friendship for the British Government and the British Government has as constantly shown its goodwill towards the Government of Nepal; and whereas the Governments of both the countries are now desirous of still further strengthening and cementing the good relations and friendship which have subsisted between them for more than a century; the two High Contracting Parties having resolved to conclude a new Treaty of Friendship have agreed upon the following Articles:

Article I. There shall be perpetual peace and friendship between the Governments of Great Britain and Nepal, and the two Governments agree mutually to acknowledge and respect each other's independence, both internal and external.

II   U   .

Article II. All previous Treaties, Agreements, and Engagements, since and including the Treaty of Segowlie of One Thousand Eight Hundred and Fifteen, which have been concluded between the two Governments are hereby confirmed, except so far as they may be altered by the present Treaty.

Article III. As the preservation of peace and friendly relations with the neighbouring States whose territories adjoin their common frontiers is to the mutual interests of both the High Contracting Parties they hereby agree to inform each other of any serious friction or misunderstanding with those States likely to rupture such friendly relations, and each to exert its good offices as far as may be possible to remove such friction and misunderstanding.

Article IV. Each of the High Contracting Parties will use all such measures as it may deem practicable to prevent its territories being used for purposes inimical to the security of the other.

Article V. In view of the long-standing friendship that has subsisted between the British Government and the Government of Nepal, and for the sake of cordial neighbourly relations between them, the British Government agrees that the Nepal Government shall be free to import from or through British India into Nepal whatever arms, ammunition, machinery, warlike material, or stores may be required or desired for the strength and welfare of Nepal, and that this arrangement shall hold good for all time as long as the British Government is satisfied that the intentions of the Nepal Government are friendly and that there is no immediate danger to India from such importations. The Nepal Government, on the other hand, agrees that there shall be no export of such arms, ammunition, etcetera, across the frontier of Nepal either by the Nepal Government or by private individuals.

If, however, any Convention for the regulation of the Arms Traffic, to which the British Government may be a party, shall come into force, the right of importation of arms and ammunition by the Nepal Government shall be subject to the proviso that the Nepal Government shall first become a party to that Convention, and that such importation shall only be made in accordance with the provisions of that Convention.

Article VI. No Customs duty shall be levied at British Indian ports on goods imported on behalf of the Nepal Government for immediate transport to that country provided that a certificate from such authority as may from time to time be determined by the two Governments shall be presented at the time of importation to the Chief Customs Officer at the port of import setting forth that the goods are the property of the Nepal Government, are required for the public services of the Nepal Government, are not for the purpose of any State monopoly or State trade, and are being sent to Nepal under orders of the Nepal Government.

(ii) The British Government also agrees to the grant in respect of all trade goods, imported at British Indian ports for immediate transmission to Katmandu without breaking bulk *en route* of a rebate of the full duty paid, provided that in accordance with arrangements already agreed to between the two Governments, such goods may break bulk for repacking at the port of entry under Customs supervision in accordance with such rules as may from time to time be laid down in this behalf. The rebate may be claimed on the authority of a certificate signed by the said authority that the goods have arrived at Katmandu with the Customs seals unbroken and otherwise untampered with.

Article VII. This Treaty, signed on the part of the British Government by Lieutenant-Colonel W. F. T. O'Connor, C.I.E., C.V.O., British Envoy at the Court of Nepal, and on the part of the Nepal Government by General His Highness Maharaja Sir Chandra Shumshere Jung, Bahadur Rana, G.C.B., G.C.S.I., G.C.M.G., G.C.V.O., D.C.L., Thong-lin Pimma-Kokang-Wang-Syan, Prime Minister and Marshal of Nepal, shall be ratified and the ratification shall be exchanged at Katmandu as soon as practicable.

Signed and Sealed at Katmandu, this the Twenty-first day of December in the year One thousand nine hundred and twenty-three Anno Domini corresponding with the Sixth Paush Sambat Era One thousand nine hundred and eighty.

The following were the addresses delivered by the Envoy and the Maharaja on the occasion of the Signature of the Treaty:

SPEECH MADE BY THE ENVOY AFTER THE SIGNATURE OF THE TREATY, 21ST DECEMBER 1923

YOUR HIGHNESS AND GENTLEMEN,
The new Treaty between Great Britain and Nepal has now been signed and sealed, and I esteem it a high privilege to have the honour of representing my Government and of being associated with Your Highness in this auspicious ceremony. The last formal Treaty between Great Britain and Nepal was signed at Segowlie in the month of December 1815, one hundred and eight years ago, and was ratified in March 1816; and during the long interval which has since elapsed, uninterrupted peace has prevailed between our two countries, and the friendship which was then begun has been steadily strengthened and cemented with the passage of time.

Such a prolonged period of peace and friendship between two neighbouring countries cannot but be to the benefit of both. It implies the constant progress of commercial traffic across the frontiers; the steady improvement of personal and diplomatic relations; and the building up of a tradition of mutual goodwill and understanding which becomes year by year more stable and less liable to disturbance.

I do not propose here to refer in detail to the services which Nepal has rendered from time to time to Great Britain, but the generation in which we live can never be forgetful of the world crisis from which we have so recently emerged, and I feel therefore that I cannot allow this opportunity to pass without some special mention, however brief and imperfect, of Nepal's attitude and services to the Allied Nations during the Great War. For so small a country Nepal's efforts may well be described as magnificent, and in proportion to the resources and population of the country they compare favourably with those of any of the Allies. A Nepalese contingent, the strength of which averaged over 10,000 men, served in India and on the frontiers of India from early in 1915 until they were reviewed by His Excellency the Viceroy at Delhi in January 1919 and returned to their native country. The number of the Gurkha Battalions of the Indian Army, normally twenty, was doubled for the period of the War, and Gurkhas were enlisted in many other corps and served everywhere with credit. It has been estimated that no less than 200,000 men, or nearly one quarter of the total of the men of the fighting classes of Nepal, served in some capacity during the Great War.

It is needless for me to descant at length on the services of these most gallant troops. The fighting qualities of the Gurkhas are known and appreciated throughout the world. These are matters of history and are within the personal recollection of all those now present in this Durbar, and I see here, as I look around, and as I saw on the breasts of the troops whom I passed just now outside, the British medals and decorations so well and bravely earned by many Nepalese subjects of all ranks.

Nor was Nepal backward in supplying assistance in other forms. Gifts of money, machine guns, and the indigenous products of the country, such as timber, etc., followed one another in quick succession and in generous profusion. In fact, Nepal's services to the British Empire are worthy of the bold and warlike nation which has rendered them, and there is no need for me to assure Your Highness that they never have been, and never will be, forgotten by my Government and fellow subjects.

It is my pleasant duty, therefore, as the representative of Great Britain in Nepal, to congratulate Your Highness and all Nepalese subjects on the proud position thus occupied by your country, and on the independence so well maintained and the reputation so bravely gained by the valour of the Nepalese fighting men.

Courage and valour indeed are fine qualities, but they are of little avail unless wisely directed. And it is in this matter of wise and skilful guidance that Nepal has been so fortunate in having as her Prime Minister during the critical times through which we have passed, so prudent a diplomat and so enlightened a statesman as my friend Sir Chandra Shumshere Jung, Bahadur Rana; and the British Government is no less fortunate in possessing as their ally so true and loyal a friend. This friendship was put to the acid test on the outbreak of the Great War, and nobly it rose and responded to the call. Not only has it stood the strain, but it has emerged stronger than before. Nepal in helping the cause of civilization has at the same time confirmed her own sturdy independence and has enhanced a reputation already high and honourable amongst the nations of the world;

and the results of Your Highness's bold and sagacious policy redound at once to your own personal honour and to that of your country. The Treaty which we have just signed, whilst it has secured a satisfactory settlement by mutual agreement of various questions which were outstanding between the two Governments, may fitly be termed, as indeed it has been termed by His Highness, a " Treaty of Friendship," and it may be regarded as symbolizing a situation so honourable to Nepal and so gratifying to both the parties concerned. And it is my earnest hope that for many long years to come it may fulfil its purpose and may be instrumental in binding yet closer the ties of mutual respect and friendship which now unite Great Britain and Nepal.

SPEECH BY THE MAHARAJA OF NEPAL AFTER THE SIGNING OF THE TREATY

COMMANDER-IN-CHIEF, BHARADARS, OFFICERS, AND GENTLEMEN,

You have heard the contents of the new Treaty and seen us put our hand and seal to the document. The structure of our friendly relations with the British Government, built as it is upon the solid foundation of mutual regard and esteem as much as sympathy and trust, may now be said to have received by this Treaty a magnificent dome crowning the whole. These friendly relations which have now lasted for more than a hundred years, pregnant with momentous events, have helped to remove whatever barriers there were to a thoroughly good understanding of each other, and have thus led up to the signing of this Treaty of Friendship. It is fervently hoped that, strengthened and reinforced by to-day's work, this friendship between the two Governments will continue unabated and grow in solidarity for centuries to come. Let us bow in all humility to the Almighty for having watched over us during all these years and supplicate Him, with every sincerity, to make this occasion auspicious and to prosper both the Governments in their undertakings of to-day, aye, and for ever.

COLONEL O'CONNOR,—Your concise, though eloquent, recital of the near past makes us live the days over again. They were strenuous days with their burden of hope and fear, hope to prove equal to the self-imposed task of helping our friend, and fear lest we might fail on account of the limited resources of our mountainous country. It would be affectation on my part to deny the pleasure that we feel in listening to the assurances, now repeated, that the appreciation of our efforts at the time has carved an abiding place in the memory of the British nation. Please accept our warm and sincere thanks for the kind words—I may say, too kind words— about my own share in the matter, and for your congratulations to us on this occasion. More than to any one present here it is known to me how much we are indebted to your zeal, tact, patience, and sympathy, and the large share you had in bringing about the conclusion of this Treaty. In offering you thanks on behalf of my Sovereign, myself, and the people of Nepal I hope you will realize the depth of my feeling, and the very real pleasure I have in doing so.

GENTLEMEN,—There is not much to add to what has already been said by our friend, Colonel O'Connor, about the Treaty. The conclusion of it I take as an indication of our steadfast confidence reposed in the honesty of purpose and the high sense of justice which ever characterized the mighty British Government. While we have here the acknowledgement in an unequivocal manner of the place we occupy as an independent nation, it dispels for all time the misconceptions about this that seemed to have hovered over our country.

The significance and importance of the other clauses will also have been made clear to you. The motive underlying them is our one desire to live in peace with all our neighbours; and good neighbours would not, as a matter of course, like to see their respective territories used to the prejudice of the other. Situated far inland as our country is, the British Government have given us the friendly assistance of allowing us to utilize freely their Indian ports for imports of our military requirements and trade needs. I value all these very much, as no doubt you all do, but what I value most is the goodwill at the back of all which, like a speckless mirror, reflects the mind from which it emanates.

I cannot pass on without expressing my appreciation of the tactful manner in which Colonel O'Connor has conducted the negotiations throughout the long discussions, protracted over so many months. He had, as representative of Great Britain, to uphold the claims of his own Government; and as I had to do the same on behalf of my country, there were occasions when we found ourselves in opposition. It was at such times as these that we learnt to appreciate more fully the patience and fairness of Colonel O'Connor. But for his diplomacy and unvarying courtesy these discussions might have led to a deadlock. Colonel O'Connor, however, while doing his duty to his own Government, was able at the same time to weigh fairly the claims of Nepal—a matter of no small difficulty at times—and his personality has been a very strong factor in enabling us to bring the negotiations to this happy conclusion.

I turn now to the pleasant duty of offering our hearty felicitations on this happy occasion to our friend Colonel O'Connor, who now is with us here as the representative of Great Britain and of requesting him kindly to convey the same, with expressions of grateful thanks, to His Excellency the Viceroy and His Majesty the King Emperor of India on behalf of His Majesty the King, myself, and the people of Nepal.

———————

TO GENERAL HIS HIGHNESS MAHARAJA SIR CHANDRA SHUMSHERE JUNG BAHADUR RANA, G.C.B., G.C.S.I., G.C.M.G., G.C.V.O., D.C.L., PRIME MINISTER, MARSHAL OF NEPAL

MY ESTEEMED FRIEND,

On the 27th August last I wrote to inform His Majesty the Maharajadhiraja of Nepal and Your Highness that I had conferred on our Envoy at the Court of Nepal full powers to conclude a new Treaty between the

British Government and the Government of Nepal.   I now write to convey, through Your Highness, to His Majesty the Maharajadhiraja of Nepal, my warm congratulations on the successful termination of the negotiations, and to express my firm conviction that the Treaty now concluded will serve still further to cement the bonds of traditional friendship which have existed between the two countries for so many years.

I remain, with much consideration,

Your Highness' sincere friend,

READING

Viceroy and Governor-General of India.

Delhi.

The 21st December 1923.

Copy of Telegram dated 22-12-23.

From Viceroy's Camp,
Rangoon.

TO HIS HIGHNESS THE PRIME MINISTER OF NEPAL, NEPAL, RAXAUL

I have much pleasure in transmitting to Your Highness for delivery to His Majesty the Maharajadhiraja of Nepal the following message from His Majesty the King Emperor. Begins: To His Majesty the Maharajadhiraja of Nepal on the occasion of the conclusion of a new Treaty of Friendship between my Government and the Government of Nepal I desire to convey to Your Majesty an expression of my sincere pleasure of this confirmation of the traditional friendly relations between us together with my earnest hope that these relations may long continue and may contribute as I am sure they will to the prosperity and peace of my Empire and of Nepal. George R.I. Ends.

VICEROY.

Copy of Reply Telegram dated 25-12-23.

TO HIS EXCELLENCY THE VICEROY, VICEROY'S CAMP

The graceful message from His Majesty the King Emperor conveyed in Your Excellency's kind telegram of the 22nd instant has been duly communicated to His Majesty the Maharajadhiraja and I am desired to request the favour of Your Excellency to please transmit the following message from him. Begins: To His Majesty the King Emperor of India. Your Majesty's very kind and inspiring message has considerably heightened the happiness felt on this auspicious occasion of the conclusion of the new Treaty of Friendship between Great Britain and Nepal so long and so cordially united in firm bonds of amity and concord, and while offering my sincerest thanks to Your Majesty for the gracious message, I take the opportunity to respectfully reciprocate the sentiments contained therein and fervently hope that the ties of friendship thus strengthened and re-strengthened may become with God's blessings as everlasting as the mighty Himalayas. Tribhubana Bir Bikram Shah Deva. Message ends.

CHANDRA SHUM SHERE,
Nepal.

HIS HIGHNESS'S SPEECH ON THE OCCASION OF THE EXCHANGE OF THE RATIFIED COPIES OF THE TREATY AT KATMANDU, 8TH APRIL 1925

By command of my Sovereign I have the honour to deliver to you the copy of the Treaty duly ratified, signed and sealed by His Majesty the Maharajadhiraja, to be taken to its destination.

COLONEL O'CONNOR AND GENTLEMEN,

By the grace of God we have now completed the last formality in connection with the Treaty of December 1923. It is indeed very gratifying to think of the happy relations subsisting between the two Governments—may God in His great mercy continue the same for ever! I heartily recipro-cate all that my friend Colonel O'Connor has said on the subject, expressive as they are of pleasure and satisfaction at the fruition of our united efforts towards drawing the traditional friendship still closer.

GENTLEMEN,

The period during which our friend Colonel O'Connor was at the head of the Legation was a time of readjustment of a world thrown out of its gear, and in which epoch-making changes were being wrought every-where. You have listened to a vivid summary of the period which no doubt will bring to your minds the anxious and troublesome days in which we then lived. Under the stress of such difficult times we had to work together, and our friendship naturally became more intimate. That friendship and sympathetic attitude, that unfailing good humour, and the great qualities of his head and heart, permitted a smooth handling of many a delicate and important issue, the last and greatest of them being this Treaty.

Colonel O'Connor, please accept my grateful thanks for all the help you have extended to lighten my work in our dealings with the great British Government, and also for the very kind expressions regarding me and my work, and the kind thoughts you entertain towards us and our country. Let me assure you that you are leaving behind as happy and pleasant memories of yourself, as you say you are carrying of us. We pray that you may live a long and happy life to enjoy the blessings of peace and rest.

COLONEL O'CONNOR'S SPEECH ON THE OCCASION OF THE EXCHANGE OF RATIFIED COPIES OF THE TREATY IN KATMANDU, 8TH APRIL 1925

(Before the exchange of the ratified copies of the Treaty.)

I rise to inform Your Highness that I have received from my Govern-ment the copy of the Treaty which was concluded between Great Britain and Nepal on 21st December 1923, duly ratified, signed and sealed by His Majesty the King Emperor; and I understand from Your Highness that the other copy has similarly been ratified by His Majesty the Mahárájadhiraja. I therefore have the honour, in accordance with the instructions which I have received from my Government, of handing to Your Highness the copy ratified by my Sovereign for preservation in the archives of Nepal.

(After the ratified copies of the Treaty have been exchanged.)

YOUR HIGHNESS AND GENTLEMEN,

It is with mingled feelings of pleasure and regret that I conclude the last official duty which falls to my lot in my capacity of British Envoy at the Court of Nepal—pleasure to think that this last ceremony marks the last stage in the conclusion of the Treaty of Friendship which I have been privileged to conclude on behalf of my Government with His Highness the Prime Minister;—regret that my happy time as Envoy in this country should now have terminated.

Your Highness will, I hope, pardon me if I give expression for a moment to my personal feelings on this occasion. It is now over six years since I first assumed the duties of Resident in Nepal. At that time (December 1918) the Great War had only just terminated, and its cinders were still smouldering. The troops which Your Highness had despatched to the support of your friend, Great Britain, and of the Allied cause generally, were still in India, under the able leadership of two of your relatives, my friends Sir Baber Shum Shere Jung and Sir Padma Shum Shere Jung, and I had the pleasure of being present at Delhi in February 1919 when these gallant troops were reviewed by Their Excellencies the Viceroy and the Commander-in-Chief. Many clouds were at that time still lowering in the political horizon, and the subsequent events which occurred during 1919 are still fresh in our memories—more especially as Nepal, with her unfailing friendship, again sprang to the support of her ally in a time of crisis and difficulty. Since then the world has gradually quieted down and peaceful relations have taken the place of the troubled diplomacy of war time, and the pleasant ceremonies in which we have just shared—that at the Hanuman-Dhoka on Monday, and the exchange of ratified copies of the Treaty to-day—are symbolical of the changed conditions prevailing in the world's atmosphere generally. I count myself fortunate to have had the privilege of representing my Government in Nepal during this critical period, and of observing the attitude of the leaders and people of this gallant country under conditions both of peace and of war. All that I have seen has only confirmed me in my belief that in Nepal Great Britain has a true and faithful friend and ally, and that this Treaty of Friendship is the final summary of years of comradeship and mutual respect and confidence.

I cannot close these remarks without a reference to my friend, your honoured Prime Minister Sir Chandra Shum Shere Jung, whose too kind references to myself in his speech on Monday deeply moved and affected me. Nepal is indeed fortunate that her destinies during all these troubled and critical years have reposed in hands at once so capable and so tactful. Alike in war and in peace Sir Chandra has guided the fortunes of Nepal with skill, prudence and courage, and her present prosperous and honourable position amongst the independent countries of the world is due in a great measure to his diplomacy and ability; and it is pleasant to find that France as well as England has recognized his outstanding merits.

May I add a personal word of thanks to him also for his unvarying courtesy and kindness to me during my term of office in Nepal. It has been a real pleasure to co-operate for the mutual advantage of our two countries with so wise a ruler and so courteous and tactful a diplomat. All the memories of Nepal which I shall carry away with me are happy and pleasant, and amongst the most cherished of these will be the recollection of the friendly relations which I have had the honour of enjoying with your Prime Minister, both in his capacity of a kind and true friend and of a wise and capable statesman.

APPENDIX XXIV

LIST OF EUROPEANS WHO HAVE VISITED NEPAL, 1881-1925

[*The following names have been given to me by the Nepal Government. I have not added to them or made any corrections except in a few obviously necessary cases. It may roughly be said that in the course of forty-four years about one hundred and fifty-three persons, excluding Residents, Envoys, and the official Surgeons, have visited Nepal for military, official, or antiquarian purposes. Fifty-five have visited Katmandu as the guests of the Maharaja.*]

1881.

Col. T. E. Webster, 9th Native Infantry, Gorakhpur (April), to inspect the Nepal Escort; Staff Officer, name not known (April), as Orderly Officer to Col. Webster; Mr. H. E. M. James, Postmaster-General, Bengal (January), to inspect the Nepal-Raxaul postal line; Mr. Mills, Engineer, to inspect the Residency buildings; Mr. White, Engineer, to inspect the Residency buildings and to prepare estimates, etc.; His Honour Sir Richard Temple, Lieut.-Governor of Bengal (in Mr. Girdlestone's time, 1872-88), as guest of the Resident.

1882.

Col. T. E. Webster, 9th Native Infantry, Gorakhpur (March), to inspect the Nepal Escort; Staff Officer, name not known (March), as Orderly Officer to Col. Webster.

1883.

Col. P. H. F. Harries, 11th Native Infantry, Lucknow (March), to inspect the Nepal Escort; Staff Officer, name not known (March), as Orderly Officer to Col. Harries.

1885.

Col. E. Venour, 5th Bengal Light Infantry, Fyzabad, to inspect the Nepal Escort; Staff Officer, name not known, as Orderly Officer to Col. Venour; Professor C. R. Bendall, on the staff of the British Museum, London (1884-85), for archaeological research.

1886.

Col. W. F. Burtleman, Commanding Bengal Light Infantry, Fyzabad (April), to inspect the Nepal Escort; Staff Officer, name not known (April), as Orderly Officer to Col. Burtleman.

1887.

Col. W. F. Burtleman, Commanding Bengal Light Infantry, Fyzabad (March), to inspect the Nepal Escort; Staff Officer, name not known (March), as Orderly Officer to Col. Burtleman.

1888.

Col. A. G. Stead, Commanding 11th Bengal Infantry, Fyzabad (March), to inspect the Nepal Escort; Staff Officer, name not known (March), as Orderly Officer to Col. Stead.

1889.

Maj.-Gen. Sir Charles Gough, Commanding Audh District, Lucknow (March), to inspect the Nepal Escort; Staff Officer, name not known, (March), as Orderly Officer to Maj.-Gen. Gough; Mr. 'B. R. Fainimore, Superintendent Engineer, to inspect the Residency buildings; The Hon. L. M. St. Clair, Engineer, on duty with Nepal Government in connection with waterworks project.

1891.

Col. A. D. C. Baich, Commanding Officer, Fyzabad, to inspect the Nepal Escort; Staff Officer, name not known, as Orderly Officer to Col. Baich.

1892.

H.E. Sir F. Roberts, Commander-in-Chief, to visit Nepal at Maharaja Bir's invitation; Lady Roberts and Staff Officers, names not known.

1893.

Col. E. A. Money, Commandant, 3rd Bengal Cavalry (April), to inspect the Nepal Escort; Staff Officer, name not known (April), as Orderly Officer to Col. Money; Major P. A. Weir, Engineer, on duty in connection with building works in progress at the Residency.

1894.

Col. E. A. Money, Commandant, 3rd Bengal Cavalry, to inspect the Nepal Escort; Staff Officer, name not known, as Orderly Officer to Col. Money; His Honour Sir Charles Elliott, Lieut.-Governor of Bengal, Lady Elliott, Capt. Currie, A.D.C. (November), to visit Nepal.

1895.

Col. E. H. Bingham, 13th Bengal Infantry, Fyzabad (December), to inspect the Nepal Escort; Staff Officer, name not known (December), as Orderly Officer to Col. Bingham.

1896.

Col. A. H. Turner, Commanding at Fyzabad (November), to inspect the Nepal Escort; Staff Officer, name not known (November), as Orderly Officer to Col. Turner.

1897.

Col. T. Pickett, Adjt.-Gen., Audh District, Lucknow (November), to inspect the Nepal Escort; Staff Officer, name not known (November), as Orderly Officer to Col. Pickett.

1898.

Professor C. R. Bendall, on the Staff of the British Museum, London (December), for literary and archaeological research, and Mrs. Bendall; Professor D. E. Boeck, a German gentleman (December), and Professor Sylvain Lévi, a French gentleman (March), for research of Sanskrit MSS.

1900.

Col. Campbell, Commanding at Fyzabad (April), to inspect the Nepal Escort; Staff Officer, name not known (April), as Orderly Officer to Col. Campbell.

1901.

Col. G. F. S. Gwatkin, Colonel on the Staff at Fyzabad (November), to inspect the Nepal Escort; Capt. M. D. Graham (November), as Orderly Officer to Col. Gwatkin.

1902.

Col. C. A. Mercer, Colonel on the Staff at Fyzabad (October), to inspect the Nepal Escort; Staff Officer, name not known (October), as Orderly Officer to Col. Mercer; Col. R. C. Sanders, Indian Medical Service (February), for medical attendance on the Maharani of the Prime Minister.

1903.

Col. C. A Mercer, Colonel on the Staff at Fyzabad (November), to inspect the Nepal Escort; Capt. C. Crogton (November), as Orderly Officer to above; Col. G. F. A. Harris, Indian Medical Service (December), for medical attendance on the Maharani of the Prime Minister.

1904.

Maj.-Gen. E. Locke Elliot, Commanding 8th Lucknow Division, to inspect the Nepal Escort; Capt. W. R. Brakespear, R.O., Gorakhpur, as Staff Officer to Maj.-Gen. Elliot.

1905.

Lieut.-Col. J. M. Stewart, 1/9th Gurkha Rifles, to inspect the Nepal Escort; Capt. W. R. Brakespear, R.O., Gorakhpur, as Staff Officer to Lieut.-Col. Stewart; Lieut.-Col. J. W. Cowley, 7th Gurkha Rifles (November), as guest of Resident.

1906.

Lieut.-Col. H. Rose, 1/3rd Gurkha Rifles (November), to inspect the Nepal Escort; Capt. B. U. Nicolay, R.O., Gorakhpur (November), as Staff Officer to Lieut.-Col. Rose; Capt. M. E. Dopping Hepenstall, 1/3rd Gurkha Rifles (June), to train the Nepal Escort; H.E. Lord Kitchener, Commander-in-Chief, Maj.-Gen. Martin, Adjutant-General in India, Col. W. R. Birdwood, Military Secretary, Capt. Wylie, A.D.C., Mr. Wheeler, Clerk (November), at the invitation of the Prime Minister.

1907.

Col. P. M. Carnegy, 2/4th Gurkha Rifles (November), to inspect the Nepal Escort; Capt. B. U. Nicolay, R.O., Gorakhpur (November), as Staff Officer to Col. Carnegy; Lieut. G. C. Wheeler, 2/9th Gurkha Rifles, to train the Nepal Escort; Mr. R. E. Holland, Secretary, F. and P. Department; Dr. Pedler, Dentist (September), to attend General Jit Sham Sher; Mr. J. H. Burkill, of the Indian Museum, Calcutta (December), to collect samples of the products of Nepal.

1908.

Maj. F. Murray, 1/8th Gurkha Rifles, to inspect the Nepal Escort; Capt. G. W. S. Shedock, R.O., Gorakhpur, Staff Officer to Maj. Murray;

Lieut. B. Orton, 39th Garhwalis, to train the Nepal Escort; Mr. Perceval Landon (November); Madame Isabelle Massieu, a French lady (September), to study ethnological geography; The Hon. C. Hobhouse, of the Royal Commission on Decentralization, Mrs. Hobhouse, and Mr. Cohen (January), as guests of the Resident; Mr. Searight, Engineer, to inspect the Residency buildings.

1909.

Col. R. C. Sanders, Indian Medical Service (February), for medical attendance on the Maharani; Dr. Bonwill, Dentist (August), for medical attendance on the Prime Minister.

1909-1910.

Mr. B. Pontet, Electrical Engineer, for service under Nepal Government; Lieut.-Col. W. G. Walker, 2/9th Gurkha Rifles, to inspect the Nepal Escort; Staff Officer, name not known, as Orderly Officer to Lieut.-Col. Walker; Lieut. H. W. Bell-Kingsley, 1/4th Gurkha Rifles, as Training Officer, Nepal Escort; Miss McNaughton, with one maid (December), as guest of the Resident; Dr. A. C. Inman, of London (October or November), to attend His Excellency the Commander-in-Chief's Rani.

1910.

Mr. Percy Brown, A.R.C.A., Principal, Government School of Art, Calcutta (October), for literary research; Mr. J. Marshall, of the Mills Equipment Co., Ltd. (November), with samples of army equipment; Mr. T. E. Lynch, Engineer (March), to erect the electric plant at Pharping; Lieut.-Col. G. S. Boisragon, 1/5th Gurkha Rifles (November), to inspect the Nepal Escort; Maj. M. R. W. Nightingale, R.O., Gorakhpur (November), as Staff Officer to Lieut.-Col. Boisragon; Lieut. W. B. Northey, 1/1st Gurkha Rifles (November), as Training Officer, Nepal Escort; Mr. R. C. Wodgson, Engineer, Champaran division (May), to inspect Residency buildings; Mr. Rutherford (May), as guest of the Resident; Mr. H. A. Kelso, Superintendent of Police, Champaran (June), as guest of the Resident; Mr. Walker and Mrs. Walker (April), as guests of the Resident; Mr. H. A. Sams, Indian Civil Service, Postmaster-General, Bengal (April), to inspect the Nepal State Post Office.

1911.

Maj. S. Hunt, Indian Medical Service (1st to 28th December), for medical attendance on the late Maharaja Deva; Col. Brown, Indian Medical Service, and Mr. H. J. Waring (August), for medical attendance on the late Maharaja Deva; Capt. C. M. T. Hogg, 1/4th Gurkha Rifles, as Training Officer, Nepal Escort; Lieut. Corse Scott, 2nd U.R. (June); Mr. R. N. Warren, of Pipra Factory, Champaran (May); Lady McMahon and niece (March); H.R.H. Prince Antoine D'Orléans (April); Capt. P. F.

Narbury, 34th Poona Horse, and Mrs. Narbury (April), as Resident's guests; Mr. H. Pedler, L.D., S.R.C.S., Dental Surgeon, Calcutta (May), to attend the Prime Minister.

1912.

Madame Alexandra David Neel, a French lady (November), for study of Buddhist philosophy; Lieut.-Col. Sir Leonard Rogers, Indian Medical Service (November), called in by the Prime Minister; Mr. D. T. Keymer, of Messrs. Keymer, Son and Co. (March), in response to an invitation; Maj. E. D. Money, 2/1st Gurkha Rifles, to inspect the Nepal Escort; Mrs. Money; Maj. M. ·R. W. Nightingale, R.O., Gorakhpur, as Staff Officer to Maj. Money; Capt. H. T. Molloy, 5th Gurkha Rifles, as Training Officer, Nepal Escort.

1913.

Mr. M. L. Smith, Dental Surgeon, of Calcutta (May), to attend the Prime Minister; Mr. J. Taka, M.A., D.Litt., Professor of the Tokio University, Mr. Ekai Kawaguchi, of Japan, two Japanese, names not known (January-February), to study Sanskrit MSS.; Mr. R. S. Underhill, Ropeway Engineer (January), employed by Nepal Government in connection with Ropeway scheme; Col. W. Beynon, D.S.O., 1/2nd Gurkha Rifles, to inspect the Nepal Escort; Capt. A. J. Chope, R.O., Gorakhpur, as Staff Officer to Col. Beynon; Lieut. G. B. Davidson, 2/8th Gurkha Rifles, as Training Officer, Nepal Escort; Miss Cholmondeley, Miss Rathbone, and Mr. P. R. Cadell, Indian Civil Service, Municipal Commissioner, Bombay (March); Baron Maurice de Rothschild, Baroness Rothschild, with European servants (March-April), as Resident's guests; Mr. H. H. Stevens, Engineer, to inspect the Residency buildings.

1914.

Lieut.-Col. F. G. Lucas, D.S.O. (November), to inspect the Nepal Escort; Maj. E. Ridgeway, R.O., Gorakhpur (November), as Staff Officer to Lieut.-Col. Lucas; Lieut. N. H. King-Salter, 1/6th Gurkha Rifles (October), as Training Officer, Nepal Escort; Mr. Parr, of Bhelwa Factory (June); Miss Lowis, from Bettia, and Miss Richardson (November); Mr. C. A. Bell, Political Officer, Sikkim (November); Mr. T. Chitty, Justice, High Court, Allahabad (September); Mr. Meyrick, of Monine Factory, Motipur (June); Mr. Wakenham, Gonda, United Provinces, and Mrs. Wakenham with a baby (April), as guests of the Resident.

1915.

Miss Parr, a sister of Mr. Parr of Bhelwa Factory, as guest of the Resident; Mr. F. A. Betterton, Engineer, Champaran (March), to inspect the Residency buildings.

1916.

Mr. F. A. Betterton, Engineer, Champaran (June), to inspect the Residency buildings.

1917.

. Lieut.-Col. Sir Leonard Rogers, Indian Medical Service (October), called in by the Prime Minister; Dr. A. Collis, Dental Surgeon (February), called in by the Prime Minister; Mr. Bayley, Secretary to the Bengal Government, and Mrs. Wheeler (May), as guests of the Resident; Mrs. Baker, as guest of the Head Clerk; Mr. H. Wardle, Engineer, Champaran Division (November), to inspect the Residency buildings.

1918.

Dr. A. Collis, Dental Surgeon, of Calcutta (December), called in by the Prime Minister; Maj. J. M. Stewart, R.O., Gorakhpur, on Recruiting duty; 2nd Lieut. W. E. Legge, 2/5th Gurkha Rifles (June), as Training Officer, Nepal Escort.

1919.

Mr. R. E. Holland, Secretary, F. and P. Department (April), to discuss some political matters with the Prime Minister; Lieut.-Col. Sir Leonard Rogers, Indian Medical Service (June), called in by the Prime Minister; Maj. Brook Northey, R.O., Gorakhpur, on Recruiting duty; Lieut. L. D. Widdicombe, 2/9th Gurkha Rifles (April-June), as Training Officer, Nepal Escort; 2nd Lieut. C. C. Williams, 2/2nd Gurkha Rifles (July-October), as Training Officer, Nepal Escort; Mr. Fremantle, Mr. Harding, Mr. Atkinson, of Champaran, and Maj. Cooper (May), as Resident's guests; Mr. J. V. Collier, Deputy Conservator of Forests, United Provinces, on duty in connection with the extraction of sal sleepers.

1920.

Maj. Brook Northey, R.O., Gorakhpur, on Recruiting duty; one Lieut. who accompanied Maj. Northey; Lieut. A. L. Fell, 3/2nd Gurkha Rifles, as Training Officer, Nepal Escort; Mr. J. V. Collier, Deputy Conservator of Forests, on duty; Mr. A. E. Marshall, Engineer, to inspect Legation buildings; Mr. Sullivan, Superintendent of Post Offices (December), to inspect Nepal-Raxaul postal lines; Dr. A. C. Inman, of London, called in by the Prime Minister, and Mrs. Inman (April-November).

1921.

Dr. F. W. Thomas, Librarian, India Office, London (May), for literary research; Lieut. H. F. C. Armstrong, 2/2nd Gurkha Rifles, as Training Officer, Nepal Escort; Capt. G. F. Hall, M.C., to inspect the Legation buildings; Mr. J. V. Collier, Deputy Conservator of Forests, on duty.

1922.

Mr. Sullivan, Superintendent of Post Offices (January), to inspect Nepal Post Office; Maj. Brook Northey, R.O., Gorakhpur, on Recruiting duty (twice); Mr. S. J. Bemfor (March); Lieut.-Col. Hunt, X-ray doctor on duty to Nepal Government; M. Sylvain Lévi, French Professor, to study Sanskrit MSS., and Mme. Sylvain Lévi; Capt. A. L. Donaldson, 2/2nd Gurkha Rifles, as Training Officer, Nepal Escort; Mr. J. J. Newton, Superintendent of Post Offices (January), to inspect Nepal Post Office; Capt. G. F. Hall, M.C. (May), to inspect Legation buildings; Mr. J. V. Collier, Deputy Conservator of Forests, on duty with the Nepal Government; Mr. A. E. Clarke, Head Master, Kshattriya School, Benares; Mr. Hemfry and Mr. Kemp, of Champaran (April), as guests of the Envoy.

1923.

Capt. Harvey, 2/1st Gurkha Rifles (April), as Training Officer, Nepal Escort; Mr. Hemfry, of Champaran, and Mr. Luby, Judge, Mazaffarpur, as guests of the Envoy; Mr. F. A. Betterton, Engineer, to inspect Legation buildings, and Mrs. Betterton (May); Mr. J. V. Collier, Deputy Conservator of Forests, on duty with the Nepal Government; Col. M. B. Bailey, 1/4th Gurkha Rifles (15th October), to inspect the Nepal Escort.

To this list the names may be added of Dr. P. Lockhart Mummery, in January, and of Mr. Perceval Landon, in May 1924; of Mr. C. T. Allen, of Cawnpore, Mr. M. Weatherall, of Darjiling, and of M. Daniel Lévi in 1925. In 1907 the name of Col. the Hon. C. G. Bruce, guest of the Resident, should have been included.

APPENDIX XXV

COINAGE

THE following account of the coinage of Nepal has been taken from a statement kindly prepared for this book by Mr. H. G. Bannerji, whose exceptional knowledge of the antiquities as well as of the present day economic system of Nepal renders his article of great value.

Copper, silver, and gold coins form the currency of Nepal. So far, no currency notes have been issued. Owing to its contiguity with British territory on three sides of its frontiers, and the extensive trade it carries on with its neighbours, British Indian rupees find free circulation in the Tarai, where, for convenience sake, the collection of Government revenues is made in that currency.

There are different denominations in the coinage of each of these three kinds of metals. Mr. E. H. Walsh in his *The Coinage of Nepal*, published by the Royal Geographical Society in 1908, has given an elaborate description of Nepalese coins as found up to the time of his writing the book.

The earlier coins had not the clear-cut and uniform shape that the present currency presents. The silver and gold coins called mohars and ashrafis respectively in local terms are finished with milled edges. The copper coins, too, have undergone a change and present a better design.

The mohar and the pice are the coins mostly used in the country and are minted in larger quantities than pieces of other denominations. The double mohar or rupee, the suka (half mohar) and suki (quarter mohar) are the most popular silver coins. In copper, the recently issued five-pice piece and the double-pice are largely used. The other pieces, both of silver and copper, do not find much currency, the former for inconvenience in handling, their sizes being too small, and the latter owing to the ruling high prices of articles of daily necessity, there being hardly anything in the bazaar which coins of smaller value than a pice could buy.

With the exception of the bakla (one-tola piece) and the patla (half-tola piece), the gold coins (ashrafis) are not in general circulation. Their value fluctuates with the market price of gold.

Much has been done by the Maharaja to standardize the coinage, as well as the weights and measures. A scheme for a reformed and up-to-date mint is ready. Of the rough machinery in use whatever proves to be usable will be retained.

The mohar rupee, which is the unit of payment, now weighs approximately 171 grains, and is exactly four-fifths fine; so that the mint par of exchange with the British Indian rupee should be 120½ mohar rupees to 100 Indian rupees. The exchange, however, fluctuates around 124 mohar rupees.

The bazaar seer in the Valley is the equivalent of the weight of 70 mohar rupees, and three such seers go to make one " dharni," which is very nearly equal to 2½ Indian seers.

Curiously enough there is a decimal relation between the primary coin of a mohar rupee and the subsidiary copper pice. One hundred pice make one mohar rupee : the sub-division is thus different from that of the currency where four pice make one anna, and sixteen annas make one rupee. Mr. Walsh, in the book referred to, mentions two systems of currency, viz., the " Pachis gandi " and the " Sorah gandi." The latter system was not actually a currency, but a fictitious sub-division used in accounts, the silver coinage corresponding to it not being usually employed in bazaar transactions. As its name implies the " Sorah gandi," or sixteen anna system, is a multiple of four, and as the sub-divisions of bazaar weight are also based on multiples of four, the adoption of it in accounts naturally followed. The Government accounts also were formerly kept in the " Sorah gandi " system. The Maharaja has changed all that, and now the mohar rupee and its decimal fractions are written and totalled separately from the Indian rupee account.

To trace the gradual evolution of coin-types in Nepal a survey of what took place in Hindu India will be of some assistance. The earliest

Hindu coins were without any inscription[1] and with simple devices such as the bull, lion, elephant, and some religious symbols. The Gaṇas and Janapadas, some of which existed prior to the foreign invasion, retained to a certain extent the purity of these coin-types. Of the two classes to which the Audumbara coins undoubtedly belong, the earlier show certain symbols only, and the latter the symbols with the name of the clan and, in a few specimens, of their kings.[2] Seven out of the eight classes of the Mālava coins of the first series depict simple devices such as the sun, a bodhi tree, a jar, bull, lion, etc.[3] The evolution can be better perceived in the Yaudheya coins. The first class of coins, the oldest of the three classes into which their coins are divided, shows a device of a bull and a pillar on one side and an elephant and a nandipada on the other, and bears the inscription of their clan-name. The second class shows some symbols on one face and a representation of a god or goddess on the other, sometimes with the name of the deity. The third class presents images of gods on both sides. It will generally be found that the coin-types in the earlier period consisted of devices connected with the religious belief of the people or the Government, which often introduced symbols of Hindu and Buddhistic faith in order to conciliate the two communities. Subsequently to this, the image of a god or goddess was inserted. Thus in Nepal the coins with the bull, etc., should precede the coins with an image of a deity, in keeping with the practice in India. But some have held that the latter class of coins is subsequent to the coins of Jishṇu Gupta, because there is one in the series with a nandipada and trident, as the symbol was interpreted, which corresponds to a similar symbol occurring in the coins of Jishṇu Gupta.[4] May it not be held with equal cogency that Jishṇu Gupta copied the symbol from the Paśupati coins which preceded his time? Śiva-worship was much earlier than any other form of religion, and the coins with the legend Paśupati are undoubtedly Śivaite. The worship of the bull is enjoined in the Tantras, together with the Dikpālas, in the installation of the Siva-linga.[5] In India, the Hūṇa Mihirakula worshipped the bull,[6] probably as a Śaiva. As being the vehicle of Śiva, the bull itself, as well as the divine weapons, was worshipped by the followers of Śiva and Śakti. The change in type from the standing bull to the recumbent one in some Paśupati coins, and the presence of a prominent trident in others, clearly connect these with Śankara Deva and probably with Dharma Deva, the grandfather and great-grandfather of Māna Deva. Many Vaṁśāvalīs mention the dedication of a huge trident and a nandi or bull to Paśupati by Śankara Deva.[7] The symbols are so prominent in the coins[8] that a connection must suggest

[1] Ancient Indian Numismatics, p. 41. [2] Prāchīna Mudrā, p. 111.
[3] Catalogue of Coins in the Indian Museum, pp. 170-174, quoted in Prāchīna Mudrā.
[4] Coinage of Nepal, p. 681.
[5] Mahā-Nirvāṇa Tantra or Tantra of the Great Liberation, p. 339, ślokas 44-45, translated by Arthur Avalon. [6] Ancient Indian Numismatics, p. 18.
[7] Wright's History of Nepal, p. 123; Sylvain Lévi, Le Népal, vol. ii, where it is mentioned that Kirkpatrick's Vaṁśāvalī says that the Nandi at Pashupati was dedicated by Dharma Deva and the Trident by Śankara Deva.
[8] Vide Plate I, Nos. 9 and 10, in Coinage of Nepal by E. H. Walsh.

itself to one conversant with the traditions in the Vaṃsàvalīs. The worship of vāhanas, such as the bull of Śiva, the lion of Mahāśakti, and the garuḍa of Vishṇu, is enjoined in books of ritual and Tantras.[1] The śastras or weapons carried by the deity are also objects of worship.[2] Similar injunctions are to be found in Buddhistic Tantras and books on ritual. There is a considerable religious merit in dedicating vāhanas and śastras in stone, metal, etc., and anything else for the service of the divinity.[3] The commemoration of such meritorious religious acts was perhaps thought to be best achieved by representation on coins, as these, being in circulation, would be most seen by the people. It may be noted here that the vāhanas dedicated are generally represented even to this day as sitting in front of the divinity. Thus the standing bull types of the Nepal coinage, at least some of them, should be considered to have been introduced prior to the recumbent type, on the analogy of Indian coins of similar type. The standing bull type of coin with the legend of Pasupati can still be obtained in some quantity, which suggests that these were in circulation for several successive reigns.[4] Besides, a change from the standing bull to the recumbent type would be more natural and in keeping with the tradition of the country and the practice in India, where the very early coins show the standing type. The Tantras provide sthūla or gross, and sūkshma or subtle worship.[5] The sthūla worship has several stages, comprising adoration of forms in three dimensions (the grossest), then of painting on the flat, then of the emblem, and lastly of the yantra or diagrammatic body of mantras.[6] This offers the key to the evolution of coin-types in Nepal and also in early Hindu India. The tri-dimensional form, called by the western world Tantric, falls again, according to Arthur Avalon, into two divisions, the one relating to the external objects associated with the divinity, and the other with the image of the divinity, the meditational or the dhyāna form, presented for the benefit of the Sādhaka or one who strives to attain unity with the Supreme Being.[7] The coins of Nepal may, on this principle, be classified as (1) those with the vāhana and sastra or praharaṇa device; (2) those of the image-type taken in its wider sense; and (3) those with the yantra device. Māna Deva the Lichchhavi first introduced the image-type. But this was not a wide departure from the practice of his predecessors, for the Tantras teach that Śiva and Śakti are but twin aspects of the same reality.[8] Whoever of his successors to the throne of Nepal introduced the

---

[1] Vide Pūjāvidhi in Ahnika-Kṛitya by Śyāmā-charaṇa Kaviratna (Gurudas Library, Calcutta), also Mahā-Nirvāṇa Tantra, p. 326, sec. 254-257; p. 339, sec. 44-45; p. 311, sec. 136, etc.   [2] Vide, for instance, Mahā-Nirvāṇa Tantra, p. 251, sec. 124.
[3] Mahā-Nirvāṇa Tantra, pp. 297-299.
[4] Kushana coins were long circulating in the Panjab even after the reigns of the Kushanas ceased, and these are found in large quantities in excavations, owing to the large number of them issued during successive reigns; vide ante.
[5] Mahā-Nirvāṇa Tantra, Introduction, pp. lxxvi and lxxvii.
[6] Indian Art and Letters, vol. i, no. 2, of Nov. 1926, pp. 75 and 76-77 in the article Psychology of Hindu Religious Ritual by Sir John Woodroffe, who under the press-name of Arthur Avalon has edited books on Tantra.
[7] Indian Art and Letters, p. 76.   [8] Indian Art and Letters, p. 70.

yantra device, followed the same principle, as _yantra_, _mantra_, and _devatā_ are the same.[1] It is true that in some coins of the Deva and Malla Rājas subsequent to the Lichchhavis there is a return to the _vāhana_ and _praharaṇa_ types, but this exception rather proves the principle. The image-type coins perhaps were not considered quite auspicious, and were therefore discarded. The coinage of Hindu India proceeded up to the second stage, at which foreign influence made itself felt so as to stop the natural further transition that took place in Nepal. From the divinity they were diverted to the ideal of sovereignty, which began to be represented in all its splendour with highly poetic similes extolling the diviner attributes of the king himself.[2]

Some of the images depicted on Nepalese coins can be tolerably well identified from _dhyānas_; but though it is known that the _yantra_ of each _devatā_ is different, the difficulty in ascribing each _yantra_ as it occurs on coins to its proper _devatā_ is great. The Tantra-worship, though open to all, is yet a secret worship. It is written, " Verily, verily and without a doubt, the Veda Shastra and Puranas are like a common woman free to all, but the doctrine of Shambhu [_i.e._, the Tantra] is like a secret house bride, to reveal which is death."[3] This spirit of secrecy is common among Hindu and Buddhistic Tāntrikas, which makes it practically impossible to obtain any information from them. The esoteric meaning of things can be learned by the initiated only. No doubt the Lichchhavis, the Ṭhākurīs, the succeeding Sūryavaṃśī kings, the Mallas, and the rest knew these as well as the Kshatriya rulers of the present time do. The goddess Māneśvarī, installed by Māna Deva I of the Lichchhavi clan, may be cited as an instance. She was his _ishṭa-devatā_,[4] but renamed _Māneśvarī_ to keep secrecy. Similarly the _yantra_ often underwent slight changes to make it appear different from what it really represents. It would be a wearisome and unprofitable task to attempt to identify the several hundred diagrams of _yantras_ which appear on the so-called Newar coins.[5] But the general similarity which these bear to the several illustrations in the works of Tantra referred to corroborates the view that they and their predecessors, the image-type and the _vāhana_ and _praharaṇa_ devices, are Tantric in origin, and result from a continuous development from the simple to the complex. The representations of some divinities in coins of foreign invaders, as for instance of Śiva in coins of Gondopharnes and Kadphises II,[6] show a departure from the meditational forms given in the Tantras, due probably to the secrecy which the adepts observed, particularly towards foreigners. The Lichchhavis, though

[1] _Mahā-Nirvāṇa Tantra_, Introduction, p. xxiv.

[2] _Vide_ inscriptions on Kushana and Gupta coins, etc., _Prāchīna Mudrā, ut supra_, as also Catalogues of Coins in the Indian and British Museums.

[3] _Principles of Tantra_, by Arthur Avalon, Introduction, p. ix ; _Mahā-Nirvāṇa Tantra_, Preface, p. xiii, and p. 279, sec. 167; also _vide_ note below on coin of Śiva Deva II.

[4] _Ishṭa-devatā_ is the special tutelary divinity whose worship is enjoined on the novice at his Tantric initiation. _Vide Mahā-Nirvāṇa Tantra_, p. 260, sec. 204. The initiate, upon full initiation, can worship the divinity in _yantra_ ; _ibid._, p. 258, sec. 183.

[5] _Coinage of Nepal_, p. 683.

[6] Vincent Smith, pp. 131-132 ; _Prāchīna Mudrā_, pp. 86-87.

Vrātya Kshatriyas,[1] did not labour under the same disadvantage, as they were entitled to study and practise the Hindu form of worship. The Guptas, much lower in caste, probably the lowest,[2] were within the circle, and thus could obtain more correct information, though in some of their coins with the image of Śiva they showed no better knowledge than their predecessors of foreign origin. At all events, the similarity between some of the Lichchhavi and Gupta coins must be traced to their common religious belief, and not to imitation. This observance of secrecy, however, greatly hampers the study of coins from the point of view of religious history, and whatever could be found and recorded here is due to the help of the enlightened Prime Minister, Maharaja Chandra Sham Sher Jang Bahadur Rana.

According to the principle here enunciated and in keeping with the tradition preserved in the Vaṃśāvalīs, the early coins of Nepal require to be arranged anew. The coins with standing bull-type will come first. Who first introduced them cannot be ascertained; but that these were Lichchhavi coins may be conjectured from the representation of the sun, which invariably occurs in this type. The Lichchhavis prided themselves on being Sūryavaṃśīs,[3] and so they adopted the sun to show their descent from that god. The Śaiva symbol of a humped bull with a crescent above occurs on these coins. In some the bull stands to the right, and in others to the left, probably indicating that the change was introduced by a succeeding king, which the variation in legend also indicates. These coins should belong to the same period as Vrisha Deva,[4] or an earlier date.

The coin with the trident on the obverse and the sun on the reverse should belong to Śankara Deva, and appears to be prior to the one with the recumbent bull, as the Vaṃśāvalīs relate that the trident was dedicated first and the Nandi erected some time afterwards. Some ascribe the Nandi to Dharma Deva, the son of Śankara Deva. He dedicated a great *Vrishabha-dhvaja*, according to some Vaṃśāvalīs,[5] and was a great devotee of Nārāyana, visiting the four Nārāyanas every day. He was told in a dream to worship the Jala-śayana Nārāyana (the god lying on the waters), by which he would acquire the same merit as through visiting the four Nārāyanas, and thenceforth he worshipped that god and Vajra Yoginī.[6] Among his contributions to Buddhistic buildings is the repair of the Dhanada Chaitya.[7] The statement that the Nandi was dedicated by Dharma Deva appears to be more probable, and the coins with recumbent bulls were perhaps introduced by h'm, as that supposition explains the existence of two kinds of coins of this type agreeing in the obverse device but differing in the reverse device.

---

[1] That is, fallen Kshatriyas according to the verse of Manu quoted in notes on Lichchhavis, *History of Mediaeval Hindu India* by C. V. Vaidya, p. 377, also Lévi, *Le Népal*, vol. ii, under heading Lichchhavis.   [2] C. J. Brown, *The Coins of India*, p. 41.
[3] Inscription of Jaya Deva at Pashupati ; see Fleet, *Corpus Ins. Ind.*, vol. iii.
[4] For illustration *vide Coinage of Nepal*, Plate I, No. 10.
[5] The Vaṃśāvalī from Bada Kaji, as also the palm-leaf Vaṃśāvalī mentioned by C. Bendall, *op. cit.* fol. 21A.
[6] The Vaṃśāvalī from Bada Kaji.   [7] Wright's *History of Nepal*, p. 124.

At all events, the coin with the recumbent bull and the symbol said to be a crude representation of the *nandipada* and trident in imitation of the one in Jishnu Gupta's coin¹ no doubt belongs to Dharma Deva. That the symbol cannot be by any stretch of imagination a trident will be apparent at a glance. The curled design on either side of the centre, which shows two closely touching round balls with a long projecting handle, does not show the three points of a trident. The figure is, without doubt, a *vajra*. In the Tantric books the *vajra*-figure is defined as being formed by placing two current Nagari sixes face to face against the handle.² The central part shows this sort of device. The scroll-like part on either side represents the strips of cloth usually placed on each side of any article dedicated to the divinity. The practice is current to this day in Nepal. As according to the Vaṃśāvalīs Śankara Deva was a thoroughgoing Śaiva, he was not likely to have introduced a *vajra*, even in its Hindu form, on his coins; but his more tolerant successor, Dharma Deva, might have done so, in the same way as he carried out repairs of chaityas. Besides, the *vajra* would be an emblem of veneration for him as a devout Vaishnava.³

Next in order is the coin with the legends *Mānānka* and *Sr̄ Bhoginī*. The legend *Mānānka* shows that the coin was issued by Māna Deva. The resemblance between this form and the *Parākramānka* of Samudra Gupta's inscription and the *Vikramānka* of some of Chandra Gupta II's coins points, it has been said, to Gupta influence.⁴ But the reason for such correspondence has already been explained. The legend *Sri Bhoginī*, from the type on the coin and the notice in the Vaṃśāvalī, appears to be connected with the goddess represented on the coin. *Bhoginī* occurs as a name for the manifestation of Mahāśakti as *Kamalātmikā*,⁵ which is another aspect of Mahā-Lakshmī. In his hymn to the goddess Māneśvarī, Māna Deva applies to her the title *Prakāśa-teja Lakshmī*.⁶ Thus though a very infrequent name is used to hide the identity, it would appear that this aspect of Mahāśakti is represented by the image, which, to preserve secrecy still further, is given the form of Lakshmī sitting on a lotus and carrying a lotus in her hand according to the *dhyāna* or meditational form⁷ of the Lakshmī-aspect. The lion has in front a lotus-flower on a stalk with a few leaves.

---

¹ *Coinage of Nepal*, p. 681, and description of coin on p. 720, No. 10.
² *Mantra-mahodadhi* (Venkateśvar Press, Bombay), in the chapter on definition.
³ *Dhvaja, vajra*, and *ankuśa, scil.* the flag, the thunderbolt, and the goad, are the special signs to be seen in the footprints of Vishṇu.
⁴ Lévi, *Le Népal*, vol. ii, pp. 106-107.
⁵ *Śakta-pramoda* (Venkateśvar Press), detailing the 1000 names of this goddess on p. 376, 74th śloka, 2nd line, mentions *Saumya-bhoga-Mahābhāga-Bhoginī Bhogadāyikā* as some of them.
⁶ Mention of the hymn will be found in Lévi's *Le Népal*, vol. ii. The Vaṃśāvalī from Bada Kaji gives a few couplets.
⁷ Raj Guru Hemrāj Pandit is of opinion that a double meaning was intended by the use of the legend, as he has found a mention in some Vaṃśāvalī that the name of the wife of Māna Deva was Bhoginī. The image was associated with a lion on the reverse. Some take the lion to be the obverse, but Mr. Walsh takes it correctly as the reverse ; *vide Coinage of Nepal*, p. 717.

312 NEPAL

The association of the lion with Mahā-Lakshmī is not uncommon,[1] though she is connected more often with the elephant.[2] The *Guṇānka* coins follow in order. There is a change in a second series of this coin from the Lakshmī type to the Kamalātmikā, which has been by a misconception identified as the figure of the king.[3] Though indistinct, the representation nearly resembles the *dhyāna* form of the goddess seated cross-legged, bearing a lotus in each of the two upper arms, the lower arms resting on the thighs. The other coin continues the representation of the goddess, as in the time of Māna Deva. The *ishṭa-devatā* of the dynasty appears to have remained unchanged from Māna Deva to Guṇakāma Deva. As the coins of Nepal are based on religion, the idea of the figure of a king appearing on a Nepalese coin is absurd. The complete portrait of the goddess can be seen in a coin of the Gauda king Śaśānka,[4] where the goddess is seated on a lotus, as in the Guṇānka coins, with an elephant on either side pouring water over her head.

In the *vajra* device on one of the Paśupati coins, and perhaps in the lion-device on the Mānānka coin, a spirit of compromise on the part of the kings may be detected. Those symbols are acknowledged by the Buddhists as within their list of symbols for worship, and so reconcile them. It is not known whether the copper coinage described was the main currency, or only a subsidiary one. It may have been the main currency, as in some parts of India, such as Vidiśā.[5] The value of copper in those days was much higher than at present, almost twenty times more,[6] and for internal currency they might have served as standard coins. If any gold coin was current, it has left no trace. Some sort of silver coin was current about the time of Śiva Deva II and Amśuvarman; but whether it circulated in the period of Māna Deva or earlier cannot be ascertained. However that may be, subsequent to the Guṇānka coin another Paśupati coin can be ascribed to a king by the help of Vaṃśāvalīs. King Śiva Deva II was known for his pious acts, the enumeration of which finds a prominent place in the Vaṃśāvalīs.[7] The restoration of the worship of Vatsalā Devī, a *śakti* specially attached to Paśupati, was an important piece of work. The image of the goddess was not to be found or shown, and so Śiva Deva II, with the help of priests well versed in Tantra, installed the goddess in a *kalaśa*.[8] The *pūjā* is still performed on a *kalaśa*, within which the *yantra* of the Devī is reported to be hidden. Śiva Deva was also, as is every true Tāntrika, a great devotee of Śiva, and installed Nṛityanāthas, Bhairavas, Śiva-lingas, and Bhūtas, and to hide his persuasion installed Ganeśas, Iśvarīs, and Śaktis with equal

[1] Lakshmī on a lion appears in a coin of Chandra Gupta I : *vide Prāchīna Mudrā*, p. 132, and *Catalogue of Coins in British Museum*, pp. 8-11, quoted there.
[2] *Vide* Guṇānka Coins, Plate I, Nos. 2 and 3, *Coinage of Nepal*.
[3] *Coinage of Nepal*, p. 718.
[4] *Prāchīna Mudrā*, p. 149 ; also *Catalogue of Coins in British Museum*, pp. 147-148, Nos. 606-612, quoted in *Prāchīna Mudrā* ; and *Coins of India*, Plate V, No. 12, etc.
[5] *Ancient Indian Numismatics*, p. 190. [6] *Ibid.*, p. 189.
[7] Wright's *History of Nepal*, pp. 125-130 ; also Lévi, *Le Népal*, vol. ii.
[8] Vaṃśāvalī from Bada Kaji.

zeal.[1] The coin with a *kalaśa* on the reverse and the legend of Paśupati and Lakshmī on the obverse was probably introduced by him.[2] The device on the obverse, by the same misconception as has been pointed out in the Guṇānka coin, has been supposed to represent a king with a crown on his head. The goddess Vatsalā is popularly regarded as one of the ten Mahā-vidyās, as was Kamalātmikā, but was so named to keep the identity secret. The doctrine of Vatsalā is kept a mystery, and little can be learned about it; but the worship of the Devī and her installation in a *kalaśa*, with the *yantra* within it, and the appearance of a *kalaśa* on a coin with the Paśupati legend, lend considerable support to the supposition put forward. In some of these coins a part of the *kalaśa* is faintly visible to the right of thr goddess, who carries a lotus in her right hand, which further confirms the supposition. Probably this *kalaśa* on the obverse formed an integral part of the die, but, being placed much to one side, has not come out in all coins. All the deities are represented in the descriptions of their meditational forms as crowned, so a crown does not necessarily imply that the image is that of a king. There is some resemblance between the deity as depicted on the coin and that on the Mānānka coin. Besides, the lotus in her right hand identifies the goddess with Lakshmī,[3] a manifestation of Mahā-Devī. This type of coin appears to be the only one issued by Śiva Deva II in at least two series.[4]

. It is difficult to fix the Vaiśravaṇa coin from the description of the kings in the Vaṃśāvalīs. This god was a favourite with the Lichchhavis, and an image of him is reported to have been installed in Khotan by a Lichchhavi from Vaiśālī.[5] He figures in the Vedic *sandhyā* prayers; and Kauṭilya gives instructions for the building of a temple to him in the city square. He is a prominent figure in Buddhist scriptures,[6] and is a great Tantric *Sādhaka*.[7] Thus the introduction of his image on the coins of the Lich-chhavis is not extraordinary. But he does not figure in the Vaṃśāvalīs, and no indication is given that any of the kings inclined to his worship. Tradi-tion has not preserved any distinguished record of King Kuveravarman, whose name suggests a connection with this coin;[8] and it is rather unlikely that such a colourless king would have introduced a coin departing from the standing bull-type, which might have been current at the time. A probable supposition is that this coin was introduced by Aṃśuvarman

---

[1] "A man may be a Śākta at heart whatever his sect may be," *vide Mahā-Nirvāṇa Tantra*, p. 53, note, also *Tantra-sāra*, *Kulāchāra-prakaraṇa*, where it is said "Śāktas in their heart outwardly Śaivas, and in assemblies Vaishṇavas," etc., etc. In the preface, p. xiii, the author relates his failure to secure a complete Mahā-Nirvāṇa Tantra from a Nepalese Pandit, who would not agree to the publication of the Shaṭkarma Mantras.

[2] The *kalaśa* of Vatsalā is very like the *kalaśa* on the coin.

[3] *Vide* Plate I, illustration No. I.

[4] *Vide* Plate I, illustration of coin No. 1, and description of that coin.

[5] Khotan has been identified with the Li-Yul of Tibetan writers, and appears to have been connected with the Lichchhavis of Vaiśālī.

[6] The Svayambhū-Purāṇa mentions Vaiśravaṇa frequently.

[7] *Principles of Tantra*, edited by Arthur Avalon, p. 117.

[8] Cunningham suggested this from Vaiśravaṇa being another name for Kuvera, the treasurer of the gods.

himself soon after he became king upon the death of Śiva Deva II, who, being sonless, nominated him as his successor.' He was not bound to respect the titular divinity of the dynasty, as he belonged to a different family, which was probably Vaishṇava, and from respect for which he may have introduced the cow and calf device with the legend *Kāmadhenu*. The design may have been meant for Surabhi, the origin of the Kāmadhenu and all cows, if the Vaishṇava tendency is accepted as correct.' The origin of the Kāmadhenu is explained by different legends; in one' she is said to be the mother of the bull of Śiva. Thus the design, both of Vaiśravana and the cow and calf, because of the manifold aspect in which those may be viewed, would appeal to the subtle genius of Aṃśuvarman. From the coins which bear his name it would appear that he wished to break away gradually from the current practice in coinage, as he did in language as a grammarian.' His close first-hand acquaintance with the religious litera-ture gave him the opportunity to apply his knowledge in practice. After this coin-type, his next must have been the one with the lion-device com-bined with the cow and calf symbol. Closely following this would be the coin with two lions. The last of the series would be the coin in which the legend *Mahārājādhirājasya* occurs and where he has boldly assumed the royal title, ranged round a raised circular device with a surround of dots. This last device has been interpreted as the sun with rays,' though the representation is more like a full moon with stars. A glance at the coin with the standing bull and crescent and the legend *Paśupati* on the other side ranged round with equal spacing between the letters' and the trident-type coin with reverse like the above,' will make the difference between the devices on Aṃśuvarman's coins and on those coins quite manifest. On the latter coins the dots are perfectly round; but on the former coins the dots below the letters are elongated like rays, and are prolonged between the letters to the periphery of the coins. It may be observed that up to this date the moon, a common deity of worship on certain auspicious days, is worshipped in Nepal on a raised circular disc with either circular dots or scollops around it. The gradual transition in Aṃśuvarman's coins is also observable in the gradual change in the language of the inscriptions,' where, step by step, he assumes the title and attributes of Śiva Deva II and other Lichchhavi kings. In coins, at each step, he retained one device from the preceding: thus he took over the *Kāmadhenu* or *Surabhi* from the coins bearing the *Vaiśravana* legend into the one with

' The Vaṃśāvalī from Bada Kaji places Aṃśuvarman immediately after Śiva Deva, following that used by Kirkpatrick.
' For the legend connected with Surabhi, the heavenly cow that fed Kṛishṇa, *vide Brahma-vaivarta-Purāṇa, Prakṛiti-khaṇḍa*, ch. 44, also quoted in *Śabda-kalpadruma*.
' *Vide Kālikā-Purāṇa*, ch. 91.
' Adopting the direction of Pāṇini (which makes optional the doubling of a con-sonant when *r* precedes it), he wrote his name on coins as *Aṃśuvarman*, with one *ma* instead of two, the usual practice. For other instances *vide* Lévi, *Le Népal*, vol. ii.
' *Coinage of Nepal*, p. 719; also Lévi, *Le Népal*, vol. ii.
' *Ibid.*, Plate I, No. 10.   ' *Ibid.*, Plate I, No. 11.
' This is elaborately noted by Lévi in *Le Népal*, vol. ii.

the legend *Śryaṃśu;* the lion from the last into the third with the two lions; and the same legend and the lion again into the fourth, with the legend *Mahārājādhirājasya.* It should be noted that the lion in the secónd series of Aṃśuvarman's coins is a winged one, better known in Tantra as the *śarabha,*[1] and in the Buddhistic scripture as the vehicle of Avalokiteśvara, thus being susceptible of interpretation according to the religious propensity of the people.

The last to be noted amongst the early coins hitherto found is that of Jishnu Gupta. His coins are very rare. The obverse of the coin has a bull,[2] and not a horse or a lion,[3] as has been supposed by some. The reverse shows a sign interpreted as *nandipada* and trident, which is really a *vajra.*[4] Jishnu Gupta's name is not to be found in any Vaṃśāvalī so far available, but that he succeeded Aṃśuvarman and reigned for some years at least is demonstrated by his coins and inscription. An explanation is suggested here for what it may be worth. The name Aṃśuvarmaṇ, the Vaṃśāvalī says, was bestowed by Śiva Deva II on his nephew when he took the boy into his family,[5] so that he apparently bore a different name in his own family. All the ·Vaṃśāvalīs so far found agree that three Gupta kings preceded Śiva Deva II. It is also mentioned that after Bhīma Deva Varman the "Gopāla Vaiśya Gupta Vaṃśa" came to the throne.[6] The Guptas, according to the Vaṃśāvalīs,[7] were Vaiśyas and Vaishnavas. Viśva Gupta married his daughter to Aṃśuvarman, who was also a Vaiśya of the Ṭhākurī clan.[8] When Śiva Deva II named Aṃśuvarman as his successor, his collaterals must have been greatly dissatisfied. The Tibetan annals mention that Aṃśuvarman's daughter was married to Srong-btsan-sgam-po, the Tibetan king.[9] Probably Aṃśuvarman, too, was without a son, and, during the lifetime of Śiva Deva II, adopted from his wife's family Jishnu Guptạ, who was renamed Kṛitavarman by Śiva Deva II, but who, on his assumption of power, resumed his old name of Jishnu Gupta. His rivals, the Devas, collaterals of Śiva Deva II, united in ousting him, and in the internecine quarrel some became kings for a short period, till the powerful Vīra Deva usurped the throne. Upon his death, his son Chandraketu had a troublesome time, till he was, in his turn, ousted by Narendra Deva, who came from Tibet on the news of the death of his uncle.

---

[1] *Puraścharyārṇava, ut sup.,* vol. ii, p. 704, and illustration at the end of vol. iii, Appeńdix, p. 17.

[2] It is said to be winged (*Coinage of Nepal,* p. 719), but really the bull bears on its hump the ornaments which are generally supplied in dedicating it; the reproduction of a Nepalese inscription in Bendall's *Journey to Nepal,* p. xiv, Appendix, shows such a decorated bull on the top of the plate.

[3] Lévi, in discussing this coin in *Le Népal,* vol. ii, says that the device is supposed to be a lion, copied from Aṃśuvarman's coin.

[4] Lévi, *Népal,* vol. ii, where the same view is taken.   [5] Bada Kaji's Vaṃśāvalī.

[6] Except Wright's *History of Nepal,* where two names occur, *Vishnu* and *Viśva,* which agree with the proper names in other Vaṃśāvalīs but differ in the family appellation, which instead of *Gupta* is given as *Deva Varman.* Kirkpatrick mentions Vishnu Gupta in place of Viśva Gupta.   [7] Bada Kaji's Vaṃśāvalī.

[8] Lévi, *Le Népal,* vol. ii; Wright gives the name as Viśva Deva Varman, p. 130.

[9] Lévi, *Le Népal,* vol. ii.

Such a reconstruction of the situation is largely conjectural, but would fairly well explain all definitely known facts of the period.

These early coins do not help us to frame a chronology owing to the absence of a date on any of them. The Vaṃśāvalī dates, even when mentioning astronomical elements such as the phases of the moon, positions of planets, days of the week, etc., are not verifiable, as the date of the year is missing. Even where the year is mentioned, the era according to which it is reckoned is open to doubt, and has not been settled satisfactorily. The intercalary month Paushya, which occurs in some inscriptions and colophons of manuscripts, is peculiar. An explanation has been sought on the supposition that in Nepal in those early days the Brahma-siddhānta system of astronomy was in vogue, instead of the Sūrya-siddhānta.[1] This intercalary Paushya is to be found in manuscripts of the thirteenth century, and even later.[2] If we take the year in Māna Deva's inscription to be of the Vikrama era, the early coins enumerated above will belong to the third century A.D., or perhaps earlier, extending to about the eighth or ninth century A.D.[3]

No specimen of any coin has yet been found for the long interval between Jishnu Gupta's coin and the one of Jagat-prakāsa Malla dated Nepal Samvat 752 (A.D. 1632); but coins were struck by some kings and were in circulation practically throughout the period. The evidence of literature is so positive that one cannot very well deny their existence. However that may be, from the period when the specimens were obtainable a change in type had already been introduced and *yantras* had begun to figure in the coins. The *yantra* is a diagram, and consists of certain permanent elements and other variable ones. It is described from the centre outward at times of *pūjā* or worship. The elements have esoteric meaning : in one aspect they represent the five elements, in another the colour, in still another the attributes or *gunas*, and so forth.[4] The combination of the representations totals up to the particular divinity with which the *yantra* becomes identical. Broadly speaking, there is a triangle, inverted, in the centre ; round this is a circle circumscribing it, with eight petals or more, generally in multiples of eight, round the circle ; the circle and petals are enclosed in a figure known as *bhūpura*. The *bhūpura* is a square, the sides of which are divided with a space in the middle of each and a parallelogram with its side next the side of the square symmetrically divided, the ends of the divided sides being joined. In the Nepalese coins of the period sometimes the whole of a *yantra* appears on one side, and the whole or part of another on the other side ; and sometimes, and this is more common, the central part appears on one side and the square on the other. In the latter case, both are to be combined to give the full representation of the *yantra*.

[1] Bendall's *Journey to Nepal*, note to inscription No. II in Appendix I, p. 76.

[2] The intercalated second Paushya is mentioned in some places in the palm-leaf Vaṃśāvalī, as in fol. 458, fol. 44A, etc.

[3] Lévi, *Le Népal*, vol. ii, has proposed for the era of Māna Deva's inscription either the Vikrama or a special Lichchhavi one ; of these the Vikrama appears to be the simpler solution.   [4] *Mantra-mahodadhi*, ch. i.

Many variations occur in the above elements. The triangle is sometimes double, one inverted over another, or in its place will be found a five-pointed star with pentagon centre and so on. The *bhūpura* again is sometimes of a single line and sometimes of more than one; the parallelograms sometimes extend to the end of the sides of the square, and sometimes stop about midway. The lines are sometimes straight and sometimes curved. In fact, variations are extensive[1] to suit the no less extensive variations in the manifestations of deity. Thus identification is rendered difficult by this variety, and much more so by the slight changes purposely introduced to guard the secret of the divinity. Other symbols such as the *mangalas*, or auspicious things, *vāhanas*, like the lion, and the *praharanas*, or weapons such as the *khadga* (sword), trident, etc., also occur, and sometimes the *kalaśa* too, but mostly as secondary to the *yantra*, which is given greater prominence. The dots on the border of the coins appear on the Paśupati coins and nearly all the early coins They reappear on the seals of the *tālapatra* deeds, and continue on all subsequent coins, thus refuting the absurd idea that they were copied from Mohammedan coins by the Mallas and subsequent dynasties in their own coins.[2] In many seals of *tālapatra* documents of the early Nepal Samvats, the elements of *yantras* appear with a *Srī*, *khadga*, or trident within, and mark the transitional period, at the same time indicating the hold it had on the imagination of the kings. The *yantras*, besides being emblematic of the divinity, were potent means in the hands of Tāntrikas for doing good or evil, known as *Tāntrika Shaṭ-karma*.[3] *Yantras* for the above purposes are commonly given, carried, or circulated to achieve certain objects, and elaborate rituals are prescribed for their preparation.[4] A passing acquaintance with these diagrams would have prevented some curious misconceptions about some of the coins, which, upon a fanciful resemblance to some Mohammedan coins when looked at upside down, were pronounced to be a copy of the latter.[5] In many of them the central circle appears on one side and the *bhūpura* or special sort of square with wavy sides on the other. The dots between parallel lines emanating from the square and the circle[6] cannot be traced in the Mohammedan coins,[7] neither can the counterpart of a square of the peculiar kind be found therein. Symbols such as *pāśa* (noose), *damaru* (double-headed drum), *matsya* (fish), *patākā* (flag), and *triśūla* (trident), etc., occur on the reverse and obverse of nearly all of them, with sometimes the *śrī*. The vertical and horizontal lines have also their counterpart in

---

[1] Illustrations of some of these will be found in *Mahā-Nirvāna Tantra*. *Pūraśchary-ārnava* and *Mantra-mahodadhi* give the largest collection.

[2] *Coinage of Nepal*, p. 688.

[3] These six magical powers consisted of *mārana*, destruction, *uchchhāṭana*, driving away, *vaśīkarana*, bringing under control, *stambhana*, arresting or staying, say a storm or striking a man dumb or motionless, *vidveshana*, causing antagonism between two persons, *svastyayana*, curative or helping power in disease, misfortune, danger, etc. *Vide Principles of Tantra* by A. Avalon, p. 112.

[4] More than a half of *Mantra-mahodadhi* is taken up with this, and many curious *yantras* will be found there. [5] *Coinage of Nepal*, pp. 686-687.

[6] *Vide ibid.*, Pt. II, Nos. 1, 2, 3, 4, 9, and 10.

[7] *Vide* illustrations, Nos. 1 and 2, on p. 687 of *Coinage of Nepal*.

some *yantras* :or *shatkarma*. The division of a circle into three parts by two straight lines found in many Gurkha coins has also been held to be the relic of the horizontal lines in the central circle in some Malla coins, reproduced from the meaningless Persian characters on those coins. But in some Pāṇḍya coins supposed to have been issued between A.D. 300 and 600 and in some Kerala coins of probably the eleventh or twelfth century, where Mohammedan influence is precluded, the same sort of divided circle occurs.[1] After the Gurkha conquest the Kshatriya kings continued their predecessors' practice of reproducing *yantras* on coins. Aberrations occurred, especially in some early Malla coins noticed hereafter, but these did not affect the broad principle. The conclusion is that the coin types and devices from earliest times to the present day are based on religion, and their development has been indigenous and on Tantric lines. The worship of Mahā-Devī begun under the name of *Māneśvarī* by Māna Deva I, revived as *Vatsalā* by Śiva Deva II, resumed under the old name of *Māneśvarī* by Jaya Sthiti Malla,[2] and enthusiastically followed by the Gurkhas since their conquest, coupled with the unmistakably Tantric devices on coins continued up till now in the *yantra* variety, make this conclusion positive and irrefutable.

DESCRIPTION OF COINS ILLUSTRATED

Many of the coins issued in Nepal have been described and illustrated in various catalogues, and the scattered information and impressions have been brought together in a contribution by Mr. E. H. Walsh[3] which makes it superfluous to reproduce them here. Such as are unrepresented in these works, and a few others of interest as conveying some more information, are brought together in the plates attached here. The coins Nos. 2, 3, 4, 5, 6, 7, and 8 are from the treasure rooms of Pashupati, and were procured by special permission of His Highness Maharaja Chandra Sham Sher Jang. The others are from private collections, the bulk being lent by His Highness.

The coin No. 1 is of copper, weighing about 94.5 grains, and measuring .8 inch across, of medium thickness. The obverse represents a deity, Lakshmī, wearing a crown, radiate, facing front, seated, holding the stalk of a lotus in the right hand, the left akimbo resting on the thigh, close to which is the representation of a small *kalaśa*, with a lotus-stalk rising from the top of it ; a dotted border. The reverse, the stamping on which is a little to the left, shows within a dotted surround, partially lost because of the shifting of the die, an image of a *kalaśa* with the *āvaraṇa*[4] ranged from the bottom upwards and a lotus-stalk rising from the mouth bearing a lotus-flower. Legend, *Paśupati: Paśu* to the left of the stalk and *pati* to the right in a straight line. In some coins of this type the legend is ranged

---

[1] Rapson, *Indian Coins*, Pl. V, Nos. 10 and 11, and p. 35, sec. 124 and sec. 125. Also Brown, *Coins of India*, Pl. VII, Nos. 3 and 9.   [2] Lévi, *Le Népal*, vol. ii.
[3] *Catalogue of Coins in the British and Indian Museums*, and *Coinage of Nepal*.
[4] The pair of cloth strips attached to the *kalaśa* or other article.

along the dotted surround in a curved line.[1] The image in these coins, though somewhat blurred, closely resembles that in our No. 1.

Nos. 2, 3, and 4 are probably Nepalese. They have features which are to be found in many Nepalese coins, and belong to the *vāhana* or *praharaṇa*

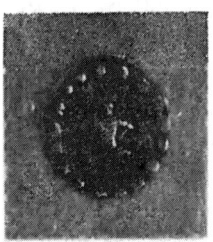 

No. 1

type combined with the *yantra* design. The dots round the border, though not exclusively Nepalese, are prominent features of the coins of that country. All are of alloyed silver.

No. 2 weighs about 158 grains and measures 1.2 inches across. Obverse: a circle, in the centre of which is *śrī śrī* in old Newari script with two crescents, one on the top of each *śrī*, with a dot above the crescent; the crescents and dots are to be distinctly seen in No. 4. On the top a

No. 2

khaḍga with its *āvaraṇa*, generally but mistakenly described as a garland; all round, an Arabic legend.[2] Reverse: two squares placed one across another to form an *ashṭaka* or complete octagon, inside which is a lion faintly visible with tail erect but curled at the end and face turned to the right. The legend in Nagari has been supposed to read *Nannesarī*; but the supposed *nna* looks very like the Newari *kshma*, as it appears in a coin

[1] *Vide Coinage of Nepal*, fig. 12, Plate I.
[2] Rubbings of this and Nos. 3 and 4 were sent to Mm. Hara Prasad Shastri, C.I.E., who obtained readings from Mr. R. D. Banerji. The readings of No. 2 were reported to be: obverse, '*Alā ud-dunyā wa'd-Dīn as-Sulṭān Abu'l-Muzaffar.* . . . Reverse, mistaken Arabic legend with *Nannesari* in Nagari script on top.

of Lakshmī-narasimha.[1] The letter *ra* is distinct on the coin, though blurred in the impression. The letter between *kshma* and *ra* may be either *na* or *sa.* The name is easily restored, and should be read as *Lakshmī-nara,* which, with the lion within the circle, read as *siṃha,* will become *Lakshmī-narasiṃha.* The use of the device of a lion as a rebus to a name is not uncommon in Nepalese coins.[2] This Lakshmī-narasiṃha was the grandson of Mahendra Malla, and became king of Katmandu in N.S. 733, or A.D. 1613.[3] As the use of the figure of a lion as a rebus to his name was made by Lakshmī-narasimha, the practice was perhaps of still earlier date. The Arabic legend, though imperfectly read, stands for some sultan of Bengal of or near the time. When the name is properly read it will probably be found to be one who reigned earlier than Lakshmī-narasiṃha.[4] It appears that Lakshmī-narasiṃha changed the coin type from this to a completely different one, more in keeping with Tantra.[5]

No. 3 in size, weight, and fabric is practically the same as No. 2. The

No. 3

obverse has the repeated *srī* within the circle, on the top of which appears the *khaḍga* or sword of Devī with a *vitāna* or top cover in the shape of a line; the ends are slightly bent in a *vitāna* where space permits.[6] This is also characteristic of Nepal. There is an Arabic legend round the circle as in No. 2, which reads the same.[7] On the reverse appears the crossed square as in No. 2, with a lion within and on the top the word *Śiva* in Newari script. Interpreted as in the case of the coin now ascribed to Lakshmī-narasiṃha, this coin should belong to Śiva Siṃha.[8] This was the name of the second son of Mahendra Malla and father of Lakshmī-narasimha, who became king of Katmandu after his licentious elder brother Sadāśiva Siṃha was expelled.

[1] *Vide* Plate II, No. 9 of *Coinage of Nepal.*
[2] *Vide* for example the coin of Siddhi-Narasimha, made up of *Siddhi-nara* and the figure of a lion, read as *siṃha,* in *Coinage of Nepal,* Plate V, No. 2, and description on p. 732.
[3] Vaṃśāvalī from Bada Kaji ; according to Bendall's list, about A.D. 1631.
[4] *Vide Coinage of Nepal,* Plate II, No. 9. [5] About 1613; *vide ante.*
[6] Illustrations of *vitāna* over *khaḍga* can be seen in Plate IV, No. 1, and Plate VI, No. 1, in *Coinage of Nepal.* [7] *Vide* footnote to No. 2.
[8] About A.D. 1600 Bendall's list ; according to Bada Kaji's Vamśāvalī, about A.D. 1580.

No. 4 of Plate III is also about the same size, weight, and thickness as Nos. 2 and 3. The device on the obverse is also the same. The Arabic legend has been read as '*Alā ud-Dunyā wa'd-Dīn as-Sulṭān Abu'l-Muzaffar Fīrōz.* The reverse is blurred, but the crossed square and the lion within are visible. The legend on top cannot be read, neither can the Arabic

NO. 4

legend, which probably is a continuation of the obverse one. The " Fīrōz " may be Fīrōz Shāh of Delhi, or the very short-lived boy king of Bengal, the son of Islām Shāh,[1] but the latter supposition is not likely. It has also been suggested that these coins may belong to some Srohiya kings of Mithila who acknowledged the suzerainty of the Mohammedan Sultans.[2] As no coins of Mithila are described in the History of Tirhut[3] or mentioned in books on coins,[4] the type and character of such, if any existed, are not forthcoming for comparison. On the other hand, the close resemblance to the design of the Nepalese coins as shown in the name ending in a rebus, and the Nagari script, which is very similar to those on coins of Lakshmī-narasimha and Siddhi-narasimha, suggest the conclusion that these are Nepalese coins. It seems that Mahendra Malla and some of his successors used the Mohammedan coins, keeping the legend on the periphery and changing the centres and tops to their own design, putting in the special traditional religious emblem of the *khaḍga*, the elements of *yantras*, and the lion, both as *vāhana* of Devī, and as rebus, to complete the name. The use of such coins might have given rise to the tradition that permission was obtained from Delhi to strike coins in Nepal.

Nos. 5, 6, 7, and 8 are Mohammedan. The rubbing of No. 5 was sent for decipherment, and was said to belong probably to Sikandar Shāh. Another coin, a rubbing of which was sent, was read as belonging to Ghiyāth ud-Dīn A'ẓam Shāh ibn·Sikandar Shāh.[5] These coins bear the marks of the conch-shell, discus, mace, and lotus. No. 5 shows clearly the conch-shell and lotus, both in relief, and the mace as a sunk mark. There

[1] *Vide Bangalār Itihās* by R. D. Banerji, vol. ii, p. 349.
[2] The suggestion came from Mahamahopadhyaya Hara Prasad Shastri.
[3] *History of Tirhut*, by Sāma-Narāin Singh.
[4] Such as the coins of India, *Prāchīna Mudrā, Bangalār Itihās*, etc.
[5] About A.D. 1332-1400 is the date given by Mm. Hara Prasad Shastri.

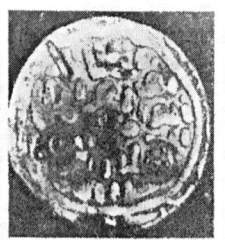 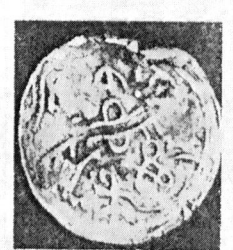

No. 5

 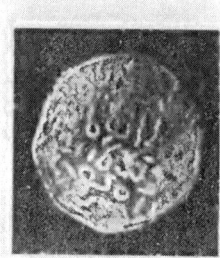

No. 6

No. 7

No. 8

are many such coins in the treasure room of Pashupati. The symbols punched on them are common to Hindus and Buddhists alike, and might have been affixed as permission to use them in the currency of the country. Apparently these are the coins referred to in the *tālapatra* deeds as current coin or *suvarṇa mūlya*. The dates of such, so far as ascertained, range from the thirteenth or fourteenth to the fifteenth or sixteenth century A.D., or from about after Jaya Sthiti Malla till some time before the time of Mahendra Malla. The class of coin shown in Nos. 2, 3, and 4 might have become current, and was probably known as *mohar* or *ṭanka*, the last a common name for coins in Mohammedan kingdoms. It will be seen ₁rom the illustrations of subsequent coins that the indigenous design with an Arabic legend did not last very long, and the kings soon returned to the pure *yantra* device. In that they exercised their ingenuity to produce a bewildering array of *yantras* from their close acquaintance with Tantric literature, both Buddhistic and Brahmanic. Identification of the divinity becomes practically impossible, not only from the variety of designs, but also from the changes purposely introduced to defeat any such attempt.

NO. 9

No. 9. This is a coin of Jaya Śrīnivāsa Malla, different from the one illustrated and described in the *Coinage of Nepal.*[1] The weight, size, and fabric are the same as for *mohars*. On the obverse appear two intersecting triangles; within the hexagon so formed a *khaḍga* with *āvaraṇa*, on top of which are a lotus and two crescents, one on each side, *śrī śrī* on left and right of the *khaḍga*, forming the top line, and *ja* and *ya* similarly placed forming the bottom line. In the six triangles, *śrī* appears within the top one, *ni* and *vā* on the left and right of the two triangles below, *sa* and *ma* in the triangles below the former pair, and *lla* in the bottom triangle. The triangles are connected by scollops, within each of which are placed four dots round a central one, with the usual dotted margin around. On the reverse: A *bhūpura* or square divided in the middle[2] in its ordinary form, and a circle in the centre of the *bhūpura*; within the circle, an elephant-goad in the middle, with a *kalaśa* with *āvaraṇa* to the left and another to

---

[1] For description *vide* p. 733, and for illustration Plate V, No. 4.
[2] The dividing space in Tantric technology is known as *dvāra* or gate.

the right; in the four corners of the square the conch-shell, discus, lotus, and mace, counter-clockwise; within the bottom *dvāra* is the date N.S. 786. In this the syllables *Nepāleśvara*, each within a *dvāra*, are absent, and probably the coin with that legend was issued later than this one.

NO. 10

No. 10, a coin of Jaya Bhūpālendra Malla, has not yet been published. Obverse: circle divided into three parts by lines said to be an imitation of Arabic letters; on the top division, a rayed sun in the centre with a *śrī* on each side; in middle division, a trident in the centre, *ja* and *ya* in the corners of the top line, *bhū* and *pā* on the left and right of the trident, *le* and *ndra* in the corners of the bottom line; in bottom division, *ma* and *lla* on left and right of a lotus on a stalk. Reverse: the circle is divided as in the obverse; in the top division, *la* and *kshmī* on the left and right of an inverted lotus on a stalk; in the middle division, in the centre, a *khadga* with *āvarana* and *vitāna*;[1] *nā* and *rā* on the top line corner, *ya* and *na* on left and right of the *khadga*; in bottom division, date N.S. 808.

NO. 11

No. 11. A coin of a somewhat similar device has been described and illustrated in the *Coinage of Nepal.*[2] This one is identical with that described so far as the obverse is concerned, but differs in the reverse, having a circle in the centre instead of an octagon. Unlike No. 9, which, with the obverse diagram placed within the circle of the reverse diagram, will make the

[1] *Vide ante.*   [2] Plate VI, No. 3, and p. 737, *Coinage of Nepal.*

yantra for ordinary *Devī-pūjā* and particularly for Sarasvatī, the goddess of learning, the coin No. 11 represents two half-designs of some practically identical *yantra*. The date on the coin is N.S. 842, and this is also the date in the illustration published, though by mistake it has been given in the description as N.S. 833.[1] The *khaḍga* rests upon a throne (not a lotus, as stated in the description referred to).

NO. 12

No. 12 is a silver coin of Yoga-narendra Malla in the shape of an equilateral triangle with the sides about .75 inch and weighing about 20 grains. The obverse has within a triangle a *khaḍga* with *āvaraṇa*; legend on the top line, *śrī śrī* to left and *vīra* to right of the *khaḍga*, on next line *yo* left and *ga* right, third line *na* left, *re* right, and below *ndra*. The reverse shows a vermilion-casket with *āvaraṇa* and a lotus on top;[2] legend, *śrī ja* and *ya la* left and right above, *kshmī* and *de* in second line similarly placed, and *vī* at the bottom. The letter *la* is read for *ra*. The coin has a dotted surround, and bears no date.

NO. 13

No. 13, a coin of Jaya Vishṇu Malla Deva, is different on the reverse from one of which an illustration has already been published.[3] The circle on the reverse is divided into three parts. In the top division are the syllables *śrī śrī* with a sun between them, in the middle a *khaḍga* with

---

[1] Plate VI, No. 3, and p. 737, *Coinage of Nepal.*
[2] This vermilion-casket, known in Newari as *sinamu*, has been wrongly described in many instances as either a *kalaśa* or a *kalaśa* in the form of a *stūpa*. The casket is a precious possession of a married Hindu lady as emblematic of Lakshmī and good luck.
[3] *Coinage of Nepal*, Plate VI, fig. v; description on p. 738.

āvaraṇa and *ka* and *ru* to left and right, in the bottom *nāmaya*. The date on this coin and the one previously published appears to be identical, and should be read N.S. 849, and not N.S. 859 as published.

No. 14

No. 14. An illustration of a coin slightly differing from this has been published. The description was not correct in certain respects. The difference lies in the omission on the obverse of *jaya*, which appears in the previously illustrated coin. The ground in this coin is ornamented, while in the other it is plain.[1] On the reverse the mirror to the left and the vermilion-casket to the right of the trident have wrongly been described as a discus and vase for offerings with cover. The two articles are found associated with pictures of Lakshmī in this country and India. In the coins of Nepal, these or one of them are found in coins where the name of a Rani occurs.

No. 15

No. 15 has never yet been noticed, nor has any description or illustration of it been published. It is of silver, size 1 inch, weight 78 grains, the fabric being the same as that of other *mohars*. The obverse contains a circle in the centre, with a *bhūpura* or square; the halves of the top parallelogram over the *dvāras* are curved, and the junction of the outer lines extends to the middle of the opening of the *dvāra*. The legend within the square appears to be as follows: top line, *śrī yu ta va*, next *ya* and *ṇha* (?) to left and right of the circle; then *da* and *śa* similarly placed; the bottom line, *bahudhānya*; below, the date 1667; within the circle, a symbol which may be a lotus or tuft of jewels. The reverse has a circle with eight petals. The circle is

[1] *Coinage of Nepal*, Plate V, No. 11.

divided into three parts, of which the top contains the legend *ratna*, the
middle a *khaḍga* with *āvaraṇa* and *ti* and *ta* (?) to left and right of it, the
bottom probably *phālā*. In the petals appear *śrī sa vi ja ka dā ya śra*.
The date can only be interpreted as a Śaka one, which would be equivalent
to N.S. 865 or A.D. 1745. This was the period when there was trouble in
Katmandu and also in Patan. As the coin refers in its quaint language to a
federation of ten, it was probably issued by the nobles of Katmandu or
Patan. The devices point to Patan, but the Vaṃśāvalī speaks of only six
Pradhāns of Patan who played the part of king-makers, and unless the
number ten is loosely used, the coin cannot be ascribed to them.[1] If it
was struck at Katmandu, it should belong to a period just antecedent to
the reign of Jyoti-prakāśa, the infant son of Jaya-prakāśa, as his coins of
N.S. 866 have been found. There is a tradition that the nobles ruled
Katmandu for a short while, and the coin may belong to that period. It is
equally probable that it belongs to Patan after Rājya-prakāśa was driven
out and Jaya-prakāśa was expelled after one or two years' experience of
the Pradhāns with him as their king. The device on the coin, as has been
said, supports this view.

No. 16

No. 16 is also a coin hitherto unpublished. It is a half-*mohar* of silver,
size about .85 inch, weight about 43 grains. This coin of Chakravartīndra
will be found to be without the so-called *bāṇāstra* which tradition affirms
to have been speedily fatal to him.[2] On the obverse is a central circle or
rather four scalloped segments joined, and above each appears a petal.
Between the petals and the intervening space is the legend *Srījayachakravar-
tīndra*; within the central figure, a trident and a lotus-stalk on either side.
On the reverse appears a design similar to that on the obverse, and within
the four petals *malla deva*; in the centre, a *khaḍga* and lotus-stalks. The
coin is undated.

Nos. 17, 18, and 19 are token-coins which must have been current in
Nepal. They are of burnt clay, thick in fabric, and of about the size of the
illustration. The obverse and reverse have the same design and legend;
the thick periphery has also a legend. They have a dotted border.

No. 17. The obverse shows a *khaḍga* with *āvaraṇa* and two crescents,
one on each side of the *khaḍga*, and the legend *rāma*, the letters being placed

---

[1] Wright's *History of Nepal*, pp. 244 *et seq.* and 250 *et seq.*   [2] *Ibid.*, p. 220.

one on each side. The reverse contains in the centre the tuft of jewels, a Buddhistic emblem. The legend on the top line is *śrī* to the left of the tuft

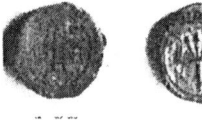

NO. 17

and 3 to the right, and below them *de* to the left and *vī* to the right. On the periphery, a lotus with projecting stalks and the words *sim-bha va-jra*, then another lotus as described and the syllable *gaja*.

NO. 18

No. 18. The obverse shows in the centre a *khadga* with a crescent on the top. The legend is *śrī hi* in a line to the left and right, on top and below *ta ma*, and at the bottom *la*, probably to be read as *Śrī Hita Malla*. The reverse shows a design like a trident with *āvaraṇa*. The periphery contains the legend *bhā ga va ta* ¹ and then *sam 862*.

NO. 19

No. 19. Obverse: a double triangle, one inverted over the other, within the hexagon, a *khadga* with *āvaraṇa*. Reverse: a circle in the centre with four petals, each entering a *dvāra*; on the periphery appears the legend *śrī ma tha sim kha siya*. In all specimens these two lines appear in the periphery placed diametrically opposite, showing that the impressions were got from a top and bottom die. The words *simha vajra gaja* may be interpreted to mean 188,² which, if read in reverse order, as the rule is,

¹ The first letter may also be read as *to* or *jo*.
² According to convention there are 8 *gajas*, 8 *vajras*, and 1 *simha*. But the legend on the coin would suggest a connection with Jaya Sthiti Malla, who (as mentioned in Wright's *History*, pp. 182-183) was a devotee of Nārāyaṇa and Rāma and at the same time a Śākta at heart. He was styled Bāla-Nārāyaṇa in a drama (*vide* Lévi, *Le Népal*, vol. ii). If we

give the number 881, which perhaps is the Samvat.[1] This and the 862 occurring in No. 18 are probably Nepal Samvat, which will place the two coins in the reign of Jaya-prakāśa Malla. The difficulty he had in meeting his expenses is mentioned in all the Vaṃśāvalīs. His vandalism did not spare the treasuries of Pashupati and even the appurtenances of the deity and the pinnacles and gilt articles of the temples.[2] Of course, such token-coins would not have served for payment of his mercenary troops, who would not have been satisfied with anything but gold and silver. But probably these token-coins were a subsidiary currency for very small payments, and give an idea of what a *turu* of Jaya Sthiti Malla may have been like. Perhaps the contemporaries of Jaya-prakāśa, the kings of Patan and Bhatgaon, may also have issued such coins. The name, however, of Hita Malla on the obverse of No. 18 would show that that was his coin. But no such name is to be found in the Vaṃśāvalīs, and if he was a king, his annals are not yet known. Some round leather pieces with a triangular hole punched in the centre and some faint markings on it are believed to have been current as coins in Nepal.

No. 20

No. 20 is a copper coin of about 1 inch diameter and about 162 grains weight, of medium thickness. The interest of it lies in the fact that the legend has been partly read as " Rāna Bahādur Shāh," and if correct would be the illustration of a new coin not yet published.

NEPALI MONEY

4 Dâms . . .	= 1 pice (paisa)
4 Pice . . .	= 1 Anna
6¼ Annas . .	= 1 Sukâ
2 Sukâs . . .	= 1 Mohar
2 Mohars . .	= 1 Rupee (Rupaiya)
1¼ Nepali Rupees	= 1 British Indian Rupee

connect the coin with him, the words *gaja*, *vajra*, and *siṃha* may be interpreted as the names of some *mangalas*, the reiteration of which is as auspicious as the representation in images. Under this aspect these coins may be the *turu* of his time.

[1] It may also be interpreted as 818, if *gaja* be read first. As the Samvat 862 can be read in No. 18, the other is probably 881.

[2] Lévi, *Le Népal*, vol. ii ; Wright's *History of Nepal*, pp. 288 etc.

For weighing Gold and Silver

Gold	Silver
10 Lâls = 1 Mâsâ	8 Lâls = 1 Mâsâ
10 Mâsâs = 1 Tolâ	12 Mâsâs = 1 Tolâ

.

INDEX

331